Beer,
and
Breakfast

Whoe'er has travell'd life's dull round,
Where'er his stages may have been,
May sigh to think he still has found
The warmest welcome, at an inn.
– William Shenstone, At an Inn at Henley

BEER, BED
AND
BREAKFAST

Edited by Roger Protz

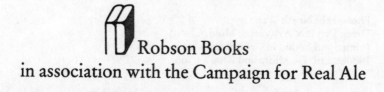

Robson Books
in association with the Campaign for Real Ale

Designed by Harold King

Maps by David Perrott

Cover picture of the Lifeboat Inn, Thornham, Norfolk, courtesy of Nicholas and Lynn Handley

First published in Great Britain in 1990 by Robson Books Ltd, Bolsover House, 5-6 Clipstone Street, London W1P 7EB

British Library Cataloguing in Publication Data

Beer, bed and breakfast.—3rd ed.
1. Great Britain. Inns. Directories
I. Protz, Roger II. Campaign for real ale.
647.944101

ISBN 0 86051 633 4

Photoset in North Wales by
Derek Doyle & Associates, Mold, Clwyd
Printed and bound in Great Britain by
Biddles Ltd, Guildford and King's Lynn

CONTENTS

INTRODUCTION

God made the wicked Grocer
For a mystery and a sign,
That men might shun the awful shop
And go to inns to dine.
G K Chesterton, 'Song Against Grocers'

And to sleep. No doubt Chesterton, in common with such literary luminaries as Dr Samuel Johnson and Robert Burns, frequently supped and slept in inns and pubs. They are pleasant, unstuffy places in which to stay. The welcome is genuine and free from the glutinous, pasted-on smile of the impersonal hotel; the food is often remarkably good; and the drink is British beer at its best.

Growing numbers of people are using pubs for holidays and breaks as the British rediscover their own country. Tired of holidaying at Gatwick-les-deux-Eglises or, if they actually get abroad, of being terrorized by their own kith and kin dressed in Union Jack boxer shorts and spraying cans of lager in all directions, they are now settling for the peace and serenity of their own island. But there are few package tours at home, and hotels can be disgracefully expensive, which is where pubs come into their own. Price is not the only consideration for choosing a pub, but for those on limited budgets it is good to know that you can still get good, simple accommodation for £10 to £12 a night.

The renewed enthusiasm for the pub as a place to stay is reflected in both the substantial growth in the number of entries in this third edition of the guide – almost twice as many as in the first edition – and the eagerness with which publicans seek to be included. Such eagerness is an indication of the growing awareness in the trade that all aspects of a pub need to be developed in order to make a good living: it is no longer sufficient just to open the doors and expect the customers to flock in.

The enthusiasm among licensees for the guide prompts me to explain how the entries are compiled. Shortly after the second edition appeared, the *Observer* newspaper revealed that the guide book *Staying Off the Beaten Track* accepted payments from small hotels that were included in its pages. Stung by this criticism, the editor, Elizabeth Gundrey, said in the 1989 edition that, 'Most annual guides of repute ... require a payment before anyone can get an entry in them.' One wonders what the editors of guides lacking repute indulge in!

Beer, Bed and Breakfast, in common with all publications produced by the Campaign for Real Ale, lacks one thing – backhanders from publicans. All entries are free in every sense: not only does the Campaign neither seek nor accept payment for entries in any of its guides, but I would reject the hidden payment of free accommodation if it were offered.

The guide is compiled from CAMRA's vast database of British pubs, which is updated continuously as the Campaign's branches inspect their local outlets for inclusion in the annual *Good Beer Guide*, local guides and the growing list of specialist books published by CAMRA's subsidiary, Alma Books. Recommendations for *Beer, Bed and Breakfast* are also made by individual CAMRA members, by readers and users of the guide and as a result of my own inspections. Publicans chosen for the guide are sent forms shortly before a new edition goes to press in order that important information concerning prices, food, and beers available is as up-to-date as possible.

They have their exits and their entrances

The substantial number of new entries this time does not mean that we have reduced our standards. On the contrary: complaints are investigated and, when judged to be fair, the pubs in question are removed from the guide.

Complaints fall into two main categories: lack of cleanliness and an unfriendly welcome. Pubs often operate with a small number of part-time staff to back up the licensees, but even so there can be no excuse for falling below acceptable standards of hygiene. When I stay in a pub, I am not bothered if the room does not have its own shower or bath, welcome though such facilities are; I can survive without an in-room tea and coffee tray, especially when the instant coffee tastes like liquid iron filings and the UHT milk appears to have passed through the wrong passage of the cow. But I do expect absolute cleanliness. There can be no excuse for grubbiness. The word pub is short for 'public house': the landlord is welcoming you into his home. When friends come to stay at my house I hurry round with the vacuum cleaner and the ozone-friendly liquid cleaner; I expect the same of publicans.

One publican in Wales had the misfortune to entertain a married couple who were professional environmental health officers. Their letter of complaint to the owning brewery, copy to the guide, was detailed and savage. I trust that the brewery in question has acted on their advice, but the pub has been omitted from this edition until I am satisfied that the standards of hygiene are exemplary.

It is reasonable to ask how such a place got into the guide in the first place. The answer is that it was recommended in good faith by people who do not accept sloppy standards. But pubs change. There is a high turnover of licensees, especially in areas that depend for a large proportion of their business on the holiday trade. An incoming licensee may have a different idea as to what constitutes a high standard of service. In the free trade, where pubs are not owned directly by brewers, little pressure can be brought to bear on owners or managers whose standards slip below those considered to be acceptable. One advantage of the tied house system is that there is an owning brewery to complain to.

I do not want to over-egg this particular pudding. The number of inns that engendered complaints concerning cleanliness did not amount to more than half a dozen entries in the last edition. But all those pubs have been removed from this edition, in one case after I had personally inspected it. In the case of another pub I inspected I was satisfied that the complaint was not justified.

Grumbles about unfriendly welcomes in pubs can also be counted on the fingers of one hand. I tend to be more tolerant of licensees who have an off day. One reader wrote complaining of surly service in a pub in Hampshire. When I visited it a few weeks later I found the licensee to be jovial and attentive to all his customers on a busy bank holiday. A friend who owns a small group of pubs told me: 'You can't expect a tenant to always have a great wide grin on his face. He's not going to be full of the joys of spring if his dog has just been run over – unless he didn't like the dog.' Complaints that I do take seriously are, again, almost always connected with a change of licensee. A reader wrote to say that a particular pub 'has changed hands. The publican seems to have no control over a largely young crowd of drinkers who use the most offensive language and forced my wife and I to leave a day early.' Such a pub cannot stay in the guide while that atmosphere prevails.

Most notable in the reports garnered for the new edition is the large number of licensees who say they have overhauled their accommodation in the past year and now offer a much higher standard in their guest rooms. The British may have an ingrained repugnance of complaining direct to publicans or hoteliers but, either by word of mouth or in letters to breweries and other owners, the word is getting through that consumers want quality accommodation.

The industry in a state

Changes in the pub and brewing industry in the next few years are likely to encourage the raising of standards. In 1989 the Monopolies and Mergers Commission took a long look at the brewing industry and did not much like what it saw. It reported that the six national brewing groups, Bass, Allied, Grand Metropolitan/Watney, Whitbread, Courage and Scottish & Newcastle, owned 74 per cent of 'tied houses', accounted for 86 per cent of loan ties in the free trade and controlled three-quarters of the beer market. It recommended that loan ties should be banned, that tenants of brewery-owned pubs should be allowed to buy a guest beer free of the tie and, most radical of all, that no brewery should be allowed to own more than 2,000 tied outlets.

After much huffing and puffing, the government reneged on a promise to implement the proposals. It has decided, however, that the major brewers, while retaining ownership of all their pubs, must turn half of them above a 2,000 ceiling into quasi free houses, with tenants able to buy not just any guest beer but a specified 'cask-conditioned ale'. It seems likely that the national brewers will prefer to sell many of these pubs; Scottish & Newcastle set the trend at the end of 1989 by putting on the market 250 of their outlets above the 2,000 ceiling. The possibility of several thousand pubs coming on to the market and being bought by independent brewers or groups of free traders can only be encouraged. From the evidence of *Beer, Bed and Breakfast* and other CAMRA guides, there is no doubt that pubs owned by independent brewers and free traders offer better service, more imaginative food and better-value accommodation. There are few 'Big Six' pubs in this guide because in general they are not interested in pub accommodation. Although Bass is now the world's biggest hotelier through their ownership of Holiday Inns worldwide, they concentrate on identikit and expensive hotel accommodation.

S&N and Grand Met have moved in the opposite direction and have sold their hotel chains; Grand Met do own a number of inns in Britain but their expensive-facilities do not win many recommendations from users of this guide. Among the nationals only Whitbread seem to have a genuine interest in bed and breakfast accommodation and they are easily outnumbered by smaller breweries who, as a result of their lack of size, remain close to their roots, their pubs and to genuine quality service.

Room for improvement

While standards are clearly rising – and the quality of food in particular puts paid to the idea that you cannot eat well in pubs – a few aspects of pubs and accommodation need to be improved. There is a small but growing trend to charge guests for their rooms only and then add extra for breakfast. I have yet to hear a coherent or logical explanation for a practice which, to many people, seems like a sharp one, as they expect the price quoted to be an inclusive one for bed and breakfast and then find an extra £3 to £5 added to the bill for morning food.

The opposite side of this coin is the trap of the Full English Breakfast, which is quoted as part of the cost of B&B. This is another way of saying No Choice. The inn is geared to producing just one mega fry-up. I am a seasoned pub user but I have fallen foul of this practice on a number of occasions by not noticing the Full English Breakfast stipulation on the tariff. Many people prefer not to have a plate of fried food at 8 in the morning. On several occasions I have returned home with soggy serviettes full of cold but still tasty bacon, sausage and black pudding for my dog while I had to make do with toast and a fried egg. Publicans should stress verbally to guests when only the FEB is offered; better still they should organize their kitchens to offer a choice. Scrambled and poached eggs are not difficult to prepare and the British pub should help in the revival of fish for breakfast. I have enjoyed kippers at a number of pubs and in Norfolk I had the great pleasure of eating my first bloater in years.

I am unhappy with the practice of charging a 'single occupancy' fee for a guest using a double room. Publicans in tourist areas may feel aggrieved in the height of the season if one person uses a room that could be let to two. But in general I think the practice is unfair to those of us who stay in pubs for business as well as pleasure and it is quite insupportable when a pub is otherwise empty.

The Best Breakfast in Britain

In the last edition of the guide I promised an award for the best pub breakfast in edition three. Many readers have reported on 'great breakfasts' but have given too little information. So on this occasion the award is based on pubs and inns that I have visited personally. Head, shoulders and half a body above allcomers is Hugh Anderson's Traquair Arms hotel in Innerleithen in the Scottish Borders. Attention was given to every detail, including butter in individual dishes, not half-melted inside impenetrable foil wrappers, hot cereals (porridge) as well as cold; and cheerfully refilled pots of tea and coffee.

When I tentatively inquired if kippers were available I was asked if I wanted one or the pair. I settled for the pair – I did have a six-hour drive ahead of me and didn't want to stop to eat in a motorway caff – and was rewarded not with filleted apologies but with two *real* kippers overflowing a large plate. I have never broken my fast so splendidly.

I have also breakfasted well in the Swan in the Rushes in Loughborough – it is good to see a town pub offering more than the conventional fry-up – the Victoria in Bamburgh, Northumberland, the Ship in Dunwich, Suffolk and the Cap and Feathers, Tillingham, Essex.

More time, gentlemen, please

Since the last edition, the government has at long last liberalized pub opening hours in England and Wales. Publicans are now free to open from 11am until 11pm. The dire warnings of an outbreak of mass drunkenness and wholesale pillage came to nothing. The British have taken the change in their stride. But only about a third of publicans have opted for the change and they are mainly in urban areas. The majority still choose to close in the afternoons, though residents in pubs and hotels have access to the premises at all times and may even get food and drink if there is staff on hand.

The price you pay

We have once again attempted to bring some order to the way pubs charge for accommodation but there is still no common style. If would be useful and simpler if Britain adopted the French system of charging for the room rather than per person. We asked publicans to quote 1990 prices but many had not yet fixed tariffs for that year when we circulated them. The prices do, however, give a good indication of the range in a particular pub or hotel, but we strongly urge readers to check the tariff carefully when booking. Children can stay on licensed premises when there are guest rooms. Where bars and restaurants are concerned, the law stipulates that no persons under 18 can be served in bars and children under 16 cannot be served in pub dining rooms. But if a pub or hotel has a residential licence then children can be admitted to dining rooms and residents' lounges.

The real thing

Real ale, also known as traditional draught beer or cask-conditioned beer, is a definition of a British beer style that is accepted by the *Oxford English Dictionary*. It means a top-fermented beer that undergoes a natural secondary fermentation in the cask and which is served without applied gas pressure. Most pubs in the guide serve real ale by a simple suction pump – a beer engine – which draws beer from the cask in the cellar when the handpump on the bar is pulled. Some pubs still serve the beer straight from the cask by gravity dispense, while others, mainly in the Midlands and the North, use electric pumps. In Scotland, while handpumps are now widespread, the traditional method of serving cask beer is the tall fount primed by air pressure.

While the guide remains primarily a pub guide, there is an increase in the number of small and not so small hotels in this new edition. It is good to see more hoteliers showing an interest in real ale. In Scotland, it should be stressed, the pub does not exist outside of the borders and Edinburgh and Glasgow. Further north, drinking is done in bars, which is why accommodation is confined largely to hotels.

Keep in touch, by gum

Your thoughts on existing entries and recommendations for new ones are eagerly sought. Use either the report forms in this guide or your own paper. Naturally we hope you never have cause for complaint, but things can go wrong in even the best-run establishments. One reader wrote to say that when she and her husband arrived at a recommended hotel in Scotland, chaos reigned as most of the rooms had been double booked. Eventually, late at night, the problems were solved and the guests finally retired to their rooms. Our correspondents were just settling down to sleep when – shades of Speedy Gonzalez – there was an urgent rapping at their door and a man's voice whispered: 'Can I come in?' 'What do you want?' they hissed in irritation. 'My teeth!' came the reply. 'My teeth are in your bathroom!'

We trust that you never have to gnash your teeth in rage in a pub or hotel recommended here. This guide does not share Robert Louis Stevenson's belief that it is better to travel hopefully than to arrive.

ROGER PROTZ

Note: All pubs serving Tolly Cobbold ales are liable to change their range; the Ipswich brewery was closed in 1989 and production switched to Cameron in Hartlepool. Cameron's Strongarm bitter is beginning to appear in Tolly pubs in East Anglia.

As the guide was about to go to press, Grand Metropolitan signed a deal with Elders IXL, owners of Courage and Foster's lager, in which Grand Met would sell its Watney breweries in return for most of the Courage pubs. Such an arrangement would remove both groups from the government's 'guest beer' policy.

JOIN CAMRA!

If you want to join the growing movement to preserve Britain's unique beers and pubs, then £9 a year will bring you a monthly newspaper, *What's Brewing*, information concerning branch, regional and national activities, including beer festivals, and generous discounts on books published by CAMRA and Alma Books. Send a cheque made out to 'CAMRA Ltd' to CAMRA, (Dept BBB), 34 Alma Road, St Albans, Herts AL1 3BW. Further details, including direct debit and credit card payments, from the Membership Secretary on 0727 67201.

ENGLAND

THE CASTLE HOTEL, BISHOP'S CASTLE

AVON

KEYNSHAM

Crown Inn
63 Bristol Road, ½ mile off A4

Licensees: Tony & Nikki Kerswell
Tel: 0272 862150

An unspoilt pub first licensed in 1745, the Crown has a large collection of photographs and prints of old Keynsham. Darts and cribbage are played in the bar. Four miles from Bristol and 7 from Bath, it has graced over ten editions of the *Good Beer Guide* thanks to the quality of its ale. A wide range of good-value, homemade food is served lunchtime and evening.

Beer: Courage BA and Best Bitter on handpumps.

Accommodation: 1 single, 3 doubles, 1 twin. B&B £14 per person. Children welcome.

MONKTON COMBE

Wheelwrights Arms
1½ miles off A36, 3 miles south of Bath

Proprietors: Marilyn Penny & Roger Howard
Tel: 0225 722287

The Wheelwrights is a fine old inn built in the middle of the 18th century and first licensed in 1871. It was once owned by a viscount and was in competition with the local monastery, which brewed its own ale. It stands in the lovely Midford Valley and is quiet and remote, yet it is just three miles from the stately pleasures of Bath. The accommodation is in a converted barn and stables. Each room has direct-dial phone, shower, colour TV, and tea and coffee making facilities. You can try your hand at darts and cribbage with the locals, and in winter you can warm yourself by a roaring log fire. There are bar snacks, lunches and evening grills (no snacks Friday and Saturday evenings).

Beer: Adnams Bitter, Butcombe Bitter, Wadworth 6X plus guest beers served straight from the cask.

Accommodation: 8 doubles/twins. B&B from £22 per person. Winter Break (Oct-March) any two days or more from £31 per day per person, includes B&B plus evening meal. Children over 14 welcome, no reductions.
Cards: Access and Visa (not accepted for meals or Winter Breaks).

RADSTOCK

Waldgrave Arms Hotel
Market Place on A367

Licensee: Graham Smith
Tel: 0761 32206

A comfortable family-run pub in countryside that was once the heart of the Somerset coalfields, where all the mines were closed some thirty years ago. The hotel is a handy base for visiting Bath, the stunning cathedral mini-city of Wells, Wookey Hole and Longleat. The Waldgrave has a pleasant lounge where meals and snacks are served every day except Sunday evening. The bar is a haven for indoor sports lovers, with two darts boards and three pool tables. There is also a skittles alley with its own bar.

Beer: Courage Best Bitter on handpump.

Accommodation: 4 singles, 3 doubles, 1 family room. B&B £15 single, £25 double or twin. Children welcome, charged half price. Residents' TV lounge.

TORMARTON

Compass Inn
B4465 off A46; junction 18 of M4

Proprietors: Mr & Mrs P Monyard
Tel: 045 421 242/577

The ivy-clad Compass is a carefully modernized 18th-century coaching inn, so named because a former landlord decorated the building with chandlery from Bristol's shipyards. The four Cotswold stone bars maintain the sea-going flavour with beams and a pair of ship's lanterns in the Long Bar. The inn has a separate restaurant with à la carte menu, specializing in local game and produce. There is also a hot and cold buffet every lunchtime and evening. There are lawns, gardens and a charming orangery. All the guest rooms have private baths and all have TVs, tea and coffee making facilities and direct-dial phones. In the heart of the Cotswolds, the Compass is close to Tetbury and its annual Woolsack race, Badminton House with its horse trials, the ancient hilltop town of Malmesbury, and the old Roman town of Cirencester.

Beer: Archers Village Bitter, Bass, Wadworth 6X on handpumps.

Accommodation: 19 rooms. 1 Apr-30 Sept, dinner, B&B 2 days £84.50 per person, 3 days, £124.75, £40 further day (£25 Sunday); single room supplement Mon-Thur £22. Winter Break (Oct-March) 2 days £74.50 per person, 3 days, £110, £35 further day (£25 Sun); single room supplement Mon-Thur £19. Dogs welcome, charged £1 per night.

WINSCOMBE

Woodborough
Sandford Road on A371

Licensee: G W Ashdowne
Tel: 0934 84 2167

The Woodborough is a mock-Tudor pub that was rebuilt in the 1930s following a fire. With live entertainment every weekend in the large skittles alley, the pub is the hub of the village and the surrounding area. The warm and welcoming lounge has snacks and bar meals and there is also an à la carte menu. It is a good base for Cheddar Gorge, Weston super Mare and Sandford Ski Centre.

Beer: Courage Best Bitter on handpump.

Accommodation: 1 single, 3 doubles. £13.50 single, £13 double per person. No children.

BEDFORDSHIRE

CRANFIELD

Swan
2 Court Road, junction 13 M1, between Bedford and Milton Keynes

Licensees: Harry & Glenda Williams
Tel: 0234 750332/750772

The Swan is a spacious 1930s pub with facilities for all the family. The Sports Bar is for snooker and skittles enthusiasts while the lounge bar has a dining area. The enclosed garden has a play area for children. Food includes bar meals, evening meals and a traditional Sunday roast. There is a separate children's menu, and a high chair is available for toddlers. Food includes fresh and toasted sandwiches, ploughman's, homemade beefburgers, croque monsieur, pizzas, pâté, swordfish steak, T-bone steak, scampi, and locally made sausages. The guest rooms have colour TVs, and tea and coffee makers. The Swan is close to a flying school that was formerly a wartime bomber base, which now offers flying lessons and hot-air ballooning. A nearby lake has a boating club.

Beer: Greene King IPA on handpump.

Accommodation: 3 doubles/twins, 1 family room, 3 rooms with en suite facilities. Double/twin £15-£20, £30-£35 en suite. No pets.

LOWER STONDON

Bird In Hand
A600 4 miles north of Hitchin, 9 miles south of Bedford

Licensees: Brian & June Cullen
Tel: 046 27 2385

The Bird in Hand is a borderline case – not for inclusion in the guide but geographically speaking. It is on the Beds/Herts border and the nearest town is Hitchin. It is a large and welcoming pub that specializes in home-cooked food, which is available seven days a week, lunchtime and evening, and has a range that covers everything from sandwiches to steaks. It also offers the complete range of Greene King beers, including the delectable dark mild.

Beer: Greene King XX, IPA, Abbot Ale on handpumps.

Accommodation: 14 rooms: 8 singles, 5 twin, 1 family room. £15 per person. Children's rates negotiable. No pets.

BEDFORDSHIRE

SALFORD

Red Lion Country Hotel
Wavendon Road: unclassified road 2 miles NW of M1 junction 13; off A421 & A507

Licensee: Bob Sapsford
Tel: 0908 583117

The Red Lion is a 16th-century inn in extensive grounds in a rural village that is only 10 minutes from Milton Keynes. There are exposed beams and cottage décor, bric-à-brac, and a roaring log fire in winter. For couples keen on nuptials as well as real ale there are six suites with four-poster beds. All the guest rooms have TVs and direct-dial telephones. The hotel is a good base for Woburn Sands, Apsley Heath, Milton Keynes shopping centre and Silverstone motor racing circuit. The Red Lion offers bar snacks, with a separate restaurant for lunch and dinner.

Beer: Charles Wells Eagle Bitter and Bombardier on handpumps.

Accommodation: 6 doubles with en suite facilities £44; 1 twin £37; 2 singles £27. Ground-floor facilities for the disabled.

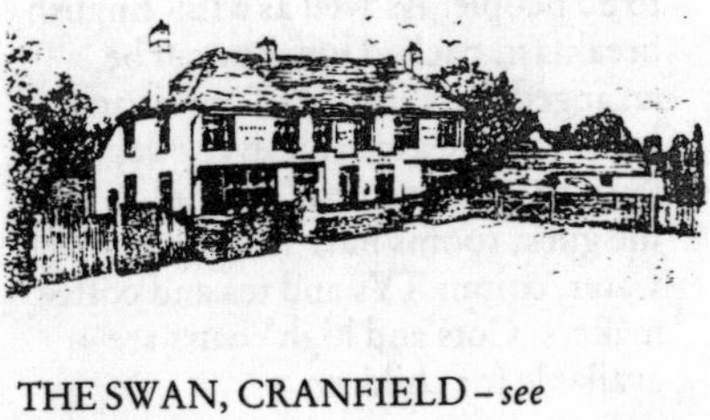

THE SWAN, CRANFIELD – *see opposite*

BEDFORDSHIRE

SHEFFORD

White Hart
2 Northbridge Street, A600

Licensees: Brian & Samantha Cullen
Tel: 0462 811144

The White Hart is a small and friendly pub on the Bedford-to-Hitchin road. It specializes in home-cooked food, ranging from sandwiches to steaks, and bar meals and restaurant meals are available every day.

Beer: Greene King IPA and Abbot Ale on handpumps.

Accommodation: 4 twin-bedded rooms, all with en suite facilities, £18 per person. Children welcome, rates negotiable. No pets.

SILSOE

Old George Hotel
High Street, just off A6; 9 miles from Bedford, 11 miles from Luton

Licensee: Irene Kirby
Tel: 0525 60218

The George is a handsome old coaching inn shaded by trees, and is well placed for visitors to Woburn Abbey and Wrest Park. It has a full range of facilities, including two family rooms, a restaurant and a conference room that can cater for up to 50 people. As well as a full English breakfast, packed lunches can be arranged for guests. Full meals and bar meals are available every day (Sunday evening residents only). All the guest rooms have hot and cold water, colour TVs and tea and coffee makers. Cots and high chairs are available for children.

Beer: Greene King IPA and Abbot Ale on handpumps.

Accommodation: 7 rooms: 3 singles, 2 doubles, 1 twin, 1 family room, 2 rooms with private baths. Single £22, double £34, evening meal £8.50. Special weekend rates: Friday and Saturday nights bed, breakfast, evening meal and Sunday lunch: £60 single, £120 double. No pets. Cards: Access, Amex and Visa.

STEVINGTON

Red Lion
1 Park Road. 1½ miles north of A428, signposted five miles from Bedford

Licensees: George & Hilary Lee
Tel: 02302 4138

The Red Lion is a friendly local next to a medieval stone cross in an attractive village. The lounge bar serves snacks, lunches and evening meals plus a traditional Sunday lunch. The emphasis is on homemade food and includes tempting pies and pasties. The cheerful public bar has darts, dominoes and crib, and there is a garden with a children's play area that includes a rabbit. Stevington has John Bunyan connections and a restored 18th-century windmill and a holy well. Bromham, two miles away, has a water mill and museum on the river Ouse.

Beer: Greene King IPA and Abbot Ale on handpumps.

Accommodation: 2 double rooms. B&B £18 single, £26 double. Children welcome, terms negotiable. No pets.

WOBURN

Bell Inn
21 Bedford Street. 5 miles from M1 junctions 12 and 13; 4 miles from A5 at Hockliffe

Licensees: T Chilton & A B Wadham
Tel: 0525 290280

The Bell is at the heart of the historic Georgian village of Woburn with its abbey close by. It is a superb country pub and restaurant, mainly 17th century but with some Victorian additions. Records show that from 1739 it brewed its own beer until 1879, when George Higgins's Bedford brewery bought the premises; some of the inn's original hops still grow in the garden. It is owned by Greene King and leased to the Chilton family, who have restored the premises to their present high standard. The superb beamed restaurant offers a choice of traditional and nouvelle cuisine food, while the bar meals have won praise from Egon Ronay. All but two of the guest rooms have en suite facilities and all have colour TVs, telephones and tea and coffee makers. The inn is a good base for visiting Woburn safari park and golf course.

Beer: Greene King IPA and Abbot Ale on handpumps.

Accommodation: 27 rooms: 14 singles, 11 doubles/twins, 2 family rooms. Single £35, double/twin £22 per person, family room £29 per person. Weekend rates on request. No pets. Cards: Access, Amex, Diners and Visa.

KNOWL HILL

Seven Stars
Bath Road. On A4 between Maidenhead and Reading, 5 miles from Maidenhead, 2½ miles from junctions 8/9 of M4

Licensees: Robin & Lyn Jones
Tel: 062 882 2967

The Seven Stars is a 17th-century coaching inn with a Georgian frontage and comfortable panelled rooms with log fires in winter. The large gardens have tree houses and swings for children while there is a children's room in the pub itself. The splendid home-cooked food is served until 9pm every day. The pub has a skittles alley and there are limited facilities for the disabled. Knowl Hill is a good base for Henley-on-Thames, home of Brakspear's traditional brewery, Windsor, Marlow – no longer the home of Wethered's traditional brewery – and the Shire Horse Centre.

Beer: Brakspear Mild, Bitter, Special and Old on handpumps.

Accommodation: 3 double rooms. B&B £18 single, £40 double. Children welcome.

EAST ILSLEY

Swan
High Street. A34 Oxford road, 5 minutes from M4, near Newbury

Licensees: Michael & Jenny Connolly
Tel: 0635 28238

The Swan is a 16th-century coaching inn nestling in the peaceful downlands village of East Ilsley and decked out with colourful hanging baskets and window boxes. It is within easy reach of Newbury and its racecourse, and the Ridgeway path, which passes through many famous prehistoric sites. Oxford is close by. Bar meals include steak and kidney pie, steak and onions braised in ale, chicken curry, macaroni au gratin, ploughman's, a range of burgers, including vegan, and sandwiches. Full restaurant meals (Tuesday to Saturday) include prawn bisque, marinated fish, seafood vol au vents, roast lamb, breast of chicken, duck, salmon and fillet of sole. Three of the guest rooms have private bathrooms and all the rooms have colour TVs and direct-dial phones.

Beer: Morland Bitter and Old Masters on handpumps.

Accommodation: 3 singles, 1 double, 1 family room. £16 single, £26 with bath; double £32, £40 with bath; family room £50. Pets accepted. Cards: Access and Visa.

GORING-ON-THAMES

Queens Arms
Gatehampton Road. A329 Reading to Oxford road. M4 junction 13

Licensee: Cyril Youngs
Tel: 0491 872825

A licensed house since 1859, the Queens Arms has been tastefully modernized to meet today's requirements. It has a large garden, car park, public and lounge bars, and serves full meals every day except Sunday, when bar snacks are available. Goring village, on the borders of Berkshire and Oxfordshire, is one of the loveliest places in the Thames valley.

Beer: Morrell Best Bitter and Varsity on handpumps.

BERKSHIRE

Accommodation: 2 singles, 2 twins. £12.50 per person. Children welcome, up to 5 years free of charge. No pets.

LAMBOURN

George Hotel
High Street, B4000, M4 junction 14

Licensee: Maureen Jackson
Tel: 048871 889

The George is less than an hour's drive from Heathrow airport yet it offers superb accommodation in tranquil countryside. It dates back to the 16th century and serves bar meals every lunchtime and early evening; there is a separate restaurant. The emphasis is on traditional English cooking and guests can enjoy not only splendid cask ale but a fine range of crusted ports, too.

Beer: Arkell BBB on handpump.

Accommodation: 1 single, 3 doubles/twins, 1 family room, 2 rooms with en suite facilities. Single £22.50, double £38, family room rates negotiable. Winter weekends negotiable. Pets accepted. Cards: Access and Visa.

REMENHAM

Two Brewers
Wargrave Road, junction of A321 and A423

Licensees: Graham & Deana Godmon
Tel: 0491 574375

A warm welcome is waiting in this cosy panelled pub with a roaring log fire in winter, hanging baskets and a children's room. An excellent bar menu is served every day with additional daily specials. You can enjoy riverside walks or stroll across the attractive 18th-century bridge with five arches into Henley, home of Brakspear's brewery and the annual Royal regatta.

Beer: Brakspear Bitter, Special and Old on handpumps.

Accommodation: 1 single, 2 twins, 1 double with en suite facilities. B&B £18 single, £35 twin, £40 double. Children welcome, no reductions.

WARGRAVE

Bull Hotel
High Street on A321

Licensees: Noel Harman & H Bill
Tel: 073522 3120

The Bull is a 16th-century listed building with exposed beams and unusually decorated brick walls in the bars and dining area, and two enormous fireplaces with blazing log fires in winter. Wargrave is an attractive Thames-side village four miles from Henley. The pub has a garden and patio. Guest rooms have central heating and colour TVs. The restaurant, known as Mo's Kitchen, has a good local reputation for the quality of its meals, and features such dishes as smoked salmon Norwegian, Portuguese sardines, poulet Basque and fresh grilled trout.

Beer: Brakspear Bitter and Special on handpumps.

Accommodation: 2 singles. 3 doubles. B&B £18 single, £30 double. Evening meals available. No children.

BERKSHIRE

WOOLHAMPTON

Angel Inn
Bath Road on A4 between Reading and Newbury

Licensees: Roger and Lyn Jarvis
Tel: 0734 713307

The Angel is a delightful ivy-covered pub near the Kennet and Avon canal. Roger Jarvis is a compulsive collector of bric-à-brac and crams the bar with his garnerings, including 70 blow lamps. The beer garden is a lovely setting in good weather, with a bridge over a large pond. Lyn Jarvis specializes in first-class home-cooked food. Constantly changing bar snacks include such unusual delicacies as upside-down pie (Stilton and bacon) and spiced Mexican beef with bananas and coconut. The restaurant dishes range from rump steaks and fresh local trout to vegetarian meals. The Angel has a skittles alley available for group bookings and conference facilities at reasonable prices.

Beer: Flowers Original, Wethered Bitter, SPA and Winter Royal, Strong Country Bitter and such guest beers from the Whitbread range as Chesters and Fremlins, all on handpumps.

Accommodation: 3 singles, 4 doubles, including an annexe, 5 with en suite showers. B&B £22 single, £38 double. Children welcome, no reductions. Cards: Access, Amex, Diners and Visa.

BUCKINGHAMSHIRE

AYLESBURY

Bell
Market Square on A41

Licensee: Ross Whelan
Tel: 0296 89835/82141

Built in the 16th century as a private house, the Bell was vigorously extended and developed in the 19th century, its history reflected in the varying sizes of the beautifully appointed guest rooms, all of which have colour TVs, phones and tea and coffee making facilities. There are welcoming log fires in winter in the cocktail and market bars. The hotel is based at the quiet, lower end of the old market square, which stresses Aylesbury's historical connections with statues of John Hampden, a leading parliamentary opponent of Charles I, and Benjamin Disraeli. The Bell is also a good vantage point for visiting St Mary's Church, one of the town's oldest buildings, the Bucks County Museum, and the County Hall designed by Vanbrugh. Further afield is Waddesdon Manor, re-created along the lines of a French château by Baron de Rothschild, Mentmore Towers and Winslow Hall. Back at the Bell you can enjoy both hot and cold snacks lunchtime and evening, as well as full meals in the Chaucer restaurant. There are cots, high chairs and baby-listening facilities for parents with young children.

Beer: Courage Directors Bitter, Webster's Yorkshire Bitter and Wethered SPA on handpumps.

Accommodation: 6 singles, 11 doubles/twins, 16 with own bathrooms. Prices are for rooms only; breakfast is extra. Singles £50, doubles/twins £55. Weekend Breaks £33-£38 single, £29-£33 doubles/twins per person per night: prices include breakfast and dinner, service and VAT. Children welcome, terms on application. Cards: Access, Amex, Diners and Visa.

BENNETT END

Three Horseshoes
Bennett End, Radnage, near High Wycombe. 3 miles from junction 5 on M40

Licensees: Tim & Rene Ashby
Tel: 024 026 3273

The Three Horseshoes is an 18th-century country inn in the secluded Hughenden Valley, nestling down narrow lanes. It has old beams and open fires and a fine garden with splendid views over the rolling Chilterns. Woodstock, Windsor and Oxford are close by. The pub offers lunchtime snacks, a full evening menu and a traditional roast lunch on Sundays. The guest rooms all have colour TVs and tea and coffee making facilities, and one room has a king-size waterbed.

Beer: Brakspear Bitter and Flowers Original on handpumps.

Accommodation: 3 doubles. B&B £38 single, £48 double. Children welcome.

CUDDINGTON

Crown
Aylesbury Road, off A418

Licensee: Barry Jones
Tel: 0844 292222

A fine old thatched building dating from the 13th century, the Crown has low beams and inglenooks plus such 20th-century attributes as central heating and tea and coffee making

BUCKINGHAMSHIRE

facilities in the guest rooms. The excellent pub food is all home made and the bar has a wealth of traditional pub games. Cuddington won the coveted Best Kept Village in Bucks award in 1989. Aylesbury is six miles away and nearby attractions include Waddesdon Manor and Wotton House in Wotton Underwood, which is almost identical to the original Buckingham House before it became Buckingham Palace. To the north, steam trains run to Aylesbury in the summer from Quainton Railway Centre.

Beer: ABC Best Bitter, Everard Tiger and Wadworth 6X on handpumps.

Accommodation: 1 single, 1 twin. B&B £17.50 per person. Evening meals available.

HIGH WYCOMBE

Bell
Frogmore, close to junction with A40

Licensee: Mr H W J Lacey
Tel: 0494 21317

The Bell is a 17th-century pub that has retained its charm and character. Its proximity to a multi-storey car park may detract a little from that character but it does make parking easy for visitors. The Bell serves food lunchtime and evening, including full meals in a restaurant area. It is close to High Wycombe town centre and West Wycombe caves are a short drive away.

Beer: Fullers Chiswick Bitter, London Pride and ESB on handpumps.

Accommodation: 2 singles, 3 doubles. B&B £17.50 per person. No reductions, no children.

LONGWICK

Red Lion
Thame Road, B4129 near Princes Risborough

Licensees: Anthony & June Goss
Tel: 084 44 4980

The Red Lion is some 200 years old, a listed building that is thought once to have been a chapel. It serves as a centre for the village but a warm and informal welcome is extended to visitors. Bar meals – soup, ploughman's, pâté, burgers, scampi – are available as well as grills in the restaurant. The pub is a splendid base for walkers in the Chiltern Hills, and Blenheim Palace and the Hell Fire Caves at West Wycombe are close by.

Beer: ABC Best Bitter, Fullers London Pride and Hook Norton Best Bitter on handpumps.

Accommodation: 4 singles, 4 doubles, all with en suite facilities. B&B £31.50 single, £41.50 double. Children over 12 welcome, no reductions. Cards: Access and Visa.

WENDOVER

Red Lion
High Street. A413, 5 miles south of Aylesbury

Licensee: Mr B Hickin
Tel: 0296 622266 Fax: 0296 625077

The Red Lion Hotel is a coaching inn that was built in 1619 and combines the best of the old world and the new: log fires in the inglenook in winter back up the central heating. The fine exterior has dormer windows and impressive tall chimneys. Wendover nestles at the foot of the Chiltern Hills and is close to Blenheim, Chequers, Woburn, Luton Hoo and

BUCKINGHAMSHIRE

Hughenden. There are facilities within the area for fishing, riding, walking and golf. The hotel has a cheery lounge bar with a buttery section where children can sit and enjoy informal meals with their parents. The oak-panelled dining room offers an à la carte menu. Bar and buttery meals include crab soup, smoked salmon, steaks, burgers, chicken surprise, devilled kidneys, smoked haddock, omelettes, Welsh rabbit, pizzas, ploughman's, filled jacket potatoes, vegetable pie, and there is a separate children's menu. All the guest rooms have private baths.

Beer: Fullers London Pride, Greene King Abbot Ale, Marston Pedigree Bitter, Morland Bitter and occasional guest beers, all on handpumps.

Accommodation: 2 singles, 15 doubles/twins, 3 family rooms. B&B £39 single, £49 double/twin, £59 family room. Weekend rates: double room 2 nights £70, 3 nights £95, single £58 2 nights, £78 3 nights. Well-behaved pets accepted. 6 more rooms are being added. Cards: Access, Amex, Diners and Visa.

WESTON TURVILLE

Chandos Arms
1 Main Street, B4043, 1 mile from A413, 2 miles from A41

Licensee: Kenneth Nickels
Tel: 0296 61 3532

The Chandos is a 200-year-old pub with log fires in winter and a great range of traditional games, including dominoes, darts, crib, bar billiards and Aunt Sally. The large garden has 20 picnic tables and a children's corner. Zena Nickels specializes in homemade, traditional English food; lunch and dinner are available every day. Morris Men perform in the summer, there are golf and fishing facilities close by as well as the Prime Minister's residence at Chequers.

Beer: Benskins Best Bitter, Burton Ale and Tetley Bitter on handpumps.

Accommodation: 2 singles, 2 doubles. B&B £15 per person, weekend £30, week £60. Children welcome, no reductions.

WEST WYCOMBE

George & Dragon
On A40

Licensee: Philip Todd
Tel: 0494 464414 Fax: 0494 462432

The George & Dragon, in a delightful National Trust village, is a 500-year-old coaching inn, renovated and restored in 1720. An archway leads to an attractive cobbled courtyard, large walled garden, play area and parking space. The inn retains some half-timbers and has ancient pigeon lofts: pigeons used to carry messages when bad weather delayed coaches. The George & Dragon is also reputed to have the ghost of a 'White Lady', thought to be a young girl named Sukie who came to an unfortunate end in the Hell Fire Caves. The caves are close by, as are West Wycombe Park and the Church Mausoleum, all open to the public. Three of the en suite rooms have four-poster beds. Bar meals are available lunchtime and evening, and the extensive menu includes homemade soup, ploughman's, smoked mackerel, savoury mushrooms and courgettes, Cumberland lamb, steak and kidney pudding, beef Wellington, spinach and blue cheese pancakes, chicken curry and a wide range of sandwiches.

Beer: Courage Best Bitter and Directors Bitter on handpumps.

Accommodation: 1 single, 5 doubles, 3 twins, 1 family room (1 double and twin) all with en suite facilities. B&B from £36 single, £46 double or twin. Weekends from £66 double for 2 nights. Children's room; children sharing a guest room are charged £10 per night.

WINSLOW

Bell Hotel
Market Square. A413 between Aylesbury and Buckingham

Licensee: William Alston
Tel: 0296 71 2741/3206

The black and white hotel dominates Winslow market square. An inn has stood on the site since Tudor times and has always been the focal point of the town. It was once used as the local magistrates' court and petty sessions were held there on alternate Wednesdays; stage coaches to and from London stopped at the Bell every day except Sunday. The Winslow Bar has a welcoming atmosphere with its ancient oak beams and comfortable seats and its log fires in winter. The Verney bar has some wattle and daub panels and an open fire. It is named after the Verney family of Claydon House, which is a few miles from Winslow and has Florence Nightingale connections. The Claydon Restaurant offers modern English and French cuisine, and bar meals are also available daily. The Stables Bar has facilities for children. Winslow is handy for Silverstone motor racing circuit, Towcester racecourse and Buckingham golf course.

Beer: Adnams Bitter, Hook Norton Old Hookey and Marston Pedigree Bitter on handpumps.

Accommodation: 4 singles, 10 doubles/twins, 1 family room, all with en suite facilities, colour TVs, telephones and tea and coffee makers. Single £45, double/twin £50-£60 per room, family room £65 per room. Children's and weekend rates on application. Pets accepted. Cards: Access, Amex, Diners and Visa.

CAMBRIDGESHIRE

BYTHORN

White Hart
On A604

Licensees: David & Madeline Rogers
Tel: 080 14 226

The White Hart, in common with many pubs in East Anglia, is a former Watney pub that is now free of the tie. It stands in a pleasant village on the Cambridgeshire–Northants border and has been extensively modernized without losing its essential character as a village local. Hood skittles and darts are played and excellent home-cooked food is available in the restaurant, which is a partitioned section of the lounge bar.

Beer: Adnams Bitter, Ind Coope Burton Ale and Marston Pedigree on handpumps.

Accommodation: 1 single, 2 doubles. B&B + evening meal £18.50 single, £30 double. Weekend Break £15 single, £25 double per person per day.

CAMBRIDGE

Clarendon Arms
35 Clarendon Street

Licensee: Pauline Milton
Tel: 0223 313937

The Clarendon is a bright and cheery local with a tasteful colour scheme of chocolate and cream and complementary blue curtains, light shades and a collection of dinner plates. There is a sun-trap patio at the back. The splendid, uncomplicated food ranges from massive crusty sandwiches to salads and ploughman's, with a daily hot special. The pub, run with enormous verve and enthusiasm by Mrs Milton, is close to the great open greensward of Parker's Piece.

Beer: Greene King IPA and Abbot Ale on handpumps.

Accommodation: 1 double, 1 twin. B&B £15 per person.

Spreadeagle
67 Lensfield Road

Licensee: Paul Smith
Tel: 0223 359571

The Spreadeagle is proof that inside every boring boozer there is a smashing pub struggling to get out. Paul and Tricia Smith took over the Spreadeagle in 1986 and concentrated on stripping away the unnecessary trappings that had accumulated over the years. The result is a traditional pub, unfussy but comfortable, with a superb collection of old Cambridge pub photos adding a touch of bibulous nostalgia. The food is remarkable value for money, all home cooked with main dishes costing not more than £2.50. The Spreadeagle is within easy walking distance of the town centre, and all the guest rooms are centrally heated and have tea and coffee making facilities.

Beer: Castle Eden Ale, Flowers Original and IPA, Wethered Winter Royal and Marston Pedigree Bitter on handpumps.

Accommodation: 2 singles, 1 double. B&B £15 per person.

EARITH

Old Riverview Inn
High Street, A1123 near Huntingdon

Licensee: Paul Ceeney
Tel: 0487 841405

The inn is an old beamed riverside free house on the Ouse, with gardens leading down to the river where the pub has a landing stage for river traffic: the gardens are currently being landscaped and a new landing stage will be built. The inn has an à la carte restaurant that specializes in game and traditional English food. The historic town of St Ives, with its Oliver Cromwell connections, is just five minutes away and Cambridge is 15 minutes' drive.

Beer: Arkell BBB, Courage Directors Bitter, Marston Pedigree Bitter and a regular guest beer all on handpumps.

Accommodation: 3 singles, 3 doubles, 3 with en suite bathrooms. B&B £16 per person. Children welcome, half price. Cards: Access, Amex and Visa.

CAMBRIDGESHIRE

EATON SOCON

White Horse
103 Great North Road. A45, off A1

Licensees: Mr & Mrs Caine and Mr & Mrs Stableford
Tel: 0480 74453

The White Horse is a 13th-century coaching inn that was once on the coaching route from London to York; it is now mercifully by-passed by the dreadful A1. The exterior is creeper-clad and there are two porches – one topped by the figure of a white horse – bow windows and miniature trees. A large garden at the back has a children's play area. The interior is a wonderful ramble of small, interconnected rooms with massive beamed ceilings, exposed timbers in the rough plaster walls, thick oak doors, a great inglenook with a copper hood and some ancient settles. Bar food includes chicken chasseur, turkey cordon bleu, steak and kidney pie, spicy mince pie, gammon and pineapple, shark satay, and jacket potatoes with a choice of fillings: chilli, prawn, coleslaw and cheese.

Beer: Flowers IPA, Original, and Strong Country Bitter, Marston Pedigree Bitter on handpumps.

Accommodation: 3 doubles. B&B £37.50-£40 per room. All rooms have colour TVs. Children by arrangement. Cards: Access and Visa.

ELY

Lamb Hotel
Lynn Road, city centre, off A10 and A142

Manager: David Highfield
Tel: 0353 663574

In the shadow of the magnificent and historic cathedral, the Lamb is an old coaching inn with high standards of accommodation. The Fenman Bar in the old stable block has been developed for ale lovers but draught beer is also available in the cocktail bar. The 32 beautifully appointed rooms all have private bathrooms, colour TVs and tea and coffee making facilities. The spacious Barton Restaurant offers à la carte and table d'hôte lunches and dinners and there are tasty snacks in the Oak Room Bar.

Beer: Greene King IPA on handpump.

Accommodation: 6 singles, 22 doubles, 2 triples, 4 rooms with four-poster beds. B&B £50 single, £64 double, £72 triple, four-poster room £85. Weekend Breaks from £35. Children welcome; stay free if under 14 and sharing with parents.

GODMANCHESTER

Black Bull
Post Street. A604

Licensee: Neil Woodrow
Tel: 0480 53310

The Black Bull is rich in history and dates back some 380 years. The warm welcome, good food and ale are underscored by the blazing log fires in cold weather. There is a separate function room that holds 150 people. There is a full restaurant menu, while bar food, served every day lunchtime and evening, includes pizzas, cannelloni, fresh trout, steaks, salads and sandwiches.

Beer: Flowers Original, Wethered Bitter, Winter Royal and a guest beer on handpumps.

Accommodation: 3 singles, 6 doubles, 1 family room. B&B £16 single, £30 double. Children welcome.

GREAT EVERSDEN

Hoops
High Street. 1 mile off A603

Licensee: Alan S Hawkins
Tel: 0223 262185

The Hoops is a splendid old village local down a country road yet close to Cambridge. Parts of the building date back to the late 17th century and you can tuck into the excellent home-cooked food under ancient beams. The Hoops has a welcoming log fire in winter and is a good base for visiting Grantchester and Wimpole Hall. The guest rooms have TVs and hand basins.

Beer: Charles Wells Eagle Bitter on handpump and Bombardier straight from the cask.

Accommodation: 3 singles, 1 double. B&B £15. Quiet dogs welcome.

CAMBRIDGESHIRE

HOLYWELL

Olde Ferry Boat Inn
Near St Ives; signposted from A1123 at Needingworth

Licensee: Richard Jeffrey
Tel: 0480 63227

Mr Jeffrey took over in 1989 from Joyce Edwards, who had run this historic thatched and timber-framed inn for 21 years. It is one of the country's oldest pubs, standing on the banks of the Great Ouse, and was recorded as selling ale in 1068. The rambling beamed bar of the inn has panelled and timbered walls with ancient settles and rush seats. No fewer than four fires belt out welcome heat in the winter. A stone in the centre of the inn marks a 900-year-old grave and it is haunted by the ghost of Juliette Tewsley, who hanged herself in 1050 when she was rejected by the local woodcutter. There is a large beer garden outside, and a terrace; both have fine views of the river. Mr Jeffrey gets his produce fresh from London markets and offers homemade soup, chicken liver pâté, ploughman's, omelettes, lasagne, venison burgers, smoked boar in red wine sauce, a mild curry with fruit called chicken Maori, and seafood pilaff.

Beer: Adnams Bitter, Draught Bass, Greene King IPA and Abbot Ale on handpumps.

Accommodation: 6 doubles, 1 twin, all en suite. B&B £32.50 single, £39.50-£55 double. Cards: Access and Visa.

CAMBRIDGESHIRE

MOLESWORTH

Cross Keys
100 yards off A604

Licensee: Frances Bettsworth
Tel: 08014 283

The Cross Keys is a handsome inn in a quiet village midway between Huntingdon and Kettering. 'It is a *pub* not a restaurant or a hotel,' says Frances Bettsworth. The wide range of home-cooked food – soup, sausage and chips, shepherd's pie, smoked haddock, prawn curry, salads, sandwiches – is served informally in the bar and there is a traditional Sunday roast lunch for £4.25, £3.50 for children. The modern guest rooms have tea and coffee making facilities and central heating and all have their own bathrooms. The welcome is warm and genuine and visitors are encouraged to try their hand at darts and skittles with the locals. Molesworth is just three miles from Kimbolton Castle.

Beer: Adnams Bitter on handpump.

Accommodation: 1 single, 7 doubles, 1 family room. B&B £15.25 per person. Full board available. Children welcome.

ST NEOTS

Old Falcon
Market Square. A45, off A1

Licensee: G T Payne
Tel: 0480 72749

The market square dates back to 1135 when the monks of the former priory were granted a market charter. The Old Falcon's origins are as a 16th-century coaching inn and today it has a thriving lounge bar and a separate restaurant with an extensive menu. There are several other fine buildings around the square, including the former Cross Keys, another coaching inn that has been transformed into a shopping mews, and Paines Brewery, taken over by Tolly Cobbold of Ipswich and closed in 1987.

Beer: Adnams Broadside, Mansfield Riding Bitter, Charles Wells Eagle Bitter and Younger IPA on handpumps.

Accommodation: 6 singles, 1 double, 1 twin. B&B from £36 per person. Cards: Amex and Visa.

SIX MILE BOTTOM

Green Man Inn
London Road. A1304; off M11

Licensees: Gordon & Clare Neall
Tel: 063 870 373/361

By one of those inexplicable quirks understood only by the Post Office, the official address of the Green Man is Newmarket, Suffolk, but Six Mile Bottom is geographically in Cambridgeshire. The inn is made up of two buildings, a pub with a restaurant and a fine old period barn with original oak beams. The quality of the accommodation can be judged by the fact that King Charles and Nell Gwynn stayed there in the 18th century: one presumes they had separate rooms! The restaurant can seat 30 people, while homemade bar snacks include a wide range of pies and Newmarket sausage.

Beer: Bateman XB, Greene King IPA and Abbot Ale, Nethergate Bitter and one regular guest beer, all on handpumps.

Accommodation: 6 doubles, 1 family room, 2 rooms with en suite facilities. B&B from £20 single, £30 double, £40 family room. Children half price. No dogs.

STOW-CUM-QUY

Quy Mill Hotel
Newmarket Road. B1102, off A45

Licensee: Ingrid Fisher
Tel: 0223 853383

The Quy Mill is a family-run hotel that dates back to the time of the Domesday Book. It is set in 14 acres of unspoilt countryside and yet is just three miles from Cambridge. Newmarket and its racecourse, historic Anglesey Abbey, Duxford air museum and the nature reserves of Welney, Wicken Fen and Ely are all within easy reach. The hotel maintains its original mill wheel. Its restaurant seats 66 and there is also an extensive range of bar meals, lunchtime and evening. All the guest rooms have private baths, telephones, colour TVs, radios and tea and coffee makers.

Beer: Adnams Bitter, Charles Wells Bombardier and a guest beer on handpumps.

Accommodation: 3 singles, 24 doubles/twins, including 2 honeymoon suites and one suite for disabled people. B&B £46 single, £54 double per room. Children's rates depend on age. Weekend Breaks: £45 per person for 2 nights. Dog kennels available. Cards: Access, Diners and Visa.

CAMBRIDGESHIRE

WEST WICKHAM

White Horse
3 High Street. A604 Cambridge to Haverhill road; signposted from Horseheath

Licensees: Vic & Beryl Terry
Tel: 0223 290871

The White Horse is a friendly and homely village pub. The Terrys have delved into the pub's history and discovered that it has been licensed since 1795, and that it was at one time used as the local court house. The bars and upstairs rooms still have many original beams. The lawn and patio at the back are safe for children. The surrounding countryside is fine walking territory and West Wickham airfield is at the top of the High Street: the village was known as Wratting Common during World War II to avoid confusion with West Wickham in Kent. Beryl Terry offers some superb homemade food, and several dishes have a beery flavour: try boozy beef and kidney pie cooked with Guinness and Abbot Ale, tipsy rabbit pie cooked in IPA, gah-gah game pie with Abbot gravy, and sloshed shepherd's pie with a dash of mild ale. Alcohol-free food includes curry, scampi, whitebait, beefburgers, seafood platter and blackberry and apple puff.

Beer: Greene King XX, IPA and Abbot Ale on handpumps.

Accommodation: 1 double. B&B £12.50 per person. Children half or third price according to age. No pets.

WISBECH

White Lion Hotel
5 South Brink. A47, Peterborough–King's Lynn road

Licensee: Michael D Gregory
Tel: 0945 584813

The White Lion is a family-run hotel on the banks of the River Nene: North and South Brink have some of the finest Georgian houses in the country, including the National Trust's Peckover House, built by a local banker. The White Lion was called the Queen's Head until 1773 when it changed to its present name. Extensive renovations and improvements were made in the middle of the 19th century. Food is available every day and ranges from sandwiches, salads, fish dishes and steaks at the bar to table d'hôte and à la carte menus in the restaurant.

Beer: Bateman XXXB on handpump.

Accommodation: 4 singles, 12 doubles, 2 family rooms, 16 rooms with en suite facilities. B&B £22 per person, £41.25 in en suite room, £27.25 per person in double room, £23.15 in family room. Children sharing £13.50. Weekend Breaks including dinner: terms on application. Dogs welcome. Cards: Access, Amex, Consort, Diners and Visa.

CHESTER

Pied Bull
Northgate Street

Licensee: S Cox
Tel: 0244 325829

The Pied Bull is an old coaching inn in the heart of the historic city and on the former London to Holyhead route. There is a plaque on an exterior pillar indicating the number of miles to such coaching destinations as London, Worcester, Ludlow, Bristol and Bath. The façade is Georgian, the interior much older, opened into one room but with many smaller sections. The striking fireplace has the painted coats of arms of city companies. The hot pub lunches are a feature of this welcoming old inn, where the accommodation has been thoroughly renovated since the last edition of the guide.

Beer: Greenall Bitter and Original on handpumps.

Accommodation: 11 rooms, all with en suite facilities. B&B from £39 single. Four-poster room available. Weekend rates on application.

COTEBROOK

Alvanley Arms Inn
A49 near Tarporley

Licensee: Doreen White
Tel: 082 921 200

The red brick and creeper-clad 17th-century inn is located in tranquil countryside close to Cheshire and the M6. Nearby attractions include Delamere Forest, Beeston Castle and

Oulton Park motor racing circuit, and there are facilities for golf, fishing and riding in the surrounding area. Visitors are guaranteed a genuine welcome in the bars and the Cobbles restaurant, which specializes in home-cooked food.

Beer: Robinson Best Mild, Best Bitter and Old Tom (winter) on handpumps.

Accommodation: 1 single, 2 doubles. B&B £25 per person. A cot is available in one room: children's rates on application. Cards: Access and Visa.

FARNDON

Greyhound Hotel
High Street, on B5130, off A534

Licensees: Christopher & Wendy Gray
Tel: 0829 270244

The Greyhound is close to the River Dee: cross the river and you are in Wales. Farndon is a picturesque village, popular with fishermen. Local salmon is a speciality of the pub, where Chris and Wendy Gray run a popular and welcoming local with a pottery attached. There are traditional games in the bar and a family garden where children can play with the donkeys, Henry and Guinness, and three goats. Farndon is a good base for Chester, Beeston and Cholmondley castles, Oulton Park, Stretton Water Mill and Snowdonia. Shooting can be arranged at a new and nearby clay shooting range. The guest rooms have colour TVs and tea and coffee making facilities.

Beer: Greenall Mild, Bitter and Original on handpumps.

Accommodation: 2 singles, 1 double, 1 family room. B&B £18 single, £24 double, £28 twin plus VAT. There are also self-catering cottages: terms on application. Children welcome, terms negotiable.

GEE CROSS

Grapes Hotel
Stockport Road (A560), near Hyde; 3 miles from junction 15 of M63 and 1½ miles from end of M67

Licensees: Brian & Hilary Samuels
Tel: 061-368 2614

An old coaching house that has retained its stables, the Grapes was first licensed in 1778 and modernized in Victorian times. It has its own bowling green and is the centre of life in the village. It is a good base for the Peak District, the Cheshire plains, and Manchester and its international airport. For walkers, the hotel is close to the Tame Valley, Werneth Low and Etherow country parks, and both Lyme Hall and Satton Hall and their parks are close by. Bar snacks are available and the guest rooms have colour TVs, tea and coffee makers, hand basins and electric blankets.

Beer: Robinson Best Mild and Best Bitter on electric pumps.

Accommodation: 1 single, 2 doubles (all rooms have space for extra bed). B&B £20-£22 single, £30-£32 double. Family and children's rates on application. Loose box occasionally available for horse up to 16 hands high.

HAZEL GROVE

Woodman
60 London Road. A6, 7 miles from Manchester, 2 miles from Stockport

Licensee: Mrs L Birtwistle
Tel: 061-483 7186

The Woodman was once a home-brew house run by the Simpson family. It was bought by Robinson of Stockport in the 1930s and was the company's first pub in the Hazel Grove area. The pub has recently been thoroughly renovated in a traditional style and has a games room with darts, pool and TV (with satellite as well as terrestrial programmes), and a comfortable lounge and bar, together with a separate restaurant. The pub is close to Lyme Park, the Peaks, Etherow Park and Bramhall Hall. Bar food includes chilli and garlic bread, beefburger, hot beef barm, sandwiches, and a children's menu. The restaurant offers curries, chilli, moussaka, deep-fried chicken, plaice, scampi, roast beef, and lasagne verde. Food is available lunchtime only.

Beer: Robinson Best Mild and Best Bitter on handpumps.

Accommodation: 4 doubles. B&B £18 single, £35 double. All rooms have TVs. No pets.

MALPAS

Red Lion Hotel
Old Hall Street, on B5069 off A41 Whitchurch to Chester road

Licensee: Shelagh Lever
Tel: 0948 860368

The Red Lion is an hospitable and historic brick-and-timber frame building, one of the oldest hostelries in south Cheshire, with wood-panelled walls and several rambling rooms. It was host to James I in 1624 when Malpas was a major stopping place for traffic between London, Wales and Liverpool. A relic of the king's visit remains in the bar – a chair known as the King's Chair. Customers must pay a penny to sit in it or stand drinks for everybody in the bar. In the heyday of coaches, the famous London-to-Liverpool coach known as the Albion used to stop here. Guest rooms are furnished to a high standard. Each room is individually named and the exposed timbers point up the antiquity of the inn. There is a solarium and sauna for visitors.

Beer: Bass and Marston Burton Bitter on handpumps.

Accommodation: 9 rooms all with en suite facilities, one suitable as family room. B&B £17.95 per person. Half and full board available. Some of the accommodation is in the attached Tudor Cottage.

CLEVELAND

HARTBURN

Stockton Arms Hotel
Darlington Road, ½ mile off A66

Licensee: Ron Gough
Tel: 0642 580104

A friendly, welcoming pub on the outskirts of Stockton, with open fires, and brasswork on the walls. There are excellent, good-value bar snacks and separate dining facilities, including Sunday roast lunch, plus summer barbecues in the garden. The guest rooms have en suite facilities, colour TVs, tea and coffee makers and trouser presses. Hartburn is in easy reach of the coast and the North Yorkshire moors while Yarm and Darlington are close by.

Beer: Bass on handpump.

Accommodation: 1 single, 2 doubles, 1 twin. B&B £22.50 single, £30 double and twin.

MIDDLESBROUGH

Eston Hotel
1 mile off A1005 Middlesbrough to Redcar road

Licensee: David Grice
Tel: 0642 453256

An early-1960s pub of unusual design, with three attic peaks at the front and large bay windows. There are three bars – lounge, cocktail and public – with darts and pool in the public. Places of interest to visit include the National Trust Ormesby Hall, the Captain Cook Museum in Stewarts Park, and the North Yorkshire Moors. To reach the pub, turn right at Eston Baths traffic lights, then first left.

Beer: Samuel Smith Old Brewery Bitter on handpump.

Accommodation: 3 singles, 3 doubles. B&B from £11 per person. Evening meals available. Children welcome, no reductions.

THE RISING SUN, ALTURNUN – *see opposite*

CLEVELAND

STOCKTON-ON-TEES

Parkwood Hotel
Darlington road. ½ mile off A66 on old Darlington to Stockton road

Licensees: Bob & Evelyn Smith
Tel: 0642 580800

The Parkwood is a friendly and inviting pub converted from the former mansion of the local ship-owning Ropner family. The hotel has a large garden popular with families. The bar features a large range of liqueurs and whiskies and a renowned variety of sandwiches. There is a separate dining room for lunch and dinner. The pub is next to Ropner Park and a mile from Stockton town centre.

Beer: Ward Sheffield Best Bitter on handpump.

Accommodation: 6 singles, 5 doubles. B&B £24 single, £35 double. Weekend rates on application. Children welcome, no reductions. Cards: Access and Visa.

CORNWALL

ALTARNUN

Rising Sun
Camelford Road, off A30 1 mile N of village, on 5 Lanes to Camelford

Licensee: Les Humphreys
Tel: 0566 86332/86636

The Rising Sun is a popular 15th-century inn built with granite from Bodmin Moor. The large bar, often packed with local farmers, has fireplaces at both ends. There are pub games and children's rooms and the locality offers pony-trekking and sea and reservoir fishing opportunities. You can visit the Altar of St Nonna Church with 79 richly carved bench ends. St Clether Church, with its holy well, is two miles to the north-east. You can tramp over the raw beauty of Bodmin Moor, and the famous tourist pub, the Jamaica Inn, made famous by Daphne du Maurier's novel, is just a few miles away along the A30. The Rising Sun serves hot and cold food every day, with roast lunch on Sundays. Don't miss the homemade pasties. There is a beer garden. a family room and a special children's menu.

Beer: Butcombe Bitter, Cotleigh Harrier SPA, Flowers IPA and Original, Marston Pedigree Bitter and regular guest beers, all on handpumps.

Accommodation: 1 single, 1 twin, 2 doubles, 2 family rooms. B&B £10.50 per person. Reductions for long weekends or weeks. Children welcome, rates by arrangement.

BUDE

Brendon Arms
Inner Harbour

Licensee: Desmond Gregory
Tel: 0288 354542/352713

The Brendon is a charming old country pub overlooking the harbour. A warm welcome is guaranteed – the 'warmest in the West' claims landlord Desmond Gregory. The pub is a few minutes from a spacious beach and is within easy distance of Bude's boating canal, which has some of the finest coarse fishing in the south-west. Sea fishing trips can be arranged. The pub serves breakfast and dinner in the restaurant, plus pub lunches. Fresh seafood, including local crab and lobster, are regular specialities.

Beer: Bass, St Austell Tinners Bitter on handpumps.

Accommodation: 3 twins, 3 doubles, 1 with private bathroom. B&B from £12 per person.

CALSTOCK

Boot Inn
Tamar Valley, near Albaston, off A390 and A388

Licensees: Paul & Lindsay Winterton
Tel: 0822 832331

The Boot is a 17th-century inn in a small Cornish village on the banks of the Tamar. There is a lively bar popular with locals and anglers, with good homemade bar meals and traditional bar games. A separate restaurant has full à la carte meals and a Sunday lunchtime carvery. The guest rooms all have en suite facilities, colour TVs and tea and coffee makers. The inn is a good centre for touring the Tamar Valley, east Cornwall and Dartmoor. Places of interest include Colehele House and Quay and Morwellham Quay and mine. Plymouth and its continental ferry port are half an hour away.

Beer: Flowers IPA, Flowers Original, Wadworth 6X and a guest beer on handpumps.

Accommodation: 2 doubles. 1 family room. B&B from £13.50 per person. 7 days' accommodation for the price of 6 if you book using this guide. Children welcome, reductions by arrangement (cot available).

CAMBORNE

Old Shire Inn
Pendarves Road, B3303

Licensee: Chris Smith
Tel: 0209 712691

The Old Shire is a tastefully converted lodge in beautiful countryside outside Camborne. The inn stands in large grounds with its own car park. The guest rooms are spacious and well-furnished and have colour TVs and tea and coffee making facilities. The pub is pleasingly quiet, without electronic distractions. There are log fires and excellent meals lunchtime and evening, including a carvery serving roast beef, turkey, pork and gammon as well as steaks.

Beer: Tetley Bitter. 'Old Shire' (Plympton Pride by another name) on handpumps.

Accommodation: 1 single, 5 doubles, 1 family room, all with en suite bath or shower. £25 single, £35 double, including full English breakfast. Children welcome, terms by arrangement. Cards: Access and Visa.

CAMELFORD

Darlington Hotel
Fore Street. A39 north of Wadebridge

Licensee: Dick Grimshaw
Tel: 0840 213314

'It *is* a pub,' Mr Grimshaw stresses. The 15th-century coaching inn gets its rather grandiose name from its former owner, Lord Darlington, in the time of the infamous 'Rotten Boroughs' – parliamentary seats that were bought rather than part of the democratic process. It is a striking black and white building in the centre of Camelford. It has two ghosts, one of a young soldier who appears on the first-floor landing, and one of an old lady who occupies the top floor. Food ranges from sandwiches and ploughman's to steaks; there are daily home-cooked specials (beef in Guinness, beef stew, liver and bacon, lasagne) and a traditional Sunday roast. Guest rooms have colour TVs and tea and coffee makers.

Beer: St Austell Tinners on handpump.

Accommodation: 1 double, 1 family room. B&B £15 single, £12 double/family. Children ½ price under 10. £10 per person per night Nov–March. Family room. Pets accepted.

Mason's Arms
Town centre. A39, 25 yards from free car park

Licensee: J Kellow
Tel: 0840 213309

The Mason's Arms is a cheery old three-storey pub that has mercifully not been changed and still has old beams, low ceilings and open fires in its two bars. The lounge bar is a haven of peace and quiet, while the more boisterous public has darts, pool and games machines. Food, lunchtime and evening, ranges from filled jacket potatoes to fresh steaks and there is always a good-value homemade daily lunchtime special for around £1.60. A beer garden leads down to the river.

Beer: St Austell Tinners and HSD on handpumps.

Accommodation: 3 doubles. B&B from £10 per person.

CARNKIE

Wheal Bassett Inn
Globe Square, off B3297 Redruth–Helston road (OS 690401)

Licensees: Terry Donnelly & Tom Purvis
Tel: 0209 216621

The Wheal Bassett is a cheery Cornish pub in the heart of the village with open fires in winter, and male voice choir singing in the bar and which is the base of local Morris Men. The pub is named after a nearby derelict tin mine and there are many relics of the defunct industry in the vicinity. There are striking views of Carn Brea from the pub, which is an ideal base for Redruth, Camborne and west Cornwall. The guest rooms have been renovated recently and have tea and coffee making facilities.

Beer: Butcombe Bitter, Plympton Pride, Tetley Bitter on handpumps.

Accommodation: 3 double rooms, £10-£15 per person, children welcome.

CONSTANTINE

Trengilly Wartha
Nancenoy, Constantine, off B3291, 4 miles off A394

Licensees: Nigel Logan & Michael Maguire
Tel: 0326 40332

A lovely old inn with extensive grounds set in a peaceful valley close to the Helford river and well-placed for Helston and Falmouth, it offers a comfortable bar and has an excellent restaurant that is open every evening. Locally produced meat, fish and shellfish dominate the menu, and you may find such dishes as kipper pâté, prawn and grape strudel, stir-fry beef, rack of lamb, roast guinea fowl, fillet of salmon, local lobster, and John Dory stuffed with mushrooms, peach and grapefruit and poached in white wine. The guest rooms have central heating, colour TVs, direct-dial phones and tea and coffee making facilities and there is a separate lounge for visitors.

Beer: Bass, Butcombe Bitter, Courage Directors Bitter, Exmoor Ale, Marston Pedigree Bitter, St Austell Tinners, Tetley Bitter and guest beers, all straight from the cask, plus 'Really Fowl Cider' from Bodmin.

Accommodation: 6 doubles, 3 with en suite facilities. B&B £15-£25. Half and full board available. Winter Break £25 per person per day B&B + evening meal. Children's room. Cards: Access, Amex, Diners and Visa.

CRIPPLESEASE

Engine Inn
Nancledra. B3311 St Ives–Penzance road

Licensee: Bob Knight
Tel: 0736 740204

The Engine Inn is a true Cornish pub, a magnificent granite building in the heart of the moorland, that once served as the counting house for the local tin mine. Locals tend to burst into song and visitors enjoy the meat roasted on the pub fire. There are stunning views of the Atlantic coast to St Ives and beyond. The guest rooms have private showers, TVs and tea and coffee making facilities. The Engine Inn is the ideal base for walking holidays, and free camping is available.

Beer: Cornish JD Dry Hop Bitter, Cornish Original and Royal Wessex on handpumps.

Accommodation: 3 doubles, 1 family room. B&B from £11.50 per person. Evening meal available. Children's room. Cards: Visa.

LISKEARD

Fountain Hotel
The Parade. A390

Licensee: Roy Towle
Tel: 0579 42154

The Fountain is a comfortable and welcoming old Cornish pub with wood panels and oak beams. It is in the centre of a busy market town, and is popular with town folk and people from the surrounding rural areas. There is splendid homemade grub, including generous portions of steak and kidney pie, plus full restaurant facilities.

Beer: Courage Best Bitter and Directors Bitter on handpumps.

Accommodation: 1 single, 2 doubles, 2 family rooms. B&B £15 per person. Children welcome, terms by arrangement.

LOSTWITHIEL

Royal Oak
Duke Street off A390

Licensees: Malcolm & Eileen Hine
Tel: 0208 872552

The Royal Oak is a 13th-century inn in a Cornish town that claims once to have been the county capital. The Royal Oak's interior has been sympathetically renovated in keeping with the pub's age and character. The back bar is popular with younger people, while the lounge and dining room are quieter. An underground tunnel from the pub is reputed to connect the cellar to the dungeons in the courtyard of Restormel Castle. The pub is a cask-beer lover's paradise with up to seven ales on tap. The food is equally renowned for its quality and its quantity; bar food includes soup, pâté, ploughman's, scallops in cheese and white wine sauce, curries, and salads in summer. The guest rooms have TVs, tea and coffee makers and most have en suite facilities. Close by you can enjoy strolls along the banks of the River Fowey and visit Lanhydrock House and the 14th-century church of St Bartholomew. Fishing, sailing and golfing are all within easy reach of the inn.

Beer: Bass, Eldridge Pope Royal Oak, Flowers IPA and Original, Fullers London Pride and ESB, Marston Pedigree Bitter plus guest beers, all on handpumps.

Accommodation: 4 doubles, 2 family rooms. B&B £19.80 single, £24.20 en suite, £32.20 double for room, £41.80 en suite. Children half price sharing.

MABE BURNTHOUSE

New Inn
Church Road. B3291, ½ mile off A394

Licensee: Mark Kessell
Tel: 0326 73428

The New Inn is a very ancient inn – a 300-year-old pub on the site of a monk's hospice and part of the heritage of the old Cornish granite-quarrying industry. The walls are featured granite; there are many old and fascinating tools in the bars, and a collection of rare photographs. The lounge bar has a vast log fire while the traditional Cornish card game of euchre is played in the public bar. There is an extensive cold buffet and hot meals, including Sunday lunch. Mabe Burnthouse is a good centre for visiting Falmouth, Helston, Truro and Frenchman's Creek, and facilities for trout and coarse fishing are close by.

Beer: Cornish JD Dry Hop Bitter and Cornish Original on handpumps.

Accommodation: 2 doubles, one with additional single bed. B&B £12 single, £22 double. Full board available. Children's room; children half price if sharing.

MEVAGISSEY

Fountain Inn
Cliff Street, 5 miles south of A390

Licensees: William & Trudy Moore
Tel: 0726 842320

The Fountain dates from 1550 and it is wonderfully placed to enjoy the tumbling cliffs and streets of this charming and historic old fishing town. The inn is just a few yards from the harbour and trips for mackerel, pollack and even shark fishing can be booked. The Fountain is an unspoilt local with darts in the bar. The bar food is generous, and a separate restaurant specializes in steaks and local fish dishes. Car parking is difficult: use the main public car park as you enter the village.

Beer: St Austell Tinners on handpump.

Accommodation: 1 double, 1 twin. B&B £12 per person.

MULLION

Old Inn
Churchtown, off A3083 and B3296

Licensees: Ray & Eve Parker
Tel: 0326 240240

A whitewashed and partially thatched inn with parts dating back to the 11th century, the Old Inn has one bar with a lounge area. A summer-time restaurant serves buffet lunches and full à la carte dinners; there are bar snacks all the year round. The inn is on the Lizard Peninsula and you can visit the spectacular cliffs and harbour of Porth Mellin, Mullion and Polurrian beach. Surf-riding and even surf-fishing are available. The attractive and comfortable guest rooms all have tea and coffee making facilities.

Beer: Cornish JD Dry Hop Bitter and Cornish Original on handpumps.

Accommodation: 5 rooms, 3 with private bathrooms. B&B from £14 per person. Children over 14 welcome in summer. There is also 1 self-catering cottage.

PADSTOW

London Inn
Lanadwell Street. Take Padstow sign from A30 after Bodmin bypass and Victoria Inn

Licensee: Clive Lean
Tel: 0841 532554

The London Inn has been a pub since 1802. It was formerly three fishermen's cottages and a recent facelift has carefully pointed up the original features. Nautical memorabilia and brass decorate every available area. Mr Lean tells me, 'We have attracted mature drinkers of all ages over the years and, apart from the cask-conditioned beers and White Shield Worthington, have a large collection of malt whiskies. Most international and selected club Rugby Union matches are discussed and re-played too often!' The White Shield Fan Club meets there daily. Bar and restaurant food is available lunchtime and evening, with a roast lunch only on Sunday.

Beer: St Austell Bosun's Bitter, Tinners and HSD on handpumps.

Accommodation: 2 doubles, 1 family room. B&B £13 per person, £5 supplement for one person in a double. Children over 14: rates by negotiation. B&B only in summer months; B&B + evening meal 1 Nov–31 Mar.

PENZANCE

Fountain Tavern
St Clare Street, off town centre. A30

Licensee: Dave Pryor
Tel: 0736 62673

Mr Pryor's heartening message is the same every time he writes to the guide: 'NO juke box!' – underlining the tranquil and traditional atmosphere in this friendly town pub, a fine centre to enjoy the local beaches, coves, Land's End, the cathedral town of Truro, and St Michael's Mount reached by a causeway at low tide from Marazion. Lunchtime bar food includes pasties and sandwiches. 'There's no food in the evening – we're too busy drinking,' Mr Pryor says. 'It doesn't matter where you come from, you will soon feel at home.'

Beer: St Austell Bosun's Bitter and HSD on handpumps.

Accommodation: 1 double, 1 family room. B&B £9 per person. Children welcome, terms by arrangement. Pets by arrangement.

PORT GAVERNE

Port Gaverne Hotel
Off A39 and B3267/3314, 5 miles north of Wadebridge

Licensees: Freddie & Midge Ross
Tel: 0208 880244

The Rosses have been running the 380-year-old hotel for 20 years and have a deserved reputation for the quality of the welcome, the food and the ale. Port Gaverne is a tiny, isolated cove near Port Isaac. The hotel's front bar is decorated by old photographs and paintings that are sometimes for sale. There are two tiny snug bars at the back and all the floors have ancient and worn Delabole slate floors. The bar meals are sea-food-based and feature lobster and crab in season from Port Isaac. The restaurant offers à la carte and carte du jour menus plus a special vegetarian menu. There is seating outside in the summer, and facilities for golf, fishing, pony trekking, sailing and surfing within easy reach. As well as the hotel accommodation, the 18th-century Green Door cottages offer self-catering in restored fishermen's houses.

Beer: St Austell HSD and Flowers IPA on handpumps.

Accommodation: 19 rooms all with private baths, colour TVs and direct-dial phones. B&B £25.50–£27.50. Special weekly and 2 night breaks: rates on application. Phone for details of self-catering rates (most cottages sleep 4).

PORTHLEVEN

Harbour Inn
Overlooking Inner Harbour. B3304, 2 miles from Helston

Licensees: Dave & Wendy Morton
Tel: 0326 573876

The inn is 300 years old. It was known first as the Commercial and offered victuals and accommodation in a small fishing village known as Port Elvan until the 19th century. The village grew with the building of a harbour that allowed a thriving fishing industry to develop. The Mortons have completely refurbished the inn but they have sensibly retained all its old charm. It is an excellent base for visiting Land's End, Goonhilly, the Lizard, St Ives and Truro. Bar food includes homemade soup, garlic mushrooms, crab pâté, smoked mackerel, tuna and prawn, pasties, filled jacket potatoes, ploughman's, Dover sole, lemon sole, fillet of plaice, and steaks. 'Sprats Corner' has a children's menu. There is a separate restaurant.

Beer: St Austell Bosun's Bitter and HSD on handpumps.

Accommodation: 1 single, 8 doubles/twins, 1 family room, 8 rooms with en suite facilities. B&B £22 single, £21 double per person, family room £62 for 4 people. Children half price sharing. Weekend rates on application. Family room. No pets. Cards: Access, Amex and Visa.

THE CROWN INN, ST EWE – *see p 46*

CORNWALL

PROBUS

Hawkins Arms
Fore Street. A390 between St Austell and Truro

Licensee: Vanessa Slater
Tel: 0726 882208

The Hawkins Arms in a delightful and unspoilt old one-bar pub with a coal fire in winter, a large garden with an eating area and a children's assault course. There is also an indoor children's room. Bar meals are served lunchtime and evening and are mainly home-cooked, with such dishes as ham, lasagne, chilli, curry, and sweets. Probus is famous for its church, which has the highest tower in Cornwall, and for the village's two lovely gardens.

Beer: St Austell Tinners and HSD on handpumps.

Accommodation: 1 single, 2 doubles/twins. B&B £12.50 single, £12 per person in double room. Children by arrangements. Pets welcome.

ST AGNES

Driftwood Spars Hotel
Trevaunance Cove

Licensees: Gordon & Jill Treleaven
Tel: 087 255 2428

Built in 1660, the Driftwood Spars over the years has been a tin mining store, chandlery, sail makers' loft and fish cellar. The old beams come from driftwood washed up on the beach from the many ships wrecked off the rugged coast. The hotel has log fires, guest ales, an extensive range of malt whiskies, three bars and live music at weekends. Food ranges from bar snacks, including real pasties, steak and kidney pie and fisherman's pie, to four-course meals or an à la carte menu in the restaurant. Breakfast can be taken as late as noon. There are fine cliff walks to be enjoyed, mine workings, a model village, surfing, sea fishing, swimming, good rock pools and nearby Truro. Most of the guest rooms have en suite facilities, sea views, TVs, tea and coffee making facilities and hair dryers.

Beer: Tetley Bitter and Burton Ale on handpumps plus a wide range of guest beers.

Accommodation: 1 single, 9 doubles, 1 family room, 5 with en suite facilities. B&B £19 low season to £20 high season per person. Single rooms with hand basins only: £11. Pro rata reductions, e.g. 2 days low season £35, 3 days £52. Children sharing bunk-bedded rooms half price. Dogs £1 a night. Cards: Access and Visa.

ST AUSTELL

Duke of Cornwall Hotel
98 Victoria Road, Mount Charles. A390

Licensee: John Avery
Tel: 0726 72031

The Duke has been open since 1868. In Mr Avery's words, 'It is just a good pub.' The public bar has no less than three dart boards, a pin table and two pool tables. The large lounge has a blazing log fire in winter. Bar meals range from sandwiches to steaks.

Beer: St Austell Tinners and HSD on handpumps.

Accommodation: 6 doubles. B&B £12 per person. Children's room. Pets welcome.

Queen's Head
Fore Street, town centre

Licensee: Jerry Ogilvie
Tel: 0726 75452

The Queen's Head is 600 years old and has everything you would expect from such an ancient tavern – oak beams, a cellar, a smugglers' tunnel and a ghost. In harsher times, the town square was the scene of public executions, including the burning of witches. St Austell has its own brewery of the same name. The town is a good base for visiting such coastal splendours as Mevagissey, Fowey and Looe. Bar food in the pub includes a wide range of pizzas, soup and crusty bread, garlic mushrooms, cauliflower cheese, steakburgers, boozy cottage pie, plaice, lasagne, chilli con carne, omelettes, and salads.

Beer: Courage Best Bitter and Directors Bitter, St Austell Tinners on handpumps.

Accommodation: 2 singles, 2 twins, 4 doubles, extra beds available for children. B&B from £14 per person. Full board available.

ST EWE

Crown Inn
5 miles SE of St Austell between B3287 and B3273

Licensees: Ruth & Norman Jeffery
Tel: 0752 84 3322

The Crown is a superb old inn bedecked with hanging baskets, flowering tubs and window boxes outside and with two Union flags on the whitewashed walls. The small main bar has an ancient fireplace with a wood surround, and a high-back

settle on a slate floor. A small adjacent restaurant specializes in homemade pies and also offers steaks, scampi and chicken. Both full meals and bar meals are served every day, lunchtime and evening. You can eat in the pleasant garden in good weather. The pub is a good base for visiting Mevagissey and the nearby beaches.
Beer: St Austell Bosun's Bitter on handpump.

Accommodation: 1 single, 2 doubles. £10 per person. No children.

ST JUST-IN-PENWITH

Star Inn
Fore Street, town centre, A3071

Licensees: Peter & Rosie Angwin
Tel: 0736 788767

A former coaching inn, the Star is St Just's oldest hostelry, a traditional Cornish building of mellow stone, with a spacious bar and cosy snug. There is a large stepped mounting block outside, used by horse-borne travellers in earlier times. One of the guest rooms is in the converted stables and has its own bathroom, TV and tea and coffee making facilities. Bar food ('absolutely no chips!') is available at all times and includes homemade soups, casseroles, real Cornish pasties, ploughman's and local crab and prawns. St Just is close to Cape Cornwall, Land's End airport and the skybus to the Scillies and is a fine base for a walking holiday, with Sennen close at hand.

Beer: St Austell Tinners and HSD straight from the cask.

Accommodation: 1 single, 2 doubles, 1 with private bath. B&B £10.50 single, £12.50 per person in double, £15 per person in room with shower. No children. No pets.

Wellington Hotel
Market Square. 6 miles from Penzance on B3306

Licensee: R D S Gray
Tel: 0736 787319

The Wellington is an imposing granite building overlooking the main square of St Just. It has a cosy, character-filled bar with attractive brass fittings and paintings on the wall. There is a separate pool room and a picturesque garden at the rear. Families are welcome, and the hotel has a deserved reputation for the quality of its bar meals, including locally caught fish, crab, steaks and light snacks. There is a roast lunch on Sundays. Food is served every day, lunchtime and evening. All the guest rooms have colour TVs and tea and coffee making facilities. St Just is close to Land's End and Cape Cornwall and the beaches at Sennen Cove, Porthcurno and St Ives. Cliff walks, hiking and climbing are all available locally.

Beer: St Austell Tinners and HSD on handpumps.

Accommodation: 3 doubles. B&B £15 single, £25 double. Rates for children and weekend breaks on request. Family room. Pets welcome.

ST MAWES

Victory Inn
50 yards up alleyway from quayside, off A39

Licensee; Alan Heffer
Tel: 0326 270324

The Victory, which dates from 1792, is a haunt of fishermen and was once the headquarters of Channel pilots who guided ships in and out of Falmouth. The pub is often full of music as local boatmen burst into song. The Victory has one bar and an adjoining room that serves hot and cold meals all year. From St Mawes you can catch the ferry to Falmouth and visit St Mawes Castle.

Beer: JD Dry Hop Bitter, Cornish Original on handpumps.

Accommodation: 5 doubles. B&B £12.50 per person. No children or dogs. Steep climb to pub makes it unsuitable for disabled people.

ST MERRYN

Farmer's Arms
A389 Newquay to Padstow road

Licensees: Bob & Sally Mann
Tel: 0841 520303

The Farmer's Arms is some 250 years old and was formerly three cottages. It is a charming old Cornish inn with a large public bar and a lounge with a low beamed ceiling, log-burning stone fireplaces and a Delabole slate floor. St Merryn takes it name from a religious figure, the Patroness Sancta Merina, and the village is famous for St Merryn Church which has the lovely font rescued from the ruined church at Constantine. Near the shore at Harlyn Bay is an ancient burial site, discovered in 1900 when more than 2,000 tons of sand were removed to reveal 130 slate coffins. It is thought, from tools and ornaments found in the coffins, that the people buried there lived some 300 years before Julius Caesar. Food in the carefully renovated Farmer's Arms includes a hot and cold carvery and the emphasis is on homemade dishes. You may find soup, garlic mushrooms, farmer's pâté, fisherman's pâté, smoked mackerel, ploughman's, burgers, filled jacket potatoes, salads, seafood platter and steaks. A separate dining room is open from September to July.

Beer: St Austell Tinners and HSD on handpumps.

Accommodation: 3 doubles, 1 family room, all with en suite facilities. B&B £15 per person. Children half price. Children's room. Pets welcome. Cards: Access, Amex and Visa.

TREBARWITH

Mill House Inn
Off B3263 Tintagel–Camelford road

Licensee: Kevin Howard
Tel: 084 0770 200

The Mill House is a former corn mill in the dramatic scenery of the Trebarwith Valley. The mill is surrounded by sycamores and a small trout stream, which once provided the power for the mill, runs outside. The main bar has massive beams, a Delabole stone-flagged floor, oak tables and settles. There are food and terrace bars, a pool, and boules in the garden. The beach is a few minutes' walk. Bar food includes homemade soup, sandwiches, pâté, ploughman's, fish platter, salads, steaks, vegetable bake and beef in beer. The separate evening restaurant specializes in local produce. The inn is a superb base for visiting Tintagel, Port Isaac, Boscastle and Wadebridge. A children's play area is planned for the garden.

Beer: Flowers IPA, Flowers Original and Marston Pedigree Bitter on handpumps.

Accommodation: 1 single, 7 doubles, 1 family room. 6 rooms with private baths, 3 with showers. B&B from £21.80 per person. Evening meals available. Children's room; children over 10 years welcome.

VERYAN

New Inn
Off A3078

Licensee: John Dandy
Tel: 0872 501362

The New Inn is a small, unspoilt, one-bar granite pub in the heart of a picturesque village famous for its roundhouses, with a warm welcome from the landlord and the locals. Veryan is close to some superb beaches at Pendower and Carne and the breathtaking scenery of the Roseland peninsula. Falmouth and Trelissick Gardens can be reached by the King Harry Ferry, and Truro and St Austell are just 11 miles away. There is good pub grub in the inn, served lunchtime and evening.

Beer: St Austell Bosun's Bitter and Tinners Bitter straight from the cask.

Accommodation: 3 doubles. B&B £11.50 per person.

PORT GAVERNE HOTEL,
PORT GAVERNE – *see p 44*

BARNGATES

Drunken Duck
Near Hawkshead. From Ambleside take the B5286 to Hawkshead; turn left at Outgate and the inn is 1 mile along the road at crossroads

Licensees: Peter & Stephanie Barton
Tel: 09666 347

The energetic Bartons have flung themselves into a major renovation and extension to this famous old Lakelands pub. There are now additional bedrooms with en suite facilities, a residents' breakfast and dining room and a modern kitchen to cope with the demand for food. But the idyllic old inn remains, with its oak beams, thick stone walls, old oak settles and log fires. The original name of this superb pub set in stunning scenery of mountains and lakes was for 300 years the Barngates Inn. Its Victorian nickname stems from a legend that a landlady in the late 19th century found her ducks stretched out in the road. She thought they were dead, though in fact they were squiffy from drinking ale from a leaking cask in the cellar, and began to pluck them in preparation for the oven. This roused them from their stupor in time to be saved from a hot end. To cover their nakedness, the landlady knitted them jerseys until their feathers grew again. The pub nickname quickly took over from the original one.

Duck didn't feature on the latest menu but it offered such tempting bar meals as aubergine and garlic pâté, ploughman's, soup, boeuf bourguignon, lamb and vegetable casserole, red bean moussaka, ravioli in basil and bacon, red onion and gruyère tart, fennel, orange and butterbean bake, red cabbage and prunes in a chestnut purée, lasagne, spinach and mushrooms tortellini,

CUMBRIA

beef curry and a wide range of old-fashioned nursery puds such as jam roly-poly. Residents can have dinner in their own lounge for £12.50. The Duck is a splendid base for visiting Ambleside, Coniston, Hawkshead and Tarn Hows.

Beer: Jennings Bitter, Marston Pedigree Bitter, Tetley Bitter, Theakston XB and Old Peculier on handpumps.

Accommodation: 1 single, 9 doubles/twins. All rooms en suite with colour TVs, tea and coffee makers and direct-dial phones. B&B £25 per person single, £22.50 in double/twin. Children welcome, rates on application. Pets welcome. Cards: Access and Visa.

BECKERMET

Royal Oak
Off A595

Licensees: Barry & Jane Jackson
Tel: 0946 84551

The Royal Oak is a delightful and homely inn, popular with anglers who enjoy access to one of Cumbria's finest salmon rivers or sea angling from boat and shore. Fishing weekends for up to eight people can be arranged. It is also superb and rugged countryside for walkers and hikers. The lounge bar of the Royal Oak offers the comfort of open fires in winter. Excellent bar meals are supplemented by a barbecue when the weather allows. There is a separate restaurant and a beer garden. The pub has folk nights on Sundays, which are popular with the locals. The eight guest rooms are in a well-appointed annexe. All have en suite facilities, colours TVs and tea and coffee makers.

Beer: Jennings Bitter on handpump.

Accommodation: 6 doubles, 2 singles. B&B £25 single, £42.50 double. Special Rate: £45 per person for 2-night weekend B&B + evening meal. 3 doubles and 1 single are on the ground floor.

BOTHEL

Greyhound Inn
A596 Carlisle to Cockermouth road

Licensee: Ian Taylor
Tel: 06973 20601

The Greyhound is a busy local that serves several surrounding Cumbrian villages. The warmth of the welcome from Mr Taylor and his staff attracts visitors en route between the Lakes, Carlisle and Scotland. Bar meals are available every day, lunchtime and evening. The pub has a wealth of old beams and an open fire in the lounge and there is live entertainment every Wednesday and Saturday. Bothel is a short distance from the market town of Cockermouth, birthplace of William Wordsworth and of Fletcher Christian, leader of the mutiny on the Bounty, and the home of Jenning's brewery. It is also a good base for the northern Lakes and the Solway coast.

Beer: Jennings Bitter on handpump.

Accommodation: 1 twin, 1 double. B&B £10 per person.

CUMBRIA

BOWNESS ON SOLWAY

Kings Arms
In the village, off A595 and A74

Licensee: Angela Bates
Tel: 06973 51426

The Kings Arms is built on the site of the last Roman Fort at the end of Hadrian's Wall and, in common with many of the houses in this isolated village, is built of stone from the wall. On the banks of the Solway Firth, the pub has superb views across to Dumfries and Galloway. The views at sunset are spectacular and unforgettable. In season, the local haaf fishermen, in a scene locked in time, can be seen standing patiently in the tidal streams of the estuary waiting for the catch. The warmth of the welcome at the Kings Arms is underscored by the open fire in winter. There are fascinating species of marine life in a large tank and a collection of photos of old Bowness decorate the walls. The restaurant features locally caught salmon and a choice of Cumbrian dishes. All the guest rooms have colour TVs.

Beer: Jennings Bitter on handpump.

Accommodation: 5 singles, 2 doubles, 1 twin, 1 family room. B&B £12.50 per person.

BOWNESS-ON-WINDERMERE

Albert Hotel
Queen's Square. Off A592

Licensee: Peter A Steen
Tel: 09662 3241 Fax: 09662 88067

The Albert is a Victorian hotel in the heart of the delightful village of Bowness. It is guarded by a chestnut tree in the middle of the road and is just 300 yards from Windermere's steamer pier. The Regency Bar, often open all day, has a roaring fire in winter months. The Victoria Bistro is open for lunch and dinner all year and opens all day Sunday. It serves steaks, fish and salad meals. Bar meals are served in the Regency. The six guest rooms all have en suite baths or showers, colour TVs and Teasmaids.

Beer: Hartley XB and Robinson Old Tom on handpumps.

Accommodation: 5 doubles, 1 family room. B&B from £17 per person; rates depend on length of stay. Weekend Breaks, autumn, winter and spring: from £87 per couple, 2 nights, including evening meals. Cheaper rates mid-week. Children under 16 with 2 adults charged only for breakfast. Children's room. Pets welcome. Cards: Access and Visa.

BROUGHTON-IN-FURNESS

Black Cock Inn
Princess Street, off A595

Licensee: Mr K Howarth
Tel: 0229 716529

The Black Cock is a popular 16th-century country inn in a charter town in southern Lakeland, with a fascinating collection of vintage motor bikes in the town square. On Tuesday, which is market day, the pub is open all day and local farmers flock into Broughton with their animals. The Black Cock has comfortable, modern guest rooms with TVs and tea and coffee making facilities.

Beer: Websters Yorkshire Bitter and Choice, Ruddles County on handpumps.

Accommodation: 3 doubles, 1 family room. B&B £12.50 per person. Weekend £24, Week £70.
Children welcome, half price under 12.

Eccle Rigg Manor Hotel
Foxfield Road, SW of village, off A595

Proprietors: Howard & Susan Loxley
Tel: 06576 398

The Manor Hotel is an imposing 19th-century mansion in 35 acres of gardens and woodland, with stunning views of Coniston Old Man and the Duddon estuary. Eccle Rigg was built by Lord Cross, whose varied parliamentary career encompassed Home Secretary, Secretary of State for India, and Lord Privy Seal (one later holder of the third office observed, 'I am neither a lord, a privy nor a seal'). Lord Cross used Eccle Rigg as his summer retreat and brought parts of the demolished Ashton Old Hall at Ashton-under-Lyne to Broughton: the old dungeon towers from Ashton now stand at the entrance to Eccle Rigg. The lounges and restaurant are elegantly furnished and the 13 guest rooms have colour TVs, in-house video, and tea and coffee making facilities. Bar food includes Morecambe Bay shrimps, Cumberland sausage, jacket spuds with a variety of fillings, chilli, and homemade steak and kidney pie. The hotel has a heated swimming pool, sauna and solarium.

Beer: Whitbread Castle Eden Ale on handpump.

Accommodation: 13 rooms, 10 with private bathrooms: 7 doubles, 6 family rooms. B&B £27.50 single, £34.50 en suite; £48.50 double, £55.50 en suite. Weekend £56, week £165.

CUMBRIA

Special rates for honeymoon couples. Children welcome, reductions on room rates and meals. Facilities for the disabled but no lift.

CARTMEL FELL

Masons Arms
Strawberry Bank, off A5047

Licensees: Helen & Nigel Stevenson
Tel: 04488 486

This delightful and welcoming old pub is devoted to good beer and good food. The seriousness with which Nigel Stevenson takes his beer is measured by the fact that the pub has a beer menu as well as a food one, with a vast range of foreign bottled beers to try in addition to the draught beers. The imported beers include both top and bottom fermented styles and Mr Stevenson ensures that they are all served at the correct temperatures. As well as the regular draught ales, he has a guest beer always on tap and serves more than a hundred a year. He also serves such genuine imported lagers on draught as Fürstenberg: he wouldn't give a XXXX for anything else. The pub got its name in the 18th century when Kendal freemasons had to meet in secret. The Masons Arms is set in lovely countryside close to the heart of Lakeland. Excellent pub grub includes homemade curries, houmous and coachman's casserole, washed down with a Belgian Trappist beer, a Czech Pilsner Urquell or a straightforward pint of ale.

Beer: Bateman XB, Thwaites Bitter and Yates Bitter on handpumps, with James White and Westons cider.

Accommodation: 3 doubles, 1 family room in converted barn next to the pub. £7.50-£15 per person depending on season; breakfast extra. Children welcome, no charge if sharing.

COCKERMOUTH

Bush
Main Street, off A66

Licensees: Joe & Brenda McKenna
Tel: 0900 822064

The Bush, in the centre of a bustling market town, sports one of the oldest of pub names. In Saxon times, when a brewster – a woman brewer – had produced fresh ale, she would hang a bush of evergreens outside her house. The McKennas are content to receive their ale from the local brewer, Jennings. The hotel is an old coaching inn. Its buttery room used to be the place where farmers' wives would bring butter to sell; it is now a cosy lounge but has retained its traditional decor. The main lounge has welcoming open fires in autumn and winter, and serves good-value bar meals every lunchtime except Sunday. Visitors can see Cockermouth Castle, Wordsworth House, birthplace of the Lakelands poet, Fletcher Christian's birthplace at Wellington Farm and Jennings Brewery, to which visits can be arranged. The less commercialized lakes of Ennerdale and Loweswater are close at hand.

Beer: Jennings Bitter on handpump.

Accommodation: 2 doubles, 1 family room. B&B £11 per person. Children 14 and under £8. No pets.

CUMBRIA

CONISTON

Crown Hotel
A593

Licensee: Mrs A I Tiidus
Tel: 05394 41243

A cheerful old pub nestling between Coniston Old Man and the famous lake where Donald Campbell broke the world speed record. There are disused copper mines and the home of writer and artist John Ruskin nearby, and you can take a trip on the lake in the steam-powered gondola owned by the National Trust. The Crown has a beer garden, a log fire in winter, and generous hot food is served lunch and evening.

Beer: Hartley Mild and XB on handpumps.

Accommodation: 3 doubles, 3 family rooms. B&B £15.50 single, £14 per person in double room. Family room £35. Children sharing half price. Two-day Break £75 for 2 with all meals. Children's room. Pets welcome. Cards: Access, Amex, Diners and Visa.

Ship Inn
Bowmanstead. A593, ¼ mile from village on Torver road

Licensees: Derrick & Linda Freedman
Tel: 05394 41224

The Ship is a traditional old pub with beams, a stone fireplace and a log blaze in winter, close to Coniston Hall camp site and Park Coppice caravan park. The inn is a popular venue for campers, hikers and sailors. Pub food is served lunchtime and evening and includes soup, grills, burgers, salmon and meat salads, sandwiches and ploughman's, plus daily specials and a children's menu. There are summer barbecues. A separate games room has darts, shove ha'penny and pool.

Beer: Hartley Bitter and Robinson Old Tom on handpumps.

Accommodation: 1 double, 1 twin, 1 family room. B&B £12 per person. Children 2-12 years £7; under 2 years free. Single supplement £3 per night.

DALTON IN FURNESS

Miners Arms
19 Crooklands Brow. A590 between Ulverston and Barrow-in-Furness

Licensee: Stewart Ainsworth
Tel: 0229 62341

The Miners Arms is a small and friendly local, the first building on the brow of the hill as you enter Dalton. The bar meals, which include vegetarian dishes, are all home-cooked. Dalton is on the fringe of the Lake District and the pub is a good base for exploring south Cumbria. It is close to the ruins of Furness Abbey.

Beer: Hartley Mild and XB on handpumps.

Accommodation: 2 twins, 1 family room. B&B £11 per person, £12.50 single. Weekly rate on application. No pets.

MASONS ARMS, CARTMELL FELL – *see p 52*

DOVENBY

Ship Inn
A593 Maryport to Cockermouth road

Licensee: Judith Wright
Tel: 0900 822522

The Ship is a true Cumbrian pub with a welcoming atmosphere that is hard to match. It has been sensitively updated to provide all the modern comforts while its original features have been left intact. The menu is varied and children are welcome in the beer garden and there is a play area for them, located behind the pub and away from the road. The guest rooms have all been recently refurbished and have colour TVs, tea and coffee making facilities and hot and cold water. Dovenby is just ten minutes from Cockermouth and close to the Solway coast and Maryport Marina.

Beer: Jennings Mild and Bitter on handpumps.

Accommodation: 2 doubles, 1 twin. B&B £12.50 per person.

DRIGG

Victoria Hotel
Off A595 west of Holmrook

Licensees: George & Christine Richardson
Tel: 09404 231

The hotel dates from 1850 and was for a time renamed the Station Hotel when the iron way reached the area. It is close to the delightful Furness line that links Carlisle and Lancaster. Its many original features include an open fire, beams and a framed collection of knots, jugs and maps. Children are welcome, and bar meals, renowned for miles around, are

CUMBRIA

served lunchtime and evening. There is a separate dining room for residents and a beer garden. All the guest rooms have central heating, colour TVs and hot and cold water. There is salmon fishing on the River Irt, and an 18-hole golf course close by. Drigg is on the fringe of the Lake District and within easy reach of England's highest mountain, deepest lake and smallest church. There is a fine sandy beach a mile away, and the hotel is also close to the La'al Ratty railway that runs between Ravenglass and Eskdale. If you send a postcard home you can pop it into one of the few remaining Victorian pillar boxes just outside the hotel.

Beer: Jennings Bitter on handpump.

Accommodation: 2 twins, 3 singles, 1 family room. B&B £12 per person.

ELTERWATER

Britannia Inn
Near Ambleside, off B5343 and A593

Licensee: David Fry
Tel: 096 67 382/210

A friendly, homely, 400 year-old inn set in the great beauty of the Langdale Valley, the Britannia is a popular centre for keen walkers and specializes in superb four course dinners – you must book well in advance as there is a long waiting list. A typical menu may include avocado pear stuffed with crab meat, chicken in a mild curry salad, leek and bacon soup, grapefruit sorbet, fresh Scottish salmon, roast ribs of beef, sirloin steak, fresh fruit Pavlova, homemade blackcurrant ice cream, and Athol Brose. Children are made welcome and can choose from the bar menu if they join their parents in the dining room. Bar meals include homemade soup, ploughman's, cheese and broccoli flan, rainbow trout and daily hot specials. There is a residents' lounge and walkers are welcome, even with muddy boots, in the bar. The cheery front bar has an open coal fire, oak benches and settles.

Beer: Bass Special Bitter, Hartleys XB, Jennings Bitter, Marston Pedigree Bitter plus draught cider on handpumps.

Accommodation: 8 doubles, 1 family room. B&B £21.25 per person, £24 with private shower, dinner £12.25 extra. Week £138.25. Children half price when sharing.

FAR SAWREY

Sawrey Hotel
B5285 towards Windermere Ferry on Hawkshead road

Licensees: David & Sheila Brayshaw
Tel: 09662 3425

The hotel is an attractive whitewashed, early-18th-century inn made up of three separate buildings. The old stables now form the bar, with the guest rooms above. The pub's original name is thought to have been the Angler's Rest, and it was later called the New Inn. The stables were converted in 1971 and named the Claife Crier bar after the ghost of a monk in Furness Abbey whose mission in medieval times was to save 'fallen' women. He fell in love with one of them, was rejected and went mad and died. The hotel has beams in the bar that are thought to have come from wrecks of the Spanish armada, many of which perished off the Cumberland coast. The bar has old stable stalls for seating, harnesses on the walls and a variety of traditional games. There are full restaurant meals, while the bar offers soup, hiker's lunch, Cumberland sausage and local trout. The guest rooms have colour TVs and telephones.

Beer: Jennings Bitter, Tetley Bitter, Theakston Best Bitter and Old Peculier on handpumps.

Accommodation: 3 singles, 11 doubles, 3 family rooms, most with private bathrooms. B&B from £16 per person, B&B + dinner from £22.50. Week from £148, Weekend from £40 B&B + dinner. Children half price.

KESWICK

Bank Tavern
Main Street, off A591 and A66

Licensees: Jack & Olive Hobbs
Tel: 07687 72663

The Bank Tavern is in the centre of one of Lakeland's most popular and picturesque towns. The pub has been carefully updated to meet modern demands but retains such original features as beams, open fires and old church pews. Bar food is served from 11.30am to 9pm in the friendly lounge bar or, in good weather, in the beer garden to the side of the pub and away from the main street. The guest rooms are all heated and have hot and cold water and tea and coffee making facilities. A residents' lounge has a colour TV and is used for breakfast.

Beer: Jennings Mild and Bitter on handpumps.

Accommodation: 1 twin, 4 doubles/twins. 1 double and 1 twin also have single beds. B&B £10 per person.

CUMBRIA

Pheasant Inn
Off A66 towards Keswick on Crossthwaite road

Licensees: David & Marion Wright
Tel: 07687 72219

The Pheasant, a traditional old Cumbrian local, was a 'Jerry House' in the early 19th century, when short-lived parliamentary legislation allowed anyone to run a pub on payment of two guineas for a licence. The Pheasant today does not have a rough, ale-house reputation though it has retained such original features as open fires in stone hearths and wood panelling. The walls are decorated with cartoons by a local artist. Bar food is served lunchtime and evening and is based on home-cooked Cumbrian dishes, using fresh local ingredients, from Cumbrian farm recipes and served in farm-size portions. A separate dining room for residents has an à la carte menu. The Pheasant is host to the Blencathra Foxhounds, which meet there twice a year. There is outside seating for families in the summer months. Guest rooms are heated and have tea, coffee and chocolate making equipment. Dogs up to labrador size are accepted.

Beer: Jennings Bitter on handpump.

Accommodation: 1 single, 3 doubles/twins, 2 family rooms. B&B £15 single, £25 double. Children half price in family rooms. Dogs welcome.

CUMBRIA

Twa Dogs Inn
Penrith Road

Licensee: Gordon Hallett
Tel: 07687 72599

Rebuilt in 1967 on the site of a traditional 17th-century Cumbrian inn, the Twa Dogs is home to the only captured specimen of the legendary Bogart Vulgaris, a cross between a fox and a badger. The bogart pole used in the capture now hangs above the bar in the spacious lounge. Gordon Hallett boasts a certificate to prove his runaway success in the 1981 'Biggest Liar in the World' competition, which means you can take the fox-cum-badger tale with an outsize pinch of white condiment. Bar meals are served all day and there is a pleasant beer garden. The pub takes its name from a poem by Robert Burns, the 'Twa Dogs', which is a discussion between two dogs about their differing lifestyles. A photograph in the pub, taken at the Burns Museum in Alloway, Ayrshire, shows the original Burns chair with the two dogs carved as the arms. A series of caricatures of locals by artist Billy Wilkinson decorates the pub. All in all, a lively sort of place. All the guest rooms have colour TVs, hot and cold water and tea and coffee making equipment.

Beer: Jennings Bitter on handpump.

Accommodation: 3 doubles, 2 family rooms. B&B from £13 per person.

TOWER BANK ARMS,
NEAR SAWREY – *see p 58*

LANGDALE

Old Dungeon Ghyll Hotel
B5343 at end of Langdale Valley, off A593 and A591

Licensees: Neil & Jane Walmsley
Tel: 096 67 272

The Old Dungeon Ghyll is a famous rock climbers' inn in a breathtaking setting at the heart of the Great Langdale Valley. The inn takes its name from the nearby Dungeon Ghyll Force waterfall. It is a simple and homely pub with great thick walls to keep out the winter blasts, sing-songs in the bar and generous home-cooked meals, including hot soup, curries and Cumberland sausage ... and a choice of snuff.

Beer: Marston Pedigree Bitter and Merrie Monk, Theakston Best Bitter, XB (summer) and Old Peculier, Yates Bitter, Bulmer medium cider and a regular guest beer, all on handpumps.

Accommodation: 3 singles, 4 doubles, 1 twin, 2 family rooms, 4 rooms with showers. B&B from £17.75 per person, evening meal £12 extra. Reduced rates for minimum of 2 nights. Winter Breaks (from Oct) 4 nights mid-week £88 per person B&B + dinner. Reduced rates for children under 12.

MARYPORT

Golden Lion Hotel
Senhouse Street, off A596

Licensee: Allan Watson
Tel: 0900 812663

The Golden Lion was once a farmhouse, built in the early 18th century by the Lord of the Manor, Humphrey Senhouse. It was the first house in Maryport and overlooks the harbour of this now bustling and busy port. The original village was called Ellenfoot and was renamed Maryport after the wife of Senhouse's son. Many of the building's original features remain from the time when the port was just a few fishing huts. George Stephenson stayed in the hotel in 1836 and the result of his visit was the building of the Maryport and Carlisle Railway: the first locomotive arrived at Maryport on a raft. The hotel today has its ancient roots supported by all the modern amenities, including first-class guest rooms (several with en suite facilities), and a nightclub as well as a good locals' bar. Bar food is based on local produce and includes soup, steak and kidney and shepherd's pies, Aberdeen haddock, Cumberland sausage, cheese and onion quiche, lasagne, salads, filled jacket potatoes, sandwiches, sweets, and a children's menu. A marina is being built in Maryport and the hotel is handy for the town's squash club.

Beer: Jennings Bitter on handpump.

Accommodation: 2 singles, 3 doubles/ twins, 1 family room, 3 rooms en suite. B&B £13 per person. Children sharing half price. Pets welcome.

NEAR SAWREY

Tower Bank Arms
B5285 Hawkshead road near Windermere Ferry

Licensee: Philip J Broadley
Tel: 09666 334

The Tower Bank is a charming cottage pub next to Hilltop, the home of Beatrix Potter. The pub is known to generations of children as the small country inn featured in *The Tale of Jemima Puddleduck*. There is a kitchen range, stone-flagged floors, high-back settles and a grandfather clock. A good range of bar meals includes Cumberland sausage, game pie, local trout and home-roast ham. Dinner is served in a separate dining room. You can enjoy good ale and food in the beer garden in summer. The guest rooms have showers and toilets en suite, colour TVs, central heating and tea and coffee making facilities.

Beer: Matthew Brown Mild, Theakston Best Bitter and XB, Younger Scotch Bitter and No 3 on handpumps.

Accommodation: 2 doubles, 1 twin. B&B £21 per person, £32 per room. Weekly £100 per person sharing a room.

ROWRAH

Stork Hotel
Frizington, 7 miles from Whitehaven, B5086 Cockermouth to Egremont road, junction 40 M6 to Cockermouth, turn left on B5086 for 9 miles

Licensee: Mrs E L Heydon
Tel: 0946 861213

The Stork dates from 1864 and is a good, welcoming Cumbrian village local with blazing fires in winter, hunting memorabilia, and darts and dominoes teams. Regulars are active participants in the area's pub quiz league. Rowrah is at the northern end of the Lake District, close to Ennerdale, and offers clay pigeon shooting, a scrambling track, an international go-kart track and the famous Melbreak foxhounds.

Beer: Jennings Mild and Bitter on handpumps.

Accommodation: 4 twins, 1 family room. B&B £8.50 per person.

CUMBRIA

SILECROFT

Miners Arms
½ mile off A595, near Millom

Licensee: R A Sawdon
Tel: 0657 2325

The reason is lost in the mists of time, but on Easter Sunday every visitor to the Miners Arms is given a free glass of mulled ale. This welcoming old pub has, nearby, a golf course, sea fishing, fine beaches and a mining museum. There are bar snacks and meals lunchtime and evening, with such tasty specialities as homemade steak pie, curries and gammon steaks. The guest rooms are centrally heated.

Beer: Matthew Brown Mild, Theakston Best Bitter, Younger Scotch Bitter and No 3 on handpumps.

Accommodation: 2 doubles, 2 twins. B&B £12-£13 per person. No children under 14. No pets.

SWINSIDE

Swinside Inn
Newlands Valley, off A66 and A591, 2½ miles from Keswick

Licensees: Robert & Nigel Peck
Tel: 0596 82253

Swinside Inn has breathtaking views across the Newlands Valley to Barraside, Causey Pike and Cat Bells. It is a superb 17th-century Cumbrian inn with open fires and low beams, an ideal spot for fell walking, climbing, fishing, sailing and windsurfing, with Keswick close at hand. The bar menu specializes in Cumbrian dishes, including local sausage and ham, plus steaks and shepherd's pie. There are two lounge bars, often packed with locals who play darts and pool and participate in the winter quiz teams. Children are welcome and have their own menu. There is a residents' dining room and the beamed guest rooms have heating, colour TVs, hot and cold water, and tea and coffee making equipment.

Beer: Jennings Bitter on handpump.

Accommodation: 1 single, 3 doubles, 1 twin, 4 family rooms. B&B from £14 per person.

TALKIN

Hare & Hounds Inn
Talkin Village near Brampton, 1 mile off B6413, 2½ miles off A69

Licensees: Pauline & John Goddard
Tel: 06977 3456/3457

This multi-award-winning inn has new owners after years of careful tendering by the Stewarts. The Goddards will not tamper with the atmosphere of what many believe to be the friendliest inn in Britain, offering the very best food and accommodation. Close to the serenity of the lovely Talkin Tarn, the Hare and Hounds has beams, stone fireplaces, lots of etched glass and superb meals lunchtime and evening. (It is closed at lunchtime in November, January and February). Meals include Talkin Tattie Specials (baked spuds with a choice of fillings) homemade soup, rainbow trout, deep-fried scampi, and there is a special children's menu. The inn, once used by monks as a stop-over on the way from Armathwaite to Lanercost Priory, is close to Brampton and its golf course, while the tarn offers boating, fishing, swimming and windsurfing. Carlisle is a short drive away, and Talkin is a good resting place en route for the Borders.

Beer: Hartleys XB, Theakston XB, Best Bitter and Old Peculier on handpumps, plus Bulmer traditional cider.

Accommodation: 1 single, 1 double, 1 family room, 2 with private bath. B&B from £16 per person. Week £7 reduction. Children's room; children half price if sharing.

ULVERSTON

Armadale Hotel
Aradd Foot, Greenodd. A590, 2 miles north of Ulverston

Licensee: Stephanie Gibson
Tel: 0229 86257

A convivial village welcome is guaranteed in this 19th-century hotel, once a doctor's house, that now serves the communities of Aradd Foot and Greenodd on the outskirts of the town. It is the ideal base for touring the southern lakes and it overlooks the grand sweep of Morecambe Bay. Bar meals, lunch and evening (not Mondays), include homemade steak pie, Stilton pasties, tagliatelle carbonara, crispy coated vegetables, roast duckling, lasagne, curries, grilled trout, Cumberland sausage, and vegetarian dishes such as vegetable curry and cheese and broccoli quiche. The guest rooms have tea and coffee making facilities; cots for children are available.

Beer: Matthew Brown Bitter, Theakston Best Bitter on handpumps.

Accommodation: 7 doubles, 1 family room, 2 rooms with en suite facilities. B&B £14 single, £25 double, £5 extra en suite. Family room £40 per night (sleeps 4).

Canal Tavern
Canal Head. Take A590 from M6; follow signs for Barrow; pub is 200 yards on left past lighthouse on hill

Licensee: Ray Burgess
Tel: 0229 57093

The Canal Tavern is 200 years old and has been sensitively modernized to win a two-crown rating from the tourist board. It is close to Ulverston's market town, and offers coarse fishing in the canal at the rear. Home-cooked food is available lunchtimes and evenings, and includes soup, corn on the cob, snails, local fish and chicken. Meals are available in the bar or in the separate dining room.

Beer: Hartley Mild, Fellrunners and XB on handpumps.

Accommodation: 3 singles, 5 twins, 2 family rooms. B&B £12.50 single, £9.50 per person in twin, £25 family room. Children 7 and under £3, 8-14 £6. Children's room. Pets welcome.

Kings Head Hotel
Queen Street

Licensees: Jack & Margaret Lowther
Tel: 0229 52892

The Kings Head is a cosy old oak-beamed, low-ceilinged pub in the centre of Ulverston, with two blazing fires in winter and crown green bowling at the back – woods are available for hire. Drinks and food can be enjoyed on the terrace in warm weather. Children are welcome. The pub is open all day except Tuesday.

Beer: Theakston Best Bitter plus guest beers on handpumps.

Accommodation: 2 doubles, 1 family room. B&B £13 per person. Children under 12 half price when sharing with parents.

ASHBOURNE

White Lion Hotel
Buxton Road. A515, 50 yards from market place

Licensee: Richard Gregory
Tel: 0335 46158

The White Lion is an old coaching inn in a market town that is a fine base for touring the peaks and dales and is within easy reach of Chatsworth House, Haddon, Hardwick Hall and Kedleston Hall. The hotel has cheery log fires and a welcoming, old-world atmosphere. The guest rooms have TVs, hot and cold water, controlled heaters and tea and coffee making equipment; most rooms have private showers or baths. Cask beer is served in two bars, the restaurant offers an à la carte menu and there is also an extensive range of bar meals, available lunchtime and evening. Trout fishing can be arranged on the River Dove, once fished by that Compleat Angler, Isaak Walton. Buxton is close at hand, and there are family pleasures at Alton Towers and the American Adventure Park.

Beer: Marston Border Mild and Pedigree Bitter on handpumps.

Accommodation: 6 doubles/twins, 1 family room, 4 rooms with en suite facilities. B&B £17.25 single, £23 en suite, £32.20 double/twin, £36.80 en suite, family room £46.20. Children half price sharing. No pets. Cards: Access and Visa.

DERBYSHIRE

BAMFORD

Derwent Hotel
Main Road. A6013, 2 miles off A57 at Ladybower

Licensees: Angela & David Ryan
Tel: 0433 51395

The Derwent is a superbly situated hotel in the heart of the Peak District, with Jane Eyre connections and close to the spectacular Ladybower reservoirs. The hotel lounges have old sewing machines, harnesses, copper, brass and fascinating pictures and prints, while the guest rooms all have TVs, tea and coffee making facilities and fine views of the Derbyshire hills. The emphasis is on home-cooked food; the bar menu includes soup, sandwiches, lasagne, steak and kidney pie and homemade deserts. There is a separate dining room and seats in the garden. Boat and tackle can be hired for fishing in the reservoirs.

Beer: Stones Best Bitter, Wards Sheffield Best Bitter and Tetley Bitter on handpumps.

Accommodation: 2 singles, 8 doubles, 2 with private baths. B&B from £21 per person. Children welcome, terms negotiable.

BIRCH VALE

Sycamore Inn
Sycamore Road. B6015, off A6 at New Mills

Licensees: Christine & Malcolm Nash
Tel: 0663 42715

The Sycamore is a cheerful family pub near Stockport, on the banks of the River Sett and standing in large grounds that include a beer garden, children's play area and barbecue area. There are patio seats at the front, too, and the two bars, three eating areas and guest rooms are beautifully appointed, the latter enjoying colour TVs, en suite bathrooms and tea and coffee making facilities. Food is served every day lunchtime and evenings, and ranges from lasagne to Mexican-style grills, fish and vegetarian dishes, and a children's menu. The inn is well placed for visiting Kinder Scout, the Blue John Mines and Chatsworth House.

Beer: Jennings Bitter and Tetley Bitter on handpumps.

Accommodation: 5 doubles. £22.50 single, £32.50 double. Full English breakfast £5, Continental £4. Children welcome. Cards: Access and Visa.

BRADLEY

Jinglers Fox & Hounds Inn
Near Ashbourne. A517 Ashbourne to Belper road

Licensee: Paula Catlin
Tel: 0335 70855

If you approach this old coaching inn from Ashbourne the inn sign says the Jinglers. From the Belper side it is called the more traditional Fox & Hounds. It was given the nickname of the Jinglers by locals in the time when the road outside was a gated one with a toll: presumably drovers on the road had to jingle a bell to attract the gateman's attention. The accommodation is all in six self-contained flats with their own kitchens and entrances. It is a splendid family pub: the family room has a pool table, video machine and juke box and the large garden has swings, slides, a heifer, Shetland ponies, a peacock and peahen, ducks, parrots, two dogs and a rabbit named Christopher Columbus. Bar meals served lunchtime and evening include chicken nuggets, chicken tikka, steak in a cob (roll), drover's pie, pizzas, ploughman's and salads. The pub is close to Alton Towers, Ashbourne, Chatsworth, Buxton and High Peak.

Beer: Marston Pedigree Bitter on handpump.

Accommodation: (all self-catering) 1 single, 3 doubles, 2 family rooms, all en suite. Room prices: single £15, double £25, family room £45-50. Children £8 sharing. £5 reduction on price of room for an extra night. Pets welcome.

BUXTON

Grove Hotel
Grove Parade

Proprietor: David E Kershaw
Tel: 0298 23804

This commanding 18th-century listed building in the centre of the famous spa town, close to the Opera House, The Crescent and Pavilion Gardens, offers great comfort, bar meals lunch and evening and the perfect base for such nearby delights as Chatsworth House, Bakewell and Dovedale and the Goyt and Manifold valleys. The guest rooms have TVs and tea and coffee making facilities. Bar food is available in Charlie's Bar and the Rowan Room has both à la carte and table d'hôte menus.

Beer: Robinson Best Mild and Best Bitter on electric pump.

Accommodation: 21 rooms including 14 doubles/twins and 5 family rooms, 7 rooms with en suite facilities. B&B £22 single, £33 en suite, double £37, £44 with bath. Children welcome. Cards: Access, Amex, Diners and Visa.

CASTLETON

Castle Hotel
Main Road, Hope Valley, A625

Licensee: José Luis Rodriguez
Tel: 0433 20578

The Castle is a 17th-century coaching inn in a lovely village of narrow twisting streets and limestone cottages at the foot of the ruins of Peveril Castle, immortalized by Sir Walter Scott in *Peveril of the Peak*. The hotel is 10 minutes from the Peak Cavern and is close to the Blue John Mine, Speedwell Cavern and Treak Cliff Cavern. The Castle's lounge and public bars have old stone walls, beams, open fires and flagstoned floors.Bar food includes sandwiches, crudités, ploughman's, stuffed pancakes, macaroni cheese, curry, and seafood Mornay. The Regency Restaurant has cosmopolitan menus. The Minstrel Gallery, which can be used for functions, is reputed to be haunted by the ghost of a jilted bride.Two of the comfortable guest rooms have four-poster beds and all rooms have colour TVs and tea, coffee and hot chocolate making facilities. Some rooms have jacuzzis and there is a bridal suite.

Beer: Stones Best Bitter on electric pump.

Accommodation: 5 singles, 5 doubles, 2 family rooms. B&B £35 single, £45 double, four-poster double £49, honeymoon suite from £55. Children welcome, from £8 per night. Bargain Breaks April–Sept, Sunday to Friday: from £27 per person per night.

NR DERBY

Holly Bush Inn
Holly Bush Lane, Makewey, Milford. A6 Derby to Belper road. Turn right at Milford Bridge; at garden centre turn left into Holly Bush Lane

Licensee: John James Bilbie
Tel: 0332 841729

The Holly Bush, sporting an ancient pub name, is 16th-century and has retained its oak beams. It is a simple, no frills, friendly old local where beer is still served by jugs, straight from the casks. Bar food is available, including evening meals.

Beer: Bateman XXXB, Marston Pedigree Bitter and Owd Rodger, Ruddles County and always two or three guest beers, all served by gravity

Accommodation: 1 single, 2 doubles. B&B £12.50 single, £24 double. Children half price. Children's room. Pets welcome.

GLOSSOP

Manor Inn
77 High Street, A57

Licensee: Kenneth Batty
Tel: 04574 5605

The Manor is an 18th-century coaching inn on the infamous 'snake' main road between Sheffield and Manchester. It is a mile from Snake Pass and a short drive to the heart of the Peak District. It is a fiercely traditional pub with a separate lounge and games room. Excellent bar food is served lunchtime every day except Sunday.

Beer: Boddingtons Bitter and OB Bitter on handpumps.

Accommodation: 1 double, 1 family room. B&B £17 single, £27 double. Children by arrangement.

HAYFIELD

Royal Hotel
Market Square, off A624 in centre of village, near junction with A6015

Licensee: Bob Hadfield
Tel: 0663 42721

The stone-built hotel dominates the square of this picturesque village bounded by the River Sett. Built in 1755 as a vicarage, the Royal has retained some of its old atmosphere. It has well-appointed rooms and a restaurant serving à la carte meals. Home-cooked bar meals are also available and parties are a speciality. Hayfield stands on the highest part of the Peak and is the natural gateway to Kinder Scout, where a 'mass trespass' in 1932 struck a major blow for ramblers' rights.

Beer: Websters Yorkshire Bitter and Websters Choice, Wilsons Original Mild and Bitter on handpumps.

Accommodation: 1 single, 1 double, 3 twins. B&B £15 per person. Children charged £7.50 under 12, babies free; children's room. Special rates for 3 nights or more.

HURDLOW

Bull I'Th' Thorn
A515, Ashbourne–Buxton road

Licensees: Judith & Bob Haywood
Tel: 0298 83 348

This famous hostelry on the old Roman road between Chester and Buxton has acted as a coaching inn and resting place for travellers for more than 500 years. There was a farmhouse on the site nearly 700 years ago which in 1472 became an inn called the Bull. The name changed to Hurdlow House in the 17th century and documents of the time refer to it as Hurdlow Thorn: the present name is a combination of its two main associations. At the height of the horse-drawn coaching period it was a major stopping place for coaches on the Derby to Manchester route. All this fascinating history is caught by the rich atmosphere of Tudor panelling, period carvings and stone-flagged floors. Bar meals – soup, ploughman's, fish and chips, steaks, salads, sandwiches, children's meals, plus Sunday roast – are served lunchtime and evening. As well as the accommodation in the inn, there is a self-catering flat.

Beer: Robinsons Best Bitter on handpump.

Accommodation: 1 double, 1 twin with private bath. B&B £11 per person. Children's room; children's terms on application. Self-catering holiday flat £100 a week.

ILKESTON

Durham Ox
Durham Street, off B6096, M1 junction 26

Licensee: Frank Barton
Tel: 0602 324570

An old-fashioned (in the best sense) backstreet pub where beer, grub, accommodation and companionship are all marvellous value. The pub is a real community centre, hosting cricket, football and quiz teams as well as offering such games as darts, skittles and pool. Durham Street is a back road and you can get to this splendid boozer, the oldest pub in the town, from either Station Road or Bath Street. The pub fare is simple and nourishing: sausage, egg, chips and beans, fish, chips and peas, and chicken, chips and peas, all at £1.60.

Beer: Wards Mild, Sheffield Best Bitter and a guest beer on hand and electric pumps.

Accommodation: 1 single, 1 double. B&B £8.50 per person.

KIRK IRETON

Barley Mow
Off B5023 Wirksworth to Derby road

Licensee: Mary Short
Tel: 0335 70306

The Barley Mow is a splendidly unspoilt 17th-century village inn. From the outside it looks like a private house, set behind stone walls, standing three storeys high and with two dormer windows. Inside it is a ramble of small, interconnecting rooms with a plethora of wood-panelling and ale that comes straight from the casks. Mrs Short is proud of her beer quality: 'We did have Theakston's but it has not been satisfactory since it has become S&N owned.' The guest rooms have been thoroughly updated and offer en suite facilities, colour TVs and tea and coffee making equipment. There is a residents' lounge and guests can have a three-course evening meal. Winter lunchtime bar meals include sandwiches, ploughman's and a hot dish of the day. The High Peak Trail is two miles away, there is trout fishing in a nearby lake, and Alton Towers, the Derbyshire dales and the many stately homes in the area are all close at hand.

Beer: Hook Norton Best Bitter and Old Hookey, Marston Pedigree Bitter, regular guest beers and Thatcher's Cider straight from the cask.

Accommodation: 5 doubles/twins, 4 rooms en suite. B&B £18 single, £30 double. One room has a double and single bed, suitable for families. Pets welcome.

TADDINGTON

Waterloo
On A6 midway between Buxton and Bakewell

Licensee: Tony Heathcote
Tel: 0298 85230

The Waterloo, high in the Peak National Park, has superb views of the dales, is within easy reach of the old market towns of Buxton and Bakewell, and is a short drive to Chatsworth House, home of the Duke and Duchess of Devonshire. The Waterloo Bar has open log fires and a beamed ceiling, a small and cosy dining room seats 22, and a larger room with seats for 120 acts as function room and larger dining room. There are singalongs on Sunday evenings with a regular pub pianist. Bar meals (not Tuesday evenings) include such homemade dishes as steak and kidney pie, chilli con carne, cheese and asparagus flan and beef curry, with steaks, fish and chips and ploughman's. The dining room offers soup, garlic mushrooms, whitebait, steaks, fresh trout, grilled salmon and boeuf bourguignon. All the guest rooms have colour TVs and tea and coffee making equipment.

Beer: Robinson Best Bitter on electric pump.

Accommodation: 2 singles, 2 doubles. B&B £12.50 per person. Children's room. No pets. Cards: Access and Visa.

TIDESWELL

George Hotel
Commercial Road, ¼ mile off A619 Chesterfield–Stockport road

Licensee: Dale Norris
Tel: 0298 871382

The George is a much-photographed, handsome 18th-century coaching inn in a medieval market town and next to the soaring Cathedral of the Peak. The friendly atmosphere of the George is underscored by a log fire in winter and a cheerful informality that happily allows guests to choose to eat in either the separate dining room or by the fire in the lounge. The menu, lunch and evening, includes daily specials chalked on a board, soup, old ale and mushroom pâté, poacher's pie, lasagne, beefburgers, and a wide variety of fillings for wholemeal rolls. Within a 10-mile radius of the hotel you can visit Chatsworth, Castleton, the Derwent Valley, Buxton, Bakewell and Hathersage, the legendary burial place of Little John. The guest rooms in the George have colour TVs.

Beer: Hardys & Hansons Kimberley Best Mild and Best Bitter on handpumps.

Accommodation: 1 single, 3 doubles, 1 family room. B&B £16 per person. £15 per day for a stay of 2-3 days. Half board available. Children's room; children 20% reduction.

DERBYSHIRE

WHALEY BRIDGE

Jodrell Arms Hotel
39 Market Street. A6, next to railway station

Licensees: Mr & Mrs J D Bond and Mrs L Jenkins
Tel: 066 33 2164

The Jodrell is a fine old pub in the centre of the village close to the canal basin terminus. It was built in the late 17th century and is a grade two listed building with a Tuscan porch and Elizabethan gables. There is a welcoming fire on winter days, good-value bar snacks and a separate restaurant for lunch and dinner. All the guest rooms have colour TVs and tea and coffee making facilities. Whaley Bridge is at the entrance to the lovely Goyt Valley with sailing on the reservoir and canal cruises. Mr J D Bond is former Lancashire county cricket captain Jackie Bond, who held one of the most remarkable catches ever seen in a Lord's one-day final when Lancashire won the Gillette Cup.

Beer: Websters Yorkshire Bitter, Wilsons Original Mild and Bitter on handpumps.

Accommodation: 2 singles, 9 doubles/twins, 2 with private showers. B&B £23 single, £35 double. Children welcome, terms negotiable. Cards: Access and Visa.

JODRELL ARMS HOTEL, WHALEY BRIDGE

WHITEHOUGH

Old Hall Inn
Chinley, ¼ mile off B6062

Proprietors: Michael & Ann Capper
Tel: 0663 50529

The inn, a grade two listed building and part of Whitehough Hall, is in a quiet hamlet with panoramic views of the Peak District. The hall dates back to the 16th century and for generations it was the home of the Kirke family. Sir David Kirke's sister, Mary, was maid-of-honour to Queen Catherine of Braganza. George Kirke was groom to the royal bedchamber of Charles I and was present when the monarch lost his head on the block. Colonel Percy Kirke put down the Monmouth Rebellion with terrible severity after the battle of Sedgemoor in 1685. The inn retains splendid beamed ceilings, mullioned windows, and a minstrel gallery in the Rafters Restaurant where there is a three-course menu for residents. Comprehensive bar food is also available. Accommodation includes private baths or showers, colour TVs, central heating, direct-dial telephones and tea and coffee making facilities.

Beer: Jennings Bitter, Marston Pedigree Bitter and Tetley Bitter on handpumps.

Accommodation: 4 doubles B&B £29.50 single, £40 double. With table d'hôte dinner: single £37.50, double £56. Children welcome; reductions up to 100% according to age. Cards: Access, Amex, Diners and Visa.

BLACKAWTON

Normandy Arms
2 miles off B3207, near Totnes, A381

Licensees: Jos & Mark Gibson
Tel: 080 421 316

The Normandy is a friendly old village pub with 16th-century origins and a warm and cosy atmosphere in an unspoilt village close to Totnes, Kingsbridge and the beaches of the South Hams. There are facilities for sailing, boating, windsurfing and sea and trout fishing. The Normandy Arms has a small, comfortable bar, a separate restaurant and a children's room upstairs with toys, games and books. It plays up the Normandy theme with photos of General Montgomery and other World War II memorabilia. Bar snacks offer homemade soup, hot smoked mackerel, vegetable pancake, ploughman's and sandwiches, while the restaurant (open lunch and dinner) has a sensibly short menu that includes such house specials as pork fillet cooked with local cider, and sauté of game Normandy. There is a beer garden for warmer days, and the brews include ales from the local Blackawton Brewery, one of the first of the new crop of small independent brewers to set up in the late 1970s.

Beer: Bass, Blackawton Bitter, 44 (summer only) and Headstrong (winter), Ruddles County on handpumps.

Accommodation: 3 doubles, 1 twin, 1 bunk-bedded room. 2 rooms with private bath. B&B from £15.50 per person. Children's terms by arrangement.

BRANSCOMBE

Masons Arms
In village centre, off A3052

Licensee: Janet Inglis
Tel: 029 780 300

The Masons is a delightful, 14th-century creeper-clad inn with beamed ceilings and stone-flagged floors. Joints are spit-roasted over the great open hearth in the main bar, which has wall benches and old settles as well as a casement clock. Outside there are seats on a terrace that leads into a small garden. Lunchtime bar food includes soup, ploughman's, jacket potatoes with a choice of fillings, and homemade steak and kidney pie. More adventurous evening dishes may include chicken curry with poppadums, braised pigeon in port and pickled walnut sauce, and pork with pineapple and ginger. There is a Sunday roast lunch. Darts, shove ha'penny and dominoes are played in the bar, and the sea is just a mile away. Some of the guest rooms are in a cottage across the road.

Beer: Bass, Hall and Woodhouse Badger Best Bitter and Tanglefoot on handpumps, plus Inch's cider.

Accommodation: 19 rooms. 1 single, 6 twins, 10 doubles, 2 family rooms, 13 rooms with private bath or shower. B&B £22.50 single, £30 en suite, double £45, £60 en suite, executive suite £35 single, £70 for 2 people. Dogs welcome. Cards: Access and Visa.

BUTTERLEIGH

Butterleigh Inn
Near Cullompton. 3 miles from M5

Licensees: Mike & Penny Wolter
Tel: 08845 407

The Butterleigh is a small 16th-century, mid-Devon pub in a tiny hamlet between Tiverton and Cullompton, set in delightful countryside. Food ranges from granary rolls and venison sausages to Butterleigh Grill or quail in port wine. The modern guest rooms have tea and coffee making facilities. The main bar is divided into two areas; one part is a standard lounge bar while the other is for locals (and guests) dedicated to such pastimes as darts, shove ha'penny and dominoes. There is also a small snug bar. Bickleigh Castle is close at hand.

Beer: Cotleigh Harrier SPA, Tawny and Old Buzzard, plus guest beers on handpumps.

Accommodation: 2 twin rooms, sharing a bathroom. B&B £14.50 single, £10.50 per person sharing. Children over 14 years welcome. Half and full board available.

CHILLINGTON

Chillington Inn
4 miles east of Kingsbridge on A379 Dartmouth road

Licensee: D R Mooney
Tel: 0548 580 244

The Chillington Inn's origins date back to the 17th century and while it serves high-class food in its restaurant it still retains the atmosphere and attitudes of a traditional country ale house. The two comfortable bars have many original furnishings and other artefacts and welcoming open fires. It is just two miles from some of the area's finest beaches. The beautifully appointed guest rooms have private bathrooms, are centrally heated and have colour TVs and tea and coffee making equipment. Bar snacks are available, while the restaurant food is based on fresh ingredients and home-cooking, with such dishes as salade niçoise, crab and lobster in season, local fish and steaks.

Beer: Flowers Original and Palmer IPA on handpumps.

Accommodation: 2 doubles, 1 family room. B&B £14.50 per person; single occupancy £16. Family room £17.50 per person. Children half price. 2 nights dinner, B&B from £27 per person per night. Pets welcome. Cards: Access and Visa.

COLEFORD

New Inn
2½ miles from A377, near Crediton

Licensee: Paul S Butt
Tel: 0363 84242

The New Inn is a very old inn, built in the 13th century. Many New Inns were so-called because they were built by monasteries to provide ale and victuals for travellers. The New Inn in Coleford has a thatched roof and cob and granite walls. It was formerly a monks' retreat and was later a staging post for coaches on the Exeter to Plymouth road. The bars have oak beams, large log fires, and stone walls with a profusion of gleaming brass and copper and old prints. A small stream runs by the inn and the village has many other old and attractive houses. The bar menu is chalked on a blackboard and based on home-cooked meals, including chilli, curry, steak and kidney pie, grills, plaice or haddock and chips, a daily vegetarian dish, Hungarian mushrooms, avocado and Stilton, beef and walnuts, and such good old nursery puds as spotted dick and bread pudding. There is a separate restaurant. Fishing and golf are available nearby.

Beer: Flowers Original and IPA, Wadworth 6X plus a a regular guest beer, all on handpumps.

Accommodation: 3 doubles, 1 room with en suite facilities. B&B £22-£24 single, double £16-£17 per person. Children welcome; under 10 years charged £10 when sharing with parents. A self-contained holiday flat with 2 bedrooms is also available.

DODDISCOMBSLEIGH

Nobody Inn
2½ miles from A38 at Haldon Hill (signposted Dunchideock & Doddiscombsleigh)

Proprietor: Nicholas Borst-Smith
Tel: 0647 52394

A famous old 16th-century inn six miles from Exeter and close to Dartmoor and the coast, its name, according to local legend, stems from an unknown landlord who locked the doors and refused hospitality to travellers seeking bed and refreshment. They went wearily on their way, reporting that 'nobody was in the inn'. You are assured of a welcome today, backed by fine food, ale, 200 whiskies and 700 wines, ports and brandies. The restaurant is open Tuesday to Saturday evenings and offers dishes made from local produce; local trout cooked in pastry is a speciality. Bar meals, served lunchtime and evening, include homemade soup, sandwiches, hot

Nr Exeter

EX6 7PS

smoked mackerel, butter bean casserole, sausage and mash, vegetable or lamb casserole. The inn has old beams and carriage lamps, and high-back settles. You can eat in the lovely garden in good weather. Guest rooms have tea and coffee making facilities; breakfast is served in the rooms.

Beer: Bass, Flowers IPA, Wadworth 6X, Youngs Special and guest beers on handpumps and straight from the cask.

Accommodation: 1 single, 7 doubles, 5 with en suite facilities. Double rooms can be used as singles. B&B £13-£22 single, £20 per person in double room. 10% reduction per person for stays of 4 days or more. No children. No pets. Cards: Access and Visa.

ERMINGTON

Crooked Spire Inn
B3211, 2 miles off A38 near Ivybridge

Licensee: Jim Shield
Tel: 0548 830202

A cosy and welcoming village inn, with such traditional games as darts and euchre in the bar and excellent pub food. Bar snacks include pasties, ploughman's and sandwiches. The separate restaurant has local trout, moussaka, steak and kidney pie, grills, salads, lasagne and curries.

Beer: Flowers Original and IPA on handpumps.

Accommodation: 3 doubles. B&B £19.50 per person. Half and full board available. Cards: Access and Visa.

FREMINGTON

Fox & Hounds
A39 on Barnstaple to Bideford road

Licensees: Brian & Geraldine Hannam
Tel: 0271 73094/42317

A small village inn and genuine local where darts, skittles and shove ha'penny are played with enthusiasm. It is a good base in north Devon for Exmoor and Dartmoor and the beaches of Lynton, Lynmouth, Woolacombe and the Taw estuary. There are facilities for riding and fishing. Pub food includes soup, trout, ploughman's, salads, and a children's menu with bangers and chips and fish fingers. There are daily home-cooked specials and a roast dinner on request.There is a sitting room for guests with colour TV, and there is live music at weekends.

Beer: Ruddles Best Bitter, Ushers Best Bitter and a guest beer on handpumps.

Accommodation: 3 doubles, 2 family rooms. B&B £13 per person. Weekend £24 for 2 nights. Children's room; 30% reductions. Cot available. Pets welcome.

HATHERLEIGH

George Hotel
Market Street. A387. A30 from Okehampton (6 miles)

Licensees: John Dunbar-Ainley and Veronica Devereux
Tel: 0837 810454

The George is an old coaching inn with a thatched roof, timbered cob walls and an impressive balcony overhanging the street. It was built as long ago as 1450 as a retreat for monks. The inn has retained its period charm with a cobbled courtyard and low beamed ceilings. The small front bar, used mainly by residents, has a great fireplace and thick stone walls. A second lounge has a wood-burning stove and old settles. A third bar is open only on market days for local farmers and other market folk. Bar food, available every day, includes ploughman's, sandwiches, soup, spinach and mushroom roulade, and steak and kidney pie. A separate restaurant offers à la carte meals. There are seats outside in the courtyard and the hotel also has a heated swimming pool. Some of the guest rooms have four-poster beds and all have colour TVs and telephones.

Beer: Bass, Exmoor Ale, Flowers Original, Theakston Old Peculier (winter) and Wadworth 6X on handpumps.

Accommodation: 1 single, 10 doubles, 3 family rooms, 9 rooms with en suite facilities. B&B £27 single, double £30.75 per room, £40.75 en suite, four-poster with bath £45. 3 nights or more out of season: 10% discount. Children's room; children welcome to stay. Pets welcome. Cards: Access and Visa.

Tally Ho
14 Market Street

Licensees: Gianni & Annamaria Scoz
Tel: 0837 810306

By the time this edition of the guide appears, the Tally Ho should be brewing its own Nutters Ale. Signor Scoz from Milan fell in love with Devon on a holiday, decided to stay, and runs a highly traditional English pub. He has now got planning permission to install a three-barrel brewery in an outhouse and will brew a pukka traditional draught beer. The inn is 15th-century, and one bar has a wood-burning stove and all the rooms have antique furnishings to point up the atmosphere, which is enhanced by candelight. Annamaria Scoz is the power behind the kitchen and supplies homemade pasta and pizzas for the bar while the restaurant offers such delights as Parma ham with melon, antipasto misto, insalata tricolore, piccata melone, scaloppine al Marsala, chicken Kiev, trout, and scampi. Signor Scoz has a good Milanese attitude to enjoyment: a leaflet in the guest rooms reads: 'As the Tally Ho is above all a country inn, the locals are likely to become a little boisterous at times, especially on darts night. If you are finding it difficult to sleep, then why not come downstairs and join in the fun.' *Salute*!

Beer: Butcombe Bitter, Eldridge Pope Royal Oak and Fullers London Pride straight from the cask.

Accommodation: 3 doubles, all with en suite facilities. B&B £20 single, £36-£38 double. Children sharing with parents charged for breakfast only. Pets welcome. Cards: Access and Visa.

HAYTOR VALE

Rock Inn
Moorland road to Widecombe; signposted from B3344 west of Bovey Tracey; 6 miles from Newton Abbot

Licensee: Christopher Graves
Tel: 03646 305

The Rock has a long and fascinating history. Down the centuries it has been an alehouse for Haytor granite quarrymen and iron miners, a meeting place for farmers and landowners, and a coaching inn. It has an unspectacular façade but the interior is a delight with half-panelled walls and high-back settles. Other rooms have log fires in handsome fireplaces, and many old prints and paintings on the walls. The inn is set in a small village nestling in Dartmoor National Park below the stark beauty of Haytor Rocks. The wide-ranging bar food includes sandwiches, pasties, homemade soup, filled jacket potatoes, ploughman's, lasagne, curries, vegetarian dishes, rabbit and cider casserole, fish casserole, local trout, and good desserts such as apple cheesecake, treacle tart and bread and butter pudding. There is a separate restaurant with such dishes as venison marinated in real ale, duck à l'orange and local salmon. The inn has a pleasant garden and there are nearby facilities for golf, horse riding and fishing.

Beer: Bass, Eldridge Pope, Thomas Hardy Country Bitter and Royal Oak and regular guest beers on handpumps.

Accommodation: 1 single, 9 doubles, seven rooms with en suite facilities, 1 four-poster bedroom; all rooms have colour TVs, direct-dial phones and tea and coffee makers. B&B £18.50 single, £35 en suite, £25.50 double per person, £27.50 family room. Winter Breaks: dinner for 2 with free overnight accommodation. Children's room. No pets. Cards: Access, Amex and Visa.

HIGH BICKINGTON

Old George Inn
Take B3217 from Barnstaple to Winkleigh; pub signposted at entrance to village

Licensee: Clive Stanton
Tel: 0769 60513

The Old George is a delightful and picturesque 16th-century thatched pub with old beams and a large open fireplace. It is beautifully situated between Dartmoor and Exmoor and is eight miles from Barnstaple and four miles from Torrington. While it does not have a separate restaurant, one section of the lounge is set aside for customers eating and children are welcome there. Bar food ranges from sandwiches to homemade pies, fish, chicken and steak dishes. Visitors can enjoy walking, fishing and riding in the area.

Beer: Butcombe Bitter from the cask and Ruddles Best Bitter on handpump.

Accommodation: 1 double, 1 family room. B&B £12.50 per person. Pets welcome.

HOOPS INN, HORNS CROSS – *see opposite*

HEDDONSMOUTH

Hunter's Inn
Near Lynton and Parracombe, signposted on A39 Lynton to Barnstaple road

Licensee: Chris Moate
Tel: 05983 230

Hunter's Inn, well signposted in the area, is set in one of the loveliest and most spectacular parts of Exmoor National Park. Several inns have stood on the spot over the centuries and some of them were haunts of smugglers. The present building is turn-of-the-century Edwardian, designed like a Swiss chalet, built when the previous inn was destroyed by fire. The large bars are partitioned to give a cosy atmosphere while outside there is no less than five acres of garden with a wide variety of wildlife. The guest rooms are sumptuous, a few have four-poster beds and most have en suite facilities, colour TVs and hospitality trays. Bar food, served lunchtime and evening, includes cold platters – eg cheese, honeyroast ham, smoked mackerel, trout, salmon, served with salad – steaks, fried chicken, spicy sausage, haddock or plaice, homemade lasagne, chilli con carne, vegetarian dishes and a children's menu. There is a separate restaurant.

Beer: Exmoor Ale, Flowers Original, Wadworth IPA and 6X on handpumps and regular guest beers.

Accommodation: 9 doubles/twins, 1 family room, 8 rooms with en suite facilities. B&B £19.50-£22 per person. Children under 12 half price sharing. 3-day breaks (not bank holidays) Nov-March: 10% reductions. Children's room. Cards: Access and Visa.

HORNS CROSS

Hoops Inn
A39 midway between Bideford and Clovelly

Licensees: Derek & Marjorie Sargent
Tel: 02375 222/247

The Hoops dates from the 13th century and has a reed thatched roof, thatched porches and great white cob walls. It stands 500 feet above sea level on the main road to Cornwall and is less than a mile from the coast. The atmosphere and antiquity of the inn is caught by the stone fireplace and period furniture, while some of the guest rooms have four-poster and half-tester beds. The Hoops has been a smugglers' inn and a home-brew house and was used by such famous old sea dogs as Sir Richard Grenville, Drake, Raleigh and Hawkins. They all sponsored the parliamentary bill of 1566 to build a quay at nearby Hartland where potatoes and tobacco were first imported to Britain. The picturesque village of Clovelly is just four miles away. The restaurant offers French and English cuisine while the bar food includes steaks, fish, salads, ploughman's, homemade soup and filled jacket potatoes.

Beer: Flowers Original, Marston Pedigree Bitter and Wadworth 6X on handpumps.

Accommodation: 1 single, 13 doubles, 3 family rooms, 8 rooms with en suite facilities. B&B single £10-£12, double £15 per person, family room £12 per person. Weekend £40 per person for 2 nights B&B + dinner in en suite room. Children's room. Small dogs welcome. Cards: Access, Amex, Diners and Visa.

KNOWSTONE

Masons Arms Inn
1½ miles NE of A361 between South Molton and Tiverton

Licensees: David & Elizabeth Todd
Tel: 03984 231

The Masons is an unspoilt, thatched 13th-century rural inn opposite the village church and close to Exmoor. The bar has a stone floor, settles and old farming tackle on the walls, with a beamed ceiling and a large open log fire. A smaller room is used mainly for games, including bar billiards and table skittles. Bar food includes homemade soup, smoked mackerel, salade niçoise, ploughman's, homemade pies, fritto misto, curry and rice, and steaks. There is a separate restaurant for evening meals. All the guest rooms have colour TVs and tea and coffee making facilities.

Beer: King & Barnes Sussex Bitter, Hall & Woodhouse Badger Best Bitter and Wadworth 6X from the cask.

Accommodation: 1 single, 4 doubles, 2 rooms with private facilities. B&B £18 per person, £22 in en suite room. Reductions for stays of 2 nights or more: eg 5 nights or more £17.50 per night. Children under 5 free. Pets accepted but speak to the management first.

LIFTON

Lifton Cottage Hotel
A30 between Okehampton and Launceston

Licensees: N H & F P Beer
Tel: 0556 84439

The small hotel is a 350-year-old Gothic building that is grade two listed. It has a cosy bar with a cheery open log fire in winter. Lifton is on the edge of Dartmoor and Bodmin Moor, and Roadford reservoir is some five miles away. Facilities for fishing and golf are available locally. Bar food and restaurant meals are served lunchtime and evening.

Beer: St Austell HSD on handpump.

Accommodation: 3 singles, 7 doubles, 2 family rooms, 9 rooms with en suite facilities. B&B £18.25 per person, £22.50 en suite. Family room £22 per person, children half price under 11. 10% discount for stays of 3 days or more. Children's room. Pets welcome. Cards: Access, Amex, Diners and Visa.

LYDFORD

Castle Inn
Next to Lydford Castle, 1 mile off A386 Okehampton to Tavistock road

Licensee: David Grey
Tel: 082 282 242

The Castle is a small, snug inn with beams, log fires and low ceilings in a lovely Devon village that was once an important Saxon borough with its own mint: the inn's Foresters Bar has seven original Lydford pennies made in the mint during the reign (circa AD 1000) of Ethelred the Unready. The bar also has old lamps hanging from the beams, a collection of old plates and a great Norman fireplace. The Tinners' Bar has a unique collection of antique stallion posters. There is a buffet lunch every day as well as bar snacks lunchtime and evening. Bar food includes steak and kidney pie, smokey bowl, Somerset chicken, Torbay sole, lasagne, lamb and mushroom cassoulet, and vegetable risotto. A separate à la carte restaurant is open every evening. All the guest rooms have colour TVs, central heating and tea and coffee making facilities. There is a small garden and a family room.

Beer: Bass, Courage Best Bitter and Directors Bitter, Wadworth 6X on handpumps.

Accommodation: 1 single, 7 doubles, 2 family rooms, 6 with en suite facilities. B&B £25 single, £30 en suite, double £17.50 per person, £20 en suite. Children half price sharing. Autumn and Winter Breaks £59 per person any 2 nights dinner B&B, £87.50 any 3 nights. Pets welcome. Cards: Access and Visa.

Dartmoor Inn
On A386

Licensees: Paul & Margaret Hyde
Tel: 082 282 221

The Dartmoor Inn is a 16th-century pack-horse inn on an old route from north to south Devon, an excellent base for walking and riding holidays, with the moors close at hand. New owners since the last edition of this guide have recarpeted and carefully decorated the inn without tampering with its essential charm and character. There are two welcoming bars, and darts and dominoes are played. Bar meals range from sandwiches to three-course meals featuring local rainbow trout and steaks. There is a separate candle-lit restaurant. All the guest rooms have colour TVs, central heating and tea and coffee making facilities.

Beer: Bass, Charrington IPA, St Austell Tinners and HSD on handpumps and scrumpy cider in summer.

Accommodation: 1 twin, 1 double, 1 family room, all with en suite facilities. B&B from £16 per person. Children welcome, 60% reduction. Cards: Access, Diners and Visa.

MORETON HAMPSTEAD

White Hart Hotel
The Square. Leave A38 at Newton Abbot/Bovey Tracey junction; take A382 to Moretonhampstead

Licensee: Peter Morgan
Tel: 0647 40406

The White Hart is based in a small former wool town with the longest single-word name in England. The hotel was built in the reign of George II and was a coaching inn on the Exeter to Plymouth run; coaches stopped there to change horses. During the Napoleonic Wars it was a meeting place for captured French officers on parole from Princetown prison on Dartmoor. The hallway has a vast road map of Devon, some 160 years old. The back bar has rough whitewashed walls, beams and horsebrasses and serves bar food, lunchtime and evening, that includes renowned ploughman's with great generous chunks of Cheddar, along with curry, steak and kidney pie, king prawns, local trout and quail. The restaurant has full à la carte meals, and the impressive breakfasts offer kippers as well as fried food. Moretonhampstead is in the heart of Dartmoor National Park and has 16th-century alms houses, a 14th-century church, and offers facilities for fishing and riding nearby. All the hotel guest rooms have en suite facilities and are furnished to a high standard.

Beer: Bass and Halls Dartmoor Best Bitter on handpumps, with regular guest beers and ciders.

Accommodation: 2 singles, 16 doubles/twins, 2 family rooms. B&B

£30-£35 single, £48-£55 double/twin, £58-£65 family room. Special Rates any 2 days from £64 per person dinner B&B. Children's room. Pets welcome. Cards: Access, Amex, Diners and Visa.

NORTH BOVEY

Ring of Bells
Off A382, 1½ miles from Moretonhampstead

Licensees: Tony & Brenda Rix
Tel: 0647 40375

The Ring of Bells is a 13th-century inn in a stunning village of whitewalled, thatched and slated cottages. It was originally built by stonemasons as their lodging place while they were erecting the parish church. The Ring of Bells has great oak beams, and next to the vast inglenook, in the dining room there is an old oven, in which the village baker used to bake his bread. The small bar has another large inglenook and a brass-faced grandfather clock built into the three-foot-thick wall. The guest rooms all have en suite facilities, and four-poster beds are available. A buffet lunch is served during the summer, with hot lunches on cold days and throughout the winter. There are evening bar meals every day. The à la carte restaurant offers daily specials that include local fish and game pies.

Beer: Flowers IPA, Eldridge Pope Royal Oak, Halls Dartmoor Best Bitter and Dartmoor Strong, regular guest beers, winter warmers and Grays cider on handpumps.

Accommodation: 1 single, 4 doubles, 1 family room, all rooms with en suite facilities. B&B from £17.50 per person. Full board from £27.50. Outdoor swimming pool. Children and pets welcome.

PRINCETOWN

Plume of Feathers Inn
The Square, A3212 Plymouth to Moretonhampstead road

Licensee: James Langton
Tel: 082 289 240

In a village famous for the Dartmoor prison – completed in 1809, once the jail of renowned villains but now just the local lock-up – the inn is Princetown's oldest building, dating from 1785. It has slate floors, granite walls, copper bars, exposed beams and log fires. The large garden is a delight for children, with rabbits and domestic animals. Bar food is served lunchtime and evening all week and includes ploughman's, curry, scampi, lasagne, chilli, filled jacket potatoes, homemade soup, and burgers.

Beer: Bass, St Austell Tinners and HSD on handpumps.

Accommodation: 2 singles, 1 double. B&B £8.50-£10.50 single, £17-£21 double. Pets welcome.

SHEEPWASH

Half Moon Inn
5 miles west of Hatherleigh off A3072

Licensees: Benjamin & Charles Inniss
Tel: 040 923 376

This fine old inn, commanding one side of the village square, has been run by the Inniss family for more than 30 years. The exterior has steeply sloping roofs, porches, creepers and plants. Inside there are ancient oak beams, an open log fire and slate floors. Riding and pony trekking are available in the area. The guest rooms all have private bathrooms, heating, colour TVs, direct-dial phones and tea and coffee making facilities. Three of the rooms are on the ground floor. Lunchtime bar food includes snacks, sandwiches and salads, and there is a separate evening restaurant.

Beer: Bass and Courage Best Bitter on handpumps.

Accommodation: 2 singles, 11 doubles, 2 family rooms. B&B £20-£25 single, £40-£50 double and family room. Rates for children and off-season rates on request. 2 children's rooms. Pets welcome. Cards: Access and Visa.

SIDFORD

Blue Ball Inn
On A3052 between Exeter and Lyme Regis

Licensee: Roger Newton
Tel: 0395 514062

A cob and flint inn dating from 1385, with a thatched roof, large inglenook fireplaces in both bars and low beamed ceilings. The public bar has a stone-flagged floor and there are carpets and comfortable furnishings in the lounge. Food ranges from chunky sandwiches, through a ploughman's that will satisfy the most ravenous appetite, to salads and hot dishes that include steak and kidney pie, chicken Mornay, chilli con carne, steaks, locally-made sausages and vegetable moussaka or lasagne. There are summer barbecues in the attractive garden. Farway Countryside Park and Salcombe Donkey Sanctuary are close by, as are Honiton, and Sidmouth, the stately Regency seaside town. Guest rooms have tea and coffee making facilities and there is a residents' TV lounge.

Beer: Cornish JD Dry Hop Bitter, Steam Bitter and Royal Wessex on handpumps.

Accommodation: 3 doubles. B&B £15 per person, single room supplement £4. Children welcome, no reductions. Residents' lounge. No dogs. Cards: Access and Visa.

SILVERTON

Three Tuns
14 Exeter Road, off A396, 7 miles south of Tiverton

Licensees: Lyn & Nick Radmore
Tel: 0392 860352

Among Silverton's attractions are its own small brewery, Barrons, and the oldest row of cottages in the county. The Three Tuns is a 15th-century inn that has carefully retained much of its original atmosphere with all the modern comforts. There is a cheerful locals' bar and bar food (lunchtime and evening) includes homemade soup, smoked mackerel pâté, homemade lasagne and cottage pie, plaice or scampi, steaks, ploughman's, and puddings, including homemade fruit pie. There is a separate restaurant.

Beer: Courage Best Bitter, Directors Bitter and John Smith's Bitter, Fullers London Pride on handpumps.

Accommodation: 5 doubles/twins all with en suite facilities. B&B £30, double £40. Family room. Pets welcome. Cards: Access, Amex and Visa.

SLAPTON

Tower Inn
Off A379 between Dartmouth and Kingsbridge; up track after the Queen's Arms

Licensees: Keith & Kim Romp, and Jan Khan & Carlo Cascianelli
Tel: 0548 580216

The Tower is a 14th-century inn up a narrow and tortuous track. The flagstoned bar has settles, a wood-burning stove, chairs made from old beer casks and a log fire. The rear garden has picnic tables and overlooks a 14th-century chantry. There is also a separate restaurant. Food is served lunchtime and evening every day. As one of the partners' names suggests, there is a strong Italian bias in the cooking, which features seafood pasta, broccoli pasta bolognese, plus curries, tandoori chicken, vegetarian dishes and a children's menu.

Beer: Blackawton Bitter, Eldridge Pope Royal Oak, Exmoor Ale, Gibbs Mew Bishop's Tipple, Hall & Woodhouse Tanglefoot, Palmer IPA, Ruddles Best Bitter and County, Wadworth 6X on handpumps.

Accommodation: 3 doubles, 1 family room. B&B £15.50 per person. Children half price. Children's room. Pets welcome.

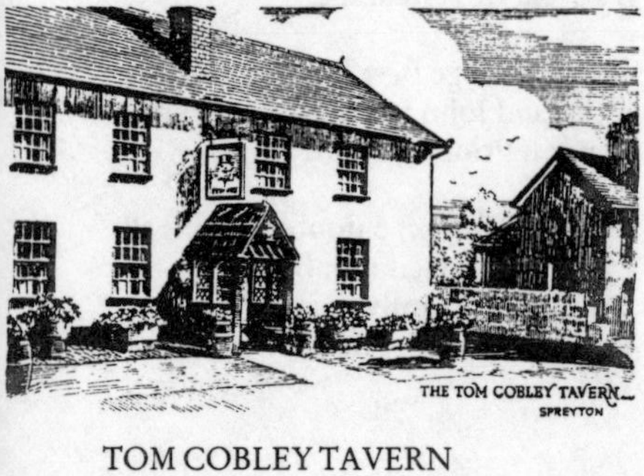

TOM COBLEY TAVERN

SOUTH ZEAL

Oxenham Arms
Village signposted from A30 at A380 roundabout

Licensee: James Henry
Tel: 0837 840244

This ancient inn has been licensed since 1552 and its creeper-clad granite exterior gives testimony to its age. Inside there are original beams and half-panelled walls, mullioned windows and old fireplaces. The walls are thick stone, and fine stone steps lead up to the garden at the back. Bar food has won wide acclaim in the area and is served lunchtime and evening every day; there is a separate restaurant. Food in the bar includes soup, ploughman's, fish and chips, homemade steak and kidney pie cooked in Guinness, and daily specials such as coq au vin. All the guest rooms have colour TVs, direct-dial phones and tea and coffee making facilities.

Beer: St Austell Tinners and HSD from the cask.

Accommodation: B&B from £28 per person. Additional accommodation in cottage across road (2 double rooms). Dogs welcome, 50p per day.

SPREYTON

Tom Cobley Tavern
Leave A30 at Merrymeet roundabout. Follow B3219 and pick up signs for Spreyton

Licensees: John & Holly Filor
Tel: 064 723 314

The Tom Cobley was where Uncle Tom and his assorted topers set off on their ill-fated journey to Widdecombe Fair in 1802. An inn is reputed to have stood on the site since 1589. The exterior has a striking porch and a riot of flowers in season from tubs and pots. There is a simple and cheerful bar, popular with locals, and a plusher back bar where homemade food is served every day except Tuesday. There is also a separate restaurant. Bar food includes pies, lasagne, moussaka and toasties. A traditional roast is served on Sundays, while there are barbecues in summer.

Beer: Cotleigh Tawny Bitter and Marston Pedigree Bitter straight from the cask, with regular guest beers.

Accommodation: 1 single, 2 doubles. B&B £12.50 per person. 10% reduction for 3 or more nights. Pets welcome.

TRUSHAM

Cridford Inn
Off A38. Take B3193 Christow and Trusham road; signposted after quarry

Licensees: Tony & Mike Shepherd
Tel: 0626 853 694

The inn is based in the lovely Teign valley, just one mile from Dartmoor. The building dates back to the 14th century and has a wealth of old beams. It has been a pub for just a few years; it was a farmhouse before that and many old farming implements have been retained and you can buy free-range eggs from the bar. There are two spacious and homely bars and the beer is stillaged behind them. The guest rooms all have en suite facilities, colour TVs and tea and coffee making equipment. Bar snacks are served every day, lunchtime and evening, and the restaurant is open Friday and Saturday evenings with an à la carte menu.

Beer: Bass, Cotleigh Old Buzzard and Exmoor Ale on handpumps and straight from the cask

Accommodation: 3 doubles. B&B from £15 per person. Pets welcome.

UPLYME

Black Dog Hotel
Lyme Road. A3070

Licensee: John Govier
Tel: 02974 2634

The postal address is Dorset, but the Black Dog is just a smidgen over the border, the first and last pub in Devon. It has an imposing roadside exterior, with tall chimneys and a large free-standing inn sign. It is an excellent base for visiting Lyme Regis and the Abbotsbury swannery. The hotel runs a courtesy service for guests arriving by train at Axminster. It is a cheerful and genuine local and the piano in the bar is often used for impromptu sing-songs. Bar meals are served lunchtime and evening and there is a traditional Sunday lunch. There is a beer garden, and the guest rooms have colour TVs.

Beer: Palmer IPA on handpump.

Accommodation: 1 single, 2 doubles, 3 family rooms. B&B £12.50 per person, children £8.50. Dogs welcome.

BRIDPORT

George Hotel
4 South Street, A35.

Licensee: John Mander
Tel: 0308 23187

'I came for a weekend twelve years ago,' Mr Mander said. He fell for this splendid small country town a mile and a half from the sea at West Bay and with good walks, a golf course, a small museum, and Palmer's brewery, a superb piece of architecture with a partially thatched roof and a great waterwheel. Mr Mander stayed to run a simple and unfussy local – 'unplasticized' is his good word for it. The bar has a log fire in winter, and there are wheel-back chairs set round wooden tables. The atmosphere is unspoilt by juke boxes or fruit machines. There is one ancient pin-ball machine, and music is either Radio 3 or classical and jazz tapes. (Trivial Pursuit question: how many pubs in Britain play Radio 3?) There are no optics and, at the last count, four different versions of Calvados. The food is home-cooked and is based on fresh local ingredients without recourse to chips or peas. Dishes include crudités, smoked fish pâté, ploughman's, Welsh rabbit, kippers, Finnan haddock, local eels fried in garlic and such tempting sweets as lemon meringue pie and bread-and-butter pudding. Food is available every day lunchtime and evening except Sunday lunch, Bank Holidays ... and the evening of the last Thursday in August. I wonder why.

Beer: Palmer Bridport Bitter, IPA and Tally Ho on handpumps.

Accommodation: 1 single, 3 doubles. All rooms have colour TVs and satellite TV is coming. B&B £15 per person. Children 5 and under free. Pets welcome.

Tiger Inn
Barrack Street, off A35

Licensees: Geoff & Gill Kenyon
Tel: 0308 27543

The Tiger is a modernized and redecorated free house 1½ miles from the coast. At West Bay you can take the coast path over the dramatic cliffs as far as Lyme Regis, following in the steps of the French Lieutenant's Woman. The Tiger offers a warm welcome, with full meals and bar snacks in the restaurant or garden patio. Local trout and steaks are a speciality, and there are always vegetarian dishes. Visitors can join the locals in skittles and pool.

Beer: Bass and Wadworth 6X on handpumps, Taunton dry cider from the cask.

Accommodation: 1 single, 2 doubles. B&B from £10 per person. Children's reductions on application.

BROADSTONE

Broadstone Hotel
Station Approach, off A349

Licensees: Wilf & Diane Dawkins
Tel: 0202 694220

The Broadstone is a cheery, traditional local with an emphasis on entertainment. There are live music evenings, and there is a separate skittles alley. The beer garden has a patio and a barbecue. The hotel offers hot and cold bar food, and the guest rooms all have showers, TVs, central heating, and tea and coffee making equipment. Broadstone is handily placed for Wimborne, Bournemouth and Poole.

Beer: Flowers Original, Strong

Country Bitter and guest beers on handpumps.

Accommodation: 5 doubles, 1 family room. B&B £13.50 per person. Reduced rates for 3 days or more. Bargain Breaks: details on request.

BURTON BRADSTOCK

Three Horseshoes
Mill Street. B3157, off A35

Licensee: W H Attrill
Tel: 0308 897259

The Three Horseshoes is a long and low-slung thatched pub with dinky thatched porches, in a village close to Chesil Beach on the Bridport-to-Weymouth coast road. West Bay is near at hand with its fleet of fishing boats and a golf course. The low-beamed lounge has an open fire and the separate dining room and bar seats 40 people. Food includes curry, crab and lobster salads, and steaks, served in the lounge, the dining room or the fine walled garden at the rear. There is a large children's room with activities to the side of the garden. The guest rooms have hot and cold running water, colour TVs and tea and coffeee making facilities.

Beer: Palmer Bridport Bitter, IPA and Tally Ho on handpumps.

Accommodation: 3 doubles. B&B from £12.50 per person. No children or pets.

LODERS ARMS

KINGSTON

Scott Arms
On B3069, near Corfe Castle

Licensees: Philip & Marcelle Stansfield
Tel: 0929 480 270

There are breathtaking views of the chilling ruins of Corfe Castle as well as of Poole Harbour and the rolling Purbeck hills from this fine, ivy-clad pub 400 feet above sea level. There are two comfortable bars with log fires in winter, one of them a family room. Excellent pub fare includes homemade soups, ploughman's, pasties, quiche, chilli, lasagne, vegetarian meals and Dorset apple cake. The guest rooms have central heating and tea and coffee making facilities. Kingston is a fine base for Corfe, Poole, Lulworth, Tolpuddle, Swanage, Chesil Beach and the Abbotsbury swannery and tropical gardens.

Beer: Cornish Royal Wessex on handpump.

Accommodation: 6 doubles, 1 family room. B&B £15 per person. Children welcome, half price.

LODERS

Loders Arms
Off A35 north-east of Bridport. Leave main road at Askerswell or Walditch and pick up signs for Loders and Uploders

Licensee: Mrs C Jennings
Tel: 0308 22431

The Loders Arms has a delightful position in the heart of a small village of stone-built and thatched cottages. The bar is popular with locals and in summer the terrace and garden, both

DORSET

bright with flowers and with fine views of the sheltering hills, attract many visitors. It is a good base for exploring the west Dorset coast stretching from Weymouth along the Chesil Beach to Lyme Regis, while Hardy country is all around. An 18-hole golf course is nearby. Lunchtime bar snacks are available every day and include ploughman's, sandwiches, pasties, soups and scampi. The evening restaurant serves steaks cooked in creamy Stilton sauce or peppercorn sauce, along with local fish, all served with fresh vegetables and followed by such tempting puddings as walnut pie. The guest rooms all have showers or baths and tea and coffee making equipment. A cosy residents' lounge has a colour TV.

Beer: Palmer Bridport Bitter and IPA on handpumps.

Accommodation: 3 doubles. B&B £15-£17.50; single occupancy £20. Children's room. Pets welcome. Cards: Access and Visa.

MILTON ABBAS

Hambro Arms
3 miles off A354, near Milton Abbey (OS 018812)

Licensee: K A Baines
Tel: 0258 880233

The Hambro is a delightful 18th-century thatched inn in a picturesque village. Milton Abbas was the first purpose-built village in England and all the cottages are in the same thatched style. The Hambro Arms has two charming guest rooms, one with a four-poster bed, both with en suite facilities. There is splendid pub food, plus a separate restaurant and a Sunday carvery.

Beer: Cornish JD Dry Hop Bitter and Royal Wessex on handpumps.

Accommodation: 2 doubles. B&B from £20 per person.

NETTLECOMBE

Marquis of Lorne
From Bridport take A3066 towards Beaminster; turn right at crossroads, signposted Powerstock; from Powerstock follow Nettlecombe sign

Licensee: Robert Bone
Tel: 030885 236

The Marquis is a 16th-century stone inn in a remote location beneath the old Roman hill fort of Eggardon. It has two bars with open fires, large gardens and a children's play area. The main bar has settles and many photographs of Dobermanns and Rottweilers. Bar food is available every day lunchtime and evening and includes sandwiches, homemade lemon and lentil or onion soup, ploughman's, daily specials such as rabbit pie or lobster, and a roast Sunday lunch. The intimate, 40-seater restaurant offers game, salmon, lobster, mussels, Dover sole and a special vegetarian section.

Beer: Palmer Bridport Bitter and IPA on handpumps.

Accommodation: 6 doubles, including 2 rooms suitable for families, 4 rooms with en suite facilities. B&B £17 per person, £19 en suite. Dinner B&B £26, £28 en suite. Children under 8 half price. Nov–March B&B £8 per person eating dinner from à la carte menu. No pets.

POOLE

Inn in the Park
26 Pinewood Road, Branksome Park

Licensees: Paula & Alan Potter
Tel: 0202 761318

This is a comfortable inn converted from a handsome Victorian house, with log fires in a bar decorated with postage stamps and old cigarette cards. In pleasant weather you can enjoy drink and food on a patio. There is an extensive hot and cold menu lunchtime and evening. All the guest rooms have colour TVs and tea and coffee making facilities. The inn is a good base for visiting Bournemouth and Poole.

Beer: Ringwood Bitter, Wadworth IPA and 6X on handpumps.

Accommodation: 5 doubles, 1 family room, 4 rooms with private bath. B&B £13 to £22.50 per person in double rooms, plus £7.50 for single occupancy. Rates for children on application.

POWERSTOCK

Three Horseshoes
Take Askerswell turn from A35 and drive round Eggardon Hill; or take West Milton turning from A3066 and follow Powerstock signs

Licensees: Pat & Diana Ferguson
Tel: 030 885 328/229

The 'Shoes' is a remote Victorian stone-built pub, well worth the effort of finding. The village has a Norman church, and cows wander down the main street. There are fine views and country walks, and trout and sea fishing facilities. The pub has a separate restaurant built with local stone and with pine-clad walls. Two of the guest rooms have en suite facilities. There are good bar meals such as fish soup, mussels, Lyme Bay plaice, squid, baked red gurnard and scallops. The restaurant specializes in local seafood as well as steaks and venison and a Sunday roast.

Beer: Palmer BB, IPA and Tally Ho on handpumps, and Taunton traditional cider from the cask.

Accommodation: 1 single, 2 doubles, 1 family room. B&B £20 per person. Single occupancy of double room £45. Bargain Breaks: 3 days half board £175 for 2.

SHAFTESBURY

Royal Chase Hotel
Royal Chase roundabout off A30/A350

Licensee: George Hunt
Tel: 0747 53355

The Royal Chase is a small, beautifully appointed 3-star hotel in the old Saxon hill town in the heart of Wessex, with its tumbling cobbled streets, thatched cottages and breath-catching views over Dorset. The hotel was a monastery until 1922 and it still enjoys a wonderful serenity and seclusion. It has an indoor swimming pool. There is a genuine locals' bar with an open fire and a fine old-fashioned cash register. The Country Kitchen restaurant offers fine food based on local produce. It is a good base for visiting the Fox Talbot Museum of Photography, Montacute House Tropical Bird Garden, Wookey Hole, Thomas Hardy's cottage and Stonehenge.

Beer: Eldridge Pope Royal Oak (usually in winter), Ushers Best Bitter, Wadworth 6X plus regular guest beers, all on handpumps.

Accommodation: 3 singles, 18 doubles, 10 family rooms, all with private bath or shower. B&B from £27.50 per person. Weekend (B&B plus evening meal) £58-£86. Real ale breaks from £58. Children's room; children free if sharing.

STOKE ABBOTT

New Inn
A3066 from Beaminster; village signposted. From Broadwindsor take Bridport road, turn left at Stoke Knapp farm

Licensee: Graham Gibbs
Tel: 0308 68333

The New Inn belies its name. It is ancient, with thatched roofs and cobbled walls outside and a bar sporting old beams decorated with horse brasses, tables and wheel-back chairs. The walls are decorated with pictures showing the wide variety of birds that visit the pub garden. There is a separate dining room which children can use. Stoke Abbott is a secluded village set among rolling Dorset hills and with picturesque thatched houses and a 12th-century church. Local places of interest include Parnham House at Beaminster, Forde Abbey and Clapton Court Gardens. Bar meals in the inn are available lunchtime and evening Tuesday to Sunday and include homemade steak and kidney pie, lasagne, Stilton flan, quiche, pizza, curries, steaks, salads, ploughman's, fish, and vegetarian meals plus a daily hot special. A traditional Sunday lunch is served from October to April.

Beer: Palmer Bridport Bitter, IPA and Tally Ho on handpumps.

Accommodation: 2 doubles, 1 twin. Rooms can be let as singles, and one double is large enough for a family. B&B £11 per person, £12.50 single. Family rates by negotiation. Children's room. No pets. Cards: Access and Visa.

STUDLAND

Bankes Arms Hotel
Manor Road, off B3351. 3 miles from Swanage. Studland can be reached from Wareham and Corfe Castle or via the Sandbanks chain ferry near Bournemouth

Licensee: T Lightbown
Tel: 092944 225

This is as near to being idyllic as you can get. The hotel, parts of which date back to the 15th century, is built of Purbeck stone and covered in attractive red-tinged creeper. It overlooks the great sweep of Studland Bay, and you can walk over the downs to Swanage, with many more stunning sea views on the way. The inn was once a smugglers' haunt and the single long bar retains all the atmosphere of a traditional fishermen's bar. A large room across the passage acts as a dining room. In good weather you cross the narrow lane on to a broad, grass-covered area of the cliff overhanging the beach. There are seats here where you can enjoy a pint, a superb crab lunch or a cream tea. A large room to the side of the pub doubles as a family room and for live music some evenings. Bar food, lunchtime and evening, includes ploughman's, salads, garlic prawns, crab, sardines, quiche, lasagne, hot pot, and jacket potatoes with choice of fillings. All the food is homemade. The evening restaurant offers steak, gammon, rainbow trout, chicken and sea bass. The guest rooms all have colour TVs and tea and coffee making facilities.

Beer: Flowers Original (summer) and Winter Royal (in season) and Marston Pedigree Bitter on handpumps.

Accommodation: 1 single, 4 doubles, 4 family rooms, 5 rooms with en suite facilities. B&B £15.50 single, double £31. Children half price sharing with adults. Winter: £2 reduction per person on all rates. Pets welcome. Cards: Access and Visa.

STURMINSTER NEWTON

White Hart
Market Cross, A357

Licensee: D G Rice
Tel: 0258 72593

The White Hart is an early-18th-century thatched coaching inn in the heart of the Blackmore Vale and Hardy country. Coarse fishing is available in the picturesque River Stour nearby. The lovely old pub is free from noisy music, has a small and pleasant garden, fires in winter, and such traditional games as skittles, crib and darts. Pub food is served lunchtime and evening.

Beer: Hall & Woodhouse Badger Best Bitter on handpump.

Accommodation: 1 twin, 2 doubles, 1 family room. B&B £15-£18 per person.

WEST LULWORTH

Castle Inn
B3070

Proprietors: Patricia & Graham Halliday
Tel: 092941 311

A picturesque thatched cottage pub near Lulworth Cove, the Castle is some 450 years old and takes its present name from the castle at East Lulworth designed by Inigo Jones and destroyed by fire in 1929. The inn, first known as the Jolly Sailor, has two bars, rolling gardens and outdoor seats at the front. The bar has a flagstoned floor and leatherette seats round the tables. The lounge has tankards hanging from a beam and rural prints on the walls. Bar food is served whenever the pub is open and includes soup, tuna cocktail, egg mayonnaise, spaghetti bolognese, plaice or cod and chips, steak and kidney pie, crofters pie, rabbit and pork casserole, curry and rice, salads, ploughman's, and filled jacket potatoes. There is a separate restaurant; children can eat in the restaurant or part of the bar reserved for diners. The guest rooms have central heating, colour TVs and tea and coffee makers. There are facilities for fishing, shooting and golf in the area.

Beer: Cornish JD Dry Hop Bitter and Royal Wessex on handpumps.

Accommodation: 1 single, 4 twins, 1 family room, 1 four-poster room, 5 doubles, plus 2 ground-floor double rooms (no stairs). 9 rooms with en suite facilities. B&B £18 single, twin £30 (£36 en suite), family room £45, four-poster £40, double £36. Winter Breaks: terms on application. Cards: Access, Amex, Diners and Visa.

WIMBORNE

Albion Hotel
19 High Street, town square A31

Licensee: Marion Edmonds
Tel: 0202 882492

The Albion is the oldest licensed premises in Wimborne, the last surviving part of an ancient coaching inn, with an original inglenook fireplace. This is very much a locals' pub, with a warm, friendly atmosphere, where dominoes, crib and darts are played. Marion Edmonds specializes in traditional food such as beef cobbler and Minster pie, jacket potatoes and ploughman's. There is a large garden with a swing. The pub is a fine base for Wimborne Hall and Kingston Lacy House (NT).

Beer: Hall & Woodhouse Badger Best Bitter on handpump.

Accommodation: 2 doubles, 1 with bath, shower and colour TV. B&B £9–£14.50 per person.

DURHAM AND TYNE & WEAR

GRETA BRIDGE (CO DURHAM)

Morritt Arms
Signposted from A66 west of Scotch Corner

Licensees: David & John Mulley
Tel: 0833 27232/27392

'We're old-fashioned and this is an old-fashioned place,' say the Mulleys, which means that the Morritt Arms is quiet and civilized and the service is impeccable. It is set close to a bridge

by the imposing gates of Rokeby Park. The lounges have high ceilings, oak settles, Windsor armchairs, and there is a model traction engine in one of them. One bar is named after Charles Dickens, who stayed there while researching *Nicholas Nickleby*. The bar has a Pickwickian mural all round the room, drawn by J V Gilray who also drew the famous pre-war Guinness posters – there are six in the hotel. Bar food offers sandwiches, homemade soup, smoked mackerel and salmon salads, ploughman's and homemade pâté, with such daily hot specials as rack of lamb or pork cutlets. There is a separate restaurant. In the public bar you will find darts, dominoes, shove ha'penny and a juke box – the only canned music in the hotel. The Mulleys do just one cask beer because they believe in serving it in tiptop condition: 'We fly a flag from the flagpole when we run out!'

Beer: Theakston Best Bitter on handpump.

Accommodation: 23 rooms, 16 with en suite facilities. B&B from £31 single. Cards: Access, Amex, Diners and Visa.

GATESHEAD (TYNE & WEAR)

Old Fox
Carlisle Street, off Sunderland and Durham roads (A6127)

Licensee: David White
Tel: 091 438 0073

The Old Fox is a cheery, one-roomed local with an open coal fire and an area for darts and pool. It is a good base for Newcastle city centre and the new Metro Centre at Dunston; the splendid and cheap Metro light railway makes sightseeing and shopping in the area a pleasure.

DURHAM AND TYNE & WEAR

Gateshead is also a handy base for visiting the Tyneside coast at Whitley Bay, South Shields and Tynemouth, and for touring 'Cookson Country'. Bar meals are available in the pub lunchtimes, and the guest rooms have central heating, colour TVs and tea and coffee making facilities.

Beer: Ruddles Best Bitter, Websters Yorkshire Bitter and Websters Choice on handpumps.

Accommodation: 2 doubles. B&B £10 per person. Children half price. No dogs. Cards: Access.

NEASHAM (CO DURHAM)

Newbus Arms Hotel
Hurworth Road, off A1 and A67

Licensee: John Able
Tel: 0325 721071

A fine old country house hotel approached along an avenue of trees, it is a 17th-century listed building with 19th-century embellishments. It has an ornate Victorian bar and first-class restaurant. The management can arrange fishing rights on the Tees.

Beer: Cameron Traditional Bitter and Strongarm, Tolly Original on handpumps.

Accommodation: 3 singles, 12 doubles, 4 family rooms. B&B from £45 per person. Facilities for the disabled.

PIERCEBRIDGE (CO DURHAM)

George
B6275 south of village

Licensees: Jennifer & John Wain
Tel: 0325 374576

A warm welcome is guaranteed in every way in the George, which has no less than five open fires in its bars and lounges. It is well sited on the old coaching route between Scotch Corner and Edinburgh. The bars have old farming implements on the walls as well as plates and prints, and the furniture is solid wood with a few Chesterfields. The lounge has good views over the Tees, and a splendid garden runs down to the river. Bar food, available all day, includes soup, ploughman's, curries, such special vegetarian dishes as vegetable Stroganoff, green pepper risotto or mushrooms in Stilton, plus all-day breakfast, steaks, chicken in mushroom sauce and a range of puddings.

Beer: John Smiths Bitter on handpump.

Accommodation: 25 double rooms, all en suite. B&B single £35, double £45. Cards: Access, Amex and Visa.

ROMALDKIRK (CO DURHAM)

Rose & Crown
Village green, off B6277 and A67

Licensees: Christopher & Alison Davy
Tel: 0833 50213

The Rose & Crown has a lovely bucolic setting on the green, which still has a water pump and the original village stocks. The bar has cream-painted walls, a large clock, farming implements and an open fire. Locals play dominoes. Bar food offers homemade vegetable soup, ploughman's, chilli con carne, haddock in tomato sauce, chicken breast in barbecue sauce, steaks, and sweets. The pub is well-placed for High Force waterfall and the Bowes Museum.

Beer: Theakston Best Bitter and Old Peculier, Younger No 3 on handpumps.

Accommodation: 1 single, 10 doubles. B&B from £25 per person. Single occupancy of double £42. Children sharing £10. Pets welcome. Cards: Access and Visa.

WOLSINGHAM (CO DURHAM)

Bay Horse Hotel
59 Upper Town, B6296 Tow Law road

Licensees: Mandy & Jan Ellila
Tel: 0388 527220

The Bay Horse is a traditional two-bar pub with old oak beams in a quiet Dales village close to the Beamish Museum and within easy reach of High Force, Durham and Killhope Wheel. Bar food is served every day, lunchtime and evening, and includes homemade rabbit and steak and kidney pies, steaks, mixed grills and fish dishes. A traditional roast is served Sunday lunchtime. Darts, dominoes and pool are played in the lower bar. All the guest rooms have colour TVs and tea making facilities.

Beer: Tetley Bitter on handpump.

Accommodation: 1 double, 6 singles, 3 with en suite facilities. B&B £15 single, £25 double, £30 en suite. Pets welcome. Cards: Access and Visa.

BRAINTREE

Hare & Hounds Hotel
High Garrett, A131 Halstead to Sudbury road

Licensees: Barry & Margaret Auitabile
Tel: 0376 24430

The 17th-century Hare & Hounds is a fine stopping place if you are en route for Bury St Edmunds, Lavenham, Cambridge, Newmarket, or Stanstead airport. It is close to Finchingfield, the most attractive village in Essex, and Gosfield sporting lake. The inn is just a few minutes from Braintree town centre but is in lovely countryside and there are steam train rides close by. The inn has been sensitively updated by the Auitabiles to provide both modern facilities and a charming period atmosphere. A restaurant has been incorporated in the design, and the inn opens all day. You can enjoy table d'hôte meals or hot and cold bar snacks, and morning coffee, sandwiches and afternoon tea are also available. There is a traditional Sunday lunch.

Beer: Greene King IPA and Abbot Ale on handpumps.

Accommodation: 5 doubles/twins, 1 family room. 2 rooms with en suite facilities. B&B £10 per person in double, £30 for en suite room with TV and tea and coffee maker. Family room £40. Children's room. No pets. Cards: Visa.

BURNHAM-ON-CROUCH

Olde White Harte Hotel
The Quay, B1010, off A12

Licensee: G John Lewis
Tel: 0621 782106

A good pull-up for yachtsmen on the River Crouch is this fine old waterside inn that is popular with landlubbers too. The front bar has comfortable seats, oak tables and parquet floors. There are several other rooms, some with bare brick walls covered with emotive seascapes. Excellent bar snacks include lasagne, fish pie and lamb chops while the restaurant – open for lunch and dinner – offers Dover sole, lobster, steaks and salads plus a children's menu. There are riding, fishing and golf facilities available.

Beer: Adnams Mild and Bitter, Tolly Cobbold Bitter on handpumps.

Accommodation: 2 singles, 11 doubles/twins, 3 rooms with private bath. B&B £18.15 single, £26.40 with shower, £28.60 with bath and shower, £31.90 double, £44 with shower, £47.30 with bath and shower.

COLCHESTER

Rose & Crown Hotel
East Gates, off A12 and A133

Manager: J De Andrade
Tel: 0206 866677/867676

The Rose & Crown bills itself as the oldest inn in England's oldest recorded town. It is an imposing building with an impressive half-timbered edifice and a sumptuous interior with low beams, wooden pillars, log fires and beautifully appointed guest rooms, including some with four-poster beds. Built in the 15th century, the hotel has stood at the corner of the old Ipswich and Harwich roads and was once a leading coaching inn. Food is available every day of the year: the restaurant offers fresh turbot, Dover sole, lobster, steaks, roast duckling, and pheasant and venison in season, while there are bar meals in the Prison Bar – the present building incorporates the site of an old jail.

Beer: Tolly Cobbold Original and Old Strong (winter) on handpumps.

Accommodation: 15 singles, 13 doubles, 2 family rooms, 21 rooms with en suite facilities, all rooms with colour TVs. B&B £27.50 single, £38.50–£42.50 with bath/shower, double/twin £38.50, £49.50–£52.50 with bath/shower, £54.50 with four-poster bed. Additional accommodation in adjoining cottages: single £42.50, double/twin £54.50. Children welcome, terms negotiable. Cards: Access, Amex, Diners and Visa.

DEDHAM

Marlborough Head
Off A12

Licensee: Brian Wills
Tel: 0206 323250

An impressive medieval inn in the heart of Constable country with, inevitably, a Constable Bar with alcove seating, beams and timbers, and a comfortable lounge. Constable went to school over the road. There is a garden with seats in fine weather. There is a vast range of food at reasonable prices, including soup, jacket potatoes with choice of fillings, ploughman's with homemade chutney, bacon, tomato and mushroom quiche, halibut and prawn bake, steak and kidney pie and a daily vegetarian dish such as carrot and cashew-nut roulade and treacle tart and sherry trifle.

Beer: Adnams Bitter and Benskins Best Bitter on handpumps.

Accommodation: 2 singles, 2 doubles, most with en suite facilities. B&B £20 single, £35 double with continental breakfast, cooked breakfast extra.

EARLS COLNE

Castle Inn
77 High Street, A604 between Halstead and Colchester

Licensee: Ron Davis
Tel: 0787 222694

The Castle is a splendid and ancient inn with exposed beams and inglenook fireplaces with welcoming fires in winter. The east wing was built before the 12th century and is thought to have been a priest's house. Other parts date back to the 16th century. The saloon bar is a popular meeting place for locals, and the pub is close to Constable Country and the steam railways in the Colne Valley. Bar meals are served lunchtime, evening meals are available in the dining area and guests have a TV lounge.

Beer: Greene King XX, IPA and Abbot Ale on handpumps.

Accommodation: 1 single, 1 double/twin. B&B £12.50 per person. Children's rates negotiable. No pets.

ELMDON

Kings Head
Heydon Lane, near Saffron Walden, just off B1039, 4 miles from M11 at Duxford

Licensees: Graham & Lynn Anderson
Tel: 0763 838358

A delightful 350-year-old Essex inn with tables on the lawn, a beer garden and clay shooting. It has two bars, a separate dining room, and accommodation in a modern adjoining building. The Kings Head has a wide range of pub games, including darts, pool and a quiz league. Food is served seven days a week, with both bar snacks and full restaurant meals. The pub is a good base for visiting Duxford air museum, Linton Zoo, Audley End and Saffron Walden.

Beer: Friary Meux Best Bitter and Tetley Bitter on handpumps.

Accommodation: 1 twin, 1 double, both en suite. B&B from £15 per person. Children welcome to stay.

MANNINGTREE

Crown & Trinity House
47/51 High Street, A137 between Colchester and Ipswich

Licensee: E J W Chapman
Tel: 0206 392620

Trinity House was a rectory until 1985 and is now a small private hotel. With the George pub next door, it faces Manningtree's charming Georgian high street, while at the rear of the buildings is a quayside with fine views of the Suffolk countryside across the Stour estuary. It is a good base for visiting Dedham, Constable Country and Colchester, and is a useful stopping place for people en route to Harwich and the continent. Bar snacks and full lunches are served and private parties in the evening are catered for by arrangement.

Beer: Greene King XX, IPA and Abbot Ale on handpumps.

Accommodation: 2 singles, 2 doubles, 2 family rooms. B&B £14.50 per person. Pets welcome. Cards: Access.

TILLINGHAM

Cap & Feathers
South Street, off B1021, A130 and A12

Licensees: Olly & Carol Graham
Tel: 062 187 212

The Cap & Feathers is a superb weather-boarded, listed building in a remote part of Essex, close to the coast, Dengie Marshes and St Peter's on the Wall, England's oldest church. The pub is the first tied house owned by the tiny Crouch Vale brewery and the Grahams' aim is to keep it as a firmly traditional pub with blazing fires, pub games and 'no flashing lights'. It has a resident ghost authorized by Willie Rushton and seen by Olly Graham. The Grahams smoke their own food and you can tuck into smoked fish, trout, eels, ham and other meat. There are also such daily specials as venison in ale, lamb and cider pie, pork in orange and cream, and fish and prawn pie. Vegetarian dishes include homemade vegetable burgers, savoury sausages mixing hazelnuts and peas, and leek and lentil slice. The only bought-in food comes from a local butcher, Tillingham Pie cooked with Willie Warmer ale. Not surprisingly, the pub features in CAMRA's guide to Good Pub Food.

The Cap & Feathers has won many awards, including CAMRA's East Anglian Pub of the Year and was runner-up in the Campaign's national Pub of the Year competition in 1989. It has no canned music and has live folk music on the first and third Sundays of the month. There is a garden at the back, and one small room acts as a family room, meeting room and tea room for the local cricket team, which defeated a rather portly side from the Guild of Beer Writers by one wicket in 1989.

Beer: Crouch Vale Woodham IPA, Best Bitter, Strong Anglian Special, Willie Warmer and Essex Porter on handpumps (the last two beers are seasonal).

Accommodation: 3 twin rooms (including 1 family room). B&B £15 single, £28 twin.

GLOUCESTERSHIRE

AMPNEY CRUCIS

Crown of Crucis
A417, 2½ miles east of Cirencester.

Licensee: R K Mills
Tel: 0285 85806 Fax: 0285 85735

The Crown is a 16th-century Cotswold stone building which has been thoughtfully refurbished as a pub and restaurant. Old oak beams and open log fires have been retained in the large bar. The inn stands beside Ampney Brook and is close to Cotswold Water Park, Cotswold Farm Park, Slimbridge wild fowl sanctuary founded by the late Sir Peter Scott, Cirencester's Corinium Museum, craft workshops and golf course. Bar food in the inn is available lunchtime and evening and includes sandwiches and ploughman's, homemade lasagne verde and steak

GLOUCESTERSHIRE

and kidney pie, a dish of the day and a children's menu. There is a separate evening menu. A lawn at the back runs down to the brook with tables on the grass. Most of the guest rooms have private bathrooms and all have colour TVs and tea and coffee making facilities. Most of the rooms overlook the brook and village cricket ground.

Beer: Archers Village Bitter, Marston Pedigree Bitter and Tetley Bitter on handpumps.

Accommodation: 26 doubles/twins, 2 family rooms, 26 room with en suite facilities. B&B £39 single, £50 double. Children's room. Pets welcome. Cards: Access, Amex and Visa.

BROCKWEIR

Brockweir Country Inn
30 yards over Brockweir Bridge off A466, 6 miles from Severn Bridge (M4)

Licensee: George Jones
Tel: 0291 689548

A 17th-century inn in the Lower Wye Valley, a few yards from the river and close to Tintern Abbey, the Forest of Dean, and Chepstow and its race course, it stands on Offa's Dyke. Fishing, riding and walking can be enjoyed in the area. The inn has oak beams, an open fire, two bars and a dining room with excellent food. Outside there is a covered courtyard, a walled beer garden, and beyond there are beautiful forests and pastures. Brockweir is a fascinating village with a rather shady past: it was a port in the 19th century, feeding the Severn, had all the usual port side associations and was chosen by Lord Nelson as the place to court Lady Hamilton.

Beer: Boddingtons Bitter, Flowers Original, Hook Norton Best Bitter plus guest beers and Bulmers traditional cider, all on handpumps.

Accommodation: 3 doubles, 1 family room. B&B from £14 per person. Half board available. Children's room.

CLEVE HILL

High Roost
A46 between Cheltenham and Winchcombe

Licensee: John English
Tel: 0242 67 2010

The High Roost gets its name from its commanding position overlooking the Cotswolds and the Severn Valley towards Wales, with one of the finest views in the county. It is a welcoming, family-run free house close to a golf course, Sudeley Castle, and the ancient town of Winchcombe. There is always a choice of 20 meals or more on the lunchtime menu, with homemade pies and baps with a variety of fillings.

Beer: Hook Norton Best Bitter and Old Hookey and Woods Special Bitter all on handpumps.

Accommodation: 2 singles, 2 doubles, 1 room with en suite facilities. B&B £12 single, £26 for 2 in en suite room. No children.

BROCKWEIR COUNTRY INN

GLOUCESTERSHIRE

FOSSEBRIDGE

Fossebridge Inn
On Fosse Way (A429) between Cirencester and Northleach

Licensees: Hugh & Suzanne Roberts
Tel: 0285 720721

The Fossebridge is a Cotswold inn with stone walls, stone floors and open fires that blaze cheeringly in winter. The Bridge Bar is the oldest part of the building and dates back to the 15th century. The most recent addition was in 1858. It is beautifully situated for visiting all the towns and villages of the Cotswolds, and a Roman villa is within walking distance. The Bridge Bar serves meals lunchtime and evening and the imaginative dishes include cream of tomato and coriander soup, garlic mushrooms, chicken and ginger warm salad, local smoked sea trout, black pudding with apples and walnuts, cured herrings in dill, steamed Dart salmon, lamb cutlets with Madeira sauce, Cornish crab with garlic mayonnaise, a selection of cheese and such tempting nursery sweets as bread-and-butter pudding, apple pie and apple and blackberry crumble. There is a separate restaurant. All the guest rooms have private bathrooms or showers, direct-dial telephones, colour TVs, radios, and tea and coffee making facilities.

Beer: Marston Best Bitter and Pedigree Bitter on handpumps.

Accommodation: 12 doubles/twins. B&B £35 single occupancy, £25 per person in double. Children £5 if sharing with parents. Fossebridge Breaks and Champagne Breaks are available throughout the year (not bank holiday weekends or Cheltenham race week). Pets welcome. Cards: Access and Visa.

GREAT BARRINGTON

Fox
Signposted from A40; pub between Little and Great Barrington

Licensees: Pat & Bill Mayer
Tel: 045 14 385

The Fox is a low-ceilinged inn with stone walls, rustic seats, and welcoming fires in winter. There is a skittles alley and seats by the River Windrush; the pub was originally called the Wharf Inn when locally quarried stone was taken down the river to build St Paul's Cathedral. Bar food includes sandwiches and toasties, steak and kidney pie, chicken and mushroom pie, ploughman's and soup. The Mayers are the longest-serving tenants of Donnington's brewery and have been running the pub since 1967.

Beer: Donnington XXX, BB and SBA on handpumps.

Accommodation: 5 rooms. B&B £16 single, £30 double.

GREAT RISSINGTON

Lamb Inn
6 miles off A40 near Bourton

Licensees: Richard & Kate Cleverly
Tel: 0451 20388

The Lamb is a Cotswold stone inn with parts dating back to the 17th century but offering such modern accoutrements as an indoor swimming pool and central heating. It has fine views over the surrounding countryside from its delightful garden. The bar is comfortably carpeted, with wheel-back chairs, round tables and wall decorations of plates, pictures and old cigarette tins. Bar food, lunch and evening, includes soup, seafood platter, curry, local trout, chicken breast with cheese and smoked ham filling, and steaks. There is a roast lunch on Sunday, and the inn has a separate restaurant. Mr Cleverly says there is a resident ghost 'but he does not use the four-poster bedroom' – clearly an inducement to book the most expensive room! The inn offers a residents' lounge with colour TV and there are several golf courses nearby.

Beer: Flowers Original, Hook Norton Best Bitter, Wadworth 6X and regular guest beers, all on handpumps.

Accommodation: 8 doubles, inc 1 four-poster room. 5 rooms with en suite facilities. B&B £21 per person, £25 en suite, double £32, £36 with private bath. Four-poster room, en suite, £41. Cards: Access and Visa.

KINGSCOTE

Hunters Hall Inn
A4135 4 miles west of Tetbury

Licensee: David Barnett-Roberts
Tel: 0453 860393

Hunters Hall is a superb, unspoilt 16th-century creeper-clad Tudor coaching inn, a maze of rambling rooms with old beams and open fires. It is one of the finest family pubs in the country with an enormous and beautifully kept garden with climbing frames and a children's walk-way linked by old wooden casks with thatched roofs. There is a garden barbecue in summer. Inside, the lounge that opens on to the garden is set aside for customers who are eating: the buffet menu is chalked on a board and includes mussels in white wine, steak and kidney pie, seafood pancakes, steaks, turkey and ham pie, and smoked trout. Children can eat in this room, the separate restaurant and an upstairs gallery. Buffet food is available every day, lunchtime and evening; the separate evening restaurant is open Tuesday to Saturday. Other rooms are like small parlours with comfortable chairs and sofas. The public bar is large and atmospheric with a flagstoned floor, settles and heavy wooden tables. Guest rooms are in a converted building next to the inn. Mr Barnett-Roberts and his staff run a smoothly efficient and friendly inn, and support the local micro-brewery, Uley, which brews wonderfully tart and fruity ales.

Beer: Bass, Hook Norton Best Bitter, Smiles Best Bitter, Uley Bitter on handpumps.

Accommodation: 11 doubles/twins, 1 family room, all with en suite facilities. B&B £39 single, £49 double, £64 family room. 2-day breaks £45 per person, £72 with dinner. Children's room. Pets welcome. Cards: Access, Amex, Diners and Visa.

LECHLADE

Red Lion Hotel
High Street, A417

Licensees: Keith, Judy & Mark Dudley
Tel: 0367 52373

The Red Lion offers a cheery oak-beamed atmosphere in an old Costwold building busily regenerated by the Dudley family since 1985. It is just 100 yards from the river, and offers fine food and comfort. Meals, lunchtime and evening, include soup, pâté, filled jacket potatoes, ploughman's, chicken, scampi, steaks, lemon sole, plaice, haddock, and local trout. There is a traditional roast lunch on Sunday. The hotel is a

GLOUCESTERSHIRE

fine base for visiting the Cotswolds, Oxford, Cheltenham and Gloucester. Fishing and boating facilities are close by, and you can follow in the poet's footsteps along Shelley Walk. There is yet another pub ghost: this one is claimed to pop out of the wardrobe in the family room to say goodnight and turn back the bed covers – Arkell's ale does have that effect on some people. The rooms, with or without ghost, have colour TVs and tea and coffee making facilities.

Beer: Arkell Bitter and BBB straight from the cask.

Accommodation: 1 double, 1 family room. B&B £14.50 per person, £38 for family room (sleeps 4). Reductions for children under 12. Special rates all year for 3 nights or more. Pets welcome.

LOWER SWELL

Golden Ball Inn
B4068, 1 mile from Stow-on-the-Wold

Licensees: Stephen & Vanessa Aldridge
Tel: 0451 30247

The Golden Ball, in keeping with its beer supplier, Donnington, the most picturesque of all Britain's country breweries, is a delightful old building of mellow Cotswold stone, dating back to the 17th century. There is a log fire in winter, a profusion of pub games – darts, shove ha'penny, dominoes and cribbage – and a garden with a stream where Aunt Sally is played. Bar snacks (not Sunday or Wednesday evenings) include homemade soups and pies, filled jacket potatoes, salads and sandwiches, with steaks and fish dishes in the evening. You can visit Broadway, Stratford, Warwick or Donnington's brewery, 20 minutes' walk away.

Beer: Donnington XXX, BB and SBA on handpumps.

Accommodation: 2 doubles. B&B £32-£36 per room; rates depend on time of year. No pets.

NAUNTON

Black Horse Inn
1 mile from B4068 Andoversford to Stow road, near Guiting Power

Licensees: Adrian & Jennie Bowen-Jones
Tel: 04515 378

The Black Horse is a 17th-century inn in a lovely old Cotswold village by the River Windrush and close to the unnervingly named hamlets of Upper and Lower Slaughter. The inn is a superb base for walking through the Cotswolds and visiting such famed beauty spots as Bourton-on-the-Water. Excellent pub food is served lunchtime and evening and includes homemade soups, salads, daily specials on a blackboard, curry, lasagne, scampi, ploughman's, fresh salmon in season, steaks, chops, and duck.

Beer: Donnington BB and SBA on handpumps.

Accommodation: 2 doubles. B&B £15 per person. No children.

NYMPSFIELD

Rose & Crown Inn
1½ miles from B4066

Licensees: Bob & Linda Woodman
Tel: 0453 860240

The Rose & Crown is a 300-year-old stone-built coaching inn in an unspoilt village close to the Cotswold Way and with easy access to the M4 and M5. The Woodmans run the Rose and Crown as 'a real pub – we don't worry too much about muddy boots'. They have bought the pub from the former brewery and now offer a wider range of beers. Food ranges from simple bar snacks to full meals and special buffets. You can enjoy delicious homemade soups, ploughman's, sandwiches, pasties, faggots, steaks, and steak and kidney pie, and there is a special children's menu.

Beer: Flowers Original and Whitbread West Country Pale Ale, Marston Pedigree Bitter and Wadworth 6X on handpumps and Bulmer traditional cider.

Accommodation: 4 family rooms. B&B £13 per person. Children welcome, reductions by arrangement. Cards: Access and Visa.

SHEEPSCOMBE

Butchers Arms
Off B4070; 1½ miles off A46

Licensee: Alan Meredith
Tel: 0452 812113

Of all the Cotswolds pubs, the Butchers Arms has arguably the finest view out over a lovely valley of woods and fields with a few nestling houses. The pub certainly has the most unusual sign around – a carving of a butcher drinking next to a bound pig. The pub has a single cheerful room with bay windows and rustic benches and a collection of bottled beers from around the world. It is the HQ of the local cricket club and there is a pleasant, steep garden with seats. Bar food includes soup, toasties and ploughman's.

Beer: Flowers Original and Whitbread West Country Pale Ale, Marston Pedigree Bitter plus guest beer on handpumps, Bulmer traditional cider on electric pump.

Accommodation: 1 double, B&B £11 per person (£13 for single occupant). No children under 14.

TEWKESBURY

Berkeley Arms
Church Street, A38

Licensee: R J Jones
Tel: 0684 293034

The Berkeley Arms is a 15th-century inn with a fine timbered exterior and original interior beams in this famous and historic old abbey town. The pub has darts and cribbage but, says Mr Jones, 'no place for a pool table': Bacchus be praised. There are lounge and public bars, and excellent pub grub.

Beer: Wadworth Devizes Bitter, 6X, Farmer's Glory and Old Timer on handpumps.

Accommodation: 1 single, 1 double, 1 family room, all with colour TVs. B&B £10 per person. Evening meals available. Children welcome, up to half price, according to age.

UPPER ODDINGTON

Horse & Groom Inn
Off A436 near Moreton-in-Marsh

Licensees: Cyril & June Howarth and Nicholas & Sally Evans
Tel: 0451 30584

The Horse & Groom is a 16th-century inn built of Cotswold stone, with original beams and timbers in the bars and some of the guest rooms. The delightful village of Upper Oddington has an ancient church, St Nicholas', dating back to the 12th century. The inn has a splendid beer garden with a stream, fishponds, an aviary and a children's area with swings and a climbing frame. Inside, the bars have wood panelling, masses of brass on the beams and fireplaces, and a dining room where local produce abounds. Bar and restaurant meals are available lunchtime and evening. The guest rooms all have en suite facilities and tea and coffee makers. French, German and Spanish are spoken. The inn is a fine base for touring the Cotswolds and visiting Broadway and Chipping Campden.

Beer: Hook Norton Best Bitter, Wadworth 6X on handpumps.

Accommodation: 6 doubles, 1 family room, all with en suite facilities. B&B £24.50-£26 per person. Double £19.50-£21 per person. Family room £52. Winter Weekend Breaks: £52-£56 per person for 2 nights with choice of à la carte menu; £5 supplement for single occupancy. Children welcome, terms on application. Guide dogs only. Cards: Access.

GLOUCESTERSHIRE

WATERLEY BOTTOM

New Inn
North Nibley, Dursley, off B4058, B4060 and A4134. (OS ST758963)

Licensee: Ruby Sainty
Tel: 0453 543659

Ruby Sainty is the kind of character that makes finding this remote old pub in a lovely wooded valley worth the effort. 'There are two golf courses two miles from the pub, where you can work off excess ale,' she says. As for the accommodation: 'Although I only let two bedrooms I have in the past put up a cricket team, and a party of six lads who bring their own sleeping bags – they're only here for the beer!' Don't let that put you off – the inn has every modern comfort, with central heating, colour TVs and tea and coffee making facilities in the guest rooms. Part of the building was a cider house more than 200 years ago, and the old cider press stands in the garden. The lounge bar has a magnificent beer engine, 160 years old, rescued from the New Cut market in London where it was being used to dispense paraffin! There are many other old beer engines on display in the bar, including one called the 'Barmaid's Delight'. Darts, dominoes, draughts, chess and crib are played in the bar. The New Inn has a fine range of pub food, including homemade soups, pâté, ploughman's, salads, steak and kidney pie, toasted sandwiches and brown baps with a choice of fillings. If you can tear yourself away, Berkeley Castle is just four miles distant.

Beer: Cotleigh Tawny and a house brew, Waterley Bottom, Greene King Abbot Ale, Smiles Best Bitter and Exhibition, Theakston Old Peculier, guest beers and Inch cider.

Accommodation: 1 twin, 1 double with children's beds if required. B&B from £12 per person. Half price for children under 12.

HAMPSHIRE

CHERITON

Flower Pots
Off A272, on B3046

Licensee: Patricia Bartlett
Tel: 096 279 318

The Flower Pots is an unspoilt village pub in an award-winning village near Tichbourne and Alresford and the Watercress Steam Railway. The pub has two bars with striped wallpaper, hunting scenes and old copper distilling equipment. Mrs Bartlett offers a homely welcome and excellent bar snacks such as ploughman's and toasted sandwiches. There are seats at the front of the pub and, inside, locals join in darts, crib, dominoes and shove ha'penny. The beer is tapped from casks on a stillage behind the bar. The guest rooms are small and cosy, with a separate bathroom.

Beer: Flowers Original and Strong Country Bitter from the cask.

Accommodation: 1 single, 1 double, 1 twin. B&B from £11 per person.

DAMERHAM

Compasses Inn
East End, 3 miles west of Fordingbridge on B3078

Licensees: H & J C Reilly
Tel: 072 53 231

The Compasses is a fine old inn in a pleasant rural setting, with a jolly landlord and an antique brewery at the rear. There are two bars, a separate dining room with food lunchtime and evening, and live jazz every Friday evening. It is a good family pub with a large garden, and in winter there are three blazing fires.

Beer: Burton Ale and Wadworth 6X on handpumps.

Accommodation: 2 doubles, 2 family rooms. B&B £15 per person. Children welcome, terms on application. Full board available.

EAST STRATTON

Plough Inn
Just off A33 near Micheldever, between Basingstoke and Winchester

Licensees: Richard & Trudy Duke and Gill Moran
Tel: 0962 89 241

A former 17th-century farmhouse, the Plough is set amid pretty thatched cottages in a tiny hamlet surrounded by farmland. The pub has its own green with swings, a seesaw and an ancient tractor. The public bar has darts and a quiet jukebox, while there is a cosy lounge and seats in a courtyard. The thriving skittles alley also has a bar. Accommodation includes an en suite family bedroom in the old bakehouse off the courtyard. Food is available lunchtime and evening and ranges from snacks, including homemade soups, to three-course meals. Children's portions are available. The guest rooms have tea and coffee making facilities and are large enough to accommodate two adults and two children.

Beer: Gales BBB and HSB, Ringwood Fortyniner on handpumps.

Accommodation: 3 twins. B&B £32 per room with colour TV; en suite £45. Children under 10 £8.50.

FACCOMBE

Jack Russell
Near Hurstbourne, off A343

Licensee: Paul Foster
Tel: 026487 315

The Jack Russell is a remote but comfortable and carefully renovated inn overlooking the village pond, on a private estate midway between Andover and Newbury. The pub is quiet and free from electronic devices. There are fires in winter, a garden for summer drinking and eating, and good pub food is served lunchtime and evening. Don't miss such delights as Jill Foster's beef stew with dumplings. It is a splendid base for the Wayfarers' Walk, which begins three miles north at Inkpen Beacon, site of the Combe gibbet. The Bourne Valley, with its painted railway viaduct, is close at hand, and Newbury and Andover are both a short drive away. The guest rooms in the Jack Russell have TVs and tea and coffee making facilities.

Beer: Palmer Bridport Bitter and regular guest beers, all on handpumps.

Accommodation: 2 doubles, 1 twin with en suite facilities. B&B £20 per person. Double £35. Half and full board available. Dogs (including Jack Russells) welcome. Cards: Access and Visa.

GRATELEY

Plough Inn
On main road through village, 1½ miles south of A306, near Andover

Licensees: Chris & Joy Marchant
Tel: 0264 88221

The Plough is a splendid old country inn run by an enthusiastic couple, with darts, crib, pool and ring the bull played in the bar, while a restaurant leads off the comfortable lounge. Pub food ranges from snacks to full meals, including Sundays. Both Grateley and nearby Quarley have 13th-century churches, while the flying museum at Nether Wallop and the Hawk Conservancy at Weyhill are just short journeys. The guest rooms in the Plough have tea and coffee making facilities.

Beer: Gibbs Mew Wiltshire Traditional Bitter, Salisbury Best Bitter (occasional) and Bishop's Tipple (in winter) on handpumps.

Accommodation: 1 single, 1 double. B&B £15 per person. Evening meals available. Children under 11 half price. Cards: Access and Visa.

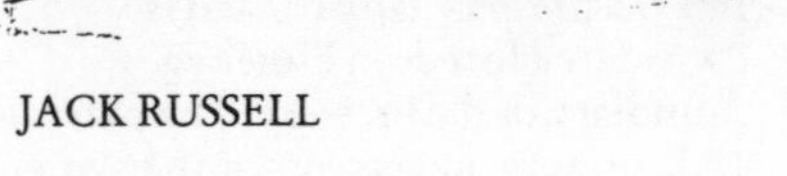

JACK RUSSELL

HAMPSHIRE

HAVANT

Bear Hotel
East Street, off A27

Licensees: J Carruthers & I Todhunter
Tel: 0705 486501

A handsome old coaching inn, the Bear combines the comfort of an AA three-star hotel with the genuine cheer of a country-town pub. There is a large public bar, and a restaurant which has à la carte and set meals, with quick lunches such as a platter of mackerel, pâté, prawns and avocado, lasagne, seafood risotto, and tagliatelle. There is a Sunday lunch and a separate children's menu. The guest rooms all have en suite showers and baths, colour TVs and tea and coffee making facilities. Havant is a good base for the New Forest, Portsmouth and Chichester.

Beer: Flowers Original and Wadworth 6X on handpumps.

Accommodation: 14 singles, 9 twins, 19 doubles. B&B £58 single, £68 double. Weekend terms on application. Children welcome, terms by arrangement. Cards: Access, Amex, Diners and Visa.

HORNDEAN

Ship & Bell
6 London Road, take Horndean exit from A3

Licensee: S R Williams
Tel: 0705 592107

The Ship & Bell is the original site of Gale's sturdily independent brewery. It is the brewery tap now and is owned by Horndean Hotels, a subsidiary of the brewery. The pub is 18th-century and is reputed to have a lady ghost in a blue dress who is seen from time to time descending the back stairs. There is an excellent range of reasonably priced food in the bars, while pub games are played with great enthusiasm.

Beer: Gales XXX, BBB, HSB and 5X (in winter) on handpumps.

Accommodation: 3 singles, 3 twins, 3 rooms with bath or shower. B&B £16 single, twin with shower £30, with bath £35. (1989 prices: check when booking.) Small, well-behaved dogs welcome. Cards: Access and Visa.

HURSTBOURNE PRIORS

Hurstbourne
On B3400 between Whitchurch and Andover, off M3

Licensees: Dave & Joy Houghton
Tel: 0256 892000

The Hurstbourne is a century-old inn, recently renovated with open-plan rooms and cosy niches in the bar, where darts, pool, shove ha'penny, dominoes and crib are played. The nearby River Test offers trout fishing and walks along its banks. The inn's food ranges from a light snack to a full meal in the restaurant, seven days a week. The guest rooms have central heating and tea and coffee making facilities.

Beer: Flowers Original, Wadworth 6X and regular guest beers on handpumps.

Accommodation: 4 twin rooms, 1 family room. B&B £17 single, £28 twin. Children welcome, terms by arrangement.

LYMINGTON

King's Arms
St Thomas Street, off A337

Licensee: Paul Elford
Tel: 0590 72594

The King's Arms is a 15th-century coaching inn in an historic old town mentioned in the Domesday Book and with a street leading down to the quay. It is a thriving sailing town today and both the town and the pub are popular with yachting people. There is a jolly, welcoming atmosphere in the pub, where Mrs Elford provides good-value bar food seven days a week. The meals have been praised by the *Sunday Times* while the *Washington Post* has raved about the breakfasts. The guest rooms have TVs and tea and coffee making facilities. Lymington is close to the New Forest and has rail links via Brockenhurst to Southampton and the Isle of Wight.

Beer: Flowers Original and Strong Country Bitter straight from the cask.

Accommodation: 1 double, 1 family room with 3 beds. B&B from £15–£16 per person.

MINSTEAD

Trusty Servant
1 mile off A337 between Cadnam and Lyndhurst

Licensee: David Mills
Tel: 0703 812137

This delightful, small and friendly two-bar pub lives up to its name. The welcome, the food, and the accommodation are so good that guests – 'friends' is Mrs Mills's term – come back year after year. She prefers not to give details of prices for B&B because she likes people to phone and discuss what they want with her, but the rates are extremely reasonable. The pub overlooks the village green, and its name is picked out on the end of the building. It is in the heart of the New Forest close to Furzey Gardens and the part-Saxon Minstead Church, the last resting place of Conan Doyle. There is an excellent range of hot and cold snacks. Friday night is music night, when Mr Mills is known to burst into song and play the washboard.

Beer: Flowers Original and Strong Country Bitter on handpumps.

Accommodation: 3 doubles. Phone for details of prices. No children.

NORTH WARNBOROUGH

Jolly Miller
Hook Road, A32 towards Alton, junction 5 off M3

Licensees: David & Stephanie Metcalfe
Tel: 0256 702085

The Jolly Miller is a half-timbered inn just a minute or two from the M3. It has a large garden where summer barbecues are held, a skittles bar that can hold up to 80 people and is used for parties and club meetings, and pleasant bars and a restaurant with 20 covers. Bar food ranges from snacks and toasted sandwiches to steaks, with daily specials on a board, and is available lunchtime and evening.

Beer: Hall & Woodhouse Badger Best Bitter, Marston Pedigree Bitter and Wadworth 6X on handpumps.

Accommodation: 3 doubles, 2 family rooms, 2 rooms with en suite facilities. B&B £25 single, £35 en suite. Double £35, £45 en suite. Family room £45-£50. All rooms have colour TVs and tea and coffee making facilities. Reductions on application for children sharing. Pets by arrangement. Cards: Access and Visa.

PETERSFIELD

Old Drum
16 Chapel Street, off A3

Licensee: Brian Barnes
Tel: 0730 64159

The Old Drum is a friendly pub with a relaxing atmosphere, just north of the market square in a bustling and prosperous town. Mr Barnes has a singular approach to pub music: 'There is recorded jazz played on tapes at a reasonable level, from Erroll Garner to Grover Washington. This frightens the morons in this town to death so they stay away, leaving the pub to the regulars and music lovers.' There are pub games and excellent bar food at lunchtimes. The large back garden, once a bowling green but now laid with lawns and fishponds, is a past winner of the Friary Meux Best Garden award. The guest rooms have colour TVs.

Beer: Friary Meux Best Bitter and Ind Coope Burton Ale on handpumps.

Accommodation: 3 doubles. B&B £10-£15.

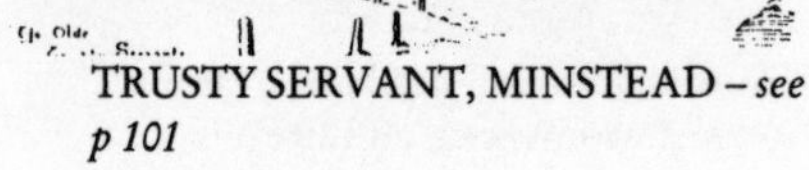

TRUSTY SERVANT, MINSTEAD – *see p 101*

HAMPSHIRE

PORTSMOUTH

Sally Port
High Street, Old Portsmouth

Licensee: C A Galloway
Tel: 0705 821860

The Sally Port is ideally placed in historic old Portsmouth with its Round Tower, the Cathedral of Thomas of Canterbury and the gate in the old fortified sea wall known as the sally port: naval officers 'sallied forth' from there to the ships. The original tavern dates back to the 17th century and was rebuilt in the 1970s from a bomb-damaged site. The present imposing four-storey hotel includes many of the original beams and more 'modern' ones from the early 19th century. The bars and guest rooms have beams and sloping floors and there is a magnificent cantilever staircase, the hub of the fine Georgian building. Most of the delightful guest rooms have en suite facilities and all have colour TVs and tea and coffee making equipment. There is excellent bar food and an à la carte restaurant.

Beer: Flowers Original, Gale HSB and Marston Pedigree on handpumps.

Accommodation: 10 rooms including 3 singles. B&B £28 single, £47 double. Cards: Access and Visa.

Surrey Arms
1–3 Surrey Street

Licensee: Liam McKee
Tel: 0705 827120

The Surrey Arms, in Portsmouth's city centre and close to the railway station, was originally a free house and was bought by the former Brickwoods Brewery in 1924: the bar on the right-hand side of the pub was once the bar from the brewery itself, while the fireplace came from another defunct brewery, Mews Langton on the Isle of Wight. To add to the nostalgia and breweriana, two doors leading into the bar were rescued from the George & Dragon at Cosham. The Surrey Arms, rich in pub and brewing history, is sumptuously done out with wood panels and etched glass mirrors. Families are welcome at lunchtime in a separate lounge. The guest rooms have tea and coffee making facilities.

Beer: Flowers Original and Strong Country Bitter, Wadworth 6X on handpumps.

Accommodation: 7 singles, 3 doubles. Single £18, double £28. 1 double can be used as family room: rates on request. Small deposit required.

SOUTHAMPTON

Royal Albert
Albert Road South

Licensee: Ron Ousby
Tel: 0703 229697

This is a solid, unpretentious town pub dating back to the 1830s and extensively modernized a few years ago. There is one large room with a horseshoe bar, and pool and darts are played. The Royal Albert is in a side street in the shadow of Itchen toll bridge and close to the Ocean Village marina and Michel Air Museum. The pub has lunchtime food and facilities for families.

Beer: Gale BBB, HSB and 5X (winter) on handpumps.

Accommodation: 7 singles, 2 twins, 1 double. B&B £14.50 per person.

TITCHFIELD

Queen's Head Hotel
High Street, ¼ mile off A27

Licensee: K A Blackmore
Tel: 0329 42154

There is a wealth of oak beams, open fires and history in this 17th-century inn in the centre of a small and historic village. The hotel is named after Catherine of Braganza, the second wife of Charles II, who built Titchfield Abbey. Bar food is available lunchtime and evening, and offers soup, ploughman's, jacket potatoes, burgers, plain and toasted sandwiches, steak and kidney pie, salads and fish and chips. There is a separate à la carte restaurant. The hotel is handy for Portsmouth, Southampton and the cross-Channel ferries.

Beer: Strong Country Bitter and Marston Pedigree Bitter on handpumps.

Accommodation: 3 singles, 4 doubles, 1 family room. B&B £20 single, £35 double. Children welcome, no reductions. Dogs welcome. Cards: Access, Amex, Diners and Visa.

WINCHESTER

Rising Sun
14 Bridge Street, B3404

Licensees: Paul & Becki Platten
Tel: 0962 62564

The Rising Sun is a superb timber-framed Tudor town inn just a minute's walk from King Alfred's statue in this stunning old city that was once the capital of England, with architecture so ancient and remarkable that even its branches of Barclays Bank and Dixons look like listed buildings. The Rising Sun is one pub where you may hesitate before asking to see the cellar: it was once a prison. The pub has hot and cold food, including vegetarian dishes.

Beer: Courage Best Bitter and Directors Bitter on handpumps.

Accommodation: 3 twins. B&B £13.50 per person.

HEREFORD & WORCESTER

BROADWAY

Crown & Trumpet
Church Street, off A44

Licensees: Andrew & Stella Scott
Tel: 0386 853202

A fine 16th-century inn behind the village green in the famous and lovely village of Broadway, the Crown & Trumpet has oak beams, log fires and first-class food lunchtime and evening. The menu includes soups, steak and kidney pie, lamb and aubergine pie, beef and Guinness pie, vegetable gratin, ploughman's, steaks and salads. The inn is an excellent base for visiting Warwick, Stratford, Worcester, Tewkesbury and the Malvern Hills. The guest rooms have colour TVs and tea and coffee making facilities.

Beer: Flowers Original and IPA, guest beers and Bulmer traditional cider, all on handpumps.

Accommodation: 2 doubles, 1 family room. B&B £15.50 per person. Weekend £18.50 with evening meals, Week £115 with evening meals. Off-season Weekend £17.50 per person for 2 nights with evening

meals. Children's room; children's terms on application.

BROMYARD

Crown & Sceptre
Sherford Street. A44

Licensee: Gavin Trumper
Tel: 0885 482441

Mr Trumper took over the Crown & Sceptre mid-way through 1989 and is planning to update the accommodation. By the time this guide appears, one of the double rooms may have become a twin, and eventually all the rooms will have private facilities: it would be a good idea to check the latest room situation when booking. All the rooms have colour TVs and tea and coffee making equipment. The charming old pub is in the centre of a small market town and its original cottage atmosphere has been carefully retained. The pub is famed for its hearty breakfasts, and a good selection of bar meals includes beef and venison pie and game pie, while the separate restaurant offers steaks and gammons. Bromyard is a good base for visiting both Hereford and Worcester.

Beer: Banks Bitter, Flowers IPA, Hook Norton Best Bitter and Woods Special on handpumps.

Accommodation: 2 singles, 2 doubles. B&B £12.50, £16 with en suite facilities. Children welcome, terms according to age. Dogs accepted.

HEREFORD & WORCESTER

CAREY

Cottage of Content
Off A49 1½ miles NE of Hoarwithy (OS 0565110)

Licensee: Michael Wainford
Tel: 043 270 242

The Cottage is a beautiful country pub in a remote area of gorgeous scenery. The timber-framed building was originally three labourers' cottages built in 1485. One of the conditions of tenancy was that one labourer should keep an ale and cider parlour in one room and the cottage has been licensed ever since. The bars have wooden benches and high-back settles, and darts, dominoes and cribbage are played in the public bar. Two other rooms are set aside for eating and a converted bar is also used when the pub is busy. Splendid food, lunch and evening, includes vegetable crumble or vegetable croquettes in apricot sauce, mussels in garlic, homemade pies, lasagne, and plaice, with soup, sandwiches and ploughman's. The restaurant is closed Sunday evenings. In summer there are tables at the front of the pub and on a back terrace.

Beer: Hook Norton Mild, Best Bitter and Old Hookey, Marston Pedigree Bitter and Owd Rodger (winter) on handpumps plus local draught ciders.

Accommodation: 2 doubles, 1 twin, all with en suite facilities. B&B £27.50 single, £35 double. Children welcome; terms on application; children sleeping in additional room with bunk beds charged for meals only. Cards: Visa.

FOWNHOPE

Green Man
B4224

Licensees: Arthur & Margaret Williams
Tel: 0432 77 243

The Green Man, first known as the Naked Boy, dates from 1485, and in coaching days it was on the main Hereford to Gloucester road. Petty sessions were held in the inn in the 18th and 19th centuries. Relics of those times include the iron bars to which prisoners were chained, the cell, the visiting judge's bedroom and a notice dated 1820 showing the scale of costs of prisoners' subsistence: accommodation is a little more expensive today. One former landlord was Tom Spring, bare-knuckle prize fighter and Champion of All England. This fine timbered and brick building has two bars – one with beams, exposed timbers and settles, and a smaller one where darts and dominoes are played – log fires in winter, good hot and cold bar food, a separate restaurant and Sunday roasts. Bar food includes soup, sandwiches, ploughman's, lasagne verde, trout, and steaks with children's portions available. The spacious back garden has a children's play area and bench tables; afternoon teas are served there in good weather.

Beer: Hook Norton Best Bitter, Marston Pedigree Bitter and Sam Smith's Old Brewery Bitter on handpumps, with Westons farmhouse cider from the cask.

Accommodation: 1 single, 11 doubles, 3 family rooms, all with private bath. B&B £27 single, double £36.50. Winter Breaks £49.75 per day for 2 people with evening meal allowance of £16.50. £5 reduction for third night. Reduced rates for children.

HEREFORD & WORCESTER

Well-behaved dogs welcome, £2 per night. Self-catering cottage also available.

HEREFORD

Castle Pool Hotel
Castle Street

Licensees: John & Lisa Richardson
Tel: 0432 356321

The Castle Pool is an imposing city-centre hotel; the pool in its grounds is the remains of the moat of Hereford Castle: the castle, once 'high and strong and full of great towers', has sadly all but disappeared. The hotel was built in 1850 and was once the residence of the Bishop of Hereford. The handsomely appointed hotel has guest rooms with en suite facilities, colour TVs and tea and coffee makers. There are good bar snacks, while the separate restaurant offers an imaginative range of dishes on a menu where a three-course meal costs £14.50. In summer there are barbecues on the lawn overlooking the moat.

Beer: Hook Norton Best Bitter, Wadworth 6X and guest beers on handpumps.

Accommodation: 8 singles, 7 doubles, 8 twins and 3 family rooms. B&B £39.50 single, £55 double. Children's terms by agreement. Dogs welcome. Cards: Access, Amex, Diners and Visa.

NORTON GRANGE HOTEL – *see opposite*

KINGSLAND

Angel Inn
B4360, 4 miles west of Leominster off A44 Kington road

Licensees: Nigel & Jayne Godwin
Tel: 056881 355

The Angel is a fine roadside inn with 16th-century origins and plenty of remaining beams in the lounge bar, where there is an open log fire. A smaller beamed restaurant is open seven days a week and specializes in local game and fish. The extensive bar meals (lunch and evening, including Sundays) offer soups, whitebait, several ploughman's, salads, pizzas, omelettes, and various fish dishes. There is a menu for children, too, and the garden has a play area. Nigel Godwin is a CAMRA member and keeps his ale in impeccable condition.

Beer: Banks Bitter on electric pump, guest beers on handpumps and Weston cider in summer.

Accommodation: 3 twins/doubles. B&B £15 single, £25 twin/double.

KNIGHTWICK

Talbot Hotel
Knightsford Bridge. B4197, just off A44 Worcester to Bromyard road.

Licensee: Derek Hiles
Tel: 0886 21235

The Talbot is a 14th-century inn in a lovely setting by a bridge over the Teme. The spacious lounge has comfortable seats including settles in the bow windows, coaching prints and Jorrocks paintings on the walls, and a great wood-burning stove in the fireplace. Thoughtful food (with the same menu for both bar and the small restaurant) includes vegetable

HEREFORD & WORCESTER

moussaka, vegetable kebabs, fresh sardines, boiled mutton, pork with melted cheese, lamb noisettes, and steaks, plus a tempting range of nursery puddings. You can walk that off in the Malvern Hills and visit Edward Elgar's birthplace or sit in the gardens at the front and the back of the pub. The small public bar is popular with locals who play darts, dominoes and cribbage

Beer: Bass, Banks Bitter, Flowers IPA on handpumps.

Accommodation: 3 singles, 7 doubles (including 1 family room), 7 rooms with private baths. B&B £18 single, £22 en suite. £30 double, £42 en suite. Well-behaved children and dogs welcome.

NORTON

Norton Grange Hotel
A435, hamlet outside Evesham

Licensee: M Smith
Tel: 0386 870215

There is lots of old-world charm in this spacious building with its large bar and intimate restaurant. A separate function room can be booked for parties and is also used as a skittles alley. Bar snacks include sandwiches, salads, steak and kidney pie, fish and chips, seafood platter and grilled trout. There is a large play area for children. Stratford and Worcester are nearby, and the hotel is popular with people visiting local racecourses. Fishermen will find the hotel a good base for the Avon.

Beer: Marston Burton Bitter and Pedigree Bitter on handpumps.

Accommodation: 4 singles, 3 doubles, 1 family room, 1 room with en suite facilities. B&B £15 per person. Children welcome, no reductions. Cards: Access and Visa.

PEMBRIDGE

New Inn
Market Square, on A44 between Leominster and Kington

Licensee: Jane Melvin
Tel: 054 47 427

The New Inn, despite its name, is an ancient and impressive black and white building that dominates the centre of Pembridge. It was built in 1311 and was known to travellers in coaching times as the 'Inn with No Name'. Six miles away at Mortimer's Cross is the site of a decisive battle in the Wars of the Roses in 1461; it is thought that the treaty was signed in the court room of the inn and established Edward IV as king. There is also a prison warders' room and wool market in the forecourt. There is first-class bar food – vegetable moussaka, mussels in garlic, deep-fried Brie, duck salad – and a separate restaurant. There are tables outside in the cobbled yard by the 16th-century wool market.

Beer: Flowers Original and Marston Pedigree Bitter on handpumps, and guest beers.

Accommodation: 2 singles, 3 doubles, 2 family rooms, 1 room with private shower. B&B £14 per person, £27 with dinner. Children welcome, terms by arrangement.

HEREFORD & WORCESTER

RHYDSPENCE

Rhydspence Inn
A438 Brecon to Hereford road; pub signposted 1½ miles west of Whitney-on-Wye

Licensees: Peter & Pamela Glover
Tel: 04973 262

The Rhydspence is a justly famous 16th-century timber-framed inn on a hill overlooking the Wye valley and the Black Mountains. It is either the first or the last inn in England, depending on whether you are coming to or from Wales: the border is a stream running through the pub's garden. The inn has been lovingly and carefully restored. Centuries ago it offered ale, food and accommodation to Welsh drovers on their way to English markets, and it was mentioned several times in Kilvert's *Diary*. There is a large stone fireplace in the central bar, seats built into the timbered walls and a profusion of beams. Food is served in the bar and in a pleasant dining room. The bar menu includes homemade soup, Devon farm sausages, Rhydspence pastie, pizza, baked aubergine parmesan, spinach and mozzarella crunch, lasagne, grilled sardines, fettucini bolognese, burgers, filled jacket potatoes and a range of ploughman's. Dominoes, crib and quoits are played in the bar. Cwmnau Farmhouse, a 17th-century working Herefordshire farmhouse owned by the National Trust (open 2-6 at weekends and some bank holidays) is three miles to the north.

Beer: Marston Pedigree Bitter and Robinson Best Bitter on handpump, Dunkertons cider from the cask and occasional guest beers.

Accommodation: 1 single, 1 twin, 3 doubles all with en suite facilities and colour TVs and tea and coffee making equipment. B&B £23 per person. Winter Weekend £66 per person for 2 nights.

WOOLHOPE

Butchers Arms
Off B4224, signposted from Fownhope (OS 618358)

Licensee: Bill Griffiths
Tel: 043 277 281

The Butchers Arms, found down a country lane, is a delightful 14th-century half-timbered inn with low beams in the bars and a terrace with flowers, a rockery and a small stream. In winter there are cheerful log fires. Bar food (lunch and evening) offers homemade soups, Woolhope Pie (rabbit and bacon cooked in local cider), steak, kidney and mushroom pie, mushroom biriani, salads and ploughman's. A separate restaurant is open Wednesday to Saturday evenings. Guest rooms have TVs and tea and coffee making facilities. Woolhope got its name from Wulviva's Hope or valley: she was the sister of the better-known Lady Godiva. In the 11th century Wulviva gave the manor of Woolhope to Hereford Cathedral.

Beer: Hook Norton Best Bitter and Old Hookey, Marston Pedigree Bitter on handpumps.

Accommodation: 2 doubles, 1 twin. B&B £16.50 per person; £20.50 for one person occupying a room. Children 14 and over welcome; terms by arrangement. Winter Breaks: any 2 days £43.50 per person for double room. No dogs.

WORCESTER

Kings Head
67 Sidbury, The Commandary, near town centre

Licensee: James Thomas
Tel: 0905 26204

The Kings Head is a picturesque old black and white pub that dates back to the Civil War. It is just a few minutes from the town centre, the cathedral, the Commandary Museum, and the Tudor Museum in Friary Street. Lunchtime bar food (not Sundays) includes filled rolls and a daily platter.

Beer: Banks Mild and Bitter, Hansons Bitter on electric pumps.

Accommodation: 2 doubles, 3 twins. B&B £12 per person. Children up to 8 years half price. Guests staying 7 days charged for 6. Pets welcome.

HERTFORDSHIRE

AYOT ST LAWRENCE

Brocket Arms
Shaw's Corner, near Welwyn, off A1 and B652

Licensee: Toby Wingfield-Digby
Tel: 0438 820250

The Brocket Arms, a handsome 14th-century building with a walled garden, forms part of the surrounding Brocket Hall estate. The hamlet of Ayot St Lawrence nestles down narrow lanes and yet is only a few minutes from the A1. There are timbered cottages, the ruins of a 12th-century church and its restored 18th-century Palladian successor. George Bernard Shaw lived down the road and his house, now owned by the National Trust, is open to the public in the summer. It is not known whether the writer drank in the pub, though his temperance has been exaggerated. Tackled on the subject, he declared: 'I am a *beer* teetotaller.' The pub gets very busy at weekends with visitors arriving on horse as well as car, foot and cycle. During the week, though, it has the atmosphere of a quiet country pub with its two small bars and a vast inglenook in the back room. Bar food, with a buffet in summer, includes soup, ploughman's, game pie, fish pie, shepherd's pie, coq au vin, tagliatelle and a roast lunch on Sundays. A separate candle-lit à la carte restaurant is open Tuesday to Saturday evenings and for lunch every day and specializes in game dishes.

Beer: Adnams Bitter, Greene King IPA and Abbot Ale, Marston Pedigree Bitter and Wadworth 6X on handpumps.

Accommodation: 3 double rooms, including 4-poster room for honeymooners. B&B £30–£35 per person. Children over 12 welcome, no charge if sharing with parents.

LILLEY

Lilley Arms
West Street, off A505.

Licensee: Peter Brown
Tel: 046 276 371

The Lilley Arms, close to the church and a farm shop in this picturesque Herts-Beds border area, dates from the early 18th century. It has two bars, including a traditional and atmospheric public, and a separate games room used for live music on alternate Thursday nights. The lounge bar has a dining area. The pub, a listed building, has its own stables for the Brown family's ponies and there is a hitching rail on the green in front of the pub for customers who arrive on horseback. The beer garden has several pets and is popular with children. Food is served every day and includes soup, garlic mushrooms, steaks, mixed grill, chicken Kiev, coq au vin, scampi, fillet of plaice or cod, rainbow trout, lemon sole, salads, omelettes, vegetarian spicy burger and pancake rolls, and a wide range of sandwiches. There is a roast lunch on Sundays.

Beer: Greene King IPA, Abbot Ale and Rayments BBA on handpumps.

Accommodation: 1 double, 1 family room. B&B £14 per person. Children under 16 half price. Children's room. No pets.

ODSEY

Jester Inn
Ashwell Station, near Baldock, 300 yards from A505

Licensee: Pam Mildenhall-Clarke
Tel: 046 274 2011

New licensees arrived in 1989 to run the 300-year-old pub with its oak beams, and blazing log fires in winter. It is just off the Baldock Royston road and two minutes from the Cambridge to London railway. The pub is steeped in horse-racing memorabilia, with a mass of horsey decorations and prints. The large beer garden has three aviaries with 200 birds, and there is also a goat named Lucy. The inn offers both bar snacks and full meals in a separate restaurant, with a traditional roast on Sundays. All the guest rooms have en suite facilities and TVs, and – a nice touch – there is a small library for residents. The four-poster bedroom is reputedly haunted by a ghost named Walter.

Beer: Boddingtons Bitter, Flowers IPA, Hook Norton Best Bitter, Marston Pedigree Bitter and a guest beer, all on handpumps.

Accommodation: 2 singles, 8 doubles. B&B £35 single, £49 double, £55 four-poster. Children welcome, no charge under 12. Cards: Access and Visa.

ROYSTON

Jockey
31-33 Baldock Street, A505

Licensee: J C Booth
Tel: 0763 243377

The Jockey is a cheerful town pub with red tiles on the roof and over the two bow windows at the front. Inside the theme is aviation, not equestrian; Duxford and Old Warden air museums are close by and the pub has many old aircraft prints and memorabilia. The Jockey has a large garden with summer barbecues. Bar food is served lunchtime and evening (not Sundays). There is a daily special and such regular favourites as beef Wellington, coq au vin, beef Stroganoff, venison and rabbit pie, cod steaks in cider or chicken in brandy and cream, plus ploughman's and omelettes. Curries, seafood lasagne and macaroni cheese appear in the evenings. Royston has a challenging golf course, and Royston Cave with its wall paintings.

Beer: Castle Eden Ale, Flowers IPA, Fremlins Bitter, Wethered Bitter and Winter Royal (in season) on handpumps with occasional guest beers.

Accommodation: 2 singles, 2 twins. B&B £13.50.

HERTFORDSHIRE

ST ALBANS

Lower Red Lion
36 Fishpool Street, off A1 and A405.

Licensee: J S Turner
Tel: 0727 55669

The Lower Red is a 17th-century pub in the heart of St Albans' conservation area and in a winding street of fine houses and artisans' cottages that leads to Verulam Park, an old water mill, the site of Roman Verulamium and the great abbey cathedral. There is a cheery welcome in the pub with its blazing fires in winter. Both bars have comfortable red seating and brick and half-timbered walls. The pub's name distinguishes it from the now defunct Great Red Lion by the historic Clock Tower. The Lower Red prides itself on the lack of juke box, background music, fruit machines and video games. It serves lunchtime meals from a set menu with daily special dishes. Evening meals are served during the week.

Beer: Adnams Bitter, Fullers London Pride, Greene King IPA and Abbot Ale on handpumps, plus a regular guest beer.

Accommodation: 1 single, 6 doubles, 1 family room. B&B £25 single, £35 double, £40–£45 family room. (1989 prices: check latest tariff when booking.)

White Hart Hotel
Holywell Hill

Licensee: Bill Marsh
Tel: 0727 53624/40237

A late 15th-century inn first known as the Harts Horn and built for pilgrims to the abbey, the White Hart became a major coaching inn, the first stop on the road north from London. It is immediately opposite the great abbey and cathedral, with its Norman tower and breathtaking shrine to Alban, the first Christian martyr. The inn, with its striking half-timbered exterior, has two comfortable pubby bars, a residents' lounge with a minstrels' gallery on the first floor, reached by a barley-twist staircase, and a separate restaurant. Bar meals are served every day lunchtime and evening. The White Hart is a good base for visiting the abbey, French Row – where French troops were garrisoned in 1217 during the struggle with King John – the street market on Wednesdays and Saturdays, and the Clock Tower. Bill Marsh is a member of the Guild of Master Cellarmen: publicans have to undergo daunting examinations of their ability to handle and serve Burton Ale to become members. So go for a Burton.

Beer: Benskins Best Bitter, Burton Ale and Tetley Bitter, Marston Pedigree Bitter on handpumps.

Accommodation: 11 rooms, 8 with full en suite facilities, 3 with showers, all with direct-dial phones, colour TVs and tea and coffee making facilities. B&B £50 single, £60 double. Friday/Saturday nights £35 single per day, £45 double. Children welcome. Cards: Access, Amex and Visa.

BARTON UPON HUMBER

George Hotel
George Street, Market Place, A1077

Managers: Steve & Norma Fletcher
Tel: 0652 32433

The George has undergone a major facelift since the last edition of the guide, a facelift that included the guest rooms, which now all have private baths or showers, TVs and tea and coffee making facilities. There is a 50-cover restaurant, a coffee lounge, a lounge bar, and a bar with TV area and pool room. Bar meals and restaurant meals are served every day, lunchtime and evening (not Sunday evenings), and include homemade soup, vegetable delight, peppered mackerel, taramasalata, steaks, chicken Mexican, duckling cooked in Grand Marnier, halibut steak, sole, vegetable lasagne and sweet and sour vegetables. Barton was once an important port and shipbuilding centre and has two ancient churches, including a restored Saxon one. The Humber Bridge has magnificent views and provides access to Hull and East Yorkshire. North of the town, strung along the banks of the Humber, there are a number of meres of great interest to naturalists and with facilities for anglers and weekend sailors.

Beer: Bass and Stones Best Bitter on handpumps.

Accommodation: 2 singles, 5 twins. B&B £25 single, £40 twin.
Cards: Access, Triangle and Visa.

CLEETHORPES

Crows Nest Hotel
Balmoral Road, off Humberston Road, A1031

Licensee: Bill Hayward
Tel: 0472 698867

The Crows Nest is a substantial, friendly estate pub in a quiet residential area, with a large car park and separate residents' entrance. There is a public bar and a comfortable lounge. The welcome is warm and the pub is deservedly popular with locals. Bar food is available both lunchtime and evening. There is a television lounge for residents and the guest rooms have tea and coffee making facilities.

Beer: Sam Smith's Old Brewery Bitter on handpump.

Accommodation: 3 singles, 2 doubles, 1 family room. B&B £13 per person.

DRIFFIELD

Bell Hotel
Market Place, off A163 and A166.

Licensees: Pat & George Riggs
Tel: 0377 46661

The Bell is an 18th-century coaching inn in an area of outstanding beauty and historical interest. Driffield is a market town close to York and Beverley and the country houses of Castle Howard, Sledmere and Burton Agnes. Kings Mill garden, just 800 yards from the Bell, is a 20-acre site that includes a watermill dating from Domesday times, and is also home to many birds and animals, including kingfishers, voles and wild deer. The hotel reflects its period with some four-poster bedrooms. All the guest rooms have private baths or showers,

HUMBERSIDE

direct-dial phones, colour TVs, radios, and tea and coffee making facilities. The Bell also offers a swimming pool, sauna and squash court. Bar food is available every evening and lunchtime Saturday, while the dining room is open for Sunday lunch and evenings the rest of the week.

Beer: Cameron Strongarm, Mansfield Riding Bitter, John Smith's Magnet Bitter and Younger Scotch, IPA and No 3 on handpumps.

Accommodation: 6 singles, 8 doubles. B&B £41.75 single, £29.50 per person in double room. No children under 12. Special breaks: details on request. Pets by arrangement. Cards: Access, Amex, Diners and Visa.

GRIMSBY

County Hotel
Brighowgate, A180

Licensee: Michael Hall
Tel: 0472 354422/344449/241560

A large and bustling pub with a lounge and restaurant decorated in Victorian style, there is always something happening in the County – quiz nights, discos, live music and fund-raising events, but there is a secluded area for those who want to rest or read. The restaurant has à la carte and table d'hôte menus, with the emphasis on fish and steaks. Bar meals, available lunchtime and evening, include chilli, filled jacket potatoes, and sandwiches. All the guest rooms have colour TVs and tea and coffee making facilities. The hotel is close to the main railway station.

Beer: Younger Scotch Bitter, IPA and No 3 on handpumps.

Accommodation: 3 singles, 3 doubles, 3 twins (including honeymoon suite). B&B £35 single, £50 double. Weekend one-third reduction. Cards: Access, Amex and Visa.

SLEDMERE

Triton Inn
Near Driffield, 4 miles off A1166 and B1252

Licensee: Christa Emmett
Tel: 0377 86644

An 18th-century coaching inn in a delightful Wolds village, the Triton lies in the shadow of the famous Sledmere House. The attractive lounge has blazing fires in winter, and high-back settle seats. Darts and dominoes are played in the public bar. Bar food offers soups, ploughman's, crab or prawn salads, burgers and steaks. There is a separate restaurant and the inn is famous for its vast breakfasts. Watch for the genuine sign outside: 'Licensed to let post horses'.

Beer: Younger Scotch Bitter and Tetley Bitter on handpump.

Accommodation: 2 singles, 5 doubles, 1 family room, 3 with en suite facilities. B&B from £14.50 per person. Children half price. Cards: Access and Visa.

ISLE OF WIGHT

CARISBROOKE

Shute Inn
Clatterford Shute off Newport–Shorwell road

Licensees: Tony Simmons & Trevor Stewart
Tel: 0983 523393

The Shute is a delightful old inn in a lovely rural setting a mile from Newport. There are fine views from the inn of Carisbrooke Castle, where Charles I was imprisoned, and over the Bowcombe Valley. A few yards from the inn a ford crosses Lukeley Brook, a tributary of the River Medina. The Shute's guest rooms all have colour TVs and tea and coffee making facilities. Bar food is served lunchtime and evening (not Sunday evening) and there is a family room.

Beer: Bass, John Smiths Bitter on handpumps, Burt VPA from the cask.

Accommodation: 1 single, 2 twins, 1 double. Room £11.50 single, £21 twin, £25 double en suite. Choice of breakfast from £2. 10% reduction for 4 nights or more. Cards: Access and Visa.

CHALE

Clarendon Hotel & Wight Mouse Inn
B3399, off A3055

Licensees: John & Jean Bradshaw
Tel: 0983 730431

Two for the price of one in this 17th-century hotel, with an inn attached, where there is live music every night of the week, winter and summer – jazz, country and western, and singing guitarists. The stone-built buildings have wood-panelling from a 19th-century shipwreck. There is a strong family emphasis: children are welcomed warmly and there is a garden with swings, slides and menagerie and no fewer than three children's rooms. Generous bar food, leaning on local produce and home-cooking, includes soups, ploughman's, burgers, steaks, salads, crabs, prawns, cockles, sandwiches and sweets. There is a separate restaurant. The pub is open all day every day for drinks and food (no hot food on Sundays between 3 and 7pm).

Beer: Burt VPA, Gale HSB, Marston Pedigree Bitter and Strong Country Bitter on handpumps.

Accommodation: 14 doubles, 8 family rooms, 8 rooms with private bath. B&B £19-£21 per person. Full board £28-£31. Weekend £56-£60, Week £155-£170. Top prices are for rooms with baths. Off-season: 15% reductions. Children half price.

NETTLESTONE

Roadside Inn
On Ryde–Bembridge road

Licensee: John Tuskin
Tel: 0983 612381

A splendid pub with an imposing half-timbered, mullioned and dormered exterior behind a walled garden. The inn is a combination of a good locals' local and a visitors' hotel, with a cheerful public bar and a pleasant and comfortable lounge. It is close to Seaview and the picturesque yachting harbour of Bembridge. All guest rooms have hot and cold water, colour TVs and tea and coffee making facilities.

Beer: Flowers Original and Fremlins Bitter on handpumps.

Accommodation: 1 twin, 2 doubles, 1 family room. B&B £14.50 per person. Children's room; children welcome to stay, half price.

NEWPORT

Wheatsheaf Hotel
St Thomas Square

Licensees: David & Sally Rudge
Tel: 0983 523865

A 17th-century coaching inn in the centre of the old market town, the Wheatsheaf has Cromwellian connections – the republican leader held a parliamentary meeting here. The guest rooms have all been thoughtfully modernized and refurbished, with colour TVs, tea and coffee makers and most with en suite facilities. The public rooms have beamed ceilings and the comfortable bar has a casement clock and an open fireplace, with chairs placed round circular tables. There is a family room and a separate function room overlooking the square. The bar is open all day Monday to Saturday and food is served from 11am to 9pm daily. The extensive menu includes homemade soup, corn on the cob, ham and asparagus, whitebait, steaks, chicken breast in a mushroom and celery sauce, trout, pork Mexican, plaice or cod, steak and kidney or cottage pie, stir-fried vegetables, stuffed pancakes, cauliflower cheese, filled jacket potatoes, ploughman's and sandwiches. A separate children's menu offers soup, steak and kidney pie, lamb cutlet, burgers, sausage, or fish fingers.

Beer: Flowers Original and Strong Country Bitter on handpumps.

Accommodation: 15 rooms. B&B £25 single, £33 with shower, £40 twin/double, £50 with shower.

ISLE OF WIGHT

SEAVIEW

Seaview Hotel
High Street

Licensees: Nicola & Nicholas Hayward
Tel: 0983 612711

The Seaview is an imposing and elegant three-storey hotel in a pleasant Edwardian seaside setting. The Haywards, with their own young family, welcome other families, including well-behaved dogs, and provide cots and children's menus. There are two bars – a plush cocktail bar with many naval photos, and the Pump Bar with an open fire in winter, popular with locals and yachtsmen. Elegance is everywhere, with antique clocks, watercolours and French cuisine in the acclaimed restaurant (closed Sunday evening). Bar food is out of the rut, with gazpacho, three-bean and garlic salad, hot crab ramekin, fresh fish terrine, mussels, vegetarian noodles and vegetable puff, julienne of lambs liver, fresh plaice or lemon sole, shark steak, duck breast, rack of lamb, and scallops.

Beer: Burt VPA on handpump.

Accommodation: 16 rooms, all with private bathrooms or showers and including 1 family suite. B&B from £33 single, £27.50 per person in twin/double. Dinner, B&B from £42 single, from £36 per person in twin/double. Children's terms according to age and season. Cards: Access, Amex and Visa.

KENT

ASH

Volunteer Inn
43 Guilton. A257 near Canterbury

Licensees: Terry & Pam Smith
Tel: 0304 812506

The Volunteer is an attractive Victorian pub on the Sandwich to Canterbury road, handy for Sandwich golf course, Richborough Castle, Howletts Zoo and the cross-Channel ferries: the Smiths provide dawn breakfasts for channel hoppers. The inn has a public bar and lounge, and bar billiards – a game that must not die – is played, as well as darts. Good bar snacks and meals include provision for special diets.

Beer: Adnams Bitter and Old (winter), Harvey Mild and Bitter on handpumps, Theobolds cider from the cask, and guest bitter.

Accommodation: 1 double, 1 family room. B&B £16 single, £26 double. Children welcome, half price. Reductions for stays of 3 days or more. Bargain winter breaks available.

BOUGHTON

Queens Head Hotel
111 The Street. Near Faversham and Canterbury. End of M2 take A2 Dover road to Boughton and Dunkirk

Licensee: Elizabeth Sabey
Tel: 0227 751369

The Queens Head is an historic, 400-year-old beamed inn with gardens overlooking the apple orchards and hop gardens of Kent. The hospitality is warm and locals will invite guests to join them in games of chess, cribbage, dominoes and shove ha'penny. The hotel has a small and cosy restaurant with 16 covers; bar meals and restaurant meals are served lunchtime and evening every day (not Saturday evening or Sunday lunch). Mrs Sabey concentrates on good home-cooking and offers pies, puddings, chicken with prawns, beef in red wine, sandwiches, burgers, jacket potatoes and desserts. The guest rooms all have colour TVs, central heating and tea and coffee making facilities. The Queens Head is a fine base for visiting Canterbury and the Kent coast or as a stopover for the cross-Channel ferries.

Beer: Shepherd Neame Mild and Master Brew Bitter on handpumps.

Accommodation: 4 doubles/twins, 1 family room. Single occupancy available. B&B £14-£18 per person. Children welcome. Special rates for stays of 3 days or more. Closed Xmas Day.

BROADSTAIRS

Royal Albion Hotel
Albion Street

Licensee: Roger Family
Tel: 0843 68071

The Royal Albion is a handsome building with a commanding position on the cliffs of this fine old seaside resort made famous by Charles Dickens, who finished *Nicholas Nickleby* while staying there. The original Bleak House is nearby. The hotel began life as the Phoenix Inn in 1760, and by 1816 had changed its name to the Albion. Visits by several members of the royal family added the prefix. The hotel has been run by the Marchesi family for 12 years and they have owned the separate restaurant (open every day for lunch and dinner) for more than 100 years.

Reasonably priced dishes include homemade soups, scallop and bacon salad, poached fillet of turbot, Dover sole, rack of lamb and a vegetarian dish of the day. The Bradstow Bar was once a separate house, where Dickens lived and worked for several years. The immaculate guest rooms all have en suite facilities, colour TVs and tea and coffee makers. The hotel can arrange day trips to France.

Beer: Shepherd Neame Master Brew Bitter on handpump.

Accommodation: 3 singles, 13 doubles, 4 family rooms. B&B £45 per person, £50 half board. Weekend £80 half board, Week £270. Children's room; children welcome to stay, half price. Cards: Access, Amex, Diners and Visa.

LAMBERHURST

Chequers Inn
Hastings Road, A21

Licensee: Keith Smith
Tel: 0892 890260

The Chequers is an attractive tile-hung pub in a picturesque village on the London–Hastings road. The inn dates back to the 15th century and has an abundance of exposed beams to prove the point. The public bar is popular with young people who enjoy darts, bar billiards and pool. The saloon is comfortable and relaxed, and first-class meals are available lunchtime and evening. The bedrooms all have colour TVs and tea and coffee makers, and there is also a separate family room, Lamberhurst is a good base for visiting Scotney Castle, Bewl Bridge Reservoir, and the successful commercial vineyard which takes its name from the village.

Beer: Flowers Original and Fremlins Bitter on handpumps.

Accommodation: 4 doubles, 1 family room, 4 rooms with private baths. B&B £27.50 single, £35.50 double. Children welcome, charged only for food if sharing with parents. Cards: Access, Amex, Diners and Visa.

LENHAM

Dog & Bear Hotel
The Square, A20 near Maidstone

Licensees: Robert & Sheila Hedges
Tel: 0622 858219

The Dog & Bear was built in 1602 at the height of the coaching period when the inn provided shelter for travellers, and refreshment for local market traders. It has a steeply tiled roof and an attractive claret and white fascia decked out with flowering tubs and hanging baskets. The first floor bears the bold coat-of-arms of Queen Anne who visited the inn in 1704. It is a good base for visiting Canterbury, while Leeds Castle is just 10 minutes away by car. Both bar meals and restaurant meals are available lunchtime and evening. Food in the bar includes ploughman's, salads, sandwiches, homemade soup, chilli con carne, cottage pie, fillet of plaice, sausage, bacon and egg with fried potatoes and tomatoes, grilled gammon, and scampi. The guest rooms all have en suite bathrooms, direct-dial phones, radios, TVs and tea and coffee making facilities. The inn also has a function room suitable for meetings and conferences.

Beer: Shepherd Neame Master Brew Bitter and Best Bitter on handpumps.

Accommodation: 1 single, 16 doubles/twins, 4 family rooms. B&B £33 single, £48 double/twin, £54 family. Children's room. Weekend

Break £65 per person for 2 nights B&B + evening meal. Pets welcome. Cards: Access, Amex and Visa.

PLUCKLEY

Dering Arms
Station Road. At Charing (A20) take B2077 to Pluckley

Licensee: Jim Buss
Tel: 023 384 371

A striking 17th-century hunting lodge with a Dutch gabled roof and stone and wood bars, the Dering Arms stands in what was once the Dering estate. A member of the Dering family escaped through a window of the lodge when he was pursued by the Roundheads during the Civil War; since then all the windows on the estate have been designed along similar lines and the style is now known as a Dering Window.The 30-seat restaurant specializes in fresh fish, local game and homemade dishes: you can choose from soup, Sussex smokies, local trout, seafood special, ploughman's, blacksmith's (ham), gamekeeper's (rabbit and pigeon), and squire's (Stilton) lunches. There are good puds, too: fruit crumble, banana pancake, and orange in caramel. The guest rooms all have colour TVs and tea and coffee making facilities. Pluckley is a good base for touring the county and taking in Canterbury, and Leeds and Bodium castles.

Beer: Dering Ale – a house beer brewed by Goachers of Maidstone – Adnams Bitter and Extra, Goachers Maidstone Ale, Shepherd Neame Master Brew Bitter, Young Special, all on handpumps.

Accommodation: 3 doubles (double and single bed in each room: can be used as single). B&B £20 single, £32 double room. Special rates for long stays. Children welcome, no reductions.

SANDWICH

Bell Hotel
The Quay. A257.

Licensee: M I Turner
Tel: 0304 613388

The Bell is a grade two listed building with an imposing exterior that includes a gable end. It is based in the oldest of the ancient Cinque Ports that was the second most important port in England after London. The Quay is an historic street of timber-framed houses where Tom Paine, author of *The Rights of Man* and a major influence in the American and French revolutions, lived. One street in Sandwich is believed to be the longest continuous timber-framed thoroughfare in the country. The houses were built by Huguenot weavers, who settled in England to escape repression on the continent. The Barbican Toll Gate dates from 1023 and dominates the eastern approaches to the town. Modern Sandwich is also the home of the Royal St George's golf club, where the British Open is played, and the hotel organizes special golfing weekends. There are facilities for clay pigeon shooting nearby, while Sandwich is a good base for visiting Canterbury, Dover, the castles at Deal and Walmer and local nature reserves. Magnums wine bar in the hotel has grills, pies and dishes of the day, while the restaurant offers both table d'hôte and à la carte menus. All the guest rooms are decorated and furnished to a high standard and have en suite facilities.

Beer (in wine bar): constantly

changing range of beers drawn from the cask, including Johnsons Bitter from Dover, Arkell and Ringwood.

Accommodation: 8 singles, 20 doubles/twins, 1 family room. B&B £44 single, £65 double, £70–£75 family room. Children free of charge sharing with 2 adults. Sandwich Break 2 day minimum £34 per person per night. Golf Break £44 per person per night. Children's room. Pets welcome. Cards: Access, Amex, Diners and Visa.

SHEERNESS

Seaview Hotel
Broadway, A249 Sheppey road

Licensee: Bill Wiseman
Tel: 0795 662003

A cheerful and friendly small hotel, the Seaview has a good pubby atmosphere and specializes in home-cooked food in the bar and separate restaurant. It has a large garden and two separate function rooms. All the guest rooms have colour TVs, tea and cofee makers and uninterrupted views of the Thames estuary. The Seaview is a good base for the Olau line ferry service to Holland.

Beer: Shepherd Neame Master Brew Bitter on handpump.

Accommodation: 1 single, 3 doubles, 7 twins, 1 family room, 2 rooms with private facilities. B&B £15 single, £25 double/twin, £35 family room. En suite facilities £5 extra. Pets welcome.

SMARDEN

Bell
B2077, 3/4 mile from the village, off A20

Licensee: Ian Turner
Tel: 023 377 283

A fine old Kentish inn in unspoilt countryside near Leeds and Sissinghurst castles, the Bell has three large bars with oak beams, candelight, inglenooks with welcoming winter fires, flagstoned floors and pews and chairs around wooden tables. It was built as a farmhouse during the reign of Henry VII, and granted an ale and cider licence in 1630. Smarden stems from the Anglo-Saxon for 'a fat and wooded place'. The front bar of the Bell, popular with locals, offers bar billiards, darts, shove ha'penny and dominoes. The tile-hung and rose-covered exterior is a delight in summer, when you can sit among the trees in the garden. Splendid bar food includes homemade soups, ploughman's, Greek-style shepherd's pie, sandwiches and toasties, steak and kidney pie, pizzas, and homemade chocolate crunch cake and apple crumble. Bar meals are served every day. The guest rooms have colour TVs.

Beer: Brakspear Bitter, Flowers Original and Fremlins Bitter, Fullers London Pride, Goachers Maidstone Ale, Ringwood Old Thumper and Shepherd Neame Master Brew Bitter on handpumps.

Accommodation: 4 doubles. Bed and continental breakfast £16 single, double £13 per person. Children's room; children welcome, no reductions. Closed Xmas Day. Cards: Access and Visa.

KENT

WINGHAM

Anchor Inn
On A257

Licensee: Roger Field
Tel: 0227 720866

The Anchor is a delightful old pub with tall chimneys on a rambling roof, close to Canterbury and its historic pleasures. The welcome is warm, and the inn specializes in excellent pub grub. You can tuck into soup, omelettes, homemade shepherd's pie, cold beef, hot potatoes, pickle and salad, ploughman's with Cheddar or Stilton, sandwiches, Anchorburgers, steaks, and fish and chips. The Anchor has a pleasant garden in summer, families are welcome and there are camping facilities.

Beer: Flowers Original and Fremlins Bitter on handpumps.

Accommodation: 3 singles, 2 doubles, 1 family room. B&B £10-£15 per person. Weekend £20-£30, Week £70-£105. Children welcome to stay.

WYE

New Flying Horse Inn
Upper Bridge Street, off A28, 4 miles from Ashford

Licensee: Barry Law
Tel: 0233 812297

The New Flying Horse is a fine 17th-century inn, which probably replaced an old or original hostelry called the Flying Horse, in this historic town once famous for its smugglers who dealt in French brandy and lace. Wye College, founded in 1447, is now a famous agricultural college that specializes in developing new varieties of hops that are resistant to pests and fungal attack. The inn has a wealth of beams, brasses and copper; its bar is a delight, with a fine old pub feel to it, enhanced by its beams, wooden pillars and an open fireplace. The Flying Horse is a good base for visiting Romney Marsh, Rye, Dover and Canterbury, and for a trip on the Romney, Hythe and Dymchurch railway. Bar meals are available lunchtime and evening every day and include homemade soup, grills, omelettes, seafood platter, trout with prawns and almonds, steaks, sandwiches, toasties and ploughman's. There is a separate restaurant.

Beer: Shepherd Neame Master Brew Bitter and Best Bitter on handpumps.

Accommodation: 8 doubles/twins, 2 family rooms, 5 rooms with en suite facilities. B&B £27.50 single, £32.50 en suite, double/twin £37.50, £42.50 en suite, family room from £40. Children £5 if sharing with adults. Let's Go Breaks any 2 days B&B + dinner £55 per person, £60 with bath (2 persons sharing). Children's room. Pets welcome. Cards: Access, Amex, Diners and Visa.

BELL, SMARDEN – see p 119

LANCASHIRE, MANCHESTER & MERSEYSIDE

BLACKO (LANCS)

Moorcock Inn
Gisburn Road, on A682, 3 miles from M65

Licensees: Elizabeth & Peter Holt
Tel: 0282 64186

A splendid pub high on the moors with panoramic views of the valleys and Pendleside villages, the Moorcock is just three miles from Clitheroe Castle and the Forest of Bowland. The bar is cheerful and comfortable, with bow windows, high ceilings and green seating, and with log fires in winter. The imaginative bar food, served until late in the evening as well as at lunchtime (the inn has a late supper licence until midnight during the week and 11.30 on Sundays), includes both Italian and Austrian dishes such as schweinschnitzel, bratwurst, goulash, lasagne, bolognese and cannelloni. More traditional fare includes soups, homemade steak and kidney pie, steak burger, grilled trout, omelettes, chilli, savoury pancakes, seafood platter, sandwiches, ploughman's, garlic bread and sweets – fruit tart and homemade cheesecake. There are full meals in a separate restaurant and a Sunday roast. A landscaped garden at the rear is popular and busy in summer.

Beer: Thwaites Best Mild and Bitter on handpumps.

Accommodation: 1 twin, 1 double, 1 family room, all rooms with showers. B&B £12.50 per person. Half and full board available. Children welcome, half price under 12.

BLACKPOOL (LANCS)

Empress Hotel
59 Exchange Street, North Shore

Proprietors: Chris & Jean Murray
Tel: 0253 20413

The Empress is an imposing three-storey red brick Victorian hotel with a traditional vault (public bar to Southerners) and plush lounge; there is a full snooker table in the vault, welcome relief from the ubiquitous 'keg' pool table, and a concert room. Boasting some of the most comfortable beds found anywhere in Britain, it was built by the son of a local brick merchant in 1847 using handmade bricks, and some of the ceilings were sculpted by Venetian craftsmen. The roll call of stars of stage, screen and politics who have visited the Empress over the years includes Vesta Tilley, G.H. Elliott, Florrie Forde, Elizabeth Welch, Mae West, Johnny (Tarzan) Weissmuller, Sir Robin Day and Edward Heath. It remains a genuine local, though, and Blackpudlians put on their best bibs and tuckers for dancing there four nights a week. The quality of the service can be gauged by the fact that Chris Murray has been judged Landlord of the Year in 1986 and 1987 while Jean has been nominated Landlady of the Year in 1982, 1983 and 1986.

Beer: Thwaites Best Mild and Bitter on handpumps.

Accommodation: 7 doubles, 3 twins, 3 family rooms. B&B £12 per person, £17 with evening meal. Blackpool Lights Weekend (3 nights) £45. Winter reductions, mini-breaks. 4 Day Xmas Special £140. Children welcome, reductions if sharing. 10% discount for CAMRA members.

LANCASHIRE, MANCHESTER & MERSEYSIDE

Ramsden Arms Hotel
204 Talbot Road

Licensees: Christine & Albert Caffrey
Tel: 0253 23215

An impressive Tudor-style pub on the edge of Blackpool town centre, the Ramsden has a large oak-panelled lounge, and a games room popular with darts, dominoes, pool and snooker players. Three blazing log fires help to brighten the coldest winter day. Bar lunches are served every day and include homemade pies, ham, roast beef, scampi and chilli. There is a residents' TV lounge, and the guest rooms have central heating, colour TVs and tea and coffee making facilities. The pub is close to the bus and railway stations. The Ramsden Arms has been voted the local CAMRA Pub of the Year in both 1988 and 1989 and Mr Caffrey has been awarded the prestigious title of North-west Innkeeper of the Year in 1988 and 1989, by the British Institute of Innkeepers.

Beer: Burton Ale, Jennings Bitter, Tetley Mild and Bitter on handpumps.

Accommodation: 3 twins. B&B £12 per person. Children under 12 half price.

BOLTON (GREATER MANCHESTER)

Gilnow Arms
258 Deane Road, off A666

Licensees: James & Margaret MacDonald
Tel: 0204 25254

The Gilnow is a 19th-century public house that has recently been carefully modernized but which retains its old-world charm with original oak-beamed ceilings and friendly atmosphere. There is a wide range of traditional pub games for locals and visitors. Evening meals are available and guests can use both a TV lounge and a dining room.

Beer: Boddingtons OB Mild and Bitter on handpumps.

Accommodation: 2 singles, 1 double. B&B £12 per person.

BURSCOUGH (LANCS)

Martin Inn
Off B5242 (OS 414127)

Licensee: John Mawdesley
Tel: 0704 892302/895788

The Martin is a remote, welcoming inn in the heart of the west Lancashire countryside on Martin Mere, with a wildfowl trust, leisure lakes and riding schools. Bar snacks are served lunchtime and evening until 10pm and there are full meals in the popular Cottage Grill restaurant. Bar food includes soup, mushrooms with garlic dip, a range of sandwiches, steaks, chicken, plaice, homemade steak and kidney pie, salads and children's meals. The guest rooms all have showers, colour TVs, tea and coffee making facilities and direct-dial phones.

Beer: Courage Directors Bitter and John Smiths Bitter on handpumps.

Accommodation: 4 singles, 8 doubles/twins. B&B from £36. Reduced rates for children sharing a room.

LANCASHIRE, MANCHESTER & MERSEYSIDE

ENTWISTLE (LANCS)

Strawbury Duck
Near Bolton, off B6391, north of Chapeltown (OS 726177)

Licensee: J B Speakman
Tel: 0204 852013

The oddly named Strawbury Duck, originally the more prosaic Station Hotel, is a fine, half-timbered and remote inn tucked away down narrow lanes from Bolton. The cheery bar has a flagstoned floor, rough stone walls, settees and pews, beams and old prints. The pub is Victorian and has been extended to include the adjacent Bridge Cottage, which is more than 300 years old. Bar food is available every day (not Monday evening) and includes soup, garlic bread with cheese, corn on the cob, plaice or cod and chips, fisherman's pie, Aberdeen Angus steaks, chicken or beef curries, vegetable biriani, wheat casserole, vegetable lasagne or moussaka, filled jacket potatoes, steak and kidney pie, burgers and a children's menu. The tap room, also flagstoned, has darts, dominoes and pool. In summer you can sit at tables overlooking the railway line that occasionally has trains from Bolton and Blackburn. The surrounding countryside is splendid for walking.

Beer: Marston Pedigree Bitter, Ruddles County, Timothy Taylor Best Dark Mild, Best Bitter and Landlord on handpumps.

Accommodation: 1 twin, 4 four-poster rooms, all en suite. B&B £35 twin room (£28 single occupancy), £37 four-poster room (£32 single occupancy). Weekends £5 reduction on all rooms for stays of 2 nights or more.

GARSTANG (LANCS)

Royal Oak Hotel
The Square, Market Place. B6430, off A6

Licensee: Mrs L Hewitson
Tel: 099 52 3318

The Royal Oak is a 500-year-old coaching inn and is a listed building. It once stood on the main coaching route between London and Edinburgh. Garstang is still a small but thriving market town, and the Royal Oak continues to offer excellent ale and victuals to locals and visitors. It provides both hot and cold bar snacks, has a separate dining room, and a large car park.

Beer: Robinson Best Mild and Best Bitter on handpumps.

Accommodation: 5 doubles, 2 rooms with private baths. B&B £14 per person. Weekend £42, Week £98. Children and dogs welcome.

LEIGH (LANCS)

Three Crowns Hotel
188 Chapel Street. A580

Licensee: Bernard Reid
Tel: 0942 673552

One of the oldest pubs in Leigh, the Three Crowns was originally a farm and no one is certain when it obtained a liquor licence. Records date back to 1836 when a John Taylor was the landlord, and, by the 1890s, when John Benyon was the owner, the pub could stable five horses, feed 55 travellers and offer just one bed for all of them! Facilities are better today. The pub has been sensitively up-dated to retain its old atmosphere. Bar food is available all day, every day, and there is a separate restaurant.

LANCASHIRE, MANCHESTER & MERSEYSIDE

The vault has a wide range of pub games, and there is a pleasant garden for the summer months.

Beer: Boddingtons Mild and Bitter on handpumps.

Accommodation: 2 singles. B&B £12 per person. Children free under 5.

OLDHAM (GREATER MANCHESTER)

Park Hotel
Park Road, off A62

Licensees: Steve & Marion Shaw
Tel: 061-624 5713

The Park is a cosy small hotel opposite Alexandra Park and just a few minutes from the town centre. The atmosphere is friendly and relaxed and the hotel offers traditional pub games in the bar, a beer garden and live entertainment. Meals are served lunchtime and evening.

Beer: Boddingtons OB Mild, OB Bitter and Bitter on handpumps.

Accommodation: 4 doubles, 1 family room. B&B £15 per person. Children welcome, terms negotiable.

ROCHDALE (GREATER MANCHESTER)

Reed Hotel
Reed Hill, Yorkshire Street

Licensees: Pat & Frank Williams
Tel: 0706 46696

The Reed is a 200-year-old coaching inn with an impressive three-storey façade, the name picked out above the entrance. Its name derives from the reed, a weaver's comb used for separating warp threads in the mills of the industrial revolution. The first Co-op shop was opened in Rochdale and is now a museum: it is just 75 yards from the hotel. The Williamses have extensively improved and refurbished the hotel and offer excellent lunchtime food, including homemade soups, steak pie, curry, fish and chips, vegetarian dish of the day, salads, ploughman's, sandwiches and toasties, and 'Frenchies' – cheese and ham or sausage served on hot French bread with salad.

Beer: Bass Dark Mild and Special Bitter on handpumps.

Accommodation: 1 single, 3 twins, 2 doubles, 1 family room, 5 en suite. B&B from £17.50 per person. Weekend from £35, Week from £112. Children welcome to stay.

ST HELENS (MERSEYSIDE)

Royal Alfred
Bickerstaffe

Licensee: Bob May
Tel: 0744 26786

The Royal Alfred is a handsome Victorian building that has been carefully refurbished and awarded a British Tourist Board 2-star classification. It is handily placed next to the central railway station. All the guest rooms have en suite facilities, colour TVs and tea and coffee making facilities.
Beer: Boddingtons Mild and Bitter on handpumps.

Accommodation: 9 rooms. B&B £13

LANCASHIRE, MANCHESTER & MERSEYSIDE

single, £25 twin, £30 double, £36 family room. Children welcome, rates on application.

SALFORD (GREATER MANCHESTER)

Prince of Wales
165 Oldfield Road

Licensees: D A & J M Brightman
Tel: 061-832 5716

The Prince of Wales was built in 1900 and has retained its traditional atmosphere with a central bar, a vault with an open fire, a lounge and a games room. The pub is host to six darts teams and a cricket team, and darts and dominoes are played in the vault. Meals and snacks are available every lunchtime and on request in the evening. There is a residents' lounge and dining room with a TV. A cot is available for use in the guest rooms.

Beer: Boddingtons OB Mild and Bitter, Higson Bitter, Hyde Mild, Bitter and Strong Ale all on handpumps.

Accommodation: 2 doubles, 1 family room. B&B £12.50 per person. Children welcome.

SOUTHPORT (MERSEYSIDE)

Herald Hotel
16 Portland Street

Licensee: Derek Ditchfield
Tel: 0704 34424

The Herald is a smart and welcoming pub in this stately Victorian seaside town with its Parisian style boulevards and vast beaches. It offers bar snacks lunchtime and evening, with a hot special dish for lunch and a full evening meal. All the well-appointed guest rooms have colour TVs and tea and coffee making facilities. The full English breakfast should satisfy even the heartiest of appetites.

Beer: John Smiths Bitter and Magnet on handpumps.

Accommodation: 3 singles, 6 doubles, 3 twins, 3 rooms with private baths. B&B £18 single, £32 double. Week and long-stay terms available. Children welcome, terms by agreement. Cards: Access and Visa.

STOCKPORT (GREATER MANCHESTER)

Tiviot Hotel
8 Tiviot Dale

Licensee: David Walker
Tel: 061–480 4109

A friendly, welcoming town-centre pub offering excellent value for both food and accommodation, the Tiviot is close to the historic market place and handy for the M63 and Ringway Airport. The guest rooms are quiet and secluded from the bars. Sandwiches will be made up until midnight, and breakfasts are served from 6am. The energetic and dying art of table football can be enjoyed here. Stockport is a good stepping stone for the Peak District and has an art gallery, Garrick Theatre and Lyme Park ... and Robinson's brewery.

Beer: Robinson Best Mild, Best Bitter and Old Tom (winter) on electric and handpumps.

Accommodation: 2 singles, 4 doubles, 1 family room. B&B £23 per person. Evening meals available.

LANCASHIRE, MANCHESTER & MERSEYSIDE

WHITEWELL (LANCS)

Inn at Whitewell
Forest of Bowland, near Clitheroe, 9 miles from A59

Licensee: Richard Bowman
Tel: 02008 222

The inn is a superb whitewashed and mullioned building set in remote and lovely countryside. Parts date back to the 14th century, and it has Georgian and Victorian additions. It belongs to the Duchy of Lancaster and has extensive fishing rights on both banks of the river. Inside there are carved stone fireplaces, oak beams, wood panels and sonorously ticking antique clocks. The Hodder Bar has darts, dominoes and shove ha'penny. There is also an art gallery with work by artists from all over Britain, and the inn acts as a wine merchant, which means there are exceptional vintages to enjoy if you prefer the grape to the grain. Home-cooked food includes soup, House of Commons pâté (the chef used to work in the palace of Westminster), steak and kidney pie, fisherman's pie, seafood or savoury pancake, courgette lasagne, Whitewell Trencher ploughman's (Stilton and Cheddar with apple, celery, pickled onion, hard-boiled egg and granary bread), Coniston cold smoked trout, and trout gravlax. Food is served as bar snacks or in the restaurant. In warm weather you can sit on trestles in the garden and enjoy the splendour of the setting.

Beer: Moorhouse Premier Bitter and Pendle Witches Brew on handpumps.

Accommodation: 11 doubles, 6 family rooms, all rooms with en suite or private facilities. All rooms let as singles. B&B £35 single, double £48. Children welcome, 60% reduction in family room. Cards: Access, Amex, Diners and Visa.

WIGAN (GREATER MANCHESTER)

Charles Dickens Hotel
Upper Dicconson Street, town centre

Licensee: G E Cowap
Tel: 0942 323263

The hotel has a splendid, traditional public bar that is justifiably popular with locals and visitors. Bar food is served lunchtime and evening and there is also a separate restaurant. A pianist adds to the lively bar atmosphere most nights.

Beer: Flowers IPA, Marston Pedigree Bitter, Tetley Mild and Bitter, Theakston Best Bitter, XB and Old Peculier on handpumps (range of beers liable to change).

Accommodation: 9 singles, 5 doubles/twins. 2 family rooms, all rooms en suite. B&B £21 single, £30 double/twin, £37 family room. Children half price. Children's room. Pets welcome. Cards: Access and Visa.

LEICESTERSHIRE

ASHBY PARVA

Hollybush Inn
Main Street, off M1 (Lutterworth exit) and A427

Licenseee: John Bayliss
Tel: 0455 209328

John and Mary Bayliss have been running the Hollybush since 1979 and have carried out a great deal of careful renovation to introduce new bars and en suite guest rooms. The inn was previously known as the Shoulder of Mutton and, while the building dates back to 1623, it has

LEICESTERSHIRE

been a public house since 1879. Mr Bayliss lived in part of the property from six weeks of age until he was 23 and then returned in 1979 to buy the place. The Hollybush has a separate restaurant and a function room that caters for 80 people. Food is available lunchtime and evening and there is a traditional roast on Sunday. Ashby Parva is a charming and tranquil conservation village with riding stables; the local hunt often meets at the inn, which is a good base for Birmingham, Leicester, Rugby and Coventry.

Beer: Marston Burton Bitter and Pedigree Bitter on handpumps.

Accommodation: 4 singles, 9 doubles/ twins, 3 family rooms, 13 rooms with en suite facilities. Room prices: £20 single, £35 double/twin, £42 family. Breakfast £5.50 extra. Rates for children on request. Children's room. Cards: Access, Diners and Visa.

BELTON

George Hotel
Market Place, off B5324 near Loughborough

Licensee: Hector Houston
Tel: 0530 222426

The George is a large country inn dating from 1753, noted for its excellent home-cooked food lunchtime and evening. It is next to an old church and has a may-pole in the grounds. There are summer barbecues in the spacious garden. Guest rooms with en suite facilities also have tea and coffee makers. All the rooms have TVs, radios and phones. The hotel is handy for Donington Park race circuit, and is close to the M1 and East Midlands airport.

Beer: Shipstone Mild and Bitter, Wem Best Bitter on handpumps.

Accommodation: 20 doubles, 3 family rooms, 13 rooms en suite. Room £16-£25, breakfast extra. Children and dogs welcome.

BURBAGE

Sketchley Grange Hotel
Sketchley Lane, off A5 and M69 near Hinckley

Licensee: N I Downes
Tel: 0455 251133

The Grange is a superb and much extended Tudor country house set in beautiful Leicestershire countryside, close to Stratford upon Avon and Warwick Castle. The 30 guest rooms all have private showers or baths, colour TVs, direct-dial phones and tea and coffee making facilities. Two rooms have four-poster beds. There is a first-class restaurant and conference room, and the bar has been so designed that it has a genuine 'pubby' atmosphere. Bar food is available every day, lunchtime and evening, and includes soup, garlic mushrooms, roast joint of the day, lasagne verde, chicken curry, steaks, seafood pancake, steak, kidney and mushroom pie, chilli con carne, sandwiches, and a children's menu of burgers, chicken nuggets or fish fingers. Facilities for golf, swimming, riding, diving, flying, gliding, motor racing and golf are all close at hand.

Beer: Marston Burton Bitter and Pedigree Bitter.

Accommodation: 6 singles, 22 doubles/twins, 1 family room. B&B £59 single, £68 double/twin, £72 family room. Children £15. Weekends £29 per person for 2 people staying 2 nights. Cards: Access, Amex, Diners and Visa.

LEICESTERSHIRE

HINCKLEY

New Plough Hotel
24 Leicester Road, off A5 and M1

Licensee: Mary Swain
Tel: 0455 615037

Mrs Swain was organizing a major overhaul of the guest rooms in the New Plough as the guide went to press and did not know the rates she would be charging in 1990: please check when booking. In the last edition B&B was £12.50 per person and the new rates are likely to be reasonable. There is a a warm and friendly welcome in the pub, with a real fire and wooden seats in the bar and a comfortable lounge. The locals play backgammon. At the third attempt, the guide will attempt to get the history of Hinckley correct: edition one reported a castle in the town, while edition two said no such edifice had ever existed. The truth is that Hinckley has the *ruins* of a castle.

Beer: Marston Burton Bitter and Pedigree Bitter on handpumps.

Accommodation: 1 single, 2 doubles, 1 twin. Phone for details of rates.

LOUGHBOROUGH

Swan in the Rushes
21 The Rushes. A6, 5 minutes' walk from town centre

Licensee: Julian Grocock
Tel: 0509 217014

The Swan is a fine example of a genuine and unspoilt town pub and is run with great enthusiasm by the amiable Julian Grocock, a stalwart CAMRA member and accomplished blues pianist. The pub, with some fine exterior tile work, was rebuilt in 1932 and was formerly the Charnwood and then just the plain Swan until it was reopened as a free house in 1986. The two bars have parquet floors, benches and stools, and are served from a central bar. The plainer of the two bars has a juke box with classic pop hits and a fruit machine. The second bar, where food is served, has no music and has an open coal fire. The Loughborough Blues Club meets upstairs and the local CAMRA branch convenes downstairs. There is a separate room for breakfasts, which is planned to be used for evening meals as well. Bar food is available lunchtime and evening (not Sunday evening), and is all home-cooked and comes chip-free. A typical menu includes beef and mushrooms in Guinness, lamb Madras, sausages and mash, avocado stuffed with tuna and egg mayonnaise, tuna and sweetcorn lasagne, vegetable goulash, spaghetti bolognese and chilli con carne. The Swan is a good base for visiting Derby, Nottingham and the Peak District, and canal users can pull up just across the road.

As well as impeccably kept cask beers, Julian also has a splendid range of fine bottled beers, including Trappist beers from Belgium and such Czech delights as Pilsner Urquell and the genuine Budweiser Budvar.

Beer: Bateman XB and XXXB, Marston Pedigree Bitter, Tetley Bitter and regular guest beers, including one regular guest mild ale, all on handpumps.

Accommodation: 2 doubles/twins, 2 family rooms, 2 rooms en suite. B&B £15-£25 per person, depending on number of people in room: ie £15 per person in fully occupied room. Single person en suite £25. Discounts for group bookings and CAMRA members. Children allowed in pub lunchtime if eating. Pets welcome.

LEICESTERSHIRE

OAKHAM

Rutland Angler
Mill Street, off A6

Licensees: John & Matthew Woods
Tel: 0572 755839

The Angler is a friendly and welcoming old Rutland pub, once Oakham's maternity hospital. It stages live jazz every Thursday evening in the spacious cellar bar. Based in the historic market town, it is just 1½ miles from the vast man-made Rutland Water, with walks, birdwatching, sailing and fishing facilities. Satellite TV is available in the pub.

Beer: Marston Pedigree Bitter and Tolly Original on handpumps.

Accommodation: 4 singles, 3 twins, 1 double, 2 rooms with private baths. B&B £16.50 single, double/twin £27, £30 with bath. Children welcome, terms by arrangement. Discounts for stays of more than 4 nights. 1989 rates: please check new rates when booking.

QUORN

White Horse
2 Leicester Road. A6

Licensees: Pam & Chris Davis
Tel: 0509 412338 620140

There has been a pub on the site since the 1650s and there are still a few reminders of the period in the spacious residents' room. The White Horse was the first ale house in the famous hunting village to be granted a wine and spirits licence. As well as the friendly lounge bar there is a large pool room with two full-size tables. The pub is in the centre of Quorn and has good car parking facilities.

Beer: Adnams Bitter, Everards Burton Mild, Beacon Bitter, Tiger and Old Original on handpumps, with occasional guest beers.

Accommodation: 1 family room. B&B £18 single, £22 double. Children welcome, half price. Tea and coffee making facilities and a TV are available. More rooms are planned.

WHISSENDINE

White Lion
Main Street, 3 miles from A606

Licensee: John Gray
Tel: 066 479 233

The White Lion is a cheery, friendly pub with first-class food lunchtime and evening (including vegetarian meals), and a strong emphasis on pub games: as well as darts and pool you can join in the rarer pub pastimes of Shut the Box and Devil Among the Tailors. There is a fine garden, where you can enjoy a drink and a meal in warm weather. The White Lion is well placed for Rutland Water and the lovely Vale of Belvoir.

Beer: Everard Beacon Bitter, Tiger and Old Original on handpumps.

Accommodation: 11 rooms, can be arranged as single, double or family. 2 rooms with showers. B&B £18–£35. Cards: Access, Amex and Visa.

SKETCHLEY GRANGE HOTEL – *see p 127*

ASWARBY

Tally Ho
On A15 near Sleaford

Licensees: Christopher & Rachel Davis
Tel: 052 95 205

The Tally Ho is an 18th-century inn built of Ancaster stone and topped by a fine slate roof. It stands in fields and lovely parkland close to Sleaford. It is renowned for its lively and friendly atmosphere and the bar is the meeting and watering place of the local community. Meals are served lunchtime and evening in the bar or separate restaurant. There are welcoming log fires in the winter and the guest rooms – in the tastefully modernized old stable block – have private baths, TVs and tea and coffee making facilities. It is a good base for visiting Stamford, Boston and Grantham.

Beer: Adnams Bitter, Bateman XB on handpumps and guest beers.

Accommodation: 6 doubles. B&B £25 single, £38 double. Weekend rates on request.

BOSTON

Carpenters Arms
Union Street, off Wormgate

Licensee: R Newberry
Tel: 0205 62840

The Carpenters is a lively, bustling pub hidden away in the small streets behind Boston Stump, the largest parish church in England with its tower that dominates the Fens and has acted as a navigation aid for sailors for centuries. The main bar of the pub is a meeting place for young and old, and there is imaginative lunchtime food – curries, pasta and vegetarian dishes. Evening food is by arrangement only. The five large guest rooms have brass bedsteads and pine furniture. Prices vary according to whether you want a full breakfast, continental or prefer to cook your own in the kitchen provided for early leavers. In Boston you can visit the church, the memorial to the Pilgrim Fathers, the Guildhall, and the market place.

Beer: Bateman Mild, XB and XXXB on handpumps.

Accommodation: 5 doubles, including 2 family rooms. B&B from £15 per person. Half and full board available.

BURGH LE MARSH

White Hart Hotel
19–21 High Street, A158

Licensee: Mrs C Watson
Tel: 0754 810321

A comfortable and welcoming pub five miles from Skegness, the White Hart is a good base for touring the Lincolnshire coast and Tennyson region. The hotel has a pleasant lounge with a fine collection of Crown Derby china, a lively public bar with games and juke box, and a separate restaurant called Harts that serves distinctive, good-value food. The charming guest rooms all have tea and coffee making equipment.

Beer: Bateman XB and XXXB, Marston Pedigree Bitter, and a guest beer on handpumps.

Accommodation: 3 doubles, 2 family rooms, all with en suite facilities. B&B £17.50 single occupancy, £30 double. Half and full board available. Cards: Amex.

FREISTON

Castle Inn
Haltoft End, A52

Licensee: Mrs B Thompson
Tel: 0205 760393

The Castle is an attractive inn four miles from Boston, with a comfortable and spacious bar with open fires in winter. This is a riproaring family pub with a superb adventure playground that includes an aerial runway and fishing boats. Bar food is served lunchtime and evening. The inn is well placed for visiting the Pilgrim Fathers' memorial near Fishtoft, and the Sibsey Traders Mill, a six-sailed windmill owned by English Heritage and open to the public.

Beer: Bateman Mild and XB on handpumps.

Accommodation: 3 doubles with tea and coffee makers. B&B £12. Half board available.

GREAT LIMBER

New Inn
High Street, A18

Licensee: Colin Spencer
Tel: 0469 60257

A large and popular pub in the centre of the village, with a splendid range of beers, the New Inn offers a relief from the expensive hotels in the area. It has a quiet lounge free from electronic music or games, real fires in winter, a welcome for families and a garden, plus good food at lunchtime (not weekends) and, for residents only, in the evening. The pub is owned by the Earl of Yarborough, whose family seat, Brocklesby Park, is close by. The hand at bridge or whist containing no card higher than a nine is called a Yarborough and is named after one of the earl's ancestors. The wife of the first baron is buried in a magnificent mausoleum within walking distance of the pub. It stands on a barrow with excellent views of the countryside and Humber estuary. The inn is a good base for the Humber industries and Humberside airport.

Beer: Bateman XXXB and regular guest beers on handpumps.

Accommodation: 5 singles, 2 doubles, 1 family room. B&B £12 single, £20 double. Half and full board available (no full board at weekends). All rooms have tea and coffee making facilities.

STAMFORD

Bull & Swan
High Street, St Martins. B1081 south side of town

Licensee: Maurice de Sadeleer
Tel: 0780 63558

The Bull & Swan is a fine stone-built coaching inn in one of England's most superb and unspoilt old towns. It has a wood-burning stove, low beams hung with copper kettles, and comfortable plush seating in the three-level bar. Bar food is served lunchtime and evening, and includes homemade soup, sandwiches, steak and mushroom pie, filled jacket potatoes, ploughman's, trout in sweet-and-sour sauce, seafood pancake and tempting puddings. There is a separate restaurant, and seats in a courtyard in good weather.

Beer: Cameron Strongarm and Tolly Original on handpumps.

Accommodation: 6 rooms. B&B £28 single, £30 en suite, £32 double, £38 en suite.

SPILSBY

Red Lion Hotel
16 Market Street. A16

Licensee: Peter Humberstone
Tel: 0790 53500

The Red Lion is a traditional one-bar pub with a strong emphasis on games, including pool. Bar food is available lunchtimes, and the pub has a children's room. Spilsby is a busy market town on the edge of the Wolds, and is close to Somersby, Alfred Lord Tennyson's birthplace. The parish church of St James has a monument to Captain Sir John Franklin, the Arctic navigator who discovered the North-West Passage linking the Atlantic and the Pacific; there is a bronze statue of him in the market place. The great knees-up seaside resort of Skegness is just ten miles away.

Beer: Bateman XB and XXXB on handpumps.

Accommodation: 2 doubles/twins, 1 family room. B&B £12 per person. Pets welcome.

WAINFLEET

Woolpack Hotel
39 High Street. A52

Licensee: David Phillips
Tel: 0754 880353

The Woolpack has been a licensed hostelry since the 18th century, though the building is older. Marked on the front of the hotel is one of the four measuring points for spring and winter tides to be found in the town. Home-cooked food, using locally grown fresh vegetables, is served every day (not Monday evenings) in either the lounge or the dining room, and ranges from shepherd's pie to mushroom lasagne, with a traditional Sunday roast. Wainfleet is the home of Bateman's brewery, saved from extinction in the mid-80s by George Bateman and his son and daughter when other members of the family wanted to sell up and retire to the sun. The brewery's tasty, fruity mild and bitters have won several awards at CAMRA beer festivals.

Beer: Bateman Mild, XB and XXXB, Home Bitter on handpumps.

Accommodation: 3 doubles/twins, 3 family rooms. B&B £15 per person. Children half price sharing a family room. No dogs.

LONDON

CLAPHAM SW4

Olde Windmill
Windmill Drive, Clapham Common South Side. A24

Licensee: Richard Williamson
Tel: 081-673 4578

The Windmill is just a few yards from an old Roman road that has been carrying traffic for more than 19 centuries. An inn has stood on the site since 1665, and the mill from which it took its name was once the winning post for the Clapham Races. The present building is largely Victorian in origin and the vast main bar has windmill pictures on the walls, and seats and sofas round tables. Bar food includes ploughman's, chilli, curries and salads. There are terrace seats outside, and in good weather the crowds of drinkers spill out on to the common. Accommodation is in an adjoining house that was once the home of the founder of Young's brewery. There is a resident ghost known as Croaker.

Beer: Young Bitter, Special Bitter and Winter Warmer on handpumps.

Accommodation: 9 singles, 4 doubles, 1 room with private bath. B&B £31 single, £40 double.

The Greyhound, *151–55 Greyhound Lane, Streatham, SW16 (01–677 9962) had suffered a fire as the guide was going to press and the accommodation was not available, though it was hoped that it would be operational in 1990. It is opposite Streatham Common, has a children's room and a conservatory and brews its own beers on the premises – Greyhound Pedigree Mild, Special Bitter, Streatham Strong and Streatham Dynamite. Phone to check availability of accommodation and prices.*

NORFOLK

ATTLEBOROUGH

Griffin Hotel
Church Street, A11

Licensee: Richard Ashbourne
Tel: 0953 452149

The Ashbournes are planning careful and sensitive restoration work to bring out the best features of the Griffin, a 16th-century coaching inn in the town centre. It has half timbers and a low-slung roof outside, and beams and open fires – one with a stove – inside, and a fine welcome from staff and locals. The walls and fires are decorated with old shields, brass jugs, china and guns. There are excellent bar snacks, ranging from a steak to a sandwich, and usually locally caught fresh fish, while the separate restaurant is open Monday to Saturday evenings, with a traditional roast lunch on Sundays. The guest rooms are centrally heated and equipped with TVs. Attleborough is close to Snetterton race circuit and Sunday Market, and Kilverstone Wildlife Park. The Griffin is open all day on Thursday, Friday and Saturday.

Beer: Greene King Abbot Ale, Marston Pedigree Bitter, Wethered Bitter on handpumps, with a weekly guest beer and local cider.

Accommodation: 2 singles, 6 doubles. B&B £16 single, £25-£30 double, £35 family room. 10% reduction for week's stay. Children welcome to stay, no reductions. No animals.

BROCKDISH

Olde Kings Head
The Street, 5 miles east of Scole on A143

Licensees: David & Helen Dedman
Tel: 037 975 8125

The Kings Head is a rambling 17th-century coaching inn with heavily beamed lounge bar and restaurant, a large open fire in the lounge, and a separate games room where darts and pool are played. Bar snacks such as ploughman's are served lunchtime and evening, and there is a children's menu, and a separate restaurant menu as well as a traditional Sunday roast. The inn is situated in the picturesque Waveney valley, a fine base for touring East Anglia, and close to the Otter Trust, Bressington Gardens and Steam Museum and the Broads.

Beer: Adnams Mild and Bitter and guest beers on handpumps.

NORFOLK

Accommodation: 6 doubles/twins, 1 family room, all with en suite facilities. B&B £18 single, £14 per person in double or family room. Children in cot £5, £10 if sharing with parents. Children's room. Pets welcome. Cards: Access and Visa.

CLEY-NEXT-THE-SEA

George & Dragon Hotel
On A149

Licensee: Rodney Sewell
Tel: 0263 740652

This historic building was rebuilt in 1879 but dates from the 17th century. It stands in one of the prettiest villages in North Norfolk in an area of bleak beauty by the salt marshes which lead down to the sea. It is ideal bird-watching territory, and the George & Dragon has a room dedicated to the Norfolk Naturalist Trust which was founded in the hotel in 1926. There are boat trips to see the seals on the point. The pub has many 'G&D' artefacts, including a stained glass window of England's patron saint slaying the mythical beast. Bar meals are served lunchtime and evening, and include local crab and lobster in season, mussels, venison, specialities from the hotel's own smoke house, and pan haggerty – baked layers of cheese, onion and potato with three slices of bacon, two sausages and baked beans. There is a large beer garden. Families are welcome and there is a TV lounge for residents.

Beer: Greene King IPA and Abbot Ale on handpumps, with regular guest beers including Bateman's and Rayment's.

Accommodation: 8 doubles including 1 en suite family room, 2 doubles en suite, including a four-poster. B&B £17–£29. Facilities for the disabled.

CROMER

Bath House
The Promenade, off A149

Licensees: Bert & Barbara Wheston
Tel: 0263 514260

The Bath House is a lovingly restored and elegant Regency inn on the promenade of this fine Victorian seaside resort, the county's most northerly coastal town, famous for its crab fishing, sea fret or mist and small lifeboat museum. The guest rooms of the Bath House are on the first floor and most have views of the sea. All the rooms are en suite and have central heating, colour TVs and tea and coffee makers. There is a residents' lounge, seats on the prom, and excellent lunches and evening meals (every day), including homemade soup, wings of fire, deep-fried mushrooms with garlic dip, steak and Guinness pie, lasagne, prawn or chicken curry, chilli con carne, steaks, plaice or cod, mariner's fish bake, Cromer crab salad, ploughman's, and sweets. The inn is just a few yards from the beach, the pier and the crab landing area.

Beer: Greene King Abbot Ale and Rayment's BBA, Woodforde Wherry Best Bitter and such regular guest beers as Bateman and Elgood, all on handpumps.

Accommodation: 1 single, 3 doubles, 3 twins, all en suite. B&B £19.50 per person. Off-season 3-Day Bargain Breaks £72 dinner, B&B. No pets. Cards: Access and Visa.

Red Lion Hotel
Brooke Street

Licensee: Miss V E Medler
Tel: 0263 514964

The Red Lion is a large and welcoming hotel with two bars, one with an interior flint wall, the other with an open fire and a high-back wooden settle, the two linked by the long serving area; real ale is served from the smaller bar. Leading off the main bar is the smart and wood-panelled residential area, which includes Galliano's evening restaurant. Bar food, served lunchtime and evening, includes a special dish of the day, crab, prawn and ham salads, omelettes, grilled lamb cutlets, chicken Kiev or cordon bleu and plaice Cleopatra. The hotel has impressive views overlooking the promenade and the sea, and is just a few yards from Cromer's fine flint-faced church.

Beer: Adnams Bitter, Bass, Greene King Abbot Ale and Marston Pedigree Bitter on handpumps.

Accommodation: 12 doubles/twins, 1 family room, 12 rooms with en suite facilities. B&B £34 single occupancy, £27 per person sharing. Half board £5 extra. Children half price, free under 3 years. Off-season 2 or more nights from £22 per person per night, including dinner. No pets. Cards: Access and Visa.

DISS

Cock Inn
Fair Green, off A1066

Licensee: Stevan Moyard
Tel: 0379 643633

The Cock is 300 years old and stands on the Thetford and Scole road, overlooking Fair Green. A few miles away at Redgrove two rivers, the Waveney and the Little Ouse, spring from the same well and flow in different directions. The inn's guest rooms include one four-poster, and bar snacks are available.

Beer: Adnams Mild and Bitter, Greene King XX and IPA on handpumps.

Accommodation: 1 single, 1 double. B&B £18 single, £34 double.

DOWNHAM MARKET

Crown Hotel
Bridge Street, close to market square and clock tower, off A10

Proprietor: John Champion
Tel: 0366 382322

The Crown's small frontage on Bridge Street belies the scope of the old inn that lies down a long and narrow cobbled yard to the side. The earliest parts are thought to have been built on the site of a medieval monks' hospice. It was the headquarters of the Downham Cavalry in the early 19th century and became an important coaching inn on the London to King's Lynn, Norwich and Peterborough routes. Today it is listed as a building of historical and architectural interest and its rooms retain their old atmosphere with exposed beams, bare brick walls and, in the bar, two open fireplaces. The more recent history of the area is captured by many photos of air crews stationed nearby during the Second World War. Mr Champion is well named for he is indeed the champion of independent brewers in eastern England, and serves their ales in the bar, along with lunchtime bar meals ranging from rolls to hot dishes of the day. Lunch and dinner are served in the adjoining restaurant.

Beer: Bateman XB, Greene King Abbot Ale, Nethergate Bitter, Woodforde Wherry Best Bitter and weekly guest beer, all on handpumps.

Accommodation: 1 single, 9 doubles/twins, 7 rooms with en suite facilities. B&B £18 single, £24 en suite, £28 double room, £34 en suite. 2 interconnecting rooms can be arranged as a family room. Children's rates depend on age and sleeping arrangements. Weekend rates on application. Pets welcome. Cards: Access, Amex, Diners and Visa.

GREAT BIRCHAM

King's Head Hotel
Lynn Road. B1153 off A148

Licensee: I Verrando
Tel: 048 523 265/210

A handsome country inn with steeply sloping roofs, tall chimneys and dormer windows, the King's Head is close to Sandringham and the Peddars Way. There is a gracious lawn for warm-weather eating and drinking. Bar meals are available lunchtime and evening and the candlelit restaurant uses local produce for its varied menu: it is renowned for the quality of its beef and shellfish dishes. There is a traditional roast at Sunday lunchtimes. The guest rooms all have baths or showers, TVs and tea and coffee making facilities.

Beer: Adnams Bitter, Bass and Charrington IPA on handpumps.

Accommodation: 3 twins, 2 doubles. B&B £22.50 per person. Cards: Access and Visa.

HOLKHAM

Victoria Hotel
On A149

Licensees: Geoff & Gemma Whitehead
Tel: 0328 710469

The Victoria is a late 19th-century brick-and-flint hotel on the north Norfolk coast road. It stands opposite the long drive that leads down to the great sweep of Holkham beach and wildlife reserve, one of the finest coastal stretches in eastern England. The bar enjoys darts, dominoes, crib and shove ha'penny, while the pleasant lounge has bay windows with fine views of the coast. There are tables in the old stableyard in summer. Bar meals include soups, ploughman's, sandwiches, salads, steaks and local fish and shellfish: the Whiteheads concentrate on local, freshly cooked produce. There is a residents' TV lounge and the guest rooms have tea and coffee making facilities. Holkham Hall, open to the public, is close by.

Beer: Adnams Bitter and Old (winter) on handpump and straight from the cask.

Accommodation: 3 singles, 5 doubles. B&B £17 per person Easter to October, £15 in winter. Winter Breaks 2 nights £42 per person with evening meal.

KING'S LYNN

Bankhouse
King's Staithe Square

Licensees: Fred & Jenny Hackworth
Tel: 0553 76508

A delightful and elegant Georgian building in the heart of this fine old East Anglian port and market town, the Bankhouse has risen phoenix-like from a terrible fire in 1985. As a result, the upper floors, with the guest rooms, have been rebuilt, but they retain much of the original panelling. Downstairs, the bar offers excellent bar snacks – soup, steaks, fish, sandwiches, pizzas – while the beamed restaurant, once the kitchen of the old house, serves lunch Tuesday to Friday, with a traditional roast on Sunday and an evening à la carte menu. The guest rooms, with views of the river and old courtyard, have colour TVs and tea and coffee making equipment. The exterior lies behind a walled garden with iron gates, and a large cornice has a statue of Charles I in a pink cloak with his hand on his sword.

Beer: Bass and Charrington IPA on handpumps.

Accommodation: 2 singles, 2 doubles, 1 room en suite. B&B £25.50 single, £32.50 double. Weekend £12.50 per person per night. Children welcome, half price. Cards: Access and Visa.

BARTON ANGLER LODGE, NEATISHEAD – see p 138

NORFOLK

MUNDESLEY

Royal Hotel
30 Paston Road. A1159

Licensee: Michael Fotis
Tel: 0263 720096

The Royal is a 300-year-old inn with superb views of the sea from Mundesley cliffs, with original beams and timbers, and strong connections with Admiral Lord Nelson, who stayed at the inn while he attended Paston school in North Walsham. The pub was known as the New Inn in those days, the change of name following a visit by royalty in the late 18th century. The Nelson Bar of the hotel has splendid bar meals that feature locally caught fish and shellfish, as well as cold meats and salads. The separate Buttery and Beachcomber Restaurant is open for lunch and dinner. The guest rooms all have private baths or showers, colour TVs, radios and tea and coffee making equipment. The hotel is a good base for visiting the many delights of north Norfolk, including the shrine to Our Lady of Walsingham, Blakeney, the pleasant seaside resort of Sheringham and its steam railway, and miles of unspoilt coast.

Beer: Adnams Bitter and Old, Charrington IPA, Greene King Abbot Ale on handpumps.

Accommodation: 26 singles/twins, 14 doubles. B&B £24.50 single, £37.50 double, four-poster £39.50. Weekend (2 nights) £65 for 2, £69 four-poster. Week £215 for 2. Children welcome, 20% reductions. Cards: Access, Amex, Diners and Visa.

NEATISHEAD

Barton Angler Lodge
Irstead Road, off A1151; after Wroxham take road signposted Neatishead and Barton Turf; in Neatishead village follow Irstead road for 1½ miles

Licensees: Tim & Anne King
Tel: 0692 630740

The Barton Angler is an elegant hotel on the banks of lovely Barton Broad, 280 acres of Anglian water where Nelson learnt to sail. The hotel can arrange for dinghy and boat hire. It has large, sweeping, flower-filled gardens, guest rooms that have been upgraded since the last edition and now include two four-poster rooms, two bars – the Mahogany and Tangler with lunchtime bar snacks – and top-class cooking in the Harlows Restaurant. In summer there are barbecues on the patio. Lunches range from soup, fisherman's pie. steak and Abbot Ale pie, salads and ploughman's to filled baps, and crab.

Beer: Greene King IPA and Abbot Ale on handpumps.

Accommodation: 3 singles, 4 doubles, 5 rooms with en suite facilities. B&B £20-£35 per person. Cards: Access, Amex and Visa.

NORTH WOOTTON

Red Cat Hotel
Station Road, 1½ miles off A148 and A149, near King's Lynn

Licensee: Peter Irwin
Tel: 0553 631244

Peter Irwin is a former chairman of the local branch of CAMRA, so you can be assured of a good pint in his popular marshland pub near the Wash, close to the ancient monument at Castle Rising. The Red Cat is faced with carrstone and dates back to the middle of the last century. Good-value bar snacks are available at all times and cooked evening meals are served in a fine beamed dining room. The comfortable guest rooms have tea and coffee making facilities and most have en suite showers or baths. The original red cat has pride of place in the bar, and the pub named after it has a garden, family room and open fires.

Beer: Red Cat Special Bitter, which is brewed for the pub by Woodforde, plus Adnams Bitter and frequent guest beers on handpumps, and seasonal old ales straight from the cask.

Accommodation: 4 singles, 3 doubles, 1 twin, 1 family room. B&B £24 single, £38-£48 double/twin, £44 family room. Children are included in family room price. Weekend rates on request. Pets welcome.

ORMESBY ST MARGARET

Grange Hotel
Off A149 and B1159

Proprietors: Pearl & Roy Smith
Tel: 0493 731877

The Grange is a former Georgian country house in two acres of grounds that include a children's entertainment centre in a log cabin, a pets' corner and an adventure playground. It is an ideal family pub with a room for children and parents inside, too. The bars offer excellent food, while the guest rooms have colour TVs, phones and tea and coffee making facilities. There are now also self-catering apartments.

The Grange is a good base for visiting Caister Castle and car museum, Thrigby wildlife park, and local beaches and golf courses.

Beer: Adnams Bitter, Bateman XXXB and Woodforde Wherry Best Bitter on handpumps.

Accommodation: Bed and continental breakfast: £24 single, £30 double en suite, children under 5 free, under 11 £5. Self-catering apartments £150 a week low season, £180 high season, up to 4 people sharing. Cards: Access and Visa.

SCOLE

Scole Inn
The Street, A140

Manager: Ivor Wright
Tel: 0379 740481

The Scole is a famous old East of England 17th-century coaching inn and a grade one listed building. Its most famous claim to fame – its inn sign – no longer exists. When village carpenter John Fairchild was commissioned by a wealthy Norwich wool merchant, John Peck, to build the inn, he added a gallows sign that straddled the road and cost the astonishing sum for 1655 of £1,057. It included many mythical and classical figures, including Neptune rising from the waves, with pride of place going to a white hart, the inn's original name. It was demolished about 250 years later, but an engraving of it by Joshua Kirby hangs in the bar. The notorious highwayman John Belcher used the inn as his headquarters. The inn today retains many of its original features, with a wealth of beams, oak doors and inglenook fireplaces. There is both good bar food and a separate restaurant. Food in the bar is waitress-served and includes homemade soup, ploughman's, steaks, crab salad, steak and kidney pie, and such homemade pâtés as Stilton, celery and port, or smoked mackerel.

Beer: Adnams Bitter and Greene King Abbot Ale on handpumps.

Accommodation: 20 doubles, including 3 family rooms, all with en suite facilities, 12 rooms in converted stable block. B&B £45–£48 single, £60–£70 double; 4 poster room £65–£70. Bargain Breaks £75 per person sharing double room for any 2 nights. Cards: Access, Amex, Diners and Visa.

SOUTH WOOTTON

Farmers Arms (Knights Hill Hotel)
Knights Hill Village, near King's Lynn, junction of A148 and A149

Licensee: Ken Hawkes
Tel: 0553 675566

The Farmers Arms is a pub in an eleven-acre farm complex that includes a hotel and restaurant. The pantiled and carrstone buildings have been converted from old stables, byres and a grain store, and the pub has a wealth of exposed beams, open fireplaces and cobbled floors. Above the bar, the old grain store, the Hayloft, is used to provide entertainment. Food is served from 11am to 10pm, with the same menu in both pub and restaurant, ranging from homemade soup, farmhouse terrine or farmhouse boots (filled jacket potatoes) to trout, lemon sole, gamekeeper's pie, baked lasagne, duck, grills, vegetarian pasta and vegeburger, and a children's choice. The complex has facilities for conferences and many indoor sporting activities. All the guest rooms have en suite facilities, colour TVs, direct-dial phones and tea and coffee making equipment.

Beer: Adnams Bitter and Broadside, Bass and Charrington IPA, Ruddles County, Sam Smith Old Brewery Bitter, and regular guest beers, all on handpumps.

Accommodation: 3 singles, 37 doubles/twins. Room from £52 single, £60 double or twin. Full breakfast £5.50 extra, continental £3.23. Children under 15 free when sharing with adults. No pets. Cards: Access, Amex, Diners and Visa.

SWANNINGTON

Swannington Hall
Church Lane, off A1067, Norwich to Reepham road

Licensees: Mr G Hale & Ms F Bloom
Tel: 0603 868412

Swannington Hall, just seven miles from Norwich, is a stunning Elizabethan house with the finest Tudor beamed ceiling in the county. It stands in five acres of ground, is surrounded by a moat and inside has cheering open fires. Robert Kett, leader of the mighty revolt against land enclosures in the 16th century, was arrested in Swannington and held in the hall before his execution. Bar food is served lunchtime and evening every day and includes homemade beef and stout pies, lasagne, whitebait, chilli and curries. The restaurant is open every evening, and there are Sunday barbecues in season.

Beer: Adnams Bitter, Greene King IPA, Abbot Ale and Rayment BBA and a wide range of guest beers, including Bateman, Marston and Theakston, all on handpumps.

Accommodation: 4 doubles. B&B £15 per person. Children free if sharing. Pets welcome.

THORNHAM

Lifeboat Inn
Sea Lane, ½ mile off A149

Licensees: Nicholas & Lynn Handley
Tel: 048 526 236

You wake in the Lifeboat's large and comfortable rooms to the sound of the sea, doves cooing and cows mooing across the road. It is a wonderful old pub on the edge of the vast salt flats that lead to the sea and across which smugglers struggled with their contraband centuries ago. The Lifeboat, a series of small rooms, has low beams, five crackling log fires in winter, oil and gas lamps, and pub games that include darts, shove ha'penny, and a penny-in-the-hole bench. Although it can be cold outside in winter, the pub has a flourishing vine in a terrace at the back. There are a few seats at the front, and the back garden has seats among the trees, a climbing frame and toys for children, and a donkey. Splendid homemade bar food concentrates on dishes such as soups, ploughman's, pasta, cheese and onion quiche, potted shrimps, lamb stew, mussels, fresh local fried fish, game pie, steaks, sandwiches and homemade ice creams. The small candle-lit restaurant has à la carte meals that include local seafood and game. A fine place to stay, eat and drink.

Beer: Adnams Bitter, Greene King IPA and Abbot Ale on handpumps and straight from the cask, plus such guest beers as Tetley and Woodforde.

Accommodation: 2 doubles. B&B £30 per room. Children's room; children welcome to stay, no reductions. Cards: Access and Visa.

WELLS-NEXT-THE-SEA

Crown Hotel
The Buttlands, off A149

Licensee: Wilfred Foyers
Tel: 0328 710209

The Crown is charmingly placed by a large green in this picturesque old sea port that is these days also a good hunting ground for buyers of antique furniture and paintings. The old coaching inn has a popular bar with a piano and good bar food that includes soup, ploughman's, omelettes, vegetarian tagliatelle, crab, steaks, and steak and mushroom pie. There are special dishes for children. The separate restaurant has no less than four chefs and offers acclaimed French and English cooking. There is a conservatory and also seats in a courtyard. Wells is a delightful town to stroll in, and is close to Blakeney, Holkham Hall, the North Norfolk Heritage Coast and Sandringham.

Beer: Adnams Bitter, Marston Pedigree Bitter and Tetley Bitter on handpumps.

Accommodation: 1 single, 13 doubles, 2 family rooms. 8 rooms with en suite facilities. B&B from £20 per person. Weekend from £62 for dinner B&B; Week from £217. Children's room; children welcome to stay, reductions on application. Cards: Access, Amex, Diners and Visa.

WOLTERTON

Saracen's Head
Off A140, 1½ miles from Erpingham

Licensees: R Dawson-Smith & I M Bryson
Tel: 0263 77409

The Saracen's Head is of unusual design even by Norfolk standards. It is modelled on a Tuscan farmhouse and was built by Horace Walpole as a coaching inn for nearby Wolterton Hall. Bar food, available lunchtime and evening, includes soups, homemade pies, fried aubergines, seafood, steaks and rustic lunches. There is a separate evening restaurant which also operates as a Sunday lunchtime carvery. Throughout the year there are regular feasts for a minimum of 12 people, including seafood and game.

Beer: Adnams Bitter and Broadside and one weekly guest beer, all on handpumps.

Accommodation: 3 doubles, all en suite. B&B £25-£35. Children by arrangement. Pets welcome. Cards: Access, Amex and Visa.

ASHBY ST LEDGERS

Old Coach House
Off A361 near Daventry; 4 miles from M1 junction 18

Licensees: Douglas & Frederika Jarvis
Tel: 0788 890349

Accommodation at the Old Coach House includes stabling for horses, recalling the time when the stone buildings were a farm with the front room set aside as a bar. The Jarvises have been undoing a great deal of thoughtless modernization in the 1960s and have discovered wonderful old inglenooks and stone floors. The many small rooms have settle chairs, farm kitchen tables, old harnesses and hunting prints. Table skittles, darts and dominoes are played in the front bar. The spacious garden has a climbing frame and swings for children and there are summer barbecues. Bar food includes a 'pot luck' daily special, giant prawns, Danish herrings, ploughman's with local cheese, game casserole, local trout, mackerel, and vegetarian dishes such as vegetable crêpes or mushrooms baked in small wholemeal loaves. Children's portions are available. In winter there is a carvery, too, with a hot roast. The lovely old village has stone and thatch cottages and the Gunpowder Plot was hatched in the manor, Althorp Hall.

Beer: Flowers Original, Marston Pedigree Bitter, Sam Smith's Old Brewery Bitter or Museum Ale on handpumps.

Accommodation: 1 single, 4 doubles/twins, 2 family rooms, all with en suite facilities. B&B £27.50 single, £30 twin, £35 double, £45 family room. Children welcome, £5 per night.

NORTHAMPTONSHIRE

BLAKESLEY

Bartholomew Arms
High Street, 3 miles off A5, near Towcester

Licensee: Tony Hackett
Tel: 0327 860292

A cheerful village local with, says Mr Hackett, no gimmicks – no pool, juke box, space invaders or plastic food. 'We offer good beer and company.' The beamed bars are packed with cricketing memorabilia, hams, guns and malt whiskies. The pub is the home of the National Soap Box Derby held every year in September. The championships were started by Tony Hackett and other villagers to raise funds for charity. Excellent bar food is served lunchtime, with a limited choice in the evening. All the guest rooms have colour TVs and central heating. The pub is a good base for Towcester and its race course, and the Silverstone motor racing circuit.

Beer: Marston Pedigree Bitter and Ruddles County on handpump.

Accommodation: 1 single, 4 doubles, 2 rooms with en suite facilities. B&B £15. Full board available. Children welcome, 40% reduction.

BRACKLEY HATCH

Green Man Inn
A45, 1 mile south of Silverstone

Licensee: Gordon M Bradshaw
Tel: 02805 209/632

The Green Man is a remarkable pub; a former 16th-century coaching inn that still retains much of its old charm and atmosphere inside with log fires and original beams. Mr Bradshaw has developed it brilliantly as a family

NORTHAMPTONSHIRE

pub and the large landscaped gardens are a paradise for children ... and tired parents. There is a bouncing castle, swings and climbing frames and a cabin when the weather is not kind: special children's menus are available there. The gardens are supervised and entertainment is provided by clowns and members of staff who volunteer to dress up as Mickey Mouse and other characters. The large, airy conservatory is also used by families. Mr Bradshaw, not suprisingly, won the Family Pub of the Year award in 1989 from Schweppes and *Publican* magazine. If you want to get away from the kids for an hour or two, the small restaurant at the far end of the inn away from the gardens will provide sanctuary. The Green Man is close to Silverstone motor racing circuit and five miles from Towcester racecourse.

Beer: Hook Norton Best Bitter and Old Hookey, Marston Pedigree Bitter on handpumps.

Accommodation: 10 doubles/twins, 4 with en suite facilities. B&B £25 single, £33 en suite, £15 per person sharing, £20 en suite. Cards: Access, Amex, Diners and Visa.

LONG BUCKBY

Rockhall House Hotel
Market Square. B5385, 1 mile from A5, 2 miles from M1 junction 18

Licensee: James W Jackson
Tel: 0327 843625

Rockhall House, one mile from the Grand Union canal, is a stone building dating back to 1680 and substantially renovated in the late 1980s. It stands on the market square of the village and provides good ale and food for locals and visitors. Both restaurant and bar food are available every evening and there is a traditional roast lunch on Sunday. It is a good base for visiting Guisborough wildlife park.

Beer: Bateman XXXB and Hook Norton Old Hookey with regular guest beers on handpumps.

Accommodation: 1 single, 8 doubles/twins, 2 family rooms, all with en suite facilities. B&B £35 single (£28 weekend), £45 double/twin (£40), £55 family room (£50). Children's rates depend on age. Pets welcome. Cards: Access and Visa.

LONG BUCKBY WHARF

New Inn
A5, 4 miles north of Weedon

Licensee: Mrs E A Blake
Tel: 0327 842540

The New Inn is an old canalside pub at Buckby Top Lock on the Grand Union. There are tables by the canal and it is a popular spot in the summer for families watching boats going through the lock. Bar food is served every day, lunchtime and evening, and ranges from steak and kidney pie to roast meals.

Beer: Marston Pedigree Bitter on handpump.

Accommodation: 3 doubles/twins. 1 room can be used as a family room. B&B £15 per person, £12.50 for families. Pets welcome.

NORTHAMPTONSHIRE

ROTHWELL

Red Lion Hotel
Market Hill, A6 near Kettering

Proprietors: Anne & Jim Tibbs
Tel: 0536 710409/712317

The Tibbs have carried out major renovations to the Red Lion since the last edition. They have added six new guest rooms, all with en suite facilities, and the menu now has a pronounced Mexican air. The hotel is a welcoming, 19th-century coaching inn with imposing gables and chimneys in Rothwell's market place. The lounge has many interesting brasses and the rare game of Northamptonshire skittles is played. Bar food is served lunchtime and evening and includes club sandwiches, ploughman's, salads and steaks. The separate evening restaurant offers nachos, chilli, tacos, enchiladas and beef, chicken and steaks cooked Mexican fashion. There is also a traditional Sunday roast, with children's portions. The guest rooms have TVs and tea and coffee making facilities. Rothwell is close to Rockingham Castle.

Beer: Charles Wells Eagle Bitter and Bombardier on handpumps.

Accommodation: 12 rooms, 6 can be used as single, double or family. B&B £18 single, £30 double, £32 family. Weekend rates on application. Children welcome. The 6 new en suite rooms are in a separate building.

TOWCESTER

Sun Inn
36 Watling Street, A5, M1 junction 15

Licensee: Tom Finnie
Tel: 0327 50580

The Sun is one of the oldest pubs in Towcester and stands on the old Roman Watling Street. The exterior is striking, with bow windows on the ground floor and a great dormer in the steeply sloping roof. The building dates from 1650 when it was a coaching inn. At one stage of its history it doubled as a mineral factory, using water from a natural well under the restaurant area. Bar food is served lunchtime and evening and includes soup, egg Mary Rose, whitebait, steaks, chicken, plaice, mixed grill and salads. Towcester racecourse is close by.

Beer: Courage Directors Bitter, Hook Norton Best Bitter and Old Hookey, Marston Pedigree Bitter and regular guest beers on handpumps.

Accommodation: 1 single, 4 doubles, 2 twins, all with private facilities. B&B £25 single, £35 double/twin, £45 family. Pets welcome. Cards: Access and Visa.

WEEDON

Globe Hotel
High Street, junction of A45 and A5, 3 miles from M1 exit 16

Licensees: Peter & Penny Walton
Tel: 0327 40336 Fax: 0327 349058

The Globe is a modernized and extended 18th-century farmhouse on the junction of the A45 and Watling Street. The Waltons have launched a programme of careful and tasteful refurbishment to the lovely old buildings in order to offer the best of both the old and the new worlds, along with first-class cuisine and guest rooms with en suite facilities. There is a large garden with fine views of the rolling countryside, and a welcome for families, while bar billiards and darts are played in the games room. The Globe Pantry serves food lunchtime and evening and offers soup, smoked mackerel, meat and vegetable curries, beef in beer, fisherman's bake, grilled trout, steaks, salads, vegetarian dish of the day, and, for children, there are chicken nuggets, fish fingers or beefburgers. There is a separate evening à la carte restaurant. The Globe is a good base for visiting the site of Naseby Civil War battlefield, Sulgrave Manor, Banbury, and the brave new world of Milton Keynes.

Beer: Bateman XB, Marston Pedigree Bitter, Ruddles County on handpumps.

Accommodation: 3 singles, 10 doubles, 2 family rooms, all en suite. B&B £30-£38 single, double £19-£24.50. Children free under 8 sharing. Weekend 2 or 3 nights, £38 per night per room. Children's room. Pets welcome. Cards: Access, Amex, Diners and Visa.

SCHOONER HOTEL, ALNMOUTH

ALLENDALE

Hare & Hounds
The Path, Haltwhistle Road. A6303

Licensee: Alec Fernyhough
Tel: 0434 683300

The Hare & Hounds is a fine 18th-century coaching inn standing in beautiful countryside near the Cumbrian and Durham borders. It is a vigorously old-fashioned hostelry, with stone floors and open fires in the bar and lounge. It is a good base for touring the wild and unspoilt Northumberland moors and forests. Mr Fernyhough serves food lunchtime and evening, and there is a pleasant garden for warmer months. The bars are quiet and free from intrusive canned music.

Beer: Ruddles Best Bitter and County on handpumps.

Accommodation: 3 doubles. B&B £12.50 per person.

ALNMOUTH

Schooner Hotel
Northumberland Street, 5 miles off A1

Proprietor: G T Orde
Tel: 0665 830216

The Schooner is a Georgian coaching inn and has been the hub of local life for many years in this lovely seaside village of tumbling streets, bordered by water on three sides. John Wesley described Alnmouth in 1748 as 'a small seaport town famous for all kinds of wickedness', which adds to its attractions. The exterior of the Schooner is striking, with its many shuttered windows. It has two cheerful and welcoming bars and pool, darts and dominoes are played.

NORTHUMBERLAND

Bar meals are available lunchtime and evening and include homemade soup, corn on the cob, rollmop herrings, fresh haddock or cod, Seahouses sole, seafood pie, herrings in oatmeal, Cheviot lamb chops, pan haggerty hot-pot, steaks, homemade steak and kidney pie, game pie, tacos, curry, lasagne, vegetable samosa, ploughman's, spring vegetables in cheese sauce, sandwiches, and a separate children's menu. There is also an evening restaurant. All the guest rooms in the hotel have en suite facilities, colour TVs, phones, and tea and coffee making equipment. The Schooner has a squash court and solarium, and is close to a golf course. The resident ghost is said to be partial to Belhaven 80 shilling ale – a discriminating ghoul.

Beer: Belhaven 80 shilling, Theakston XB, Vaux Samson and a regular guest beer on handpumps.

Accommodation: 3 singles, 9 doubles/twins, 11 family rooms. B&B £20–£30 per person according to season. Children's rates depend on age. Discounts for 3 days' stay. Children's room. Pets welcome. Cards: Access, Amex, Diners and Visa.

ALNWICK

Oddfellows Arms
Narrowgate, off A1

Licensee: Anthony Copeland
Tel: 0665 602695

The Oddfellows is a cheerful and welcoming pub by the castle in this cobbled and castellated historic town (pronounced 'Annick'), the centre of many long and bloody battles and sieges over the centuries. The Oddfellows offers coal fires, a public bar with darts and dominoes, 'but no pool', and a comfortable lounge. The inn is a haven of quiet, without juke boxes and other distractions, and has a pleasant beer garden for the summer months. Food is served lunchtime and evening in summer, lunchtime only in winter.

Beer: Vaux Samson on handpumps.

Accommodation: 2 doubles. 1 family room. B&B £12.50 per person.

BAMBURGH

Victoria Hotel
Front Street, junction of B1340, 1341 and 1342

Licensee: Robert Goodfellow
Tel: 066 84 431

With a host named Goodfellow, the Victoria has a head start over most pubs and hotels, and underscores the point by offering special rates for CAMRA members. The friendly hotel is in the heart of Bamburgh village in one of the loveliest coastal areas of Britain. Bamburgh was once the capital of the ancient kingdom of Bernicia and is now designated an area of outstanding beauty, and the Victoria is a splendid base for touring the area, and visiting the great castles of Bamburgh, Dunstanburgh and Lindisfarne, and the Farne Islands, Holy Island and the Grace Darling Museum. The hotel has a wide range of bar meals – toasties, ploughman's, homemade soups, fish and chips, burgers – served lunchtime and evening, in adult and children's portions, plus excellent meals in a separate dining room. Breakfasts are superb and include locally cured kippers from Craster. There is a residents' lounge and all-day coffee shop. Real ale is served in the back bar.

Beer: Belhaven 80 shilling and Tetley

NORTHUMBERLAND

Bitter on handpumps always with one guest beer, usually Marston Pedigree.

Accommodation: 25 rooms, 5 singles, 15 doubles, 5 family rooms, 18 rooms with private baths. B&B per person from £27.40 high season, £24.25 low season. Children welcome, under 2 years £2, under 13 half price. Small charge for dogs. Bargain breaks: details on application. 10% Reductions for CAMRA members. Cards: Access, Amex, Diners and Visa.

CORBRIDGE

Wheatsheaf Hotel
St Helens Street, off A69 and A68

Proprietors: Carol & Gordon Young
Tel: 0434 632020

The Wheatsheaf is a friendly inn in an ancient village with Roman connections, including the remains of a fort; Corbridge was a supply depot for Hadrian's troops and the fort includes a granary with an advanced system of grain ventilation. The granary certainly produced bread and may have supplied malt for brewing. The Wheatsheaf has a comfortable bar and lounge with live music at weekends and a darts and dominoes competition every Tuesday. Lunchtime bar meals include soup, farmhouse grill, chops and fish, sandwiches and children's meals. Full evening meals offer steaks, fish, lasagne, and a vegetarian dish. There is a large beer garden for the summer months.

Beer: Lorimer Scotch, Vaux Bitter and Samson on electric and handpumps.

Accommodation: 1 single, 3 doubles, 2 family room, 1 room with private bath. B&B from £16 per person. Off-season Weekend from £50. Children welcome, 30% reduction.

FALSTONE

Blackcock Inn
Off A68

Licensee: Alexandra Brown
Tel: 0434 240200

The Blackcock really has a warm welcome, for Miss Brown has a collection of vintage coal fires. The fire in the bar was made in Newcastle at the turn of the century and first fitted in a house in Hexham. It is complete with oven and hot water tank. The lounge has a small stove made in Fife and called a 'Beatonette', presumably in honour of Mrs Beaton of Victorian home-hints fame. The dining room has a large open fire with a handsome black marble surround, built for Allerwash Hall at Newbrough. The village-centre inn is more than 200 years old and was originally a single-storey thatched building, which has been extended and modernized over the years without losing its genuine character. The residents' lounge has a grand piano, and the dining room seats 30. Falstone, on the banks of the Tyne, is close to Kielder Forest with the largest manmade lake in Europe and facilities for water sports, walking, fishing and pony trekking.

Beer: Greenall Bitter and Original Bitter on handpumps.

Accommodation: 1 single, 2 doubles, 1 en suite. B&B £15 per person. Children welcome, half price under 12. The other rooms will have acquired private facilities during the lifetime of this edition of the guide.

NORTHUMBERLAND

LOWICK

Black Bull Inn
4 Main Street, B6353

Licensee: Tom Grundy
Tel: 0289 88228

The Black Bull is a delightful old village inn renowned for its welcome, good ale and bar food, served lunchtime and evening. There is a separate restaurant with 68 covers. The inn is a fine base for visiting the Scottish Borders, the Cheviots, the great castles of north Northumberland, and the vast stretches of unspoilt beaches. Lowick is also handy for the main A1 to the south.

Beer: McEwan 70 and 80 shilling, Theakston Best Bitter on handpumnps.

Accommodation: in self-catering cottage next to pub. Rates depend on number of guests and time of year: phone for details. Cards: Visa.

NEWBIGGIN-BY-THE-SEA

Old Ship Hotel
Front Street, off A1189

Licensee: Keith Richmond
Tel: 0670 817212

The Old Ship is a coaching inn on the seafront of this delightful fishing village, once a major port in the 15th century. Fishermen still put to sea in their traditional 'cobbles' to catch salmon and lobster. The hotel offers a good welcome and good cheer, with an extensive menu in the Captain's Pantry, including soup, pâté, salads, omelettes, homemade steak and kidney pie, curry and scampi. Wansbeck Riverside Park and Woodhorn Lake are close to Newbiggin; St Mary's Church in Woodhorn is the oldest church on the Northumbrian coast and is now a museum and cultural centre.

Beer: Vaux Bitter and Samson on handpumps.

Accommodation: 1 single, 6 doubles. B&B £12 per person. Children welcome, half price.

SEAHOUSES

Black Swan Inn
2 Union Street, off A1 between Craster and Bamburgh

Licensee: Billy Gillhom
Tel: 0665 720227

The Black Swan is a happy little stone-built, backstreet pub in this famous seaside resort, with its harbour and fine beaches. The inn has bar snacks and accommodation at extremely reasonable rates. Seahouses is a good base for visiting Bamburgh Castle, Craster with its home-cured kippers, Holy Island and the Farne Islands.

Beer: McEwan 80 shilling and Theakston Best Bitter on handpumps.

Accommodation: 1 double, 1 family room. B&B from £12.50 per person. Children half price.

White Swan Hotel
North Sunderland

Licensee: Paul Davison
Tel: 0665 720211

On the outskirts of Seahouses, the White Swan is half a mile from the harbour and close to fine sandy

NORTHUMBERLAND

beaches. It is next to a riding school and surrounded by farms. There are views of Bamburgh Castle from some of the guest rooms, and the hotel has a spacious walled beer garden. Bar food, served lunchtime and evening, includes homemade cottage pie and hot-pot, roast chicken with sage and onion stuffing, steak and kidney pie, and locally caught fish. A restaurant is open in the evening. The beer range is due to be expanded.

Beer: Belhaven 80 shilling and Vaux Samson on handpumps.

Accommodation: 2 singles, 13 doubles/twins, 3 family rooms, 7 rooms with en suite facilities (to be extended to 12). B&B £15–£25 per person; rates depend on season. Children free or 30% reduction according to age. Discounts for stays of 3 days or more for dinner, B&B. Children's room. Pets welcome. Cards: Access, Amex, Diners and Visa.

WOOLER

Anchor Inn
2 Cheviot Street. Off A697

Licensee: David Newton
Tel: 0668 81412

The Anchor is a striking two-storey building, decked out with hanging baskets and pots of flowers, in a pleasant old market town at the foot of the Cheviots in the Glendale Valley. It is a genuine family pub, and is popular with people on walking holidays or touring Northumberland. Bar meals are served at lunchtime and evening, and there are camping facilities nearby.

Beer: Lorimer Best Scotch and Vaux Samson on handpumps.

Accommodation: 1 twin, 1 double, 1 family room. All rooms have colour TVs and tea making facilities. B&B £10-£11 per person. Week: 10% discount. Children welcome, reductions if sharing.

Ryecroft Hotel
On A697 on northern edge of town

Licensees: Pat & David McKechnie
Tel: 0668 81459

Standing on the outskirts of the town, the Ryecroft is a friendly, family-run hotel with log fires. Pat McKechnie supervises the cooking and discriminating diners come from far afield for her meals that are based on local produce and include fruits of the sea, creamed mushrooms, cheese soup, pork steaks braised in cider, and smoked salmon quiche. The comfortable bar has strong local support for enthusiasts of darts, dominoes and quoits. The Ryecroft has a residents' lounge and all the guest rooms have en suite facilities. The hotel arranges special bird-watching and walking weekend holidays with guides, from March to May and in September and October.

Beer: Marston Pedigree Bitter, Tetley Bitter, Yates Bitter and guest beers on handpumps.

Accommodation: 1 single, 8 doubles. B&B £30 single, £26 per person sharing. Dinner £16 extra. Bird-watching and walking weekends £135 per person. 2 nights dinner, B&B £82 high season, £78 low season.

NOTTINGHAMSHIRE

HAYTON

Boat Inn
Main Street. 1 mile off A620

Licensee: Anthony Ralton
Tel: 0777 700158

The delightful Boat is on the banks of the Chesterfield Canal, where it has its own moorings and is a popular stopping place for boating people. The inn has a large car park and spacious gardens that run down to the water's edge. Carvery meals are served in a separate restaurant seven days a week. There are facilities for camping, too. The rooms are in converted cottages next to the pub.

Beer: Bass and Stones Best Bitter, Marston Pedigree Bitter, Whitbread Castle Eden Ale and Trophy Bitter on handpumps.

Accommodation: 3 singles, 5 doubles, 2 family room, 2 rooms with private bath. B&B from £15 single. Children can stay in the family rooms.

KIMBERLEY

Nelson & Railway Inn
Station Road, off A610

Licensees: Harry & Pat Burton
Tel: 0602 382177

If you are wondering what connection there is between Lord Nelson and the railway, the answer is that the pub's original name was 'the Lord Nelson Railway Hotel'. Although Kimberley is just a village, at the height of the railway boom it boasted two competing railway stations, both a few yards from the pub. They still exist as Kimberley Ex-Servicemen's Club and as the offices of a local timber firm. The inn is now the brewery tap, for Hardy (no connection with Nelson) and Hanson's large and imposing brewery dominates the village and looms over the pub. Both the lively bar and more sedate lounge offer a friendly welcome to visitors. There are gardens front and rear, with swings for children. The pub has darts and long alley skittles. Bar snacks are served lunchtime and early evening and include chip, bacon, sausage and fried egg butties, jacket potatoes with choice of filling, burgers, homemade quiche, cottage pie, chilli and lasagne, ploughman's, gammon, steaks, omelettes, and a children's menu. There is a roast Sunday lunch, too. Kimberley is close to Eastwood and the D H Lawrence museum.

Beer: Hardy & Hanson Kimberley Best Mild and Best Bitter on electric and handpump.

Accommodation: 2 doubles. B&B £9.50 per person. Children welcome, no reductions.

NOTTINGHAM

Queens Hotel
2 Arkwright Street, opposite railway station

Licensee: Stephen Webster
Tel: 0602 864685

The Queens is the ideal place for refreshment as you leave the railway station or head for Trent Bridge cricket and football grounds. There is a cheery basic bar with darts and pool, plus a comfortable lounge where dominoes is played. There are bar snacks, and full meals in a separate restaurant. The pub is just half a mile from Nottingham's city centre and is a good base for visiting the castle and another splendid hostelry, the Trip to Jerusalem, England's oldest pub.

Beer: Shipstone Bitter on handpump.

Accommodation: 6 singles/twins. B&B £15 single, £25 twin.

WALKERINGHAM

Brickmakers Arms
Fountain Hill Road, ½ mile off A161

Licensees: Michael & Colin Dagg
Tel: 0427 890375

The Brickmakers is a traditional old-world pub with one bar and a restaurant with good-value food. There are welcoming log fires in winter. The guest rooms have baths or showers, colour TVs and tea and coffee making equipment. Walkeringham is well placed for visiting Wesley's house at Epworth, Mattersley Priory, and the Old Hall at Gainsborough.

Beer: Tetley Bitter on handpump.

Accommodation: 17 rooms, all en suite. (A bridal suite is being added.) B&B £25 single, £30 double, £35 family room. Children welcome, terms included in price of family room. Cards: Access, Amex and Visa.

BANBURY

Britannia Inn
Windsor Street, A423

Licensee: David Spackman
Tel: 0295 256917

The Britannia is a small family pub on the Oxford road to Banbury. Children are welcome and there are bar meals every day, lunchtime and evening (not Sunday or Monday evenings). There is also a traditional lunch on Sunday.

Beer: Marston Burton Bitter and Pedigree Bitter on handpumps.

Accommodation: 2 doubles. B&B £15 per person. No pets. Cards: Access and Visa.

Elephant & Castle
6 Middleton Road, across bridge from railway station; ¼ mile from M40

Licensee: Roy K Betts
Tel: 0295 250238

Mr Betts describes the Elephant & Castle as 'just a good old beer pub'. Visitors who are keen on darts will, he says, take on players who are some of the best in the area – 'and they are all good, friendly lads'. The name of the pub, in common with the pub and district of south London, is not, as is often claimed, a corruption of 'Infanta of Castille', a Spanish princess, but comes from the sign of the Guild of Master Cutlers.

Beer: Bass and Morrells Best Bitter on handpumps.

Accommodation: 5 singles, 1 double. B&B £10 per person.

OXFORDSHIRE

BICESTER

Plough Inn
63 North Street, A421 by Banbury–Buckingham roundabout

Licensees: Per & Tracy Egeberg
Tel: 0869 249083

The Plough is a delightful 400-year-old pub with oak beamed ceilings and large open fireplaces, and is a good base for visiting Stratford-upon-Avon, Woodstock, Blenheim Palace and Oxford, which is 12 miles away. Part of the Plough's horseshoe-shaped bar is set aside as a restaurant area that serves such homemade dishes as mushroom, onion and garlic soup, fillet of pork in cider sauce, sausage casserole, tandoori chicken, steak, mushroom and Guinness pie, steaks, lasagne, trout and scampi, followed by homemade sweets such as bread-and-butter pudding or fruit crumble. Rolls and sandwiches are also available. Food is served lunchtime and evening.

Beer: Morrells Best Bitter and Varsity on handpumps.

Accommodation: 3 twins, 2 family rooms, 2 rooms with en suite facilities. B&B £15 single, £12.50 per person in twin, £10 in family room. Pets welcome.

BURFORD

Highway Hotel
117 High Street, off A361

Licensee: D N Cohen
Tel: 099 382 2136

A superb 16th-century inn, strikingly painted white with black woodwork and decked with hanging baskets, the Highway stands on the wide High Street that slopes down to the River Windrush. Old Cotswold stone houses and cottages huddle together in a town created by the Saxons in the 8th century; the Domesday Book recorded a population of 200 in 1086. The inn has log fires in winter in its comfortable rooms, many of which still retain their original beams. In warmer weather, guests may sit in a courtyard. The guest rooms all have colour TVs and tea and coffee making facilities. There is a four-poster bed in one room, where the old beams vie with modern central heating. Superb food is served in a candle-lit restaurant.

Beer: Hook Norton Best Bitter and Wadworth 6X on handpumps.

Accommodation: 8 doubles, 2 family rooms, 8 rooms with en suite facilities. B&B from £21 per person. Weekend £31.50 with dinner; mini-breaks: 2 nights B&B + dinner from £61 per person. Cards: Access, Amex, Diners and Visa.

Lamb Inn
Sheep Street, off A361

Licensees: R M & C de Wolf
Tel: 099 382 3155

The Lamb is a 500-year-old, mellow stone inn in the loveliest of the Cotswold towns. The bar has a flagstoned floor and high-back settles, while the spacious, beautifully furnished lounge has beams, panelled walls, mullioned windows and old wooden armchairs. The beer is dispensed for both bars from a remarkable old beer engine in a glass cabinet. Menus change daily but bar food may include homemade vegetable soup with crusty bread, fresh grilled sardines, tagliatelle, potato and bacon hot-pot, guinea

OXFORDSHIRE

fowl casserole, goulash, ploughman's and rolls, followed by chocolate roulade or hazelnut mousse with chocolate. The inn has a lovely sunny, flower-filled garden.

Beer: Wadworth IPA and 6X on handpumps, Old Timer in winter from the cask.

Accommodation: B&B £27.50 single, £25 double/twin per person, £29 with bath or shower. Winter Weekend Break: £68 per person for 2 nights, plus £14 dinner allowance. Extra day: £25. Midweek Breaks from £66 per person for 2 days including dinner allowance.

FRILFORD HEATH

Dog House Hotel
Off A34 and A338. From Wantage turn right at crossroads; or leave A34 at turning marked RAF Abingdon, follow signs to Frilford, take first right and continue for 2½ miles

Licensee: Clive E Haggar
Tel: 0865 390830/390896

Well, it gives a new meaning to going to the dog house. The building is some 150 years old and used to house dogs reared for hunting; the Berkshire Hunt used to meet there. It has been thoroughly overhauled and renovated, and offers top-class service in beautiful surroundings with views of pasture land with grazing cows and the Vale of the White Horse. Frilford Heath golf club is just 300 yards away. Food is available lunchtime and evening every day, with daily specials chalked on a board.

Beer: Morland Bitter and Old Masters on handpumps.

Accommodation: 1 single, 16 doubles/twins, 2 family rooms, all with en suite facilities. B&B £45 single, £55 for 2 people, £70 family room. Children over 12 £15, under 12 £3.50. Weekend £55 single for 2 nights, double £85. Pets welcome. Cards: Access, Amex, Diners and Visa.

GREAT TEW

Falkland Arms
Off B4022, 5 miles east of Chipping Norton

Licensees: John & Hazel Milligan
Tel: 060 883 653

The Falkland Arms is one of the most popular entries in the guide and the Milligans' guest book confirms this with such superlatives as 'excellent', 'superb', 'out of this world', 'heaven' and 'this has spoilt us for anywhere else – yummy ale'. A stunning old inn in one of the loveliest of Oxfordshire villages, it dates back to the 15th century and was originally named the Horse & Groom but was renamed in honour of the local lords of the manor. It has a partially thatched roof and a vast overhanging tree. Inside there is a panelled bar with high-back settles, flagstones, oil lamps and an enormous collection of pots and tankards hanging from the beams. Lunchtime food (not Monday) makes use of the Milligans' own free-range chicken and duck eggs, and dishes include homemade seafood, cheese and ale, Stilton and cauliflower and carrot mint soups, lamb cobbler, Lancashire hot-pot, pork and Stilton pie, homemade fishcakes or faggots, spicy stuffed marrow and rabbit stew, with ploughman's and salads. The guest rooms have old iron bedsteads and pine furniture. A gallon of ale is offered to anyone who sees the ghost of Lord Falkland.

Beer: Donnington BB, Hall & Woodhouse Best Bitter, Hook Norton Best Bitter and five guest beers on handpumps.

Accommodation: 4 doubles, 1 family room, 1 room with en suite facilities. B&B £25 single, £32 double, £38 family room, room with four-poster bed £40.

IFFLEY

Tree Hotel
Church Way, Iffley. ½ mile from ring road, 1½ miles from Oxford city centre

Licensee: David Bowman
Tel: 0865 775974

The Tree Hotel is based in the ancient village of Iffley, which was first recorded in 941 AD and was listed in the Domesday Book. The name stems from the Saxon 'giftelege', meaning a field of gifts. The small Victorian hotel, with a handsome exterior of bow windows, is close to the village's Norman church, which is more than 800 years old, and the Isis river and Iffley lock are close by. The excellent bar food is based mainly on homemade dishes, while all the guest rooms are en suite and have colour TVs, phones, and tea and coffee making facilities.

Beer: Morrells Bitter and Varsity on handpumps.

Accommodation: B&B £45 single, £55 double, £60 twin, £65 executive suite, £75 family room.

MOULSFORD-ON-THAMES

Beetle & Wedge Hotel
Ferry Lane, off A329

Proprietor: Kate Smith
Tel: 0491 651381/651376

Beetles and wedges are the ancient tools used by boat builders and ferrymen on this stretch of the Thames. The red-brick building dates from the early 18th century, while the adjacent cottage and the building that together form the Boathouse Bar date from the 12th century. The hotel overlooks a gentle stretch of the Thames and featured as the 'Potwell Inn' in H G Wells's *History of Mr Polly*. Since the last issue of the guide, the hotel has been extensively improved by the Smiths. All the guest rooms are en suite, with colour TVs and tea and coffee making facilities. The bars have fine copper tables, with an open fire in the main bar surmounted by a large mirror that gives a reflection of the Thames in all its moods. Bar meals in the Boathouse Bar include hot watercress and potato soup, mussels, grilled sardines, smoked sea trout, whole baked crab, avocado salad with smoked chicken and prawns, asparagus hollandaise or vinaigrette, crispy duck, stuffed aubergine, steaks, grilled halibut, cold poached salmon, tagliatelle with seafood and chive sauce, and ploughman's. There is a separate restaurant.

Beer: Adnams Bitter, Hall & Woodhouse Tanglefoot and Wadworth 6X on handpumps.

Accommodation: B&B from £55 per person. Double £65. Weekend Breaks £90 per person for B&B + dinner. Overnight mooring £15.

NEWBRIDGE

Rose Revived
A415, 7 miles south of Witney

Licensee: Mr B Jefferson
Tel: 086731 221

The Rose Revived is set in lovely countryside at one of the oldest crossing points on the Thames. It dates back to the 14th century, and the bars have flagstoned floors and open fires. There is a separate restaurant specializing in homemade dishes, and bar food is also available. In summer visitors can use the large riverside garden and patio. The guest rooms all have splendid views of the Thames, and Oxford and Woodstock are close at hand. There are facilities for fishing, and Frilford golf club is nearby.

Beer: Morland Bitter and Old Masters on handpumps.

Accommodation: 7 rooms, some with en suite facilities. B&B £30.40 single, £35.45 double.

OXFORD

Globe Inn
59-60 Cranham Street, Jericho

Licensees: Mick & Sue Simmonds
Tel: 0865 57759

The Globe is a delightful, old-fashioned local with one large bar and homemade food. It is close to St Barnabas church, the Radcliffe hospital and Park Meadow. Food is available from breakfast time and there is a daily lunchtime special and a roast on Sundays.

Beer: Morrells Bitter and Varsity on handpumps.

OXFORDSHIRE

Accommodation: 1 single, 1 double, 2 family rooms, all centrally heated and with colour TVs. B&B £12.50 per person. No pets.

NR OXFORD

Berkshire House
200 Abingdon Road. A4144, off A34 and A423

Licensee: Philip Plucknett
Tel: 0865 242423

The Berkshire House, built in the 1930s, is a spacious hostelry close to Oxford. It has three bars with one used mainly by parents and children; this bar has access to a garden where the ancient pub game of Aunt Sally is played in the summer. The main bar is comfortably carpeted, while the third bar is used mainly by customers playing pool. The pub is open from 7am for breakfast and all the food is homemade. Bar food includes steaks, curry and a range of pies.

Beer: Morrells Bitter on handpump.

Accommodation: 2 twins, 1 family room, all with private showers. B&B £15 per person, £12.50 in family room. Children free under 4, 4-10 years £8, 10-15 £10.

WITNEY

Red Lion Hotel
Corn Street, town centre. A40

Licensees: Roy & Isabel Tams
Tel: 0993 703149

The Red Lion was built as a coaching inn in the 17th century in the historic Cotswold village that is the home of the Witney blanket. The hotel has a welcoming lounge bar and a busy games room with a hexagonal pool table. Bar meals are available all day from 10am to 11pm (not Sunday afternoons). The delightful guest rooms have the air of a country cottage with attractive fabrics and furnishings.

Beer: Morrells Bitter and Varsity on handpumps.

Accommodation: 1 single, 4 twins, 1 family room, 2 rooms with en suite facilities. B&B £20.70 single, £24.15 en suite, £29.90 per person in twin, £34.50 en suite. Children's room. No pets. Cards: Access.

SHROPSHIRE

BISHOP'S CASTLE

Castle Hotel
Market Square, off A488 and A489

Licensees: David & Nicky Simpson
Tel: 0588 638403

The Castle is in the centre of this small, bustling Shropshire town. The bars are cheerful and welcoming, and the food is excellent and includes dishes for vegetarians. Dogs are welcome, there are baby-minding facilities, and fishing is available nearby. Another pub worthy of note in the town is the Three Tuns, a famous home-brew inn with a small tower brewery in the backyard that produces excellent ales. There is a traction engine rally in the town on August bank holiday. Little remains of the castle that gave the town its name but there is a profusion of fascinating architectural styles, with many half-timbered buildings of which the best known is the House on Crutches. Offa's Dyke and the rock outcrops of Long Mynd and the Stiperstones are nearby.

Beer: Bass and Springfield Bitter on handpumps, and regular guest beers.

Accommodation: 5 doubles, 3 twins, 3 rooms with en suite facilities. B&B £20-£22 single, £33-£37.50 double.

CLUN

Sun Inn
On B4368

Licensees: Keith & Bunny Small
Tel: 058 84 559/277

'The quietest place under the sun', said A E Housman of Clun, but the small town's history is anything but quiet. It was the scene of protracted battles between Britons and Romans. Later skirmishes with the Welsh forced King Offa to build his dyke to contain them, and Clun Castle was built in the 11th century in a further effort to keep back the marauding Welsh. The Sun Inn, dating from the 15th century, is a delightful place to stay, and a good base for visiting the Iron Age forts, Offa's dyke, the medieval saddleback bridge over the river Clun, the castle and the fascinating museum in the town hall. The inn has a wealth of exposed beams, a vast fireplace in the bar, flagstones and settles. The restaurant offers exotic dishes from around the world based on local produce. There are always vegetarian dishes. Bar food includes homemade soup, garlic and herb mushrooms, Spanish butter bean stew (fabada), curries, vegetarian cassoulet, beef and cashew nuts, apple and cinnamon pie, and cheesecake. Residents have the use of a comfortable lounge with an open fire, beamed ceiling and TV. Accommodation is in the converted old bakery and old stables attached to the inn.

Beer: Banks Mild and Bitter, Woods

Special Bitter and one guest beer on handpumps.

Accommodation: 4 en suite doubles, 2 singles, 1 double, 1 family room. B&B £17 single, £35 double, £38 en suite. Winter Specials: 3 nights £20 per person per night including dinner.

LUDLOW

Church Inn
Buttercross, off A49

Licensee: J B Hargreaves
Tel: 0584 2174

The Church is an extensively modernized inn, with a pleasantly painted Georgian pastel exterior. Church is the fifth name it has had in 500 years. There is a comfortable lounge bar and a separate restaurant. Bar food includes soups, stuffed mushrooms, steak and beer pie, trout, plaice and mackerel, fisherman's pancake and homemade sweets. The restaurant menu offers melon and port, salmon steak, duckling, prawn and melon salad, pork, and trout and grapefruit. The inn is close to the medieval castle where the unfortunate princes stayed before leaving for London and dying at the hands of either Henry Tudor or Richard Plantagenet, depending on which conspiracy theory you prefer. Nearby is the parish church of St Laurence, burial place of the Shropshire poet A E Housman.

Beer: Flowers Original, Ruddles Bitter and Websters Yorkshire Bitter on handpumps.

Accommodation: 9 doubles, all en suite, with TVs and tea and coffee making facilities. B&B £23 single, £35 double, family room £40. Children welcome. Cards: Access and Visa.

MARKET DRAYTON

Corbet Arms Hotel
High Street, off A53

Proprietors: John & Cynthia Beckett
Tel: 0630 2037/2961

The Corbet Arms is a creeper-clad, 16th-century coaching inn in the centre of the fine old Shropshire market town, mentioned in the Domesday Book and scene of a major battle in the Wars of the Roses. Present-day attractions include a Safari Park, the Shropshire Union canal, fishing and horse riding. The hotel has a separate restaurant that seats 50 and which can arrange for vegetarian dishes. There is a hot and cold carvery at lunchtime, and bar snacks in the evening. The hotel has a 'friendly' lady ghost. The guest rooms all have colour TVs, direct-dial phones and tea and coffee making facilities.

Beer: Springfield Bitter on electric pump.

Accommodation: 12 rooms, 10 with private baths. B&B £28 single, £30 double let as single, £40 double, £50 family room. Winter Weekend: £50 single, £56 double let as single, £72 double, £88 family room for 2 nights. Cards: Access, Amex, Diners and Visa.

OSWESTRY

Olde Boote Inn
Whittington, old A5

Licensee: K H Lawrenson
Tel: 0691 662250

The Olde Boote is an ancient inn in a suburb of Oswestry where Dick Whittington is said to have passed on his way to make his fortune in

London. The inn has a panoramic view of the ruins of an old moated Norman castle. Inside the Olde Boote there are oak beams and many horse brasses. A golf course is nearby. Lunchtime bar snacks and an evening restaurant are available every day.

Beer: Robinson Best Bitter on electric pump.

Accommodation: 4 doubles/twins, 2 family rooms, all with en suite facilities. B&B £19 single, £34.50 double/twin, £39.50 family room. Children £5 sharing. No dogs. Cards: Access and Visa.

SHREWSBURY

Swan Inn
Frankwell, on A458

Proprietors: Don & Shirley Reynolds
Tel: 0743 64923

The Swan is a small, cheery and comfortable inn in one of the oldest suburbs of Shrewsbury. There is excellent food in the inn's Victorian bar and restaurant, where bookings are required. The guest rooms all have en suite facilities with colour TVs and tea and coffee making equipment and there are fine views of Shrewsbury. Close by is the impressive Fellmongers Hall, built in 1580, while Charles Darwin's birthplace is just a short walk away. A few minutes' stroll over the Welsh Bridge brings you into the heart of Shrewsbury with its wealth of half-timbered 16th-century houses and later Georgian and Queen Anne architecture. Shrewsbury Castle guards the loop in the River Severn while Quarry Park stages the famous annual flower show.

Beer: Ansells Mild and Bitter, Burton Ale, Marston Pedigree Bitter, Wadworth 6X on handpumps.

Accommodation: 2 doubles, 2 twins. B&B £20 single, £35 double.

SOMERSET

AXBRIDGE

Lamb Inn
The Square, ½ mile from A371 Wells to Cheddar road

Licensee: Max & Jenny Wigginton
Tel: 0934 732253

A fascinating 18th-century coaching inn, the Lamb has been named both the Holy Lamb and the Lamb & Flag. The Wiggintons specialize in good plain cooking, a sensible range of ale, and comfortable accommodation in rooms with TVs and tea and coffee making facilities. Homemade bar food includes soup, ploughman's, vegetarian pizza, lasagne, tripe and onions, steak in ale pie, steaks, stuffed tomatoes, vegetarian cottage pie and a children's menu. The inn stands in the square famous for St John's hunting lodge and Axbridge church. The handsome old town nestles on the southern slopes of the Mendips and is close to Cheddar and its gorge and its much abused cheese, and to Wells, with its magnificent cathedral.

Beer: Butcombe Bitter, Flowers Original, a guest beer, and Thatcher's farmhouse cider on handpumps.

Accommodation: 2 doubles, 1 family room. B&B £16–£22. 10% reduction for week's stay. Children's room.

SOMERSET

BATCOMBE

Three Horse Shoes
1½ miles off A359

Licensees: Bob & Sue Sluggett
Tel: 074 985 359

The Three Horse Shoes is a 600-year-old coaching inn in lovely countryside overlooking the Somerset Levels. The Sluggetts specialize in home cooking, with food available in the bar or separate restaurant. It is a genuine locals' pub and you may be challenged to play darts, shove ha'penny or pool. The pub has a resident ghost named George. Local attractions include Cheddar, Wookey Hole, Glastonbury Tor, Stourhead and Longleat.

Beer: Constantly changing range of cask beers on handpumps.

Accommodation: 1 twin/family room, 1 double, both with en suite facilities. B&B £32 single, £42 double. Children welcome, with reductions. Weekend Break £22.50 single, £32 double.

BURNHAM-ON-SEA

Royal Clarence Hotel
31 Esplanade. 3 miles off M5 exit 22

Licensee: Paul Davey
Tel: 0278 783138

The Clarence is an old coaching inn with facilities that range from a skittles alley to a Regency suite. It has fine views over the beaches and sea, and it boasts its own miniature brewery where Clarence Bitter is brewed. There are good bar meals, while the elegant restaurant offers sole, rainbow trout, pork Normande in cream and cider, duck, carbonade of beef, and a daily vegetarian dish.

Beer: Butcombe Bitter, Clarence Bitter, Wadworth 6X and guest beers on handpumps.

Accommodation: 3 singles, 10 doubles, 2 family rooms, 9 rooms with private baths. B&B £22 single, £36 double. Half and full board available. Children welcome, half price under 11. Special Breaks: 2 days dinner, B&B £52 per person, 3 days £74, 5 days £130. Dogs only by special arrangement.

CASTLE CARY

White Hart
Fore Street, 6 miles from A303 at Wincanton

Licensee: Charles Anderson
Tel: 0963 50255

The White Hart is a coaching inn that dates back to the 17th century, with local Cary stone in the servery and the fireplace, while the main bar has an old wooden block floor. There is a strong emphasis on traditional pub games, including skittles, darts, bar billiards, table skittles and shove ha'penny. Bar food includes sandwiches, home-cooked ham, burgers, steak and kidney pie, pork with onion and chives, omelettes, cod, plaice and scampi with chips and peas, ploughman's, and tuna salad, plus homemade apple pie and ice cream.

Beer: Courage Best Bitter, Directors Bitter and John Smiths Bitter on handpumps.

Accommodation: 3 doubles. B&B £12 per person. Half board available. Weekend £24, Week £77. Off-season Weekend £22. Children by arrangement.

EXFORD

White Horse Hotel
Near Minehead, on B3224

Licensees: Peter & Linda Hendrie
Tel: 064 383 229

The White Horse is a welcoming outpost in the middle of Exmoor where moorland folk descend to meet, talk, drink and eat. The creeper-clad hotel, with some half-timbered upper storeys, has two children's rooms, a candle-lit dining room and a Dalesman Bar full of local pictures, scrubbed wooden tables and a high-back settle. Bar food includes soup, ploughman's, lasagne, macaroni cheese, liver and bacon, venison pie and sirloin steaks. The full pleasures of Exmoor – riding, fishing, walking and bird-watching – are on the doorstep. The guest rooms all have private baths, TVs and tea and coffee making facilities.

Beer: Bass, Cotleigh Tawny and Old Buzzard and a guest beer, all served straight from the casks.

Accommodation: 1 single, 7 doubles. B&B £28.75 per person. Children welcome.

FROME

Sun Inn
6 Catherine Street, off A361

Licensee: D J Hands
Tel: 0373 73123

Not so much a pub ... more a permanent beer festival, with seven real ales always available. The Sun is an old coaching inn and listed building with a vast and impressive fireplace dominating the interior. There is excellent pub grub every day, and a restaurant menu with a daily roast. The guest rooms all have colour TVs, and Mr Hands supplies friendly ghosts at no extra charge. Frome is four miles from Longleat.

Beer: (from) Butcombe Bitter, Greene King Abbot Ale, Felinfoel Double Dragon, Flowers Original, Hall & Woodhouse Tanglefoot, Marston Pedigree Bitter and Wadworth 6X all on handpumps.

Accommodation: 5 doubles, 2 family rooms. B&B £16.50 single, £24 twin, £30 family room. Children welcome, 20% reductions.

KEINTON MANDEVILLE

Quarry Inn
High Street, B3153 between Lydford and Somerton

Licensees: Barry & Becky Goddard
Tel: 045 822 3367

This handsome creeper-covered inn was originally the house of the quarry master from the local mine. When times were hard he paid his labourers with cider. In the 19th century the house was licensed and became a hotel. It is now a free house, with a skittles alley and beer garden. A full menu and bar snacks are available seven days a week and the Goddards have added a new 25-seat dining room. Fresh fish dishes are available Thursday and Friday and it is advisable to book for those days. The inn is just a few miles from Glastonbury, Shepton Mallet and Yeovil.

Beer: Oakhill Farmers Ale, Ruddles Best Bitter, Wadworth 6X on handpumps.

Accommodation: 3 doubles. B&B £15 per person, £25 double. Reductions for stays of 5 or 7 days.

SOMERSET

LUXBOROUGH

Royal Oak
Minor road off A39 at Washford; at Luxborough turn right over bridge (OS 984377)

Licensee: Robin Stamp
Tel: 0984 40319

The Royal Oak is a rural pub of great charm and antiquity in Exmoor national park. The inn, known locally as the Blazing Stump, dates back to the 15th century and has stone-flagged and cobbled floors, inglenook fireplaces and a wealth of ancient beams. There are three bar areas and a charming garden. Quiz night is Tuesday and music night Friday. Fresh local produce is used for both bar snacks and in the dining room and dishes include Royal Oak prawns, homemade soup, sandwiches, ploughman's, chilli, steaks, salads in season, with sweets and a children's menu of fish fingers or sausages. Mr Stamp claims that 'when you walk through the door you will think you have stepped back two centuries and you won't have changed your mind when you leave'. Except for the prices, but even they are extremely reasonable by 20th-century standards.

Beer: Cotleigh Tawny Bitter, Eldridge Pope, Thomas Hardy Country Bitter and Royal Oak, Golden Hill Exmoor Gold, Flowers IPA on handpumps.

Accommodation: 4 doubles. B&B £12.50 per person. Weekend £22 for 2 days. Week £70.

MIDDLEZOY

George Inn
Main Road, ¼ mile off A372 between Bridgwater and Langport

Licensees: Keith & Maureen Waites
Tel: 082 369 215

The George is a 17th-century inn in a fascinating village on the Somerset Levels. The Wiltshire militia lodged here during the battle of Sedgemoor in 1685 and the inn was used by 'Hanging Judge' Jeffreys during the subsequent trials. The inn today specializes in good homemade food, including some authentic Indian dishes. It stages twice-yearly real ale festivals.

Beer: Cotleigh Tawny Bitter, Oakhill Farmers Ale and twice-weekly guest beers, all on handpumps.

Accommodation: 3 doubles. B&B £13.50 per person.

MONTACUTE

Phelips Arms
The Borough, A303, 750 yards beyond entrance to Montacute House

Licensee: Roger Killeen
Tel: 0935 822557

The Phelips Arms is named after the family that built Montacute House. The pub, which dates back to the 17th century when it was a posting inn, is constructed of local hamstone and has an impressive exterior with steeply sloping roofs, hanging baskets and a porched entrance. It has been carefully renovated to provide one large bar that leads to a courtyard and a secluded walled garden. Bar meals are served every day, lunchtime and evening, with daily specials chalked on a board, that may include sweet and sour squid, smoked prawns, boozy beef, thatched pork casserole, Persian lamb kebabs, Oriental beef, whole West Bay plaice, red gurnard with peach sauce, and tuna in garlic. You can also tuck into such regulars as homemade soup, monkfish in batter, rump steak, lasagne, Montezuma's Revenge (a powerful chilli), spare ribs, beefcakes, vegetable lasagne, vegetable moussaka and mushroom Stroganoff. The Phelips Arms is the ideal base for visiting Forde Abbey, Brympton d'Evercy and other local historic houses.

Beer: Palmer Bridport Bitter, IPA and Tally Ho on handpumps.

Accommodation: 2 doubles/twins, 1 family room, 2 rooms with en suite facilities. B&B £18 single, £28 double, £35 family room. Children's room. No pets. Cards: Access and Visa.

PORLOCK

Ship Inn
High Street, A39 (bottom of Porlock Hill)

Licensees: Mark & Judy Robinson
Tel: 0643 862 507

The Ship is a splendid place to stay and useful for drivers when their vehicles refuse to go up the dreaded hill, one of the steepest in England. The delightfully rambling thatched inn dates back to the 13th century, and offers good food in the bar and dining room, a skittles alley and a beer garden with wonderful views of the surrounding Quantock and Brendon hills and the sea. The bar is a delight with window seats, benches, a flagstoned floor and an inglenook fireplace. Bar food includes homemade soup, salmon and curd cheese mousse, beef in Guinness, pheasant casserole and king prawns. The guest rooms have central heating, TVs and tea making facilities.

Beer: Bass, Cotleigh Old Buzzard, Courage Best Bitter on handpumps, a regular guest beer and Perry's local rough cider.

Accommodation: 7 doubles, 4 family rooms, 5 rooms with en suite bathrooms. B&B from £14.50 per person. Children welcome, half price under 12 when sharing with parents. Dogs welcome.

PRIDDY

New Inn
Priddy Green, 3 miles west of A39 Bristol to Wells road

Licensees: Anne & Doug Weston
Tel: 0749 76465

The inn was originally a 15th-century farmhouse owned by local alehouse keepers, who moved their business to the present building to meet the demands of the hard-drinking lead miners in the area. The tavern remained largely unchanged until the 1970s when a lounge was added from existing outhouses, the bar replaced an old staircase and a skittles alley and guest rooms were developed. The Westons concentrate on good food and ale; bar meals include specially prepared jacket potatoes mixed with cider with a wide choice of toppings, omelettes, homemade vegetarian dishes – black-eyed bean casserole in red wine, cashew nut paella, genuine Indian recipe vegetable curry – oak-smoked gammon, and trout. Priddy, surrounded by beautiful countryside, is an ideal base for walking, seeing local country crafts of cheese and cider making, and visiting Wells and its cathedral.

Beer: Eldridge Pope Dorchester

Bitter, Marston Pedigree Bitter, Wadworth 6X on handpumps, and Perry cider from the jug.

Accommodation: 3 doubles, 2 twins, 1 family room. B&B £28 double or twin, £17 single occupancy. Children welcome.

SHEPTON MALLET

Kings Arms
Leg Square, off A37

Licensee: Drew Foley
Tel: 0749 3781

The Kings Arms, a pub of great charm that covers three sides of a courtyard, was built in 1660 and has been a pub since 1680. Today it has a main bar, a heritage bar and a skittles alley.The patio is a popular drinking spot in the summer.

Beer: Burton Ale, Halls Harvest Bitter, Tetley Bitter and Wadworth 6X on handpumps.

Accommodation: 3 doubles. B&B £15.50 single, £26.50 double. Full and half board available. 10% discount for CAMRA members. No children.

STOGUMBER

White Horse Inn
2 miles off A358, 4 miles south of Williton

Licensee: Peter Williamson
Tel: 0984 56277

The White Horse is a small white-painted inn opposite a 12th-century church in a delightful conservation village near the Quantocks and Brendon Hills. The main bar has red tiles on the floor, a coal fire in winter, and old settles. Skittles, darts, dominoes and shove ha'penny are played in a separate room. Bar food (lunchtime and evening) includes homemade vegetable soup, smoked mackerel, chicken with Stilton sauce, steak and kidney pudding, vegetable curry, chilli con carne, lasagne, trout with almonds, grilled plaice, fried cod, steaks and kebabs, salads, omelettes, sandwiches, and such tasty sweets as walnut tart and cream, apple crumble, and homemade ice-creams. The separate restaurant is the village's old market house now joined to the inn, with the village 'reading room' on the top floor. There is a pleasant garden for sunny weather.

Beer: Cotleigh Tawny Bitter, Golden Hill Exmoor Ale on handpumps.

Accommodation: 1 double, 1 family room, both with en suite facilities, TVs and central heating. B&B £20 single, £32 double. Children welcome, terms according to age. Cards: Access.

TAUNTON

Masons Arms
Magdalene Street, town centre, off M5 exit 25

Licensee: J J Leyton
Tel: 0823 288916

The elegant three-storey building stands in the shadow of the superb St Mary Magdalene church and in an area of considerable historical interest. At the turn of the 19th century the present broad street was a squalid alley called Blackboy Lane, named after an inn whose landlord was accused of murdering a soldier and throwing his body into the River Tone. Cursing and swearing often drowned the singing in the church. The authorities cleared this 'sink of iniquity' in 1864 and turned the hovels and tenements into Magdalene

Street. The Masons Arms was formerly the house of the local rent collector and became a beer house in 1855. Today it offers a good selection of bar meals as well as fine ale. There is a wide range of salads, plus turkey pie, savoury flans, Cornish pasties, steak and kidney pie, curry and jacket potatoes. The pub has a traditional skittles alley. Accommodation is in a self-catering flat with colour TV, kitchen and bathroom.

Beer: Bass, Golden Hill Exmoor Ale and Exmoor Dark, Wadworth 6X and guest beers in winter, all on handpumps.

Accommodation: Self-service flat with 1 twin and 1 single room. 1 to 3 people £30 per night, discount for stays of more than 7 days. Children 10 and over welcome.

WATERROW

Rock Inn
B3227 (formerly A361), 14 miles west of Taunton

Licensee: B R P 'Brough' Broughall
Tel: 0984 23293

The Rock is a 400-year-old inn beside the River Tone in a lovely village nestling beneath the steep wooded hills of the Tone valley. It is a splendid base for touring Exmoor and the north Devon coast. The inn has a large cosy bar, and both bar and restaurant meals are available lunchtime and evening, including grills, poultry, fish, and vegetarian dishes. All the guest rooms have private bathrooms, central heating, colour TVs and direct-dial phones. There is also a residents' lounge.

Beer: Cotleigh Tawny Bitter, Hall & Woodhouse Tanglefoot and Ushers Best Bitter on handpumps.

Accommodation: 4 doubles, 2 twins. B&B £15.50 per person. Children's rates according to age. 2-day breaks from £39.50 including dinner. Discounts for 5 nights or more and group bookings. Cards: Access and Visa.

WEST PENNARD

Red Lion
Newtown, A361

Licensees: François & Wendy Bakerian
Tel: 0458 32941

The Red Lion, just three miles from Glastonbury, was built in 1678, probably as a farmhouse, and retains much of its old charm with flagstoned floors, low beams and log fires in winter. Snacks and full meals are available lunchtime and evening. Bar meals include soup of the day with croutons, ploughman's, salads, jacket potatoes, cod fillet, steak and kidney pie, ratatouille, cheese and nut croquettes and ice creams and sorbets. There is a roast lunch on Sundays and a separate evening restaurant. Accommodation is in a converted old barn and all the luxurious, carpeted rooms have private baths, colour TVs, central heating, direct-dial telephones, and tea and coffee making facilities. The Red Lion is a good centre for walking and visiting Glastonbury Abbey, Wookey Hole, Cheddar, Bath, Longleat, the East Somerset steam railway and English wine makers at Wooton, Pilton Manor and Coxley.

Beer: Bass, Butcombe Bitter and a house brew Red Lion Best Bitter on handpumps.

Accommodation: 6 doubles/twins, 1 family room. B&B from £20 per person. Weekend Breaks (Oct–

March) £60 per person, children £30; prices include dinner and Sunday lunch. Week £80 single, £135 double, children over 10 £72. Children under 10 free when sharing with parents. Cards: Access, Amex and Visa.

WILLITON

Foresters Arms
Long Street, on A39 Bridgwater to Minehead road

Licensees: Sunny & Aidan Downing
Tel: 0984 32508

The Foresters is a 17th-century building, though some parts may be considerably older. Its first name as a licensed house was the Lamb, but this was changed to the Railway Hotel with the arrival of steam – the West Somerset railway is just five minutes away. It was renamed the Foresters Arms in 1984. The Downings have extended the quality of the welcome, the food, the ale and the accommodation. There is a children's room, and spacious gardens with ornamental pools and patios. The pub offers a fine range of lunchtime bar meals, a Sunday roast lunch and grills in the evening in a restaurant seating 20. There is also a lady ghost. Williton is well placed for touring the Quantocks and visiting the picturesque town of Watchet.

Beer: Bass, Cotleigh Tawny Bitter and weekly guest beer on handpumps.

Accommodation: 1 single, 5 doubles (3 en suite), 2 family rooms, 1 coach house apartment, all with colour TVs and tea and coffee making equipment. B&B from £13 per person: all rooms available as single according to demand. Half and full board available. Children welcome. Facilities for the disabled in pub and restaurant only. Cards: Access and Visa.

SOMERSET

WINSFORD

Royal Oak Inn
Exmoor National Park, off A396 near Minehead

Licensees: Sheila & Charles Steven
Tel: 064 385 455

The Royal Oak is a 12th-century thatched inn in the heart of Exmoor. For many years it doubled as a farm as well as a licensed house. Members of the wool trade operated from the inn, working with both local wool and Irish yarn. Tom Faggus, a 17th-century highwayman, lived near the village and was a character in *Lorna Doone*. The inn today has cheery bars, a welcoming open fire, bar meals and an evening à la carte restaurant. Bar meals (lunchtime and evening) include homemade country soup, fresh salmon or trout pâté, ploughman's, vegetarian quiche, smoked trout, toasted croissant filled with Somerset brie, haddock in cream sauce, chopped bacon and mushrooms cooked in cream, baked jacket potatoes with choice of fillings, cold game pie, fish crumble, rump steak casserole, salads and homemade sweets.

Beer: Flowers Original and IPA on handpumps.

Accommodation: 1 single, 5 doubles, 2 twins in the inn, all en suite, five doubles in courtyard complex, which also has a family cottage for 2 adults and 2 or 3 small children. Prices per person: £27 room only, £35.50 B&B, £57.50 with dinner. Midweek Breaks (Sunday to Thursday): 1 & 2 nights dinner, B&B £52.50 per person per night, 3 & 4 nights £47.50, 5 nights £42.50. Single room occupancy of double room £22 supplement per night. Children in family cottage £5 per night plus food. Kennel for dogs.

ABBOTS BROMLEY

Coach & Horses
High Street, B5014 near Rugeley

Licensees: Bob & Shirley Haywood
Tel: 0283 840256

The Coach & Horses is an attractive 16th-century inn, with a comfortable lounge and a bar with inglenook fireplaces where dominoes, darts and bar billiards are played. There is a residents' dining room, a large car park and a beer garden – and a resident ghost. Bar meals, from £2 to £5, are served every lunchtime. The guest rooms all have colour TVs and tea and coffee making facilities. The inn is a good base for visiting Alton Towers and Cannock Chase.

Beer: Ansells Bitter and Burton Ale on handpumps.

Accommodation: 3 twins. B&B from £11 per person.

ALSTONEFIELD

Watts-Russell Arms
Off A515; leave the Ashbourne to Buxton road opposite New Inn hotel and follow signs for Milldale

Licensees: Stephanie & Alf Harrison
Tel: 033527 271

The Watts-Russell takes its name from the family that built nearby Ilam Hall in the 17th century. The pub is some 200 years old, and has shuttered windows and a large porch. It is built from limestone that gives the local landmark, the White Peak, its name and is in a small hamlet less than a mile from where the River Dove flows through Milldale. The pub is popular with serious walkers and those out for more gentle strolls in the lovely countryside, and the Harrisons provide generous portions of homemade food lunchtime and evening. In warm weather there is a pleasant beer garden, while colder days are cheered by two logs fires in the bars.

Beer: Marston Pedigree Bitter on handpump.

Accommodation: 2 twins. B&B £12 per person. No pets.

ALTON

Bull's Head Hotel
High Street, off A52, A515 & B5417

Licensees: Brian & Heather Harvey
Tel: 0538 702307

The Bull's Head is a fine 18th-century village inn in the picturesque Churnet Valley conservation area. The village is crowned by fairytale Alton Castle, which gives it more the air of the Rhineland than the Staffordshire moors. Alton Towers fun park is close by. The beamed hotel has a 35-seater dining room that specializes in home-cooked food that includes imaginative use of local vegetables; there is always a daily vegetarian wholefood dish. Tempting desserts include a gâteau of meringue, rum, cassis and blackcurrants. Bar food is also available every lunchtime. The guest rooms all have showers, colour TVs, and tea and coffee making facilities.

Beer: Burton Bridge Bitter and Tetley Bitter on handpumps.

Accommodation: 4 doubles/twins, 2 family rooms. B&B from £25 single, £15 per person in double or twin, family room £11.25 per person. Children's rates by agreement. Cards: Access and Visa.

BURTON UPON TRENT

Station Hotel
Borough Road, next to railway station

Licensee: Alex Hill
Tel: 0283 64955

A cheerful and welcoming pub five minutes' walk from the town centre, the Station has a lounge bar, pool room, and railway memorabilia. Hot and cold food is served every lunchtime and evening. The bedrooms have tea and coffee making facilities and colour TVs. Burton is the historic centre of the British beer industry, its roots going back to monastic brewing. Bass, Allied's Ind Coope, Marston and Burton Bridge brew in the town, and both the Bass Museum and the Heritage Brewery Museum, in the former Everard's plant, have fascinating displays depicting the industry ancient and modern. Information about both museums is available in the hotel, where Alex Hill – a former brewer, member of both the Guild of Master Cellarmen and an Ansells Master of Ales – will be happy to debate the merits of different beers over a jar or two.

Beer: Ansells Bitter and Burton Ale on handpumps, and a guest beer.

Accommodation: 1 double, 3 twins, 2 family rooms. B&B £15 per person.

BUTTERTON

Black Lion
Near Cauldon, off A52 and B523

Licensees: Ron, Derek & Marie-Pierre Smith
Tel: 053 88 232

The Black Lion is a characterful, stone-built 18th-century rural pub with several rooms off the main bar. Furnishings range from pretty sofas to settles and bar stools with back rests. There are beams, open fires, a kitchen range and a carefully restored dining room. Excellent bar food includes ploughman's, sandwiches, steak and kidney pie, lasagne, vegetarian lasagne, moussaka, liver, bacon and onions, beef in red wine, and daily specials such as chicken provençale. Games to play include darts, dominoes and shove ha'penny, while a pleasant terrace has tables and chairs for warmer weather and fine views of the hamlet of Butterton close to Dovedale and the Manifold Valley. Nearer at hand is the remarkable Yew Tree at Cauldon, a rambling old inn packed with grandfather clocks and a collection of working Victorian music boxes, including polyphons and symphonions. At the Black Lion there is a residents' TV lounge, while the guest rooms all have en suite facilities and tea and coffee making equipment.

Beer: McEwan 70 shilling and 80 shilling, Theakston Best Bitter and Younger No 3 on handpumps.

Accommodation: 2 doubles, 1 family room. B&B £14 per person.

HULME END

Manifold Valley Hotel
Off A515 and B5054

Proprietors: Todhunter & Milner families
Tel: 0298 84537

The hotel is a delightful old village inn in a hamlet in the north Staffordshire Peak District, close to the lovely Manifold Valley and the tourist centre of Hartington. The inn has one cheerful bar with an open fire, and a separate restaurant, with food served lunchtime and evening. Accommodation is in a recently renovated building next to the hotel; all rooms are en suite and have colour TVs and tea and coffee making facilities. One room is suitable for disabled people. There is a separate residents' lounge, and there are camping facilities close by.

Beer: Darley Dark Mild, Thorne Bitter and Ward Sheffield Best Bitter on handpumps, with guest beers every weekend in summer.

Accommodation: 1 single, 3 doubles, 1 twin. B&B from £19 per person. No dogs.

UTTOXETER

Roebuck Inn
37 Dovebank, A518, off A50

Licensee: Ronald Eldridge
Tel: 0889 565563

The Roebuck dates back to 1608 and has oak beams, roaring fires in the bar and quarry-tiled floors. Meals are cooked to order and Mr Eldridge concentrates on using fresh local produce. There are meals and snacks every lunchtime and evening, including a vegetarian dish. The guest

rooms have colour TVs and tea and coffee making facilities. The Roebuck is distinguished not only by its handsome features, but also by the visits of a local medium and clairvoyant who considers the inn to be a fascinating place for ghostly hauntings. The inn is a good centre for visiting Alton Towers, the Potteries and Tutbury castle and glassworks.

Beer: Bass on handpump and regular guest beers, including Burton Bridge ales from Burton upon Trent.

Accommodation: 1 single, 2 twins, 2 doubles, 1 with en suite facilities. B&B £15 single, £20 twin, £25 en suite room.

SUFFOLK

ALDEBURGH

Mill Inn
Market Cross Place, A1094, off A12

Licensee: Bryan Hurrell
Tel: 0728 452563

The Mill is an attractive old pub close to the sea front of this famous Suffolk resort with its powerful Benjamin Britten associations: Snape Maltings concert hall, founded by the composer, is just outside the town, and *Peter Grimes* is based on a story about this part of the Suffolk coast. Opposite the Mill is the medieval Moot Hall or meeting place. The inn has a large public bar that attracts both local fishermen and the gentry, while the lounge is small, cosy and sedate: the two rooms are divided by an unusual fire raised above ground level and behind a glass front. A tiny snug room is a couple of steps down from the public bar. There are

SUFFOLK

lunchtime and evening grills (not Wednesday or Sunday evening). The guest rooms have TVs, and tea and coffee making facilities. Booking is advisable for summer and the Aldeburgh Festival.

Beer: Adnams Bitter and Old (winter) on handpumps.

Accommodation: 2 doubles, 1 twin. B&B £24 double. Children 14 and over are welcome, no reductions.

BARDWELL

Six Bells Inn
The Green, ½ mile off A143
Bury to Diss road

Licensees: Carol & Richard Salmon
Tel: 0359 50820

A 16th-century inn with exposed beams and an inglenook fireplace, the Six Bells is on an old coaching route and stands close to the village green and duck pond in an acre of land surrounded by farmland. Bury St Edmunds is close by. The restaurant of the Six Bells incorporates an old Suffolk range with its original oven and copper. The Salmons specialize in prime steaks and fresh fish, and the restaurant offers turbot in lobster sauce, salmon in pink peppercorn sauce and steak Diane. Bar meals include steak and ale pie, beef and chicken lasagne, smoked breast of chicken salad, and grilled sardines. Not surprisingly, the Salmons have been regional finalists in the Pub Caterer awards for 1988 and 1989. Their food is available every day, lunchtime and evening; there is a roast lunch on Sunday. Accommodation is in a converted barn; all the rooms are en suite and have colour TVs and tea and coffee making facilities.

Beer: Adnams Bitter, Boddingtons Bitter and Wadworth 6X on handpumps.

Accommodation: 2 singles, 4 doubles/twins, 1 family room. B&B £22.50 single, £37.50 double/twin, £42.50 family room. Children £5 for additional bed in room and breakfast. 2 night B&B plus £10 meal allowance Saturday/Sunday from £40 per person. No pets. Cards: Access and Visa.

BILDESTON

Crown Hotel
High Street, B1115 between Stowmarket and Hadleigh

Licensees: Edward & Dinah Henderson
Tel: 0449 740510

The Crown is an old coaching inn built around 1500. It has a wealth of exposed beams and there are log fires in winter; it is close to the stunning medieval wool town of Lavenham and is also handy for Bury, Ipswich and Constable country. Food is available in both the restaurant and bar and includes an à la carte menu and such bar meals as toasted sandwiches, ploughman's, omelettes, chicken and chips, clam fries and egg piperade.

Beer: Adnams Bitter, Mauldon Bitter and Marston Pedigree on handpumps.

Accommodation: 9 doubles/twins, 2 family rooms, 4 with en suite facilities. B&B from £19-£20.50 single, £30-£49 double. No dogs. Cards: Access, Amex, Diners and Visa.

SUFFOLK

BRANDESTON

Queen's Head
Near Woodbridge; 2 miles off B1120 at Earl Soham

Licensees: Ray & Myra Bumstead
Tel: 072 882 307

The Queen's Head is a welcoming country pub with banquettes and old pews to sit on, and coal fires in the winter in the front bar. A new bar at the back has been opened for customers who want a quiet drink away from the food area in the main bar. The Bumsteads concentrate on home-cooked meals and offer steak and kidney pie, lasagne, kidneys in cream and mustard sauce, lamb bakes, and salads, sandwiches and ploughman's. Families are well catered for with a family room and a play area in the large garden, which has tables for summer drinking and eating. Two golf courses are close by. There is a ½-acre site at the back of the pub for camping and caravans.

Beer: Adnams Mild, Bitter, Broadside (summer), Old (winter) on handpumps, and local cider.

Accommodation: 3 doubles (let as singles if demand allows). B&B £13 per person. Children welcome, terms according to age.

BURY ST EDMUNDS

Bushel Hotel
St John's Street, town centre, off A45

Licensee: E V Groves
Tel: 0284 754333

The Bushel, sandwiched between St John's Street and St Andrew's Street in the town centre, dates back to the 15th century and is an old coaching inn. It was sensitively refurbished in 1989 to bring out the true atmosphere of the old building. Bar meals and restaurant meals are available.

Beer: Greene King XX, IPA and Abbot Ale on handpumps.

Accommodation: £18 single, double £15 per person.

Dog & Partridge
29 Crown Street

Licensee: Mr A Painter
Tel: 0284 764792

The Dog & Partridge is an inn of some antiquity, built in approximately 1689 and with many of its original features – beams, pillars and pews – left intact. It is a grade two listed building; it was first a private house, then became an inn called the Mermaid that specialized in rook pie, and later adopted the present name and, thankfully, phased out its bird dishes. Full meals and bar snacks are served at lunchtime. The bar at the rear has been fashioned from the inn's old stables. It is near the cathedral, abbey gardens and St Mary's Church, and is the 'brewery tap' for Greene King, the powerful regional group based in Bury.

Beer: Greene King XX, IPA and Abbot Ale on handpumps.

Accommodation: 1 single, 1 double, 1 twin. B&B £18 single, £28 double/twin. Children sharing with parents £8 including breakfast. No dogs.

CAVENDISH

George Inn
The Green, A1092

Licensees: Mike & Jill Vincent
Tel: 0787 280248

The George is a 15th-century village pub overlooking the green in Cavendish. It has a tall, imposing chimney and a handsome bow-windowed frontage. Inside there is a cosy public bar and a spacious lounge; excellent food is available both lunchtime and evening. This is Constable Country and the pub is a splendid base for visiting Flatford and Dedham. Closer to Cavendish are a vineyard, a working priory and the Sue Ryder Foundation headquarters.

Beer: Flowers IPA and Original on handpumps.

Accommodation: 2 doubles, 1 twin, 1 room with shower; all rooms have hot and cold water, central heating, TVs and teasmades. B&B £15 per person. Children over 5 welcome, terms by arrangement.

CHELSWORTH

Peacock Inn
The Street, B1115

Licensees: Lorna & Tony Marsh
Tel: 0449 740758

The Peacock is a superb country pub ten miles from the nearest market town and five miles from Lavenham, one of the finest examples of a preserved medieval town in England. The inn is opposite a tiny bridge over the narrow River Brett. It has five small guest rooms, most with exposed beams. The horseshoe bar divides into a stand-and-chat bar, a snug with a blazing open fire and a smart lounge with a permanent art gallery. There is an extensive menu of homemade food, including on Sundays roast beef cooked over a log fire. Lorna Marsh's special dishes include game pie in winter, seafood Mornay, pasta dishes, vegetarian quiche, steak, kidney amd mushroom pie, homemade soup, sweet and sour chicken, ploughman's and granary bread sandwiches. The saloon bar has a piano and there is live music, usually jazz, on Fridays.

Beer: Adnams Bitter and Old (winter), Greene King IPA and Abbot Ale, Mauldon Bitter on handpumps.

Accommodation: 1 single, 3 doubles, 1 twin. B&B £18 single, £35 double. Children by special arrangement only.

CLARE

Bell Hotel
Market Hill, off B1092

Licensee: Brian Miles
Tel: 0787 277741

The Bell is an imposing 16th-century posting house with a half-timbered façade, a panelled and beamed bar with an open fire, and a wine bar with fascinating memorabilia connected with canal building. The splendid accommodation is furnished with period furniture and includes a four-poster bedroom. Bar food, seven days a week, includes soup, toasties, homemade lasagne, and grills. There is a separate à la carte restaurant, too, and afternoon tea is served in the conservatory. Clare has the remains of a castle and priory and is the home of the small Nethergate Brewery: the Bell was the first outlet for its wonderfully fruity ale.

Beer: Greene King IPA and Nethergate Bitter on handpumps.

Accommodation: 20 doubles, 2 family rooms, 20 rooms with en suite facilities. B&B from £27.50 per person. Weekend £45 per person. Children welcome, no reductions. Dogs by arrangement. Cards: Access, Amex, Diners and Visa.

DUNWICH

Ship Inn
St James Street, 2 miles off B1125

Licensees: Stephen & Annie Marshlain
Tel: 072 873 219

The nautical bar of the Ship is, rather suitably, slightly sunken for the once great medieval city of Dunwich – the greatest in East Anglia and the seat of kings – lies beneath the North Sea and only the church bells can be heard tolling at night before a storm ... or so legend, embellished by a few pints, claims. The bar of the Ship has a tiled floor, wood-burning stove and captain's chairs. Homemade bar food includes soup, locally caught fish with chips, cottage pie, salads, ploughman's, and various puddings. The separate restaurant (open for lunch and dinner) has homemade boozy pâté, fresh fish dish of the day, chicken Kiev, vegetarian dish, ice creams and sorbets. There is a pleasant garden, terrace and conservatory, ideal for families. Children are allowed in all rooms except the bar.

Beer: Adnams Bitter and Old (winter), Greene King Abbot Ale on handpumps.

Accommodation: 1 single, 2 doubles, 1 twin, 1 family room. B&B £16 per person. Children welcome, terms negotiable.

FELIXSTOWE

Fludyer Arms Hotel
Undercliff Road East, off A45

Licensee: John Nash
Tel: 0394 283279

The Fludyer Arms, close to the beach in old Felixstowe, is a large and impressive Victorian building with several splendid Dutch gables and a large conservatory with fine views of the sea. There are two bars and a children's room. Extensive bar food includes a special 'spud grub' section – baked jacket potatoes with a wide range of fillings, from baked beans to curry and prawns – plus homemade soup, whitebait, fillet of cod, steak and kidney pie, chicken curry, omelettes, ploughman's, sandwiches, burgers, and such sweets as apple pie and vanilla ice cream.

Beer: Tolly Bitter and Original on handpumps.

Accommodation: 2 singles, 5 doubles/twins, 1 family room, 1 room with en suite facilities. B&B £16 single, £22 with shower, £28 double, £40 with shower, £40 family room. Pets welcome. Cards: Access and Visa.

Ordnance Hotel
1 Undercliff Road West

Licensees: Gary Cornwell & Trevor Ewing
Tel: 0394 273427

The Ordnance Arms Hotel, as it was first called, was built in 1854 close to the old coastal defence battery in Felixstowe, now a leisure centre. In the bicentary history of the Ispwich brewers, Cobbold, the hotel was described as the 'oldest hotel in

Felixstowe, well known for its catering'. Today the hotel is set in large gardens close to the town centre and the beach, and handy for the port terminal. It has a bar and lounge and also a large function room. Bar snacks are available lunchtime and evening every day (lunch only at weekends) and there are full meals in a bistro.

Beer: Tolly Bitter on handpump.

Accommodation: 6 singles, 10 doubles/twins, 1 family room, 5 rooms with en suite facilities. B&B £26 single, £36 en suite, £38 double/twin, £48 en suite, £50 family room. Children's room. No dogs. Cards: Access, Amex, Diners and Visa.

FLEMPTON

Greyhound
The Green, off A1101, near Bury St Edmunds

Licensee: David R Nunn
Tel: 028 484 400

The Greyhound is a large, lively and rambling local overlooking the green in this old Saxon village with its ancient forge. The Greyhound, which is featured on the pub weather vane, has a heavily windowed exterior and a charming, unspoilt interior with welcoming open fires. There is bar food lunchtime and evening, and a walled garden for the summer months. The pub is a good base for visiting the village, the local abbey gardens and Bury St Edmunds.

Beer: Greene King XX, IPA and Abbot Ale on handpumps.

Accommodation: 2 doubles, 1 family room. B&B £12 per person.

FRAMSDEN

Dobermann
The Street. Signposted from B1077 south of junction with A1120 Stowmarket to Earl Soham road

Licensee: Susan Frankland
Tel: 047 339 461

The Dobermann, despite its rather alarming name, is a gentle and welcoming old thatched pub tucked away down a lane. The owners raise the hounds and the many rosettes they have won adorn the lounge. Inside, the pub has been carefully rendered back to its original style, with bare brick walls, beams and wooden partitions. The plainer bar area and chintzy lounge are connected by a large see-through fireplace that is decorated with flowers in the summer. Imaginative bar food includes a daily vegetarian dish along with trout in wine and almonds, steak and kidney or chicken pie, scampi, Stilton ploughman's and turkey fricassée. There is a charming garden to the side of the pub, where boules is played, and there are picnic tables and a summertime barbecue.

Beer: Adnams Mild, Bitter and Broadside, Greene King IPA and Abbot Ale, a guest beer such as Charles Wells Bombardier and a house beer, Dobermann Bitter, which is Tetley Bitter in doggy disguise.

Accommodation: 1 double room, £15 per person.

GREAT GLEMHAM

Crown
1½ miles off A12 at Stratford St Andrew

Licensees: Roy & Eve Wood
Tel: 072 878 693

The Crown is a wonderfully welcoming pub with a massive, dominating fireplace where a log fire blazes in winter. The comfortable lounge has captain's chairs around kitchen tables, and there are local paintings and photographs decorating the white walls. There are seats on the lawn in spring and summer, and inside locals play darts, dominoes and crib. Bar food includes steaks, Suffolk ham, plaice, fisherman's platter, chilli, burgers and omelettes. There is a Sunday roast lunch. The separate restaurant seats 24, and tables must be booked in advance. Families can use the dining room at lunchtimes during the week.

Beer: Adnams Bitter, Broadside and Old (winter), Greene King IPA and Abbot Ale on handpumps, plus summer guest beers including Marston's, Flowers and Hall & Woodhouse.

Accommodation: 1 single with shower, 2 doubles, 1 family room, 2 rooms with en suite bathrooms. B&B £15 per person. Children £10. Children's room. Pets welcome.

GEORGE INN, CAVENDISH –
see p 171

IPSWICH

Lion's Head
213-215 Cauldwell Hall Road, off A45 and A12

Licensee: Barry French
Tel: 0473 727418

The Lion's Head is a turn-of-the-century building on the east side of Ipswich. It is decorated inside with a plethora of plates, and there are good value bar meals served lunchtime and until 9 in the evening (no food Sundays). A large garden has a children's play area.

Beer: Tolly Bitter and Original on handpumps.

Accommodation: 1 single, 3 twins. B&B £12 per person.

LONG MELFORD

Crown Inn
Hall Street, A134

Licensees: B & K Heavens
Tel: 0787 77666

An historic inn, with a striking black-and-cream façade embellished with hanging baskets, the Crown dates from 1610. It is a listed building and retains its Tudor cellars, exposed beams and a log fire, and a stained-glass panel in the lounge, showing a scene from Shakespeare's *A Midsummer Night's Dream* is thought to be of great value. The Riot Act was last read in England in 1885 from the steps of the Crown when Liberal voters from nearby Glemsford clashed with Tory voters at Melford's polling station. Long Melford and the Crown are more peaceful places these days. The town boasts the longest village street in England and has no less than 30

SUFFOLK

antique shops. The Crown has bar meals and a 35-seater restaurant. Local produce is used in the cooking, which ranges from roasts to vegetarian dishes. The delightful accommodation includes a four-poster bedroom.

Beer: Adnams Bitter, Greene King IPA, Mauldon Bitter, Nethergate Bitter, Tetley Bitter on handpumps.

Accommodation: 1 single, 6 doubles, 3 twins, 1 family room, 7 rooms with private baths. B&B £31.50 single, double £39, four-poster en suite £47.50. Bargain Winter Breaks: single £70.50 for 2 nights, double £50 per person, including £6.50 dinner allowance. Cards: Access, Amex, Diners and Visa.

George & Dragon Inn
Hall Street, centre of town

Licensee: Peter Thorogood
Tel: 0787 71285

The George & Dragon is an ancient coaching inn that was restored in Victorian times. It is a typical Suffolk pub with a large lounge bar and a genuine locals' public bar with darts and pool and regular folk and jazz nights. Bar food is available lunchtime and evening (not Sunday evenings) in the lounge, and traditional dishes range from ploughman's to East Anglian topside of beef. There are splendid breakfasts, too.

Beer: Greene King IPA and Abbot Ale on handpumps.

Accommodation: 3 singles, 4 doubles/twins, 1 room with en suite facilities. B&B £15 per person. Children allowed in lounge bar. Pets welcome.

ORFORD

Jolly Sailor
Quay Street. B10884, off A12, 12 miles from Woodbridge

Licensees: Pat & June Buckner
Tel: 0394 450243

The sea has receded from Orford but has left this merry matelot behind as a reminder of the town's nautical days. Parts of the 16th-century inn are built from the timbers of old shipwrecked vessels. Beer and food come from a central hatch that serves the bar, lounge and snug. Darts, dominoes, crib and shove ha'penny are played by locals and the bar is warmed by an old-fashioned stove. There is a children's room, a spiral staircase and a collection of stuffed miniature dogs thought to come from Tudor times. Bar food includes hot daily specials, seafood platter, ploughman's, steaks, sausages and salads. A large garden at the back has a children's play area. Orford has one of the finest castles in East Anglia and the renowned Butley Orford Oystery restaurant specializing in seafood.

Beer: Adnams Bitter and Old (winter) on handpumps.

Accommodation: 1 single, 3 doubles. B&B £14 per person. Children welcome, reductions if sharing with parents.

SUFFOLK

RICKINGHALL

Hamblyn House
The Street, on A143 Diss to Bury road, 4 miles from Diss

Licensees: Dennis Barrow & Brenda Wallace
Tel: 0379 898 292

James Hamblyn, who played an important role in the founding of Chicago, built his house 480 years ago. It has a striking and unusual Flemish exterior that spans two parishes: the lounge and bar are in Rickinghall Inferior while the restaurant, fittingly, is in Rickinghall Superior. Inside there is a huge stone fireplace, black timbers and copper and brassware, with a great sweeping staircase leading to the en suite guest rooms tucked away under the eaves. Food is based on local produce. The restaurant can seat up to 35 and bar meals are available lunchtime and evening (not Sunday evenings).

Beer: Greene King IPA and Abbot Ale on handpumps.

Accommodation: 4 doubles/twins, 2 family rooms. B&B £25 single, £38 double, £55 family room. No pets. Cards: Access and Visa.

SAXMUNDHAM

White Hart Hotel
High Street, off A12

Licensee: Malcolm Banks
Tel: 0728 602009

The White Hart is a 16th-century coaching inn in a small market town that stages twice-weekly auctions. The inn, thoroughly renovated and refurbished in 1989, has two bars and a restaurant and open log fires. Bar food, available lunchtime and evening, includes sandwiches, roasts, salads, liver and onions, scampi, and a daily three-course special. The restaurant is open Wednesday to Sunday. The hotel is a good base for visiting Framlingham castle, Woodbridge, Bruisyard vinyard, Minsmere bird sanctuary and the coast.

Beer: Tolly Bitter and Original on handpumps.

Accommodation: 1 single, 3 doubles/twins, 4 family rooms. All rooms have hot and cold water, colour TVs and tea making facilities. B&B £15 per person. Family room £40. Children by arrangement. Pets welcome. Cards: Access, Amex and Visa.

SIBTON

Sibton White Horse
Halesworth Road. A1120, ½ mile from Peasenhall

Licensees: Fay & Tony Waddingham
Tel: 072 869 337

The White Horse is a delightful 16th-century pub in 2½ acres of ground and surrounded by fields in a conservation area. Darts, cribbage, dominoes, shove ha'penny and pétanque are played. There is a pleasant outside seating area on shingle at the front and a children's play area at the rear with more seating. Inside, the pub has a 20-seater beamed restaurant and a raised gallery area where children are welcome. Bar meals are available lunchtime and evening and always include a vegetarian dish. Accommodation is in a separate building in the grounds; all the rooms have en suite facilities.

SUFFOLK

Beer: Adnams Bitter and Broadside on handpumps.

Accommodation: 3 singles, 3 doubles, 3 twins, including 1 family suite with double and single beds and bathroom. B&B £14.16 per person. Children's rates according to age. Pets welcome.

SOUTHWOLD

Crown Hotel
90 High Street, off A12

Manager: Simon Hawkins
Tel: 0502 722275

The green and cream Georgian hotel announces Adnams' dominant position in the town. The carefully extended brewery lies behind the Crown, which doubles as small town hotel-cum-pub and, upstairs, the brewery's fast-expanding and much-praised wine business. The food is outstanding and, like the accommodation, is surprisingly reasonably priced. Bar food includes celery and apple soup, casserole of fish, warm salad of sautéed beef with ginger, salade niçoise, fillet of cod with capers and orange, sautéed lambs' liver with shallots and bacon, braised leg of duck, and baked pepper with mixed vegetables, rice and cheese. Restaurant meals (lunch and dinner £10.50–£15 per person) are accompanied by recommended glasses of wine for each course, the wines kept under nitrogen pressure in a Cruover machine: the only form of gas pressure permitted by CAMRA. Regular jazz and classical music evenings are staged. The Crown holds frequent wine appreciation weekends: details and prices from Mr Hawkins.

Beer: Adnams Bitter, Broadside and Old (winter) on handpumps.

Accommodation: 2 singles, 9 doubles, 1 family room, 9 rooms en suite. B&B £25 single, £41 double, £62 family room. Children welcome, half price plus food. Dogs by prior arrangement. Cards: Access, Amex and Visa.

Red Lion
2 South Green

Licensee: Alan Coleman
Tel: 0502 722385

The Red Lion has one of the best positions in this delightful Victorian seaside town with its roots dating back to the 15th century when it was granted a charter by Henry VII. The famous battle of Sole Bay was fought here in 1672, with the combined English and French fleets against the Dutch. The pub, with a striking figure of a red lion, welcomes you to the wide expanse of South Green, just a few yards from the sea and the wide shingle beach. Inside there is one long panelled bar with bench seats running round the walls below the windows, and fascinating old photos of Southwold as it was before the Victorians discovered the place. To the left of the bar is a large, comfortable family room, to the right a pleasant dining room with buffet lunches – including local crab – served daily in summer and bar snacks and hot specials in winter. Mrs Coleman is renowned for her generous traditional breakfasts.

Beer: Adnams Bitter, Broadside and Old (winter) on handpumps.

Accommodation: 2 doubles, 1 en suite twin. B&B £22 per person.

STOKE BY NAYLAND

Angel Inn
On B1068 Sudbury to East Bergholt road, 5 miles off A12

Licensee: P G Smith
Tel: 0206 263245/6

The Angel is a 16th-century inn on the Essex border in the heart of Dedham Vale – Constable country. The village was much loved by the painter who immortalized its cottages and river banks on canvas. The lively inn has a garden, a wood-burning stove, original timbers and beams. Bar food is available lunchtime and evening and includes soups, ploughman's, asparagus, moussaka, homemade gravlax, chicken and prawn brochette, and a plate of three fresh griddled fish. There is a separate restaurant for evening meals. The guest rooms all have en suite facilities, colour TVs and tea and coffee makers.

Beer: Adnams Bitter, Greene King IPA and Abbot Ale, Mauldon Bitter, Nethergate Bitter on handpumps.

Accommodation: 6 singles, 6 doubles, 1 family room. B&B £35 single, £45 double. Cards: Access, Amex, Diners and Visa.

STRADBROKE

Ivy House
Wilby Road. B1117; off A140

Licensee: John O'Brien
Tel: 0379 84634

A charming thatched pub close to Eye and Diss, the Ivy House has two bars, a lounge, a dining room, and a pleasant garden for families in summer. Food is available lunchtime and evening and ranges from three-course meals to bar snacks. Daily homemade specials, with fresh vegetables, include beef and Guinness casserole, pork braised in cider, and steak and kidney pie. Wingfield Castle is close by, and it is a short drive to the Otter Trust at Bungay, Framlingham castle, and Bressingham steam museum and gardens.

Beer: Adnams Extra, Marston Pedigree Bitter and Flowers Original on handpumps.

Accommodation: 1 single, 2 doubles/twins. B&B £12.50 per person. No pets.

SUDBURY

White Horse
North Street, off A134

Licensees: John & Anne Martin
Tel: 0787 71063

Sudbury was the home of Thomas Gainsborough, once the greatest portrait painter in England, and his nephew was landlord of the White Horse for a time. The pub is 500 years old, and many architectural styles have been added to it over the years but have not tampered with its essential charm and cosiness. It has a 40-seater lounge restaurant serving a wide range of home-cooked meals lunchtime and evening, and bar meals are also available. It is a fine base for touring the Stour valley, Constable country and the old market towns of Clare and Lavenham.

Beer: Greene King XX, IPA and Abbot Ale on handpumps.

Accommodation: 3 singles, 3 doubles/twins, 1 family room. B&B £15 single, £27 double. No dogs.

WALBERSWICK

Bell Hotel
B1387, off A12. Go right through village to green, turn right for pub

Licensee: Mark Stansall
Tel: 0502 723109

The Bell is an atmospheric old fishermen's inn in a village that has no truck with such modern refinements as pavements or street lighting. The inn is 600 years old and the passage of feet has worn and bowed the old stone floors. There are high-backed settles in the main bar, photos of the village and some of the local characters in a smaller side bar and a large room where shove ha'penny and crib are played. A vast back garden with hedges, trees and tables, is ideal for summer Sundays when crowds descend for Adnams' ale and the Stansalls' buffet lunch of fresh seafood and salads. There is an inside dining room, too, for lunches and dinner. Food includes homemade fish pie, freshly caught fish, homemade quiche, smoked mackerel, prawns and crab, with additional hot dishes in winter. The Bell is a genuine local, with fishermen strolling up from the mouth of the Blyth for a pint and a crack. The ferryman will row you across to the opposite bank from where you can buy fresh fish and crabs or walk into Southwold.

Beer: Adnams Bitter, Broadside and Old (winter) on handpumps.

Accommodation: 1 single, 2 twins, 2 en suite doubles. B&B £20 per person, £22 in en suite room.

WOOLPIT

Swan Inn
The Street, 1 mile from junction of A45 and A1088

Licensees: Joseph & Gillian Thompson
Tel: 0359 40482

The Swan is a 400-year-old red-brick former coaching inn in the centre of the village with one large L-shaped bar warmed by a log fire in the winter. There are excellent lunchtime bar snacks (not Sundays) and hearty breakfasts. The guest rooms, in an annexe off the main building, all have colour TVs and tea and coffee making facilities. Bury St Edmunds is just ten minutes' drive.

Beer: Ruddles County, Websters Yorkshire Bitter on handpumps.

Accommodation: 1 single, 1 twin, 1 double, 1 double/family room en suite. B&B £13.50-£15.50 per person. Children of all ages welcome at reduced rates.

SURREY

BLETCHINGLEY

Whyte Harte
Off A25 and A22, 2½ miles from M25 exit 6

Licensees: Helen & David Cooper
Tel: 0883 843231

The Whyte Hart is a 600-year-old inn, with low beams, wood floors, an inglenook fireplace with an ancient and sagging beam, and settles and stools to sit on. The pleasant garden is bounded by a stone wall and old Tudor cottages and there are also seats at the front among flower tubs.

Homemade pub fare includes sandwiches, smoked salmon, beef Stroganoff, ploughman's, and daily hot specials such as cottage pie, spaghetti bolognese and plaice, plus vegetarian dishes.

Beer: Friary Meux Best Bitter, Tetley Bitter and Burton Ale on handpumps.

Accommodation: B&B from £27.50 single, £31.50 with private bath, £42 twin, £48 with bath.

DORKING

Pilgrim
Station Road, next to Dorking West railway station

Licensee: A Stappard
Tel: 0306 889951

The Pilgrim is a cheerful old inn tucked away from the town centre and offering a traditional pub alternative to the town's many pricey hotels. The handsome town of Dorking is close to the well-known beauty spots of Leith Hill – at 1,000 feet the highest place in the south-east – and Box Hill. The North Downs run along the northern edge of the town. The Pilgrim has a garden and serves bar food lunchtime and evening.

Beer: Friary Meux Best Bitter and Burton Ale on handpumps.

Accommodation: 5 doubles, 1 family room. B&B £18 single, £30 double.

SURREY

GODSTONE

Bell
128 High Street, B2236, 1 mile south of M25 exit 6

Licensee: Mrs Pat Avery
Tel: 0883 843133

The Bell is a splendid 600-year-old coaching inn with open log fires and a wealth of copper and brass in its large beamed bar. Food is served lunchtime and evening in the bar, and there is also a separate restaurant. Crib, backgammon, dominoes and shove ha'penny are played by the locals. The Bell has a large garden and there is a children's room equipped with games. It is close to the village green and pond, and handy for visiting the North Downs. Penshurst Place, Hever Castle and Chartwell with its Winston Churchill connections are in the area. Guest rooms at the Bell include a four-poster bedroom.

Beer: Friary Meux Best Bitter, Burton Ale and Tetley Bitter on handpumps with Benskins Best Bitter or Taylor Walker Best Bitter as guest beers.

Accommodation: 2 doubles, including a four-poster room. B&B £35 double, £42 four-poster. (Additional rooms are planned.)

GOMSHALL

Black Horse Inn
On A25

Licensee: Tony Savage
Tel: 048 641 2242

An imposing three-storey building in the centre of the village, the Black Horse was formerly the brewery of Reffell Brothers, bought by Young of Wandsworth in 1926. It has a small games bar, a large comfortable lounge with antique furniture, a spacious beer garden, and a separate restaurant. Bar food includes homemade soup, filled jacket potatoes with a choice of fillings, steak and kidney pie, local trout, macaroni cheese, chicken curry, seafood platter, ploughman's with choice of cheese, and daily specials. The Black Horse has a sloping lawn and a pleasant terrace with tables under parasols. It is a good pub for traditional games and, against intense competition, has appeared in every edition of the *Good Beer Guide*.

Beer: Youngs Bitter, Special Bitter and Winter Warmer on handpumps.

Accommodation: 1 single, 1 twin, 2 doubles. Colour TVs in all rooms. Room price £19.95 per person; breakfast extra.

HINDHEAD

Devils Punchbowl Hotel
London Road, A3

Licensee: Anthony Smith
Tel: 0428 736565 Fax: 0428 735713

This imposing hotel, with its porches, dormers in the steeply sloping roof and a central tower, stands 900 feet above sea level with superb views of the Surrey Downs and the famous Devil's Punchbowl beauty spot from which it gets its name. The building was originally the country residence of the Hon. Rollo Russell, son of Lord John Russell, the first Liberal Prime Minister. The present hotel retains a genuine pub atmosphere in a busy bar popular with locals. There is a lounge for morning coffee and afternoon tea, while Squire's restaurant offers a wide choice of à la carte meals. including steaks, lemon sole, rainbow trout, chicken Kiev, roast duckling and vegetarian lasagne. All the beautifully appointed guest rooms have en suite facilities, colour TVs and tea and coffee making equipment.

Beer: Bass, Hall & Woodhouse Badger Best Bitter and two or three guest beers on handpumps.

Accommodation: 8 singles, 30 doubles/twins, 2 family rooms. B&B £55.50 single, £65.50 double/twin. Children under 16 sharing with 2 adults free; 75% of tariff in own room. Weekend minimum 2 nights, £30 per person per night B&B + dinner.

OCKLEY

Kings Arms
Stane Street, A29

Licensee: Alec Hastings
Tel: 0306 711224

The Kings Arms is an attractive old inn on an even older Roman road in a pleasant village with a large green. The hostelry successfully trebles as pub, hotel and restaurant, with good food served both lunchtime and evening and an outdoor drinking area for the warmer months. It is popular with people using Gatwick airport and booking is therefore essential.

Beer: Fullers ESB, Flowers Original, Hall & Woodhouse Badger Best Bitter, King & Barnes Sussex Bitter, Marston Pedigree Bitter and Youngs Bitter on handpumps.

Accommodation: 3 doubles. B&B £25 per person. Cards: Access, Amex, Visa.

SUSSEX

ALFRISTON (EAST SUSSEX)

Wingrove Inn
High Street, south end of village, off A27

Licensee: Sandra Calow
Tel: 0323 870276

The Wingrove is a splendid example of Victorian colonial architecture in the heart of the South Downs with spectacular views of the village green – The Tye – the Cathedral of the Downs, and the National Trust Clergy House. The inn's restaurant serves à la carte and table d'hôte menus and the wide-ranging bar food has won Les Routiers' 'casserole' award. A garden with views of the downs and valley is popular in summer. All the guest rooms have en suite facilities, colour TVs and tea and coffee making equipment.

Beer: Bateman XXXB, Harvey BB and King & Barnes Sussex Bitter on handpumps.

Accommodation: 2 twins, 1 double. B&B £25–£30 per person. No pets.

ARDINGLY (WEST SUSSEX)

Ardingly Inn
Street Lane, off B2028

Licensees: Ian & Tricia Morgan
Tel: 0444 892214

The inn is a large village-centre pub with a spacious and comfortable lounge and a separate restaurant, with meals served lunchtime and evening. It has a real fire, and a pleasant garden, and is close to Ardingly College, the South of England Showground, and the Bluebell Railway at Horsted Keynes. The inn's guest rooms all have colour TVs and tea and coffee making facilities. If you need to ask the way, the village is pronounced 'Arding-lie'.

Beer: Charrington IPA and King & Barnes Sussex Bitter on handpumps.

Accommodation: 3 twins, 3 doubles, 3 with en suite facilities. B&B £37.50 double, £44 en suite. Cards: Access, Amex, Diners and Visa.

ARUNDEL (WEST SUSSEX)

The Swan
High Street, A27

Licensees: Diana & Ken Rowsell
Tel: 0903 882314

The Swan, with its handsome façade, striking red window shades and high dormer roof, is in the centre of this famous old Sussex town with its imposing castle. The Rowsells continue energetically to improve the facilities of the hotel and plan to add three guest rooms in 1990. The large L-shaped, partly timbered lounge serves good food based on local produce, including homemade soup, rolled smoked salmon and prawn, whitebait, a wide range of sandwiches and toasties, chicken and chips, burgers, grilled pork chop with apple sauce, fresh Sussex trout, steaks, salads, vegetarian curry and a daily vegetarian special, and filled jacket potatoes. There is an evening à la carte restaurant and a traditional Sunday roast. All the guest rooms have en suite facilities, phones and tea and coffee making equipment.

Beer: Courage Best Bitter and Directors Bitter, Hall & Woodhouse Badger Best Bitter and Tanglefoot, King & Barnes Sussex Bitter and Marston Pedigree Bitter on handpumps.

SUSSEX

Accommodation: 10 doubles. B&B £35 single, £45 double. Two-day Breaks including dinner £82 single, £116 for 2. Off-season Breaks £80.95 for 2 people for 2 nights dinner, B&B. Children welcome, 2 rooms suitable for families. Cards: Access, Amex and Visa.

BURWASH (EAST SUSSEX)

Bell Inn
High Street, A265

Licensees: David Mizel & Annick Howard
Tel: 0435 882304

New licensees are developing this 17th-century inn opposite the church. The Bell has exposed beams and a sloping floor; ale and wine are mulled on the open log fire and you can try your hand at ring the bull – one of the oldest pub games – toad-in-the-hole, darts and cribbage. The comfortable lounge has old photos of the area, which includes Batemans – not a brewery but the former home of Rudyard Kipling. Bar food includes ploughman's, Danish open prawn sandwich, beef curry, breast of chicken in leek and Stilton sauce, halibut or plaice, king crab, and homemade pizzas that can also be taken away. The inn provides daily newspapers for customers, and there are seats at the front in good weather.

Beer: Harvey BB and XXXX (winter) on handpumps, and regular guest beers such as Youngs Special and Charles Wells Bombardier.

Accommodation: 1 single, 2 doubles, 1 twin. B&B £18 single, £28 double. Children welcome, terms by arrangement. No pets.

EDBURTON (WEST SUSSEX)

Tottington Manor Hotel
Near Henfield. Take A281 from A23. At Henfield go left at mini-roundabout towards Woods Mill and Small Dole; approx 1 mile after Small Dole take left turn to Edburton

Proprietors: David & Kate Miller
Tel: 0903 815757

The food at Tottington Manor is likely to be good even by the now high standards of many small hotels and pubs, for David Miller was head chef at the Ritz in London's Piccadilly, though you may find prices a shade cheaper here. The manor, mentioned in the Domesday Book and now grade two listed, was built around 1604 and is a handsome building set in its own spacious grounds, with lovely views of the surrounding countryside. It stands between Brighton and Worthing, and guests can enjoy horse-riding, walking, tennis, squash, swimming, fishing and hang-gliding close by. Bar food (lunchtime and evening, not Sunday evening) includes sandwiches, toasties, ploughman's with Sussex Cheddar, Irish blue cheese and various meats, homemade soup, deep-fried butterfly prawns, salmon mousse, Welsh rabbit with bacon and tomato, and such daily specials as cider-baked ham, homemade sausages, grilled pork chop with black pudding, burgers, homemade pie of the day with potatoes and vegetables, Southdown lamb cutlets, steaks, and vegetarian lasagne. There is a special Sunday roast and a separate restaurant for lunch and dinner.

Beer: Adnams Bitter and Broadside, Bateman XXXB, Fullers London Pride and King & Barnes Sussex Bitter on handpumps.

Accommodation: 6 doubles, all en suite and with colour TVs and tea and coffee making facilities. B&B £35 single, from £48 double. Family room £10 extra per child over 3. 5 nights or more £28 single B&B per day, £40 double. Children's room. Pets welcome. Cards: Access and Visa.

FOREST ROW (EAST SUSSEX)

Ashdown Forest Hotel
Chapel Lane. From A22 take B2110; Chapel Lane is fourth on right

Licensees: Robin Pratt & Alan Riddick
Tel: 0342 82 4866

The hotel is an elegant Edwardian building with a creeper-clad and balconied exterior, standing in secluded grounds with its own 18-hole golf course. It has a bar, à la carte restaurant and a suite that holds up to 180 people. As well as golf, there are facilities close by for pony trekking and fishing. Bar food, lunchtime and evening, includes seafood platter, vegetable dips, sandwiches, a hot potato dish, salads, canapés and a carved buffet.

Beer: Harvey BB and a regular guest beer on handpumps.

Accommodation: 2 singles, 10 doubles/twins, 3 family rooms, 10 rooms with en suite facilities. B&B (including morning paper) £35 single, £48 double, £61 triple. (1989 prices: please check current tariff.) Golfing holidays: prices on application. Children welcome, no reductions but most meals half price. No dogs. Cards: Access and Visa.

HASTINGS (EAST SUSSEX)

Crown Inn
66 All Saints Street, off A259

Licensee: Ivan Measor
Tel: 0424 428308

The Crown is well-positioned in the old town section of Hastings, just 80 yards from the promenade. Mr Measor offers a warm welcome and will help point you in the direction of the Old Town Heritage Trail where you can discover 15th-century half-timbered houses intermingled with Georgian architecture. A miniature railway, boating lake and the historic fish market and harbour are close to the pub, which was rebuilt in the 1920s and has three bars and bar food lunchtime and evening.

Beer: Harvey BB on handpump.

Accommodation: 2 twins, 2 doubles (1 double room has an additional single bed). B&B £12 per person, £14 in July and August. Winter Weekends (not Xmas) £20 per person. No dogs.

LEWES (EAST SUSSEX)

Dorset Arms
22 Malling Street, off A227

Licensee: John Trembling
Tel: 0273 477110

The Dorset Arms is an historic Lewes pub known as the Cats. Parts have been rebuilt but it retains its essential 17th-century character, with two bars with open fires and a separate restaurant called the Georgian Room. Food is available every lunchtime and Wednesday to Saturday evenings and ranges from local fish dishes to sirloin steaks. There is a patio for warmer weather. Lewes is close to Brighton and Eastbourne, and is steeped in history, with many old timbered buildings and cobbled streets. It is also the home of Harvey's brewery, a splendid example of a Victorian 'tower' system where the brewing process flows by gravity from one floor to another. The company's draught Pale Ale was one of CAMRA's Beers of the Year in 1989.

Beer: Harvey Pale Ale, BB (winter) and Armada on handpumps.

Accommodation: 3 doubles, 2 en suite. B&B £17.50 per person, £19 single occupancy. Children's room. No dogs. Cards: Access, Amex and Visa.

MANNINGS HEATH (WEST SUSSEX)

Dun Horse
Brighton Road, A281 near Horsham

Licensee: N Goodhew
Tel: 0403 65783

The Dun Horse is a homely pub south of Horsham, with comfortable bars and guest rooms and fine windows dating back to the days of the Rock brewery. The pub has open fires, a garden, excellent pub grub lunchtime and evening, and traditional games in the public bar. All the guest rooms have colour TVs.

Beer: Flowers Original, Fremlins Bitter, Strong Country Bitter and Wethered Winter Royal (seasonal) on handpumps.

Accommodation: 2 singles, 1 double, 1 family room. B&B £15 per person.

DUDLEY (WEST MIDLANDS)

Station Hotel
Castle Hill, junction of Trindle Road, A461

Manager: Graham Hatherill
Tel: 0384 53418

The hotel dates back to 1898 and was extensively rebuilt in the 1930s. It is stone built and crescent-shaped, and was the haunt of theatre-goers to the Dudley Hippodrome in the heyday of regional theatre and music hall. It is close to Dudley Zoo and Castle, and to the Black Country Museum. The hotel has a traditional lounge bar with a daily hot buffet lunch (not Sundays), cocktail bar, a young people's music bar called Trax, and an à la carte restaurant open Tuesday, Wednesday and Thursday evenings and for Sunday roast lunch. A solarium and gym have been added and other major improvements include bringing the restaurant down to the ground floor and installing a new lounge bar. Dudley is built on the highest hill in the Black Country and is surrounded by villages created by the Industrial Revolution.

Beer: Banks Mild and Bitter on electric pumps.

Accommodation: 13 singles, 10 doubles/twins, 6 family rooms, 1 de luxe suite, many with en suite facilities, all with colour TVs and tea and coffee makers (extra rooms are being added). B&B £41 single, £52 double/twin, £63 family room. Weekend 2 people sharing £40 each. (All prices 1989: please check new tariff.) Cards: Access, Amex and Visa.

KENILWORTH (WARWICKSHIRE)

Clarendon House Hotel
Old High Street, off A452

Licensee: Martyn Lea
Tel: 0926 57668

Kenilworth and the hotel are steeped in the history of the English Civil War. The hotel, once the Castle Tavern, was used by Cromwell's troops during the siege of the town, and today has Cromwellian armour and other artefacts of the Civil War period. The original pub was built in 1538 around an oak tree that today still supports part of the main roof. There is a comfortable bar and a restaurant in the converted stables with a full à la carte restaurant. There are lunchtime bar snacks, too, and a Sunday roast.

Beer: Flowers IPA and Original, Hook Norton Best Bitter and guest beers, all on handpumps.

Accommodation: 15 singles, 14 doubles/twins, 1 family room, all with private baths. B&B £41 single, £60 double/twin. Weekend £65. Children welcome.

KINGSWINFORD (WEST MIDLANDS)

Old Court House
High Street, A4101, ½ mile from A491

Licensee: Clive Burke
Tel: 0384 271887

The Old Court, with its attractive cream and green façade and red-tiled roof and porch, was built as a court building in 1790 and still stands on the village green in this pleasant hamlet near Dudley. There is one lounge bar serving bar meals (not Sundays), a separate restaurant and a new conservatory café bar.

Beer: Banks Mild and Bitter, Burton Ale on handpumps.

Accommodation: 1 single, 1 double, 2 twins, all with en suite facilities. B&B £35 per person. Cards: Access, Amex, Diners and Visa.

LONG ITCHINGTON (WARWICKSHIRE)

Jolly Fisherman
The Green. A423, opposite village green

Licensee: Peter Hewitt
Tel: 092 681 2296

A large pub set back from the road across from the village green and pond, the Jolly Fisherman has a large public bar that sports a photo of the pub in 1903, and a comfortable lounge that stages live music on Fridays and Saturdays. A games room offers pool, Japanese 'noise boxes', darts and dominoes. Food, including bar snacks, is traditionally English in style. There is a large garden for sunny days.

Beer: Ansells Mild and Bitter and Tetley Bitter on handpumps.

Accommodation: 1 double, 2 family rooms. B&B £12.50 per person. Half and full board available. Children's room; children welcome to stay, 30% reductions according to age.

WARWICKSHIRE & WEST MIDLANDS

NETHERTON (WEST MIDLANDS)

Saltwells Inn
Saltwells Road, Quarry Bank, Brierley Hill, just off A4036

Licensees: Gill & Alan Stewart
Tel: 0384 69224

The inn is in the Saltwells woods and nature reserve in the heart of the Black Country. It has a smart 1930s appearance from the outside, with tall chimneys placed unusually either side of the main entrance. The interior has been extensively redecorated in 'modern Tudor', with ceiling beams and many old photos and advertising prints on the walls. The Stewarts offer a genuinely hospitable welcome and good food at reasonable prices: there is bar food lunchtime and evening – steaks, scampi, plaice, steak and kidney pie, burgers, a daily special, sandwiches, salads, pizzas and pasties, plus a children's menu – and Sunday lunch. The large garden is surrounded by trees, has a children's amusement area and is floodlit at night. There is a large family room with camera link, and all the guest rooms have colour TVs and tea and coffee making equipment.

Beer: Banks Mild and Bitter and Hansons Mild on electric pumps.

Accommodation: 5 singles, 5 doubles, 1 family room, 6 with en suite facilities. B&B £15 single, £17.25 en suite, £28 double, £32.20 en suite. Cards: Access and Visa.

WALL HEATH (WEST MIDLANDS)

Prince Albert Hotel
High Street, on A449 at village crossroads

Licensee: Ronald Lappage
Tel: 0384 287411

The Prince Albert is a sizeable turn-of-the-century mock Tudor pub in the centre of an urban village at the edge of the Black Country and close to the Staffordshire countryside and Broadfield House glass museum. The hotel has good hot lunchtime bar meals every day (evening meals by arrangement), a public and lounge bars, and traditional games.

Beer: Hansons Mild and Banks Bitter on electric pumps.

Accommodation: 3 singles, 2 doubles, 1 family room. B&B £14 per person.

WARWICK

Black Horse Inn
62–64 Saltisford, A41 Birmingham–Warwick road

Licensee: Simon Moore
Tel: 0926 492200

The Black Horse is a delightful 17th-century inn with mullioned windows, dormers in the eaves and a striking pub sign. Inside there are two cheerful and comfortable bars. Bar food includes soup, jacket potatoes with a choice of fillings, king-size Yorkshire puddings with fillings ranging from chicken and mushroom to beef and Guinness and sausage, plaice, cod and seafood platter, pie of the day, burgers, spaghetti bolognese, ravioli, tortelloni and lasagne, salads, sandwiches, ploughman's, ratatouille au gratin

WARWICKSHIRE & WEST MIDLANDS

and vegetable lasagne, and, for children, sausage, burgers, fish fingers and chicken nuggets.

Beer: Courage Directors Bitter, Marston Pedigree Bitter, Wadworth 6X and a house beer, Blackhorse Bitter, on handpumps.

Accommodation: 2 singles, 2 twins, 2 doubles, 1 family room. B&B £13.50 single, £27 double/twin. Children's room. Children welcome to stay. Special rates for long stays. Cards: Access, Amex, Diners and Visa.

Wheatsheaf Hotel
54 West Street, near town centre, A429

Licensees: Keith & Rachel Hinton
Tel: 0926 492817

The Wheatsheaf, near the centre of this fascinating and historic town with its castle, doll museum and medieval Shire Hall, has a most attractive three-storey exterior with white-painted brickwork and striped awnings. Keith Hinton, a self-confessed 'amiable nutter', and his wife run a small dining room that serves lunch, dinner and a traditional Sunday roast, and a lounge bar where darts and dominoes are played. The delightful guest rooms all have central heating, colour TVs and tea and coffee making facilities. One room has a four-poster bed.

Beer: Ansells Bitter, Burton Ale, Gibbs Mew Wiltshire Bitter, Tetley Bitter on handpumps.

Accommodation: 2 singles, 6 doubles, 3 family rooms, including 1 four-poster room with shower. B&B £20 single, £30 double, £38 family room, £34 four-poster. 10% discount for weekly stay. Children welcome, 10% reduction under 12 years. Cards: Access, Amex, Diners and Visa.

WOLVERHAMPTON (WEST MIDLANDS)

New Inn
Salop Street, near ring road

Licensee: Michael Maher
Tel: 0902 23779

The New Inn is a cheerful market pub which had an all-day market licence before the law changed and all pubs had the opportunity to open in the afternoons. In fact, the New Inn opens at 10am, not 11, and provides a *four-course* breakfast! Cooked lunches are served, and rolls and sandwiches are available at all times. It is a good base for visiting the Black Country, Audley, Lichfield, Cannock Chase and Birmingham. The guest rooms are served by three bathrooms and each room has colour TV and tea and coffee making facilities.

Beer: Banks Mild and Bitter on electric pumps.

Accommodation: 2 singles, 2 doubles, 2 family rooms. B&B £12.50 per person. Children welcome, rates depend on age. Pets welcome.

Wheatsheaf Hotel
Market Street, town centre

Licensee: Brian Hall
Tel: 0902 24446

A pub in the busy town centre, near the bus and rail stations, the Wheatsheaf, with its public and lounge bars and a beer garden, gets full at weekends but is quiet at other times. There is a residents' TV lounge and morning tea or coffee are brought to the guest rooms. Breakfast is the only meal provided but there are many inexpensive restaurants close by.

Beer: Banks Mild and Bitter on electric pumps.

Accommodation: 7 singles, 3 twins. B&B £14 per person. Children welcome to stay, no reductions.

WILTSHIRE

AMESBURY

Antrobus Arms
15 Church Street, ½ mile off A303

Licensee: Mrs P B Stammers
Tel: 0980 623163

The Antrobus Arms is in the heart of Salisbury Plain, close to Stonehenge. The pub is beautifully furnished with fine antiques, the bar has a cheerful, friendly atmosphere and the restaurant has a deserved reputation for quality cooking. In the garden is a cedar tree that is more than 400 years old and a Victorian pond and fountain. The guest rooms have colour TVs, phones and tea and coffee making facilities.

Beer: Bass, Wadworth Devizes Bitter and 6X on handpumps.

Accommodation: 8 singles, 12 doubles, 1 family room, 11 rooms with private bath. B&B £25 single, £30 with bath, £48 double, £50 with bath. Children welcome, charged £10 for additional bed in room.

BARFORD ST MARTIN

Green Dragon
Junction of B3089 and A30, 6 miles west of Salisbury

Tel: 0722 742242

Licensees were changing as the guide went to press – but that is the only alteration at the Green Dragon with its traditional oak-panelled bar warmed by a log fire in winter, and a games bar where darts, dominoes, shove ha'penny and pool are played. There is a play area for children. Meals are served in both bars and include soup, ploughman's and hot dishes of the day. The guest rooms are in a separate wing of the building, giving residents access at all times. The rooms have tea and coffee making facilities.

Beer: Hall & Woodhouse Badger Best Bitter and Tanglefoot on handpumps, and a weekly guest beer.

Accommodation: 1 single, 3 doubles, 1 family room. B&B £12.50 per person. Children welcome, one-third reduction.

BROAD HINTON

Crown Inn
Village centre, off A4631. At Swindon take the Devizes road; there are 3 turnings marked for Broad Hinton

Licensee: Bob Tidey
Tel: 0793 731302

The Crown is a 19th-century inn in a village at the foot of the Ridgeway Hills and close to Avebury and the historic town of Marlborough. A full range of bar food is served every day, lunchtime and evening, and there is a separate 30-seater restaurant (closed Monday evenings). Children have a play area.

Beer: Arkell Bitter, BBB and Kingsdown Ale on handpumps.

Accommodation: 2 doubles, 1 en suite. B&B £25-£35. Weekend: 2 nights for the price of 1. Cards: Access and Visa.

BURTON

Plume of Feathers
B4039, off A46 and M4 exits 17 and 18

Licensees: June & Peter Bolin
Tel: 045421 251

The Plume is a splendid 400-year-old listed building between Chippenham and Chipping Sodbury and close to Castle Combe and Badminton. The pub has a resident ghost, allegedly a young woman but, according to Mr Bolin, acts more like a young man 'with a racy sense of humour'. The Bolins offer a vast range of hot and cold food, bar snacks and full meals, seven days a week, supported by good ale and some fine Antipodean wines. Just a glimpse at the formidable menu finds mushrooms sautéed in port and cream, halibut baked with anchovies and sloes, homemade steak and kidney pie, lamb mènèhould, pork Normandy, moussaka, three types of lasagne and a selection of vegetarian dishes. Twenty years of living in the Far East are reflected in an extensive Oriental menu featuring curries, Chinese dishes and, during the winter months, a Sunday lunch of Indonesian rijsttafel (rice table) – four meat curries and three vegetable ones – and 30 other dishes selected from every country in SE Asia, and served buffet style in the Indonesian manner.

Beer: Marston Pedigree Bitter and Usher Best Bitter on handpumps.

Accommodation: 2 doubles, both en suite. B&B £25 single, £35 double.

DOWNTON

Kings Arms
9 High Street, B3080, 1 mile off A338

Licensees: Colin & Yvonne Ludswell
Tel: 0725 20446

The Kings Arms is a lively village pub near Salisbury and the New Forest. Parts of the building date back to the 14th century and there are beams and open fires. Darts and pool are played indoors while boules brings a Gallic influence to the large garden. Fishing is available on the Hampshire Avon and Stour rivers. The Kings Arms enjoys a reputation for its splendid home-cooked bar snacks and full meals.

Beer: Gibbs Mew Salisbury Bitter and Wiltshire Bitter on handpumps.

Accommodation: 2 doubles, 1 family room. B&B £11.50 per person. Children welcome, one-third reductions.

EVERLEIGH

Crown Inn
A342 between Andover and Devizes

Licensee: Jacki Chapman
Tel: 026485 223/229

New owners, who also run the Hatchet Inn at Lower Chute, have carried out extensive renovations to bring out the best features of this fine 17th-century dower house standing in extensive walled gardens. The inn now incorporates a 50-cover restaurant reached from the bar by a magnificent chandeliered mahogany staircase. Restaurant and bar meals are made only from fresh local produce; food in the bar includes the chef's locally renowned cheese herbies, kidneys in sherry, smoked chicken toasties, and a ploughman's lunch with a wide choice of cheese and bread baked on the premises. The restaurant menu may offer roast rack of lamb with port and redcurrant sauce, sirloin of pork with mushrooms and tarragon, beef wellington, grilled turbot, or homemade hot game pie. Menus change daily and there is always a vegetarian choice. Children over five are welcome to eat in the restaurant. A garden room, seating 30, is available for meetings, business functions and private parties. The beer is stored in a deep cellar, too far to pull by manual beer engine, which explains the electric pumps, rare in the area.

Beer: Bass John Smiths Bitter and Wadworth 6X on electric pumps.

Accommodation: 1 single, 1 double, 1 twin (all en suite). B&B from £30 per person. (Extra rooms will be available from 1990.)

FONTHILL GIFFORD

Beckford Arms
2 miles off A303, 1 mile off B3089 near Tisbury

Licensee: Peter Harrison
Tel: 0747 870385

The Beckford Arms is a rural 18th-century inn on a crossroads between the villages of Hindon and Tisbury in the middle of the former Beckford's Fonthill estate. The pub has a large garden and there are lakeside and woodlands walks to enjoy. The two bars, both with log fires and high ceilings, are linked by the stillage where the beer is drawn straight from wooden casks. Food includes sandwiches, homemade soup, ploughman's, home-cooked smoked ham and pâté. No chips are served. Mr Harrison, who took over in the autumn of 1989, is planning extensive improvements to the accommodation.

Beer: Courage Best Bitter and Directors Bitter, Wadworth 6X and Old Timer (winter) straight from the cask, and a regular guest beer.

Accommodation: 7 rooms, 5 en suite. Provisional 1990 tariff £30 single, £15-£23 double; please check when booking. Children welcome, one-third reductions.

FOVANT

Cross Keys
On A30

Licensee: Pauline Story
Tel: 0722 270 284

This fascinating old coaching inn, built in 1485, nestles in the village beneath the Fovant Badges carved on a ridge of hills and depicting the emblems of British and ANZAC regiments in the First World War. The Cross Keys, once a haunt of highwaymen, is homely and welcoming, but people of average height and above have to watch their heads to avoid contact with the low beams. The inn is a warren of nooks and crannies, has old open fires, a garden, camping facilities and splendid bar food served both lunchtime and evening.

Beer: Hook Norton Best Bitter and Wadworth 6X on handpumps.

Accommodation: 1 single, 2 doubles, 1 family room. B&B £10–£15 per person. Cards: Access and Visa.

HIGHWORTH

Saracen's Head Hotel
Market Place, north on A361 from Swindon; off M4 junction 15

Licensee: R Bennett
Tel: 0793 762064/762284

The Saracen's Head is an old coaching inn in the centre of Highworth. It has a comfortable lounge bar (no torn jeans, singlets or sleeveless shirts here, says the landlord) and a dining room. Bar food is served lunchtime and evening while the restaurant is open Monday to Saturday evenings. The hotel is a good base for visiting Lechlade, the Cotswolds and Cheltenham and Newbury races.

Beer: Arkell Bitter and BBB on handpumps.

Accommodation: 5 singles, 7 doubles/twins, 2 family rooms, all en suite. B&B £35 single, £47 double/twin, £51 family room. Pets by prior arrangement. Cards: Diners and Visa.

HINDON

Grosvenor Arms
High Street, B3089

Licensees: Angela & Danny Caulfield
Tel: 074 789 253

The Grosvenor is an old coaching inn that once stood on the London to Exeter road. The Caulfields are new licensees and spent their first year overhauling and sensitively renovating the 390-year-old building. The interior has been opened up and the one bar has striped wallpaper and some original brick walls, a collection of old sewing machines and pictures, books and magazines. There are singsongs round the pub piano on Sunday evenings. Mr Caulfield learnt his catering in the Merchant Navy and with J Lyons and uses fresh ingredients and avoids the microwave. Food, lunchtime and evening, includes daily vegetarian dishes, homemade trout pâté, homemade pasta, including lasagne and canelloni, fresh mackerel, steak and kidney pie, and rack of lamb. There is a Sunday roast lunch, too. Hindon is steeped in history: the Agricultural Riots broke out here in 1830 and, earlier, in 1754, the Great Fire of Hindon wiped out many of the village's 13 ale houses.

Beer: Fullers London Pride, Usher Best Bitter, Wadworth 6X and Websters Yorkshire Bitter on handpumps, and regular guest beers.

Accommodation: 1 double, 1 family room. B&B £15 per person. Cards: Visa.

PORTON

Porton Hotel
1 mile north of A30, ½ mile south of A338

Licensees: David & Jeanette Canale
Tel: 0980 610203

The Porton is an Edwardian railway hotel on high ground in a village five miles from Salisbury. The trains no longer stop there but the London to Exeter line runs nearby. The hotel has a comfortable lounge bar with a small restaurant, and there are pub games in the bar. Hot meals are available lunchtime and evening and include soup and steaks, homemade steak, mushroom and Guinness pie, Yorkshire pudding sandwich, and homemade lasagne. The Porton is a good base for Stonehenge and the New Forest, while Finsbury Rings, an ancient earth site, is five miles away. The hotel's guest rooms have colour TVs and direct-dial phones, and there is a large beer garden for summer weather.

Beer: Gibbs Mew Wiltshire Bitter, Salisbury Best Bitter and Bishop's Tipple (winter) from the cask.

Accommodation: 2 singles, 6 doubles. B&B £14 single, £12 double per person. Weekend £28, Week £98. Children welcome, no reductions. Cards: Access and Visa.

SALISBURY

Old Mill Hotel
Town Path, West Harnham, just off A3094

Licensee: Jerry Such
Tel: 0722 27517

The Old Mill is a breathtakingly ancient building dating back to 1135 and built from brick, flint and stone. It spans the River Nadder across the water meadows from the great cathedral. The mill was used to store church documents when the cathedral was being moved from Old to New Sarum and has also served as a monks' hospice and a leper hospital. It became a water mill in the 16th century and was in working use until 1931. It became a restaurant in 1983, and its low-beamed interior offers traditional English cooking, including game in season, mussels, seafood pancake, soups, local trout, poached halibut, wild duck, guinea fowl, fillet of beef and a daily vegetarian dish. Lunch and dinner, morning coffee and tea are served but in winter the restaurant is closed Sunday evenings and all day Monday. The hotel section was originally a store house for the mill and was divided into accommodation early in this century. The building includes a residents' TV lounge and a small ground-floor bar, open all year round, popular with locals.

Beer: Palmer IPA, Wadworth 6X and Old Timer (winter) on handpumps and straight from the cask.

Accommodation: *1 April–30 Nov only*. 2 singles, 4 doubles/twins, 1 en suite family room. B&B from £16.50 per person. Reductions for weekly stays. Cards: Access, Amex, Diners and Visa.

Red Lion Hotel
Milford Street

Proprietor: Michael Maidment
Tel: 0722 23334

The Red Lion is a superb 13th-century inn rooted in the history of this magnificent cathedral city. It became an extended coaching inn in the heyday of horse-drawn road travel but its earlier origins are evident from the wealth of exposed beams and wattle-and-daub, with hand-painted medieval plasterwork and brass and copper decorations. Among the many antiques is a remarkable skeleton organ clock in which the skeletal figures ring the hours: it is thought to have been carved by Spaniards taken prisoner after the defeat of the Armada in 1588. The half-timbered exterior is partially covered by a fine Virginia creeper. The dining room specializes in traditional English cooking and includes venison and jugged hare in season, local trout and roast beef.

Sumptuous accommodation includes several four-poster bedrooms.

Beer: Bass, Hook Norton Best Bitter, Ruddles County, Usher Best Bitter and Wadworth 6X and guest beers on handpumps.

Accommodation: 10 singles, 45 doubles, 4 family rooms, all en suite. B&B £50 single, £70 double, £80 four-poster, £80 family room. Spring & Summer Breaks including lunch or dinner: rates on application. Cards: Access, Amex, Diners and Visa.

TISBURY

South Western Hotel
Station Road, off A30 and A303

Licensee: Mrs P V Evans
Tel: 0747 870160

A large and imposing pub, the South Western is the 'brewery tap' for the Wiltshire Brewery, which is just 200 yards away. The hotel has one L-shaped bar and a small games area where darts, crib and bar billiards are played. A small dining room seats 20. Bar food includes soup, homemade pâté, grills, curries, chilli, burgers and vegetarian dishes. The restaurant offers grills, vegetarian dishes, trout and curries. The hotel has been recently refurbished, the guest rooms all have tea and coffee making facilities and a function room is available for hire.

Beer: Wiltshire Stonehenge Best Bitter, Olde Grumble Bitter, Old Devil Strong Ale, Ma Pardoe's Mild plus regular guest beers, all on handpumps.

Accommodation: 1 double, 4 twins, 1 with private shower. B&B £14 per person. Weekend £32.50, Week £70. Off-season Weekend £10 per night. Children welcome, half price under 5.

WHITEPARISH

Fountain Inn
The Street, A27 between Romsey and Salisbury

Licensee: Carol Pulpitt
Tel: 0794 884266

The Fountain is a cheerful, 300-year-old inn with beamed bars and dining room, and open fires. Locals mix happily with visitors. Mid-week breaks include excursions to historic buildings and places of interest in the locality, among them Salisbury, the New Forest, and Romsey where Broadlands, the Mountbatten family home, lies.

Beer: Wiltshire Stonehenge Best Bitter, Olde Grumble Bitter and Old Devil Strong Ale on handpumps and Wiltshire's real, alcoholic ginger beer.

Accommodation: 1 single, 2 twins, 3 doubles, all en suite. B&B £20 per person. Children by arrangement. Dogs welcome.

WROUGHTON

Fox & Hounds
1 Markham Road, on A361 Swindon to Devizes road

Licensee: Eddie Adams
Tel: 0793 812217

The Fox & Hounds was originally a thatched farm cottage and was granted a licence to brew and sell beer in the mid-1700s. It was rebuilt in the 1860s following a fire, and was left virtually unchanged until 1984 when it was extensively altered and refurbished, while, however, retaining the old cottage atmosphere. In 1989 a motel was opened next to the pub. The pub has a log fire in winter and a pleasant beer garden in summer. The motel rooms all have en suite facilities, colour TVs, phones and tea and coffee making equipment. Pub food, available lunchtime and evening every day, includes sandwiches, burgers, steaks, grills, trout, seafood platter, salads, pizzas and a daily special. Wroughton is a good base for visiting the Ridgeway, Marlborough, Cirencester, Avebury and the Cotswolds.

Beer: Arkell Bitter, BBB and Kingsdown Ale on handpumps.

Accommodation: 4 singles, 4 doubles/twins. Room £17.50 single, £37.50 double/twin. Full English breakfast £3.50. Cards: Access, Amex and Visa.

WYLYE

Bell Inn
High Street, junction of A306 and A36, midway between Salisbury and Warminster

Licensees: Steve & Anne Locke
Tel: 09856 338

A delightful coaching inn built in 1373 the Bell has a superb location in the centre of the village, next to a 14th-century church. The inn has a large inglenook fireplace, low beams and a warm and cosy atmosphere. There is a walled garden at the rear overlooking the church, and a patio garden to the side. Food is available lunchtime and evening, and includes homemade pâté and steak and kidney pie, prawn fritters, spare ribs, gammon steak, jambalaya, steak au poivre, vegetarian dishes, jam or treacle roly-poly and bread-and-butter pudding. It is a good base for visiting Stonehenge and Salisbury; there are lovely walks along the River Wylye and fishing can be arranged in local trout lakes.

WILTSHIRE

Beer: Wadworth IPA and 6X and a weekly guest beer on handpumps.

Accommodation: 2 singles, 4 doubles/twins. (2 rooms will have en suite facilities by summer 1990.) B&B £17 single, £30 double, £35 en suite. Children sharing half price. Pets welcome.

YORKSHIRE

ABERFORD (W YORKS)

Swan Hotel
Centre of village on old A1

Licensees: Otto & Ann Kreft
Tel: 0532 813205

The Swan is a former coaching inn on the Great North Road in an attractive village now by-passed by the new A1. The hotel has some interesting outbuildings that date back to coaching days, while inside the main building there are two bars linked together, a games room and a separate restaurant. Bar meals and full meals are served lunchtime and evening. The guest rooms all have colour TVs and tea and coffee making facilities, and the double rooms have their own showers. The Swan has a pleasant garden to enjoy in good weather, and is a good base for visiting such interesting local places as Hazlewood Castle.

Beer: Whitbread Trophy and Castle Eden Ale on handpumps.

Accommodation: 2 singles, 4 doubles. B&B £15 per person. Cards: Access, Amex and Visa.

YORKSHIRE

APPLETREEWICK (N YORKS)

New Inn
2 miles off B6160 at Barden Tower or Burnsall (OS 051601)

Licensee: John Pitchers
Tel: 075 672 252

The New Inn is a cheering sight from the riverside Dales Way footpath. It stands at the foot of the village street in an area of great historic and scenic beauty. The welcoming inn received fame and notoriety under its previous owner who banned smoking and decorated the place with warnings against the Evil Weed. Mr Pitchers has a more even-handed approach, supplying both ash trays and air purifiers. The inn is a fine Dales pub with horseshoe chairs and benches outside to enjoy the view, and Mr Pitchers wisely retains it as a genuine local not a tourist trap. As well as his good draught ale, he has a world-wide collection of bottled beers, including some bottle-conditioned Trappist monastery brews from Belgium. There is good lunchtime bar food. Appletreewick and its environs are packed with interest: the Earls of Craven supplied a Lord Mayor of London in 1610, Mock Beggar Hall was a shelter for the homeless, while Percival Hall dates back to Tudor times.

Beer: John Smiths Bitter, Younger Scotch Bitter and No 3 on handpumps, and Franklin Farmhouse cider.

Accommodation: 1 single, 3 doubles. B&B £18 per person single night; more than 1 night £16.50.

BOROUGHBRIDGE (N YORKS)

Three Horseshoes Hotel
Bridge Street, off A1

Proprietors: R S & B S Porter
Tel: 0423 322314

The Three Horseshoes is an impressive hotel rebuilt between the wars and retaining a homely, 1930s flavour. The lounge has an unusual tiled fireplace and a wealth of wood panels and leaded glass. There is a basic public bar, separate dining room and a lounge. Boroughbridge is an historic market town on the old A1, from where you may take leisurely boating trips on the River Ure, or visit the stately home of Newby Hall.

Beer: Vaux Samson on electric pump.

Accommodation: 5 singles, 5 doubles/twins, 2 family rooms, 6 rooms with private baths. B&B £16.50 per person. Children welcome, terms according to age. Limited facilities for the disabled; easy access to pub.

BRADFORD (W YORKS)

Victoria
Bridge Street, opposite transport interchange

Licensee: John Wilkinson
Tel: 0274 728706

A three-star hotel in the city centre, the Victoria is well placed for Bradford's growing tourist industry. It is an imposing stone building dating from 1880 and was originally named the Great Northern Hotel when it stood opposite the now defunct Exchange railway station.

The Victoria has a quiet residents' lounge, meals lunchtime and evening, and colour TVs and tea and coffee making facilities in all the guest rooms. Bradford's Barber Shop Singers regularly sing for their suppers in the plush public bar. The Victoria is next door to St George's Hall, which holds concerts and many other events, and is close to the National Museum of Photography, Film and Television, and the revamped Alhambra theatre.

Beer: John Smiths Magnet and Tetley Bitter on handpumps.

Accommodation: 29 singles, 30 doubles (doubles can be converted to family rooms), all rooms with private baths. B&B £67 per person midweek. Weekend £34 per night (minimum 2 nights stay), Week from £200. Children welcome, terms negotiable. Cards: Access, Amex, Diners and Visa.

West Leigh Hotel
30 Easby Road. A647 towards Halifax, ½ mile from city centre

Licensee: John Jowett
Tel: 0274 727089

The West Leigh is a spacious and comfortable pub that was once three separate Victorian houses. It has a cheerful, comfortable bar with a pool table, a separate residents' lounge, and a wide selection of bar meals. The guest rooms have colour TVs, phones, tea and coffee making facilities and central heating. The hotel is handy for the city centre, the university, the Alhambra theatre, Bradford's famous curry houses and pubs and is just a short journey to Haworth with its Brontë connections and steam railway centre.

Beer: McEwan 80 shilling, Younger Scotch Bitter and No 3 on handpumps.

Accommodation: 11 singles, 11 twins, 8 doubles, 2 family rooms, 9 rooms with private baths. B&B £20 single, £35 twin/double, £5 extra for bath. Children welcome, terms by agreement. Dogs allowed.

DALTON (N YORKS)

Jolly Farmers of Olden Times
Off A168, A19 and A1, 4 miles south of Thirsk

Licensees: Norman & Patricia Clark
Tel: 0845 577359

This much-loved small country inn is far and away the favourite pub in the guide: letters regularly praise the welcome, the food, the ale: it is as near as you are likely to get to the Perfect Pub. It is 200 years old with some of the original beams and a welcoming coal fire, in the heart of Herriot country and with the white horse cut in the chalk of the Hambleton Hills visible from the village. The Clarks are enthusiasts – for the pub, for real ale (they are CAMRA members) and for organizing rambles and long walks in the dales and on the moors. The inn offers a games room, bar and lounge, a fine garden with trees, and a welcome for families. Local produce is used for bar meals and the restaurant. Food in the bar includes steaks, chops, gammon, haddock, trout, and vegetarian dishes. Meals in the restaurant (lunch and dinner: advance booking essential) offer soup, ham cooked in wine, mushroom and cheese sauce, casserole supreme, and curried lamb. There is a traditional Sunday roast lunch, too – good value at £4.95 per person, 1990 price.

Beer: Websters Yorkshire Bitter and Choice on handpumps, with regular guest beers.

Accommodation: 1 double, 1 family room. B&B £13 per person, £12 for more than 1 night. Weekend £24, Week £84. Children and pets welcome. 6-berth residential caravan also for hire.

DANBY (N YORKS)

Duke of Wellington
Centre of village, 2 miles off A171 Whitby to Guisborough road; the village is a stop on the Esk Valley railway

Licensee: Anthony J Howat
Tel: 0287 60351

The Duke of Wellington is an 18th-century coaching inn and the Iron Duke is believed to have used the building as a recruiting centre to raise a local regiment before the battle of Waterloo. The bars are cheerful and friendly with low beamed ceilings; the public bar is popular with locals who play darts, cards and dominoes. The homemade food (lunchtime and evening) includes an enormous mixed grill, kebabs, Whitby fresh fish, soup, omelettes, salads and ploughman's, and several vegetarian dishes. Children have their own menu. The guest rooms all have colour TVs and tea and coffee making facilities. A tranquil village in the heart of the North Yorkshire Moors national park, Danby's Moors Centre was once the home of Canon Atkinson, author of the classic *Forty Years in a Moorland Village*. There is a 12th-century castle, and trout fishing is available close by.

Beer: Cameron Traditional Bitter and Strongarm on electric and handpumps.

Accommodation: 1 single, 2 doubles, 2 family rooms (double and single beds in each room), 2 rooms en suite. B&B £12.50 single, £14 per person in double, £13 in family room. £1 extra for en suite rooms. Children under 10 half price. 2 nights or more B&B + dinner from £18 per person per night. Details of autumn and winter breaks on application. Pets welcome. Extra rooms are being added. Cards: Access and Visa.

EASINGWOLD (N YORKS)

George Hotel
Market Square, off A19 York–Thirsk road

Licensees: Chris Simpson & Judy Stephens
Tel: 0347 21698

The George is an 18th-century coaching inn in a cobbled market square, with handsome white-painted bow windows and porch, and shutters on the top storey. It has all modern amenities such as central heating, colour TVs and tea and coffee making facilities in the charming guest rooms, but retains its old charm with beams, open fires and wood panelling in the bar and candle-lit dining room. Lunchtime bar snacks include homemade steak and kidney pie, ham, chicken and mushroom pie, sandwiches and salads. The dining room offers an extensive à la carte menu in the evenings. The hotel is a splendid base for visiting York, the east coast and the moors. An 18-hole golf course is close at hand.

Beer: McEwan 80 shilling, Theakston XB and Old Peculier, Younger Scotch Bitter and IPA on handpumps.

Accommodation: 12 doubles, 2 family rooms, all en suite. B&B from £19.50. Off-season weekend rates on request. Children welcome. Facilities for the disabled. Cards: Access, Amex, Diners and Visa.

GRASSINGTON (N YORKS)

Foresters Arms
Main Street, near Skipton, off A65

Licensee: W A Chaney
Tel: 0756 752349

The Foresters is a superb, welcoming pub in a lovely old Wharfedale village with a cobbled square. The lively bar offers darts, dominoes and pool and the contented chatter of the village locals. Bar and restaurant food includes homemade soup and steak and mushroom pie, grills, home-cooked ham and pork, haddock, plaice and scampi, ploughman's, and a choice of sweets. The pub has a residents' TV lounge, and the guest rooms have tea and coffee making facilities and hot and cold water. Satisfied visitors single out the 'terrific' breakfasts for particular praise.

Beer: Tetley Mild and Bitter on handpumps.

Accommodation: 1 single, 5 doubles, 2 family rooms. B&B £12 per person. Off-season Weekend £35. Children's room; children welcome to stay.

HAWORTH (W YORKS)

Brontë Hotel
Lees Lane, near junction with A6033

Licensees: Geoff & Sheila Briggs
Tel: 0535 44112/46725

The hotel was built eight years ago in the village heavy with Brontë connections. It is a mile from the Brontë parsonage (now a museum) where Anne, Charlotte and Emily wrote, despite their genteel surroundings, novels of great power and passion such as *Wuthering Heights* and *Jane Eyre*. The hotel, with two comfortably furnished lounge bars, has all the amenities of a modern hotel, with meals lunchtime and evening. It is also a handy base for visiting the moors and the Keighley and Worth Valley Light Railway (Haworth station).

Beer: Tetley Bitter and Younger Scotch Bitter on handpumps.

Accommodation: 3 singles, 5 doubles, 3 rooms with en suite facilities. B&B £15–£25 per person. Half and full board available. Cards: Access and Visa.

HELMSLEY (N YORKS)

Crown Hotel
Market Square, off A170

Licensees: Mr & Mrs B J Mander and Mrs M Hutchinson
Tel: 0439 70297

The Crown is a 16th-century coaching inn that dominates one side of the square of this picturesque old market town with its eerie and awesome castle ruins, fine parish church, a miniature Albert Memorial and, nearby, the ruins of the great monastery of Rievaulx. The hotel has a small bar with darts, and a cosy lounge bar with a blazing imitation log fire and comfortable bench seats. The pleasant Jacobean restaurant serves lunch, high tea and dinner (last orders 8pm), using traditional English cooking and fresh local produce. Some of the guest rooms in this listed building have exposed beams, and all have colour TVs, phones and tea and coffee making equipment. There are residents' lounges.

Beer: Cameron Best Bitter and Strongarm on electric pumps.

Accommodation: 6 singles, 7 doubles/twins, 2 family rooms, 14 rooms en suite. Two ground floor rooms permit dogs. B&B £25 per person. Half and full board available. Winter Break: £63.50 per person 2 nights B&B and dinner. Children welcome, child in cot charged only for meals; if in separate bed in parents' room, £2 per day plus meals. Cards: Access and Visa.

HEPTONSTALL (W YORKS)

Cross Inn
Towngate, 1 mile off A646, near Hebden Bridge

Licensees: Gerald & Joan Fisher
Tel: 0422 843833

The Cross is a welcoming 17th-century inn built on the site of a previous licensed building, and with a later Victorian frontage. Morning coffee, lunches and evening meals are available. The Cross stands in the main street of a picturesque and historic hill-top village overlooking Hebden Bridge and set in wonderful Pennine scenery.

Beer: Timothy Taylor Golden Best, Best Bitter and Landlord on handpumps.

Accommodation: 1 twin, 1 double. B&B £14 per person. Children welcome, terms according to age.

HUBBERHOLME (N YORKS)

George
Off A684, 1 mile from Buckden on Hawes road (OS 926782)

Licensees: John Frederick & Marjorie Forster
Tel: 075 676 223

There are many claims to the title, but the George is probably *the* Dales pub. It dates backs to at least the 18th century, was once the village vicarage, and has stone-flagged floors, low beams, mullioned windows and antique furniture. There are blazing fires in winter, and on New Year's Day the local parliament of 'House of Lords' (vicar and churchwarden) and 'House of Commons' (local farmers) negotiate the letting of nearby pasture land in aid of poorer parishioners. The George has a separate restaurant, while bar meals include French bread with a choice of fillings, ploughman's, pâté and hot dishes of the day such as steak and kidney pie. There are a few outside seats with stunning views of the moors rising all around. The village is named after the Viking Hubba who settled there, and remains an attractive huddle of church, bridge and inn with a few scattered farms and cottages. The road through the hamlet is the highest in Yorkshire, reaching 1,934 feet on its way to Hawes.

Beer: Younger Scotch Bitter and No 3 on handpumps.

YORKSHIRE

Accommodation: 5 doubles/twins. B&B £16 per person. Week £98. Children over 8 welcome, no reductions.

HUGGATE (N YORKS)

Wolds Inn
Driffield Road, signposted from A166 York to Driffield road

Licensees: Norris & Lynda Binner
Tel: 0377 88217

The inn dates back to the 16th century, and has a wood-panelled lounge and dining room, open fires and brasswork. The bar is popular with locals as well as ramblers and walkers. Bar and restaurant meals are available lunchtime and evening, walkers can get snacks at all times, and there is a roast lunch on Sundays. The inn is the highest pub on the Wolds, and the village is the heart of the local farming community, with one of the deepest wells in England and a fine church.

Beer: Cameron Traditional Bitter and Tolly Bitter on handpump.

Accommodation: 5 doubles/twins, 1 family room, all en suite. B&B £18 single occupancy, £14 per person sharing. Children half price; babies small charge for cot. Pets welcome.

JACKSON BRIDGE (W YORKS)

Red Lion
Sheffield Road, A616

Licensee: Mrs J Oscroft
Tel: 0484 683499

This is *Last of the Summer Wine* territory, near Holmfirth, and the success of the TV series draws visitors but cannot detract from the outstanding and unspoilt character of the countryside and its small towns and villages. The Red Lion is a delightful old inn with a cosy bar and open fire and beer garden. Home-cooked food is served lunchtime (not Sunday) and Monday to Friday evenings. The guest rooms all have colour TVs and tea and coffee making facilities. There is also a ghost named Chippy Brook, a former landlord of the inn.

Beer: Marston Pedigree, Tetley Mild and Bitter on handpumps and guest beers straight from the cask in winter.

Accommodation: 2 twins, 4 doubles, 3 en suite. B&B £18 single, £20 en suite, £28 double, £32 en suite.

White Horse
Scholes Road, off A616 3 miles from Holmfirth

Licensee: Ron Backhouse
Tel: 0484 683940

This is the heart of the *Summer Wine* saga, for this splendid old stone-built Yorkshire pub features prominently in the series and is adorned with a multitude of TV memorabilia. But it retains its character – and its genuine local characters, too. The pub is popular with walkers and offers open fires in winter, a large and attractive garden, a games room with darts and dominoes, and pub food lunchtime and evening. The guest rooms have central heating, TVs, radios and tea and coffee making facilities.

Beer: Stones Best Bitter on handpump.

Accommodation: 2 doubles, 3 family rooms, may be used a singles according to demand. B&B £14–£17 per person.

YORKSHIRE

KIRBY HILL (N YORKS)

Shoulder of Mutton
Near Richmond, 2 miles from A66 north of Scotch Corner

Licensee: Hylton Pynner
Tel: 0748 2772

The Shoulder of Mutton is a country inn in a superb hillside setting near Richmond, overlooking lower Teesdale and the ruins of Ravensworth Castle. It was built in 1800, possibly as a farmhouse, and converted to licensed premises some 50 years later. It is in a village of great antiquity, the church dating back to 1200 while the handful of cottages stem from the 15th century. The inn has two bars, traditional pub games and a separate restaurant. Bar food ranges from steak and kidney pie to gammon and steaks, local trout, lasagne and jacket potatoes with a choice of fillings. The guest rooms all have showers, colour TVs and tea and coffee making facilities.

Beer: Ruddles County, Theakston XB and Websters Choice on handpumps.

Accommodation: 5 doubles. B&B £14–£17 single, £23.50–£26 double. 3 days or more £21.50–£23.75. Half board available. Reductions for children.

LEEDS (W YORKS)

Brookfield
11 Brookfield Terrace, Hunslet Road

Licensees: Michael & Pauline Payne
Tel: 0532 451851

The Brookfield is a solidly built pub in an industrial area on a busy main road, noted for good-value food lunchtime and evening. It is a typical early 20th-century Tetley pub, built when industry was developing in the area. It is still surrounded by factories ancient and modern, and is close to the M1, the city centre and Tetley's brewery.

Beer: Tetley Mild and Bitter on handpumps.

Accommodation: 1 double with shower. B&B £15 per person. *Mid-week only; no weekend accommodation.*

MALTON (N YORKS)

Green Man Hotel
Market Street, off A64

Manager: Anne Coates
Tel: 0653 600370

The Green Man stands in a dominant position in Malton's town centre. It dates from 1862 and has retained its handsome panelled entrance hall, furnished in English oak. In winter it has a blazing log fire and in summer it is decorated with flowers. The Oak Lounge is also wood-panelled and most of the furniture was made by Robert Thompson of Kilburn, Yorkshire, whose trademark was a mouse, carved on most of his work. Bar food is served lunchtime and evening; high teas are also available and there is a separate evening restaurant. The hotel also has facilities for conferences and functions. The guest rooms are beautifully appointed, all are en suite and have colour TVs and tea and coffee making facilities. Malton is the home of a micro-brewery of the same name: its fruity and hoppy beers can be enjoyed in the Crown Hotel in Wheelgate.

Beer: Cameron Strongarm, Tetley Bitter and Younger Scotch Bitter on electric and handpumps.

Accommodation: 11 singles, 11 doubles/twins, 3 family rooms. B&B £29.50 single, £50 double/twin, £55–£60 family room. Children £5, meals extra. Any 2 nights £35 per person per night B&B + dinner. Children's room. Pets welcome. Cards: Access, Amex, Diners and Visa.

MASHAM (N YORKS)

Kings Head Hotel
Market Place, A6108 near Ripon

Licensee: Colin Jones
Tel: 0765 89295

The Kings Head is a stately, three-storey stone coaching inn built in 1685 in the home town of Theakston's brewery. The hotel has a large marble fireplace, cast-iron tables, a profusion of plants, and a shelf with pottery figures. Excellent lunchtime bar meals include soup, sandwiches, smoked meat platter, Old Peculier casserole, and fresh local trout. The evening restaurant has a full à la carte menu. There are a few seats in a courtyard in fine weather. Masham is a fine base for visiting the dales, while Theakston's brewery has a visitors' centre, open May to October, which offers a visit to the cooper's shop and a video film of the history of the company: tours by appointment only.

Beer: Theakston Best Bitter, XB and Old Peculier on handpumps.

Accommodation: 2 singles, 7 doubles, 1 twin, all rooms en suite. B&B £29.50 single, £42.50 double/twin.

YORKSHIRE

MIDDLEHAM (N YORKS)

Black Bull Inn
East Witton Road. B6108, 2 miles from Leyburn

Licensees: Howard & Maisie Fricker
Tel: 0969 23669

The Black Bull is a small village local that serves racing folk and visitors alike. This is horse-training country and you can watch horses on their daily gallops. Middleham is in an attractive Dales location and Herriot country is nearby, along with Richard III's castle. The inn serves meals at all reasonable times.

Beer: Big End Old Lubrication, Theakston Best Bitter and Younger No 3, plus guest beers in summer, all on handpumps (Big End alternates with Younger's).

Accommodation: 1 double, 1 family room. B&B £13.50 per person, £42 for 4 in family room. Children half price under 12.

MIRFIELD (W YORKS)

Black Bull
130 Huddersfield Road, A644

Licensee: Tony Woods
Tel: 0924 493180

The Black Bull was built in 1850 as a railway hotel – it is still handy for Mirfield BR – but it has come a long way since its inception. Mr Woods runs a lively regime with a disco and cabaret, yet the pub retains some of its true local character. It has bar meals at lunchtime and restaurant meals in the evening.

Beer: Tetley Mild and Bitter on handpumps.

Accommodation: 9 rooms, 4 doubles, 3 twins, 2 family rooms. B&B £16 single, £26 double/twin, £37 family room. Discounts for long-term stays. Cards: Access, Amex and Visa.

OAKENSHAW (W YORKS)

Richardsons Arms
Bradford Road, A638, ½ mile from M62 exit 26

Licensee: Tony Maskill
Tel: 0274 675722

Richardsons is a lively pub with a strong emphasis on entertainment, and has live music on Thursday to Sunday evenings. It has a single, open-plan lounge and serves bar meals lunchtime and evening. The well-appointed guest rooms all have TVs and tea and coffee making facilities. Oakenshaw is a village that is being subsumed into Bradford's outskirts and is close to the M62 and M606.

Beer: Whitbread Trophy on handpump.

Accommodation: 5 singles, 4 doubles. B&B £12.50 per person.

OSSETT (W YORK)

Crown
20 Horbury Road, 1 mile south of town centre

Licensees: Glyn & Joan Calton
Tel: 0924 272495

The Crown is a small, traditional, stone-built pub with panelled rooms and a collection of dolls in a cabinet. Pub games include darts, dominoes and ring the bull. There are two lounge bars where lunches are served every day except Sunday: the speciality of the house are Yorkshire puddings eight inches in diameter filled with beef stew, and there are many other homemade dishes, including braised steak and onions, steak and kidney pie, chilli, sandwiches and toasties. The guest rooms are in an adjoining building with a separate entrance. Each room has colour TV and tea and coffee making facilities.

Beer: Tetley Mild and Bitter on handpumps.

Accommodation: 2 singles, 2 doubles, 1 family room. B&B £15.50 single, £25.50 double. Weekend £13.50 per person per night, Week £14.50 per night. Children welcome, charged only for meals if sharing parents' room.

OTLEY (W YORKS)

Black Horse
Westgate, town centre

Licensee: Roy Golsworthy
Tel: 0943 461047

The Black Horse is a substantial and imposing building in the heart of the small, picturesque market town. The pub is of Victorian origin with lounge and public bars, and meals lunchtime and evening (no evening meals Monday). Guest rooms have tea and coffee making facilities.

Beer: Burton Ale and Tetley Mild and Bitter on handpumps.

Accommodation: 3 singles, 5 doubles, 1 family room. B&B £12.50 per person. Half board available. Business breakfasts arranged.

YORKSHIRE

PICKERING (N YORKS)

White Swan
Market Place, A169; off A64

Owner: Kenneth C Buchanan
Tel: 0751 72288

The White Swan is a superb 16th-century coaching inn, once a staging route on the Whitby run used by salt smugglers. It has a fine stone exterior with a bowed ground-floor window and several dormers. There is a fine beamed bar where lunchtime meals are available, including traditional Yorkshire puddings served as a separate course. There is a separate restaurant with a menu based on fresh local produce. The hotel guest rooms all have en suite bathrooms and direct-dial phones. There is plenty to see and to do in the area: there is Pickering's ruined castle, a parish church with fine examples of medieval wall paintings, Castle Howard, Rievaulx Abbey and the North Yorkshire Moors railway. Facilities for golf, riding, pony-trekking and fishing are close by.

Beer: Cameron Traditional Bitter and Strongarm Premium on handpumps.

Accommodation: 12 doubles/twins. B&B £25 single occupancy, £27.50 per person sharing. Children £10 sharing. Dinner B&B minimum 4 nights £32 double, £36 single occupancy, £37 in Ryedale Suite. Dogs welcome. Cards: Access and Visa.

ROBIN HOOD'S BAY (N YORKS)

Victoria Hotel
Station Road, off A171 Whitby to Scarborough road

Licensee: R S Gibson
Tel: 0947 880205

The Victoria, as its name implies, is a turn-of-the-century hotel. It has a commanding position on the cliffs with stunning views of the bay. There is a cheerful bar where locals and visitors mingle and a large restaurant. Bar meals are served lunchtime and evening; the restaurant is open for table d'hôte and à la carte meals every night in season; Friday and Saturday the rest of the year. From the hotel you can walk down the tumbling, cobbled streets to the village and the seafront, or use the Victoria as a base for touring the heritage coast and the moors.

Beer: Cameron Traditional Bitter and Strongarm, Everard Old Original on handpumps.

Accommodation: 2 singles, 9 doubles/twins, 2 family rooms, 1 room en suite. B&B from £13–£18 per person. Children sharing: rates depend on age. Children's room. No dogs. Cards: Access and Visa.

SCARBOROUGH (N YORKS)

Black Lion
North Street, off A170 and A171

Licensee: Martyn Scutt
Tel: 0723 360774

The Black Lion is a cheerful and welcoming, family-run pub in the centre of the famous seaside resort. It has a traditional bar and a lounge.

Homemade bar meals are available at lunchtime, and evening meals are supplied on request. There is a traditional lunch on Sunday. The pub is close to the beach and Scarborough castle.

Beer: Cameron Traditional Bitter and Strongarm Premium on handpumps.

Accommodation: 1 single, four doubles/twins, 2 family rooms. B&B £10 per person. Children sharing £6, under 3 years free. Stays of 3 nights or more £8.50 per person. Children's room. Pets welcome. Cards: Visa.

SHELLEY (W YORKS)

Three Acres Inn
Roydhouse, Drinker Lane, off A637 and exit 38 of M1 (OS 216125)

Partners: Neil Truelove & Brian Orme
Tel: 0484 602606

Three Acres is a substantial country pub and restaurant beautifully situated in the rolling scenery of Emley Moor, close to the TV mast. It has spectacular views of the moors, yet is within easy reach of the motorway, Huddersfield and the Holmfirth area. It has a cheerful bar with beams and brasses, and restaurants concentrating on quality English and Continental cuisine. Lunch and dinner, including bar meals, are available every day. The inn offers facilities for families and disabled people. The splendid guest rooms all have private baths or showers, colour TVs, and tea and coffee making facilities.

Beer: Burton Ale and Tetley Mild and Bitter, Timothy Taylor Best Bitter on handpumps.

Accommodation: 7 singles, 2 twins, 6 doubles, 3 family rooms. B&B £38 single, £48 double. No charge for children sharing with parents. Weekend £40 single for 2 nights, £60 for 3, £70 double for 2 nights, £105 for 3. Half and full board available. Cards: Access, Amex and Visa.

SLAITHWAITE (W YORKS)

White House
B6107 Meltham to Marsden road, 6 miles from Huddersfield

Licensee: Gillian Sykes
Tel: 0484 842245

The White House's official address is Slaithwaite but it is actually in the tiny hamlet of Holthead near the open moors of the East Pennines. The cheerful, spacious old rural pub has retained much of its original charm, with open fires, two bars, facilities for families, bar food, and full meals in the separate restaurant. There is a traditional roast lunch on Sundays. The guest rooms all have en suite facilities and tea and coffee making equipment.

Beer: Tetley Mild and Bitter, Younger Scotch Bitter and IPA on handpumps.

Accommodation: 1 single, 4 doubles, 1 twin. B&B £20 single, £30 double, £28 for single occupancy in double room. £25 double per night at weekends. Cards: Access, Amex, Diners and Visa.

YORKSHIRE

SLEIGHTS (N YORKS)

Plough
180 Coach Road, at bottom of Blue Bank, A169 between Pickering and Whitby

Licensee: Colin Buxton
Tel: 0947 810412

The Plough is a splendid old pub with a cottage-style exterior behind a walled garden. It looks deceptively small, with a bar and lounge and a 22-seater restaurant. There are fine views over the tranquil Esk valley from the garden, and swings and other playthings keep children happy. Bar food is served lunchtime and evening. The restaurant is open in the evening and there is a Sunday lunch, too. The North Yorkshire Moors steam railway is just two miles away.

Beer: Cameron Traditional Bitter on handpump.

Accommodation: 3 doubles/twins. B&B £11 per person, £15 single occupancy. Children free under 5, £7.50 over 5. Winter Weekend: £21 per couple. No dogs.

STARBOTTON (N YORKS)

Fox & Hounds
B6160, 2 miles north of Kettlewell

Licensee: Pam Casey
Tel: 075 676 269

The Fox & Hounds is set in a lovely limestone village in Upper Wharfedale, just off the Dales Way in picturesque walking country. The stone-built pub is some 160 years old, and has a large stone fireplace, beams, flagstoned floors, with settles and other old and comfortable furniture. Lunchtime bar food includes homemade cream of lettuce soup, ploughman's, sandwiches, and a hot dish in winter. There are tables and benches outside in warm weather with stunning views of the hamlet and the hills. Mrs Casey has upgraded the guest rooms and plans to expand the restaurant area.

Beer: Theakston Best Bitter, XB and Old Peculier, Younger Scotch Bitter and guest beers in season on handpumps.

Accommodation: 1 double, 1 twin, both en suite. B&B £20 per person.

WASS (N YORKS)

Wombwell Arms
From A19 York to Thirsk road, take right turn to Coxwold and follow signs to Wass

Proprietors: Kevin & Sharon Kisby
Tel: 03476 280

The Wombwell Arms is a fine old country inn with a pub sign bearing the crest of the Wombwell family who have lived for generations at Newburgh Priory two miles away. The inn is also close to the famous Ampleforth School and the ruins of Byland abbey. A small restaurant is open for weekend evenings, and the Kisbys are well-known locally for their fine bar meals, with daily specials chalked on a board.

Beer: Cameron Traditional Bitter and Strongarm Premium on electric and handpump.

Accommodation: 1 single, 1 double, 1 family room. B&B £15 single, £12.50 per person in double and family rooms. Children half price under 12. Pets welcome.

WENTWORTH (S YORKS)

Rockingham Arms
Main Street, B6090, 3 miles from M1 exit 36

Licensee: Murray Jameson
Tel: 0226 742075

An old, ivy-clad pub in an unspoilt village between Rotherham and Barnsley, the Rockingham Arms has a main bar with log fires and comfortable furnishings. The barn bar has live music three nights each week. Bar food is available lunchtime and evening and includes sandwiches, Yorkshire puddings with gravy, homemade quiche, steak pie, and daily specials. The pub has an orchard beer garden and a bowling green. The guest rooms all have tea and coffee making facilities and TVs.

Beer: Theakston Best Bitter and Old Peculier, Younger Scotch Bitter, IPA and No 3 on handpumps.

Accommodation: 13 rooms, 5 with en suite facilities. B&B from £21.50 per night.

PLOUGH, SLEIGHTS – *see p 207*

WALES

NEUADD ARMS HOTEL, LLANWRTYD WELLS – *see p 229*

CLWYD

GLYNDYFRDWY

Berwyn Arms
A5 between Llangollen & Corwen

Licensee: Les Gallagher
Tel: 049 083 210

The Berwyn Arms is a fine old coaching inn with welcoming open fires in winter, superb views of the Dee valley and 1¾ miles of salmon, trout and grayling fishing. Darts and dominoes are played in the bar, food is served lunchtime and evening, there is a beer garden and facilities for families. Camping can be arranged in the village.

Beer: Burtonwood Bitter on handpump.

Accommodation: 3 singles, 2 doubles, 4 family rooms, 4 rooms with private showers. B&B £12 per person. Half board available.

HANMER

Hanmer Arms
¼ mile off A539, near Whitchurch (OS 459399)

Proprietors: Trevor & Lesley Hope
Tel: 094 874 532

The Hanmer Arms is in superb border country between Wales and Shropshire and overlooks the lovely Hanmer Mere. The village is dominated by the ancient church of St Chad's while Chirk Castle is nearby. The heavily beamed pub has a bar used mainly by local people, a lounge with a brick fireplace and range, where hot and cold bar meals are served, plus a bistro bar and a separate restaurant. Food ranges from burgers and sandwiches to soup, deep-fried cod, whitebait, spare ribs, curries, steaks, duck, and Dover sole, with a good choice of vegetarian dishes such as vegetable pie, biriani, lasagne, moussaka and mushroom nut balls in a sherry sauce. Both the pub and the accommodation are in buildings converted from a former inn and farmhouse. The guest rooms have British Tourist Board 4-crown rating and surround a cobbled courtyard; two rooms have been specially converted for use by disabled people. All the rooms have colour TVs, video programmes, baby listening devices and private baths. The Hanmer is a good base for visiting Whitchurch, and the Saxon town of Ellesmere and its mere.

Beer: Ansells Mild, Burton Ale and Tetley Bitter on handpumps

Accommodation: 1 single, 9 doubles, 2 family rooms. B&B £30-£35 per person, £17.50-£25 if sharing double. Weekend Break: 2 people 2 nights (Fri, Sat or Sun) £17.50 per person per night. Half and full board available. Cards: Access and Visa.

LLANBEDR-DYFFRYN-CLWYD

Griffin Inn
A494, 1½ miles from Ruthin on the Mold road

Licensee: Mrs Menai Edwards
Tel: 08242 2792

The Griffin, an old coaching inn built in 1726, has an imposing exterior with a large porch supported by pillars, and latticed windows. A former toll cottage, where money was collected at the turnpike, adjoins the hotel, which stands at the foot of the Clwydian Hills, with Moel Fammau – the Mother Mountain – just three miles away. There are ample facilities for fishing in rivers and streams nearby, while walkers and ramblers

CLWYD

can visit Offa's Dyke. The old market town of Ruthin has a castle and many half-timbered buildings. The Griffin offers a blazing log fire in winter, several bars and a lounge overlooking the attractive gardens. Bar food, lunchtime and evening, includes homemade soup, steak and kidney pie, plaice or cod, burgers, lasagne, beef curry, chilli con carne, homemade pizzas, ploughman's, filled jacket potatoes and children's meals. There is a separate restaurant.

Beer: Robinson Best Bitter on handpump.

Accommodation: 1 single, 1 double, 3 twins. B&B £17.50 per person. No dogs. Cards: Access and Visa.

LLANGOLLEN

Bridge End Hotel
Abbey Road. A539, near Dee Bridge

Proprietor: Edward Coulthard
Tel: 0978 860634

The Bridge End is an extensively modernized, lively and welcoming hotel that is close to the canal and has fine views of Llangollen and the river. Fishing can be arranged for anglers, while there are facilities for pony-trekking and golf in the area. Meals are available lunchtime and evening with both bar snacks and an à la carte restaurant.

Beer: Robinson Best Bitter on handpump.

Accommodation: 9 doubles, 1 family room. B&B £15 single, £20 en suite, £30 double, £38 en suite, £40 in family room for 3, £50 in room for 4. Week £160 per person, £200 en suite. Children's room; children welcome, half price.

LLANSANNAN

Saracens Head Hotel
Near Denbigh; from A55 at Abergele take A548 to Llanfair Talhaiarn, then A544 to Llansannan

Licensee: Roger Crookes
Tel: 074577 212

The Saracens Head is a 12th-century inn with a striking black and white exterior and a porched entrance. Inside, the lounge bar has old beams and is dominated by an imposing brick fireplace, with log fires in winter, and topped by a plethora of brasswork. It is adjoined by a restaurant and children's room. All the guest rooms have hot and cold water, central heating, and tea and coffee making facilities; there is a residents' TV lounge, too. The hotel's permanent resident is a ghost called the Grey Lady. It is a good base for visiting the Aled Valley and north Wales. Bar snacks – homemade soups, home-cooked ham, beef and pork – are available throughout the day, while the evening restaurant, with 20 covers, offers local smoked salmon, trout, beef, pork and lamb dishes.

Beer: Robinson Best Mild and Best Bitter on electric pumps.

Accommodation: 1 single, 5 doubles/twins, 3 family room. B&B £12 single, £24 double/twin, £36 family room (with 1 double and 1 single). Children under 12 half price. Winter Breaks (Nov–Feb) £10 per person. Pets welcome. Cards: Access and Visa.

RUABON

Wynnstay Arms
High Street, junction of old A483 and A539 Wrexham–Whitchurch roads

Licensee: Paul Skellon
Tel: 0978 822187

The Wynnstay is an imposing stone-brick and ivy-clad building with a wood-panelled lounge and popular back bar where darts and dominoes are played. It is an old coaching inn that has refound peace and tranquillity with the opening of a new bypass. It takes its name from the estate of Sir Watkin Williams Wynn: the houses of the estate workers flank the road past the hotel. Bar lunches and the restaurant concentrate on local produce, and meals may include coq au vin, duckling, Welsh lamb, steak and kidney pie, curries, poached salmon, choice of salads, and open sandwiches. The comfortable guest rooms all have TVs and tea and coffee making facilities. Ruabon has an ancient church with wall paintings, and is a good base for visiting Llangollen, Chester and the Shropshire meres.

Beer: Robinson Best Bitter on electric pump.

Accommodation: 1 single, 6 doubles, 2 family rooms, 3 with private baths. B&B £23 single, £28 en suite, £34 double, £41 en suite, £44 family room. Children's rates depend on age. Pets welcome. Cards: Access, Amex, Diners and Visa.

WHITE LION HOTEL

LLANGADOG

Castle Hotel
Queen Square, 5 miles from Llandovery on A4969

Partners: Brian Whitney & Geoffrey Dunbar
Tel: 0550 777377

The Castle is a 500-years-old inn in a village nestling at the foot of the Black Mountains on the edge of the Brecon Beacons national park. Later extensions used original ship's timbers from vessels of Nelson's times. The inn has a 20-seater restaurant with a menu making use of local produce such as fresh salmon. Bar meals are served in the lounge and saloon bars. The light and roomy guest rooms are on the first floor and have pleasant views over the town square.

Beer: Marston Pedigree Bitter and regular guest beers on handpumps.

Accommodation: 3 singles, 1 double, 2 twins, 1 family room. B&B £15 single, £25 double, £30 family room. Children welcome. Cards: Access and Visa.

TAL-Y-BONT

White Lion Hotel
A487 near Aberystwyth

Licensee: John C Davies
Tel: 097 086 245

The White Lion dates back to the 16th century and retains some original characteristics in spite of many alterations over the years. It has an impressive façade with dormers in the roof, a balcony above the porch and fine bay windows on the ground floor. The hotel has coal and log fires in winter and, according to Mr

Davies, a 'ghost that goes *bonk* in the night' ... but there is no extra charge for this service. Darts, pool, dominoes and cribbage are played in the bar and bar meals are served lunchtime and evening. Food includes fresh poached salmon and local trout, home-cooked ham, cannelloni, salads, jacket potatoes, steaks, sandwiches, toasties, and curries, and burgers, and fish fingers for children, plus apple pie, trifle, and raspberry or lemon torte. Guest rooms all have tea and coffee making facilities. The area offers sandy beaches and golf courses, and narrow-gauge railways at Rheidol, Tal-y-Llyn and Ffestiniog. Tal-y-Bont is a keen sporting village with football, cricket, darts and pool teams, and Mr Davies is happy to arrange sporting weekends for visiting teams and clubs. Lake and river fishing is free to guests, and pony-trekking and hacking can be arranged.

Beer: Banks Mild and Bitter on electric pumps.

Accommodation: 1 single, 3 doubles, 1 family room, 3 rooms with showers. B&B £15 per person. Off-season Weekend £12 per night. Children welcome, 20% reductions. Cards: Access and Visa.

WOLF'S CASTLE

Wolf's Castle Inn
On A40 Haverfordwest to Fishguard road

Licensees: Fritz & Judy Neumann
Tel: 0437 87662

The inn is a 200-year-old stone building with a slate roof and a welcoming halo of roses, hanging baskets and trees. Inside there is a cheerful bar with a tiled floor where darts and dominoes are played, a comfortable lounge, a conservatory doubling as a restaurant, and a delightful garden for the summer months. Bar food includes homemade soup, farmhouse pâté, local smoked trout, ploughman's, fish and chips, and a wide range of salads. Dishes from the restaurant can also be eaten in the bar: you can choose from smoked salmon, fresh rainbow trout, chicken chasseur, grills, salads, and a splendid sweet trolley that includes ice creams and sorbets. Children are made particularly welcome. The area offers beaches, windsurfing and walks, and the inn is a good resting place to and from the Irish ferry. The accommodation is one self-contained suite with a kitchenette that has a fridge and tea and coffee making facilities but no cooker.

Beer: Felinfoel Double Dragon on handpump.

Accommodation: 1 double with bed for a child, with shower. B&B £18 per person. Children welcome, half price under 11 years. Cards: Access and Visa.

GLAMORGAN

COWBRIDGE (S GLAMORGAN)

Bear Hotel
High Street, off A48

Licensees: H P Lewis & M Saunders
Tel: ~~044 63 4814~~

The Bear is a cheery 12th-century inn made up of a ramble of small rooms and beamed ceilings, with a flagstoned public bar and a carpeted lounge, plus a wine bar/bistro and up-market cocktail bar. Good-value bar food includes lasagne, steak and kidney pie, and ploughman's. There is a separate restaurant in an impressive vaulted room. Two of the attractive guest rooms have four-poster beds, and all the rooms have colour TVs and tea and coffee making facilities.

Beer: Bass and Welsh Hancock's HB, Brains Bitter and SA, Buckley Best Bitter, Flowers Original, Marston Pedigree Best Bitter and Wadworth 6X on handpumps.

Accommodation: 13 singles, 23 doubles, 1 family room, 34 rooms with private baths. B&B £35 single, £45 double. Children welcome, no reductions.

NOTTAGE (MID GLAMORGAN)

Rose & Crown
Heol-y-Capel, A4299, 2½ miles off M4 exit 37

Manager: J W Rout
Tel: 065 671 4850

The Rose & Crown is a white-painted hotel with a stone porch, hanging baskets and outdoor trestle tables, in a village near Porthcawl. The pub has some original beams and stone walls, a separate restaurant and beautifully appointed guest rooms with private bathrooms, tea and coffee trays and colour TVs. The restaurant offers pâté, smoked mackerel, roast beef and Yorkshire pudding, desserts and a children's menu. There are facilities for sea fishing, sailing and golf in the area.

Beer: Ruddles Best Bitter and County, Websters Yorkshire Bitter on handpumps.

Accommodation: 2 singles, 6 doubles/twins, 1 family room. B&B £34 single, £45 double/twin. Off-season Weekends: reduced tariff on application. Babies free, children 3-12 sharing with parents £5 per night inc breakfast. Cards: Access, Amex, Diners, Visa and Grand Met.

OGMORE-BY-SEA (MID GLAMORGAN)

Sea Lawn Hotel
Overlooking beach near river mouth and castle, off A48

Proprietor: Verdun Moore
Tel: 0656 880311

Mr Moore has strong views about food: his breakfasts will 'set you up for the day – they're not a roll and jam' and other meals are made from fresh produce, 'not from plastic bags' The Sea Lawn is a small, family-run hotel with stunning views of the sea and the heritage coastline. The area offers sea and river fishing, golf, beaches and walks. The guest rooms have colour TVs, phones and tea and coffee making facilities. Lunch and dinner are served and the food may include fillets of sole, tournedos Rossini, noisette of lamb, cod Mornay, fillets of plaice, and desserts.

Beer: Bass and Welsh Worthington Dark and BB on handpumps.

Accommodation: 5 singles, 2 doubles, 2 twins, all en suite. B&B £28 single, £38 double. Weekend (3 nights) £68 single, £90 double B&B + evening meal.

ABERGAVENNY

Llanwenarth Arms Hotel
Brecon Road, A40 midway between Abergavenny and Crickhowell

Licensee: D'Arcy McGregor
Tel: 0873 810550 Fax: 0873 811880

The Llanwenarth Arms is a combination of 16th-century inn and modern hotel on the banks of the River Usk, with hills and mountains forming a backdrop. The pub has a welcoming exterior with awnings over the windows, and tubs of flowers on the forecourt. Inside there are two superb bars with beamed ceilings and bar meals, while the dining room that overlooks the river has an à la carte menu. All the well-appointed guest rooms have baths and showers, colour TVs and tea and coffee making facilities.

Beer: Bass and Wadworth 6X on handpumps.

Accommodation: 18 doubles. B&B £45 single, £55 double. Weekend £22.50 per person per day for any 2 nights. Children welcome, half price. Facilities for the disabled. Cards: Access, Amex, Diners and Visa.

CAERLEON

Roman Lodge Hotel
Ponthir Road, 3 miles from M4 exit 25. Watch for Caerleon/Ponthir signpost; go through Caerleon village, turn left, hotel ½ mile on left

Proprietors: Brian & Judith Ansen
Tel: 0633 420534

The Ansens have made such extensive changes since the last edition of the guide that the Rising Sun has changed its name. But the commitment to real ale is just as deep. There are always five cask beers available and Brian Ansen searches far and wide for choice, with an emphasis on smaller breweries. The Lodge is a splendid base for visiting the ancient Roman fortress in Caerleon, and there are no less than six castles within 15 minutes' drive, and the Brecon Beacons and Wye Valley. Meals are available in the dining room both lunchtime and evening every day.

Beer: Brain SA, Burton Bridge Porter, Felinfoel Double Dragon, Flowers Original and many guest beers on handpumps.

Accommodation: 1 single, 5 doubles, 2 family rooms, 2 en suite. B&B from £21.50 per person. Half and full board available. Children welcome, from no charge to half price depending on age. Cards: Access, Amex, Diners and Visa.

CHEPSTOW

Coach & Horses
Welsh Street, off A48

Licensee: Mr L Bell
Tel: 0291 622626

The Coach & Horses is a one-bar, split-level pub at the end – or beginning – of Offa's Dyke, with a strong emphasis on sport. The pub boasts three darts teams as well as a crib team, and there are regular quiz nights. The locals are friendly and always keen to discuss Rugby, on the firm understanding that Wales has the best national team. There are bar snacks at lunchtime and many nearby restaurants offer evening meals.

Beer: Bass, Brains SA, Ruddles Best Bitter, Usher Best Bitter on handpumps.

Accommodation: 3 singles, 3 doubles,

1 family room, 3 rooms with private baths. B&B £20 per person. Children welcome, no reductions.

LLANTHONY

Abbey Hotel
Off A465, near Crucorney

Licensee: Ivor Prentice
Tel: 087 32 487

The Abbey is a superb and ancient inn set amid the ruins of a Norman priory with the backdrop of the Black Mountains. The priory was established in 1108 by William de Lacy; his task was to put down rebellious Welsh in the area but he tired of the bloodshed and settled for the monastic life instead. The inn is part of the original prior's lodge and was restored in 1811. It has a stone-flagged and vaulted bar and a dining room with an impressive oak-backed settle and a profusion of brass. The guest rooms, reached by a perilous stone spiral staircase, include a four-poster bedroom. The restaurant is open Tuesday to Friday evenings. Bar food, available every lunchtime and every evening except Sundays, includes soup, homemade pâté, chilli, vegetable lasagne, vegeburgers and sweets. *The hotel is open weekends only from December to Easter: phone to check availability.*

Beer: Brain Bitter, Flowers IPA and Original, Ruddles County on handpump.

Accommodation: B&B from £17.50-£20 per person.

LLANTILIO CROSSENNY

Hostry Inn
B4233 by White Castle, between Monmouth and Abergavenny

Licensees: Mike & Pauline Parker
Tel: 060 085 278

The Hostry is a 15th-century village inn on Offa's Dyke, owned since 1459 by the descendants of Sir David Gam, knighted by Henry V for saving his life in battle. It has a free-standing inn sign and tubs of flowers and benches and seats by the entrance, and there is a superb 300-year-old banqueting hall. Long alley skittles, bar skittles, darts and dominoes are played in the bar. A vintage Rolls-Royce is available for hire. Food ranges from cockles and mussels or faggots and peas as bar snacks to four-course meals in the restaurant, with steaks and salmon. A good range of vegetarian dishes is also available.

Beer: Smiles Best Bitter and occasional guest beers on handpumps.

Accommodation: 1 single, 2 doubles, 1 family room. B&B £10 per person. Half and full board available. Children's room, children welcome to stay, half price. Facilities for the disabled.

TREDEGAR

Cambrian Hotel
The Circle, A65

Licensees: Neil & Val Breeze
Tel: 0495 711107

The Cambrian is a street-corner mining-valleys local dating back to 1810 and with Chartist connections, in a town associated with Nye Bevan, post-war architect of the National Health Service. The lively pub has log fires in winter, live music on Tuesdays and Thursdays, and a Sunday charity quiz. Bar food includes rolls and sandwiches, ploughman's, jacket potatoes with a choice of fillings, sausage, egg and chips and a daily special. Full meals are available in a separate restaurant. Water sports are available in Bryn Bach Park, and there are some remaining working mines and a mountain railway.

Beer: Bass and Brain SA on hand and electric pumps.

Accommodation: 3 doubles, 1 en suite. B&B £15 per person. Children welcome.

GWYNEDD

ABERSOCH

St Tudwal's Hotel
Main Street, off A499 main road from Pwllheli

Licensee: John Page
Tel: 075 881 2539

The pub, popular with locals and tourists alike, has been upgraded by Mr Page since the last edition of this guide, and has a smart and comfortable lounge, a rear bar, restaurant and a large patio. St Tudwal's has open fires in winter, a welcome for families, a garden, pub games, and good food both lunchtime and evening. Abersoch, on the Lleyn peninsula, has a good harbour and fine beaches, and is the home of the South Caernarfonshire Yacht Club, one of the biggest in Britain. All the guest rooms have TVs, central heating and tea and coffee making facilities.

Beer: Robinson Best Mild, Best Bitter and Old Tom (winter) on electric pumps and straight from the cask.

Accommodation: 12 singles, 1 twin and 5 en suite doubles. B&B from £17.50 per person. Pets welcome. Cards: Access and Visa.

BEAUMARIS (ANGLESEY)

Olde Bull's Head
Castle Street, off A545

Proprietors: Keith Rothwell & David Robertson
Tel: 0248 810329

You are in distinguished company here, for those two travellers and boozers, Dr Johnson and Charles Dickens, stayed here in the original posting house of the borough, established in 1472 and rebuilt in 1617. It is a grade two listed building and is packed with fascinating antiques including brass and copper ware, china, armour and weapons. There is a 17th-century water clock, and a high-backed chair in the beamed bar that used to be the town's ducking stool for law breakers. Access to the enclosed courtyard at the rear of the inn is through the original stage coach entrance, which has the largest single-hinged door in Britain. Bar food includes homemade soup, sandwiches, ploughman's, chicken fricassee, tagliatelle bolognese, braised oxtail, venison sausages, and delicious homemade puddings like walnut and treacle tart and cheesecake. Experienced restaurateur Keith Rothwell uses his skills in the beamed dining room to produce dishes based on such local produce as turbot, sole, salmon and

GWYNEDD

hare. There is a residents' lounge, and morning tea is brought to your bedroom. The guest rooms have been upgraded since the last edition and now have four crowns from the Wales Tourist Board.

Beer: Bass on handpump.

Accommodation: 1 single, 5 doubles, 5 twins, all en suite. B&B £32.50 single, £55 double. Children welcome; special bedroom for children adjoining parents' double: £10 per child. Cards: Access and Visa.

BEDDGELERT

Prince Llewelyn
By bridge over river, off A498 and B4085

Licensee: D C Norton
Tel: 076 686242

The Prince Llewelyn is a fine old three-storey, brick-built inn in a wonderfully peaceful setting by a river in the Snowdon mountains, with rushing streams and quiet meadows. The spacious inn offers a genuinely warm welcome, with open fires, facilities for families, disabled people and campers, and good bar meals lunchtime and evening. It is named in honour of the Welsh prince who, according to legend, slew his faithful hound, Gelert, when he thought the dog had killed his son. In fact, the dog had killed a wolf to protect the child. The anguished prince buried the dog in a spot close to the present hotel: the name of the village means Grave of Gelert. Close to the hotel there are facilities for fishing, climbing, walking, canoeing and pony-trekking.

Beer: Robinson Best Mild and Best Bitter on electric pumps.

Accommodation: 2 singles, 2 twins, 1 double, 2 family rooms, 4 rooms with en suite facilities. B&B £12–£16 per person. Cards: Access and Visa.

Tanronen Hotel
From the A5 at Capel Curig take the A498 for Beddgelert; turn left over the bridge and the hotel is on the left

Licensee: William Alun Hughes
Tel: 076686 347

The Tanronen is a small hotel in the centre of the Snowdonia national park, at the foot of Snowdon and seven miles from the coast. The grave of Gelert and the Sygun copper mine with its craft shops are close at hand. Bar meals and restaurant meals are available lunchtime and evening.

Beer: Robinson Best Mild and Best Bitter on electric pumps.

Accommodation: 4 twins, 4 doubles. B&B £15 per person. Children sharing with parents charged half price 12 years and under and 25% reduction 13 to 16 years. Mini-break 2 nights including evening meal £46.50 per person, 3 nights £67. No dogs. Cards: Access and Visa.

BENLLECH (ANGLESEY)

Glanrafon Hotel
Benllech Bay, A5025

Licensee: Jim Robinshaw
Tel: 024 885 2364

The Glanrafon is a gracious black-and-white-fronted hotel with superb views of the Irish Sea from Moelfre Bay and Ormes Head at Llandudno. The beaches of Benllech Bay are just minutes away; there are opportunities for fishing, boating and golf on the island, while Snowdonia is just across the bridge on the mainland. The hotel has a lively public bar and a quiet lounge. Darts, pool and dominoes are played; there is a separate residents' TV lounge and a restaurant with table d'hôte menu. Bar meals are also available lunchtime and evening every day from Easter to October. Most of the bright and airy guest rooms have fine sea views.

Beer: Lees Bitter on handpump.

Accommodation: 8 doubles, 4 twins, 5 family rooms, 12 with private baths. All rooms let as single when available. B&B from £16 per person, £23 with dinner. Weekend from £38 half board, Week £108 B&B, £156 half board. Children's room; children welcome to stay, 25-95% reductions according to age.

BODEDERN (ANGLESEY)

Crown Hotel
B5109, 1 mile off A5

Licensees: Reg & Candy Bryant
Tel: 0407 740734

The Crown is a fine example of a traditional village pub and is a good base for both the beaches of Anglesey and the port of Holyhead. It offers good and reasonably priced accommodation and food, with bar meals – home-baked pies, jacket potatoes and basket meals – available both lunchtime and evening. The bars have beamed ceilings and stone fireplaces, with darts and dominoes played in the public. There is a children's room and a separate small restaurant. The Crown offers plenty of live entertainment, with quizzes on Sunday nights and regular parties and fancy-dress and charity fund-raising events.

Beer: Burtonwood Bitter on handpump.

Accommodation: 1 single, 1 twin, 3 doubles, 2 family rooms, all rooms with TVs. B&B from £12 per person. Children welcome, terms by arrangement.

BULL BAY (ANGLESEY)

Trecastell Hotel
On A5025, near Amlwch

Licensees: Arthur & Iris Leese
Tel: 0407 830651

The Trecastell Hotel, with a striking bow-windowed and tall-chimneyed exterior, overlooks the rocks at Bull Bay and has magnificent views over the Irish Sea. It is next door to a golf club with an 18-hole course. There is a comfortable lounge bar with sea views, a cocktail bar, games rooms and residents' lounge and restaurant. Food ranges from bar snacks to grills. Most of the guest rooms have private baths and tea makers and all have superb views of the sea. Bull Bay has a natural harbour, and the coastline is lush with heather and alpine flowers.

Beer: Robinson Best Bitter on electric pump.

Accommodation: 9 doubles, 3 family rooms, doubles let as singles when available. B&B £19.50 single, £33 double. Off-season Breaks: details on application. Children welcome, 25% reduction 10–15 years, half price 2–10.

CAPEL CURIG

Bryn Tyrch Hotel
On A5 at eastern edge of village

Licensee: Rita Davis
Tel: 06904 223

This cheerful hotel on the A5 has a comfortable lounge with fine views across the valley to Moel Siabod, and a small public bar where darts and pool are played. There is an enterprising range of bar food lunchtime and evening, with the emphasis on wholefoods and an extensive vegetarian and vegan menu, using herbs and spices. Dishes includes spicy cabbage and onion or cauliflower soup, houmous in hot pitta bread, vegetable samosas, aduki bean chilli, ratatouille, and aubergine, mushroom and black-eyed bean curry. Carnivores can enjoy chicken tikka or cacciatore, lamb korma, beef goulash, fisherman's pie, plaice, trout, pizzas; there are also filled jacket potatoes, and the sweets include carrot cake, rhubarb crumble, treacle tart, locally made ice creams plus herb teas. There is a separate restaurant, too. The hotel offers real fires in winter, a welcome for families, a garden and camping. There are superb walks, facilities for fishing, and you can swim in the river when the weather is hot.

Beer: Castle Eden Ale and Flowers IPA on handpumps.

Accommodation: 6 en suite double rooms, all with tea and coffee making equipment. B&B £11.50–£16.50 per person, discounts for group bookings. Cards: Access, Amex, Diners and Visa.

Cobden's Hotel
On A5, 1 mile east of village

Licensees: Craig & Jane Goodall
Tel: 06904 243

Cobden's is a lively and welcoming smart country hotel with a comfortable lounge and a climbers' bar. It offers facilities for families and disabled people, a garden and excellent bar food both lunchtime and evening. It is a popular resting place for visitors who enjoy the surrounding countryside or who energetically clamber up the encircling peaks.

Beer: Courage Directors and John Smiths Bitter on handpumps.

Accommodation: 4 singles, 12 doubles, 2 family rooms, all rooms with en suite facilities and TVs. B&B £15–£25 per person. Cards: Access and Visa.

Tyn-y-Coed
On A5, 1 mile east of village

Licensee: G Wainwright
Tel: 06904 231

Thousands of visitors know the Tyn-y-Coed as the pub with the stage coach in the car park. The prominent landmark, more arresting than any pub sign, stands opposite the liveliest hotel in Capel. At weekends the bars are bursting with thirsty walkers and climbers, while residents can relax in more peaceful lounges and the restaurant. There are open fires in chilly weather, a garden and welcome for families, good bar food and full meals lunchtime and evening. Pen-y-Pass and Nant Ffrancon, two landmarks of Snowdonia, are just a few miles away and there are gentler walks and climbs for the less energetic all around. The guest rooms in the hotel all have private baths or showers as well as tea and coffee making equipment.

Beer: Castle Eden Ale and Flowers IPA on handpumps.

Accommodation: 10 doubles, 3 family rooms. B&B from £18 per person. Half and full board available. Bargain Breaks £17 per person, £26 with evening meal. Cards: Access and Visa.

CLYNNOG-FAWR

St Beuno Coach Inn
A499, near Caernarfon

Licensees: S P Williams & G M Boland
Tel: 0286 86212

A spacious and comfortable old country inn overlooking the sea on the edge of Snowdonia, the St Beuno has log fires, large gardens and cosy lounge and bar areas. Food is available all day, and includes soup, homemade steak and kidney pie, beef or chicken curry, spaghetti bolognese, chilli con carne, seafood platter, plaice or cod, beefburger, pizza, steaks, ploughman's, and a children's menu. Sports fanatics will enjoy facilities that include a full-size snooker table, three pool tables, table tennis, a skittle alley, bar billiards and shove ha'penny. Outdoors, you can play golf, go shooting, fishing or walking.

Beer: Marston Burton Bitter and Pedigree Bitter on handpumps.

Accommodation: 8 rooms – doubles, twins and family. B&B from £12 per person. Cheap winter breaks available. Children and pets welcome. Cards: Access, Amex and Visa.

DOLGELLAU

Royal Ship Hotel
Queen's Square, off A487, A470 and A494

Licensees: Mr & Mrs M Humphries
Tel: 0341 422209

The Royal Ship has a superb exterior, a dark stone, creeper-clad building with a gable end, five dormer windows and a porch supported by pillars. It was built as a coaching inn in 1813 and has been extensively refurbished in recent years, with smart and comfortable bars, lounges and a restaurant. The beautifully appointed guest rooms have central heating and colour TVs. Bar food is available lunchtime and evening, while the restaurant serves evening meals and a Sunday roast. Dolgellau has opportunities for walking, fishing and pony-trekking, and there are several steam railways in the vicinity.

Beer: Robinson Best Bitter on electric pump.

Accommodation: 2 singles, 20 doubles/twins, 2 family room, 16 rooms with en suite facilities. B&B £15 single, £24 en suite, £30 double, £48 en suite. Children half price up to 12 years, 25% off adult rate 13–16 years. Two-day Mini Break dinner B&B en suite £62 per person, 3 days £87 per person. Children's room. No dogs. Cards: Access and Visa.

GWYNEDD

LLANBEDR

Victoria Inn
On A496 south of Harlech

Licensee: Lawrence E Barry
Tel: 034 123 213

The Victoria stands on the banks of the River Artro in the picturesque Llanbedr valley with mountains, valleys, lakes and beaches all around. The inn has a superb garden with tables, chairs and benches, as well as a Wendy House and slides and swings for children. Inside, the antiquity of the building is underscored by massive beams, a rare circular wooden settle, an ancient stove, stone-flagged floors and exposed timbers. Bar food is served lunchtime and evening, and the dining room serves evening meals and Sunday lunch. All the guest rooms are en suite and have colour TVs and tea and coffee making facilities.

Beer: Robinson Best Bitter on electric pump.

Accommodation: 2 singles, 3 doubles. B&B £19.75 per person. Children half price. Two-night Stay £36, 3 nights £52. Pets welcome. Cards: Access and Visa.

LLANBEDR-Y-CENNIN

Olde Bull Inn
Off B5106 (OS 761695)

Licensees: Phillipe & Brenda de Ville Forte
Tel: 0492 69508/69359

The Olde Bull is a 16th-century inn on the slopes of the Conwy valley. The old stone bar has beams, settles and log fires, one in a vast inglenook. There is a residents' lounge, separate dining room with beams from an old Spanish galleon, and a patio with wonderful views of the lowering mountains. Homemade bar food includes soup, grills, pasta bolognese, meat pie, seafood pasta, curries, burgers, salads, sandwiches, toasties and desserts. Groups of 30 or more have the free use of a barbecue. Darts, dominoes and crib are played. As well as the guest room there is a six-berth caravan for hire.

Beer: Lees GB Mild and Bitter on handpumps.

Accommodation: 1 single, 1 double, 1 family room. B&B £14 single, £25 double, £28 family room. All rooms have tea and coffee making facilities.Children welcome, terms by arrangement. Cards: Access and Diners.

LLANBERIS

Padarn Lake Hotel
High Street, off A4086

Licensees: T Skiliki & P Ashes
Tel: 0286 870260

This stone-built hotel overlooks Padarn Lake and has magnificent views of Snowdonia. There is a public bar with darts and pool, a lounge bar, and a cocktail bar next to the restaurant. There is a wide range of bar food lunchtime and evening, and the restaurant menu includes local produce and game whenever possible. The excellent accommodation has lake and mountain views, private baths or showers, TVs, phones and tea and coffee making equipment. The hotel is a fine base for the Snowdon Mountain Railway, Llanberis Lake Railway, the Welsh Slate Museum, and Padarn Country Park where you can fish, sail or row. Dinorwig Power Station, known as the 'Underground Giant' as it is

GWYNEDD

contained within the heart of the mountain, is the largest pumped storage power station in Europe.

Beer: Marston Pedigree Bitter on handpump.

Accommodation: 21 doubles/twins, 3 family rooms. B&B £24 single, £43 double. 10% reductions for more than 3 nights. Two-day Breaks including dinner: £59 single, £110 double. Cards: Access, Amex, Diners and Visa.

LLANDUDNO

Gresham
143 Mostyn Street, off A55

Licensee: S G Capes
Tel: 0492 76120

The Gresham is a small, cheerful, one-bar pub in the famous seaside resort of North Wales. The lounge is decorated with old pictures and prints, and a lower area is reserved for pool players. There is frequent live music, aided by a piano, with singalongs most evenings in summer and at weekends in winter. The guest rooms all have tea and coffee making facilities and central heating. The North Shore beach is just 200 yards away.

Beer: Burton Ale on handpump.

Accommodation: 1 single, 1 double, 4 family rooms. B&B £10 per person. Half board available.

Sandringham Hotel
West Parade

Licensee: D Kavanagh
Tel: 0492 76513

A small, family-run hotel just 30 yards from the West Shore beaches, the Sandringham has a naval flavour to its décor, with many seascapes and sailors' hats. Pool, dominoes, draughts and cards are played in the bar; there is a garden with splendid views of Conwy Bay and Snowdonia, and bar meals are served lunchtime and evening. The well-furnished guest rooms all have en suite baths or showers, and tea and coffee making facilities.

Beer: Greenall Original Bitter on handpump.

Accommodation: 3 singles, 11 doubles/twins, 3 family rooms. B&B £15–£25 per person. Cards: Access and Visa.

Snowdon Hotel
11 Tudno Street

Licensee: R J Corris
Tel: 0492 75515

The Snowdon, which is close to the North Shore and the Great Orme tramway station, has a spacious open-plan lounge bar decorated with old photos of the pub, old mirrors and whisky jugs. One of the original Victorian windows has been preserved and framed and hangs above the fireplace. One section of the lounge is reserved for the local lifeboat crew; its walls are decorated with lifeboat memorabilia and there is a scale model of one of the old

Llandudno boats. The small public bar is a haven for darts players: the pub has three teams. The Snowdon serves bar meals every lunchtime except Sundays. The neat guest rooms have colour TVs, tea and coffee making facilities and, a nice touch, bowls of fresh fruit.

Beer: Bass on handpump.

Accommodation: 4 doubles, 2 en suite. B&B £10.50 per person, £12.50 en suite.

MENAI BRIDGE (ANGLESEY)

Anglesey Arms Hotel
On A5025

Licensee: Alex Honeyman
Tel: 0248 712305

Cross the Menai Strait by Telford's famous suspension bridge, and on the left at the far end you will find the Anglesey Arms. The Britannia Bridge is farther along the coast and the hotel has an interesting collection of photos showing the bridge in its various stages of construction. Although it is on the main road to Bangor, the white-painted hotel with dormer windows is set in lovely tree-guarded gardens with panoramic views of Snowdonia. There is an extensive bar snacks menu, while the restaurant offers both table d'hôte and à la carte meals. The spacious and comfortable guest rooms all have private baths or showers, tea and coffee making facilities and colour TVs.

Beer: Lees Bitter on electric pump.

Accommodation: 4 singles, 4 doubles, 9 twins. B&B £27 single, £42 double. Half board available. Weekend from £54 half board per person. Children welcome, terms depend on age.

RED WHARF BAY (ANGLESEY)

Min-y-Don Hotel
1 mile off A5025 between Pentraeth and Benllech

Licensee: Diana M Kitchen
Tel: 0248 852596

There is a warm, friendly atmosphere in this pleasant black-and-white hotel overlooking the cliffs and the sea. Since the last edition of the guide, Mrs Kitchen has organized an extensive refurbishment. Several of the 15 guest rooms now have en suite facilities and all can be supplied with colour TVs and tea and coffee making equipment; most rooms have fine views of the sea. Local produce features in the restaurant and bar meals. Pool, darts and dominoes are played and there is a comfortable lounge. The hotel has regular live entertainment, and is a good base for wind-surfing, sailing, boating, fishing and exploring Anglesey and Snowdonia. Accommodation is available from mid-March to the end of October; the rest of the year weekends only with advance bookings.

Beer: Burtonwood Best Bitter on handpump.

Accommodation: 3 singles, 6 doubles, and 6 rooms en suite. B&B £17 single, £38 en suite, £32 double, £44 en suite. Dogs £1.50 per night.

TRAWSFYNYDD

White Lion
Top of the hill in centre of village, off A470

Licensee: Mrs M Kreft
Tel: 076 687 277

The White Lion is a homely, unspoilt moorland village inn with solid brick walls and three small rooms in a beautiful setting between Porthmadog and Dolgellau in the hills south of Snowdonia. It is just ten minutes' drive from Blaenau Ffestiniog and its steam railway and slate museum. The pub has brasses and fascinating old photos on the bar walls; darts, dominoes and cards are played by locals and visitors, and bar meals are available lunchtime and evening.

Beer: Burtonwood Dark Mild and Bitter on handpumps

Accommodation: 1 single, 3 doubles, 1 family room. B&B £10–£15 per person.

POWYS

BRECON

Gremlin Hotel
The Watton, A40

Proprietors: Stuart & Eleanor Harwood
Tel: 0874 3829

The Gremlin is just outside the centre of Brecon and is a fine base for visiting the national park, where canoeing, sailboarding, pony-trekking, golf, fishing and canal boating are available. Parts of the building date back more than 400

years. It is a genuine popular local with open fires, a garden, and a public bar where darts and quoits are played. Food ranges from sandwiches and home-cooked snacks to full meals in the small restaurant. The Gremlin is claimed to be haunted by a piano-playing ghost named Hilda.

Beer: Bass and Felinfoel Double Dragon on handpumps with regular guest beers.

Accommodation: 2 singles, 5 doubles, 1 family room. B&B £12.50 per person. Children welcome.

ERWOOD

Erwood Inn
A470

Licensee: P J Lewis
Tel: 098 23 218

The Erwood is a happy-go-lucky old coaching inn in a village on the Cardiff road in the Wye Valley. The writer Henry Mayhew, one of the founders of *Punch* magazine, worked in the inn. The pastel-coloured exterior is prettily decked out with hanging baskets and window boxes. There are a few seats and tables at the front and a garden at the rear with fine views of the valley where salmon and trout fishing are available. The inn has a lounge and public bar, a visitors' lounge, and good, plentiful bar food lunchtime and evening. The guest rooms have tea and coffee making facilities. Petrol and oil are available 24 hours a day on the forecourt.

Beer: Flowers Original, Marston Pedigree Bitter and Wadworth 6X (summer) and guest beers on handpumps.

Accommodation: 2 singles, 2 doubles,

1 family room. B&B £10 per person. Half and full board available. Weekend £30, Week £90. Children welcome.

GLASBURY-ON-WYE

Harp Inn
B4350, off A438

Licensees: David & Lynda White
Tel: 04974 373

The Post Office thinks the pub and Glasbury are in Herefordshire but they are firmly and geographically in Wales. The inn is a former 18th-century cider house, now with a full licence, in the beauty of the Wye Valley and the Black Mountains. In summer you can soak in the surroundings from the back terrace and lawn that slopes down to the Wye. Inside there is a strong emphasis on games with shove ha'penny, cribbage, cards, dominoes and pool played in a separate room that overlooks the river. The lounge has brick walls and a log fire in winter. Bar food includes homemade hot-pot, chicken curry, lasagne verde, chilli con carne, steak and kidney pie, such vegetarian dishes as nut roast, vegetable curry, aubergine and mushroom lasagne, and vegetable pasty, plus ploughman's, sandwiches, jacket potatoes and burgers. The Whites welcome children, and sensibly ask that parents as well as offspring, should be well-behaved. The inn is a splendid base for walking, fishing, riding, golfing and canoeing; Hay-on-Wye, with its famous second-hand book shops, is close by.

Beer: Flowers Original and IPA, Robinson Best Bitter on handpumps.

Accommodation: 4 doubles/twins, 2 rooms en suite. B&B £11.50 per person. Week £75. Children under 10 £7.

LLANDRINDOD WELLS

Llanerch
Off Waterloo Road, near BR station, A483

Proprietors: John & Kenneth Leach
Tel: 0597 2086

The Llanerch is a fine old inn in the county town of Powys, and was once an important coaching inn in old Radnorshire. Llanerch is a shortened version of 'Llanerchderion' – 'resting place by the glade for coaches'. The inn was built in the 16th century and still has old beams, an inglenook fireplace and superb Jacobean staircase. It stands in spacious grounds with a beer garden, terrace and children's play area. Darts, dominoes, pool and boules are played, and golf, fishing and pony-trekking are available in the area. There is a residents' TV lounge. Food is served in the bar or in the brasserie, and includes onion soup with croutons, steak, kidney and mushroom pie, curry, rainbow trout, vegetarian pancakes, grills, toasties, filled baps, jacket spuds, fisherman's pie, lasagne, omelettes, and children's dishes. The inn is a splendid base for visiting the Elan Valley, Powis Castle, the Wye Valley and the neighbouring English towns of Ludlow and Shrewsbury.

Beer: Bass and Hancocks HB, Robinson Best Bitter on handpumps.

Accommodation: 3 singles, 7 doubles/twins, 2 family rooms, 6 rooms en suite. B&B £15-£20 per person. Two-day Break from £40 includes dinner; Week from £90. Children welcome, terms negotiable. Cards: Access and Visa.

LLANFAIR CAEREINION

Goat Hotel
¼ mile off A458 Welshpool road

Licensees: Richard & Alyson Argument
Tel: 0938 810428

The Goat is a handsome country inn in old Montgomeryshire near the town of Welshpool: Llanfair and Welshpool are linked by the narrow-gauge steam railway that operates in the summer months. The inn offers old-fashioned comfort with crackling fires, polished brasses and deep armchairs, and central heating and tea makers in the guest rooms. Bar meals include soups, ploughman's, jacket potatoes, casserole of the day, ham, sausages, chicken, curry, fish, and beef and kidney pie. The menu offers grills, Welsh lamb cutlets, duckling and rainbow trout. The area is rich in history and places of interest, including Powis Castle, St Mary's church and well in Llanfair, the working weaving mill at Dinas Mawddwy, and Montgomery Castle.

Beer: Felinfoel Double Dragon and Welsh Hancocks HB on handpumps.

Accommodation: 5 doubles, 1 family room, 4 rooms with en suite facilities. B&B £11-£17 per person. 10% discount if you carry a CAMRA guide. Children's room; children welcome to stay, half price.

HARP INN, GLASBURY-ON-WYE – *see p 227*

LLANFYLLIN

Cain Valley Hotel
High Street, A490

Licensee: Simon Acres
Tel: 069 084 366

The Cain Valley Hotel is an imposing small market-town hotel with a multi-windowed, stucco frontage, and beams and log fires in the interior. The hotel dates back more than 350 years and has every comfort in its wood-panelled bars and lounges and well-appointed guest rooms, all of which have private bathrooms and tea and coffee makers. Mr Acres and his staff have a growing reputation for good food. As well as draught beer and wine there is an interesting selection of imported lagers. Fishing by boat at Lake Vyrnwy and along the River Cain can be arranged, and places of interest include the Berwyn Mountains, Lake Bala, Chirk and Powis castles and the waterfalls at Llanrhaeadr.

Beer: Bass and Marston Pedigree Bitter on handpumps.

Accommodation: 7 doubles, 4 twins, 3 family suites. B&B from £15 per person, £20.50 with dinner. No single supplement. Reductions for children. Pets welcome. Cards: Access and Visa.

LLANGADFAN

Cann Office Hotel
A458

Licensee: G Lewis
Tel: 0938 88202

A large pub set back from the road and with trees and bushes guarding the entrance, the Cann Office dates from the 14th century and offers facilities for all ages. Food, mainly home-cooked, ranges from egg and chips to a T-bone steak. Welsh singing often breaks out spontaneously on Saturday nights. Local activities include fishing, pony-trekking and bird watching.

Beer: Marston Burton Bitter and Pedigree Bitter (summer) on handpumps.

Accommodation: 2 singles, 3 doubles, 2 family rooms. B&B from £12 per person. Children welcome.

LLANGURIG

Blue Bell Inn
A44, near Llanidloes

Licensees: Bill & Diana Mills
Tel: 05515 254

The Blue Bell is a 16th-century inn – two buildings knocked into one with an impressive double-porch façade – a fine stopping place for those touring mid-Wales. The hotel will arrange for permits for fly fishing on the Clywedog reservoir, and there are also facilities for golf, pony-trekking, bird watching and walking in the beautiful surrounding countryside. The Blue Bell has a welcome for families, open fires in winter, a public bar, full restaurant meals, hot and cold bar snacks, and packed lunches if required. Llangurig is 1,000 feet above sea level and has a 14th-century monastic church and a craft centre. Five miles away is the historic market town of Llanidloes at the confluence of the rivers Severn and Clywedog. The Plynlimon mountains, Elan Valley and Claerwen lakes are all within easy reach.

Beer: Flowers Original, Sam Powell Best Bitter on handpumps.

Accommodation: 4 singles, 5 doubles, 1 family room, 1 en suite. B&B £14.50 per person. Children welcome.

LLANWRTYD WELLS

Neuadd Arms Hotel
The Square, A483

Proprietors: Gordon & Di Green
Tel: 0591 3236

The Neuadd Arms is a splendid 19th-century hotel by the river in the smallest town in Britain. There is carefully restored Georgian and Victorian architecture, log fires, the obligatory ghost and good cooking. The traditional back bar, where quoits, darts and shove ha'penny are played, has a good local atmosphere. There is Welsh singing at weekends. Gordon Green is an enthusiastic CAMRA member and organizer of the Mid-Wales Beer Festival every November, and a Real Ale Ramble in the forests. The Greens will also attempt to order any guest beers that visitors request, and will arrange visits to Buckley's and Felinfoel breweries in Llanelli. For visitors of a less bibulous nature there are pony-trekking, horse riding, fishing, mountain cycling, para-gliding and bird watching facilities all around.

Beer: Felinfoel Double Dragon, Greene King Abbot Ale and guest beers every week on handpumps.

Accommodation: 7 singles, 7 doubles, 1 family room, 7 en suite. B&B £15.50 per person. Weekend £48, Week £100. Details of beer festival and other ale-activities on request. Children welcome, up to 50% reductions. Cards: Visa.

MACHYNLLETH

Dyfi Forester Inn
4 Doll Street, A489

Licensees: Victor Watson & Lars Sorensen
Tel: 0654 2004

The inn is more than 100 years old and has been sensitively renovated by new owners. Regulars and visitors can take part in such traditional pub games as darts, dominoes and cribbage, which are enjoyed especially in the autumn and winter in front of a blazing open fire. Food is served in both the bar and the new bistro and restaurant. The bar menu includes homemade chilli con carne, curries and shepherd's pie. There is now a pleasant residents' TV lounge and the modernized guest rooms have tea and coffee makers. The pub is popular with steam railway enthusiasts: the Severn Valley Railway runs along the glorious Cambrian coast.

Beer: Marston Burton Bitter, Pedigree Bitter and Owd Rodger (winter) on handpumps.

Accommodation: 1 single, 1 double, 1 family room (3 beds). B&B £15 per person.

PENYBONT

Severn Arms Hotel
Junction of A44 and A488

Proprietors: Geoff & Tessa Lloyd
Tel: 059 787 224/344

The Severn Arms is a splendid old coaching inn with ancient roots and a more recent, Georgian frontage. Penybont or Pont Rhyd-y-Cleifon as it was first known, dates from medieval times when it served as the fortification of Castle Cefn Llys. An inn by the bridge over the River Ithon has existed for centuries and was known as the Fleece or New Inn until 1814 when it became known as the Severn Arms; in 1840 it was moved, lock, stock and barrels, to its present site. It has a wealth of old beams and log fires, and there is a traditional bar and is a residents' TV lounge. Residents can use the fishing rights on the river, and pony trekking is available locally. The inn is in a superb location and is a good base for border hopping between Wales and Shropshire. Bar meals include steaks, lasagne, fillet of plaice, trout, smoked salmon, fisherman's platter, and steak and kidney pie. There are full meals in the beamed dining room.

Beer: Bass on handpump.

Accommodation: 4 doubles, 6 family rooms, doubles let as singles when available. All rooms en suite, with colour TVs, radios and phones. B&B £18 per person. Weekend £52.60, Week £140 including dinner. Children welcome, up to half price depending on age. Cards: Access and Visa.

PONTROBERT

Royal Oak Hotel
2 miles off A495 from Meifod

Licensee: Alyson Pullinger
Tel: 093 884 474

The Royal Oak stands in magnificent scenery. It is built of Welsh stone and has exposed beams, and log fires in winter. The locals' bar has a snug with a dart board and a pool area. The lounge is spacious and comfortable, and there is a separate family room where bar meals can be enjoyed, as well as a restaurant that seats 24. Bar food includes soup, grills, homemade lasagne, chilli, cottage pie, and curry, with trout, seafood pasta, steak and kidney, ploughman's and a children's menu. Outside there is a landscaped garden with a children's play area, and tables in warm weather.

Beer: Marston Pedigree Bitter on handpump.

Accommodation: 2 singles, 2 doubles. B&B £11 per person. Children welcome.

TALGARTH

Tower Hotel
The Square, A479

Licensees: J Poole & M J Barnes
Tel: 0874 711253

The Tower is in the centre of town and offers excellent family-run accommodation and food. The bar has a large log fire in winter, a pool table and homemade bar snacks lunchtime and evening. The lounge has a TV for residents and children, while the separate dining room is open seven days a week. The guest rooms have tea and coffee making facilities. The surrounding area offers opportunities for gliding, hang-gliding, canoeing, sailing, fishing, hill walking and golf.

Beer: Flowers Original and IPA on handpumps, Wethered Winter Royal in season and regular guest beers.

Accommodation: 6 twins/doubles, 2 family rooms. B&B from £32 double; single occupancy £18. Children welcome, reductions by arrangement.

SCOTLAND

Scottish pub hours are standard: 11–2.30 and 5–11, Sunday 12.30–2.30 and 6.30–11. Many pubs have regular afternoon and evening extensions that allow them to open all day and often until midnight or later. Not all pubs open on Sunday but hotels serve drinks to residents.

TIBBIE SHIELS INN, ST MARY'S LOCH – *see p 237*

BROUGHTON

Greenmantle Hotel
On A701

Licensees: Ken & Julie McFarlane
Tel: 089 94 302

The Greenmantle takes its name from the novel by John Buchan who lived in the village. The ranch-style roadside hotel is in the middle of this pleasant Peeblesshire village near Biggar. It has a bar and lounge, two open fires in winter, and a sitting room for residents. Families are welcome and food is available all day. Broughton is the home of the small independent brewery of the same name, set up in 1980 by a former Scottish & Newcastle executive with the splendid brewing name of David Younger. In a country dominated by two giant groups, he has had surprising but welcome success.

Beer: Broughton Greenmantle Ale on air pressure.

Accommodation: 6 doubles, 1 en suite, all rooms with colour TVs. B&B from £18 per person.

CARLOPS

Alan Ramsey
On A702

Licensee: Anthony Swift
Tel: 0968 60258

The Alan Ramsey is a 200-year-old 'howff' with blazing log fires in winter, and stone-flagged floors. There is a bar, food lunchtime and evening, family facilities and an outdoor area for picnics and barbecues in warm weather. Carlops is a tiny Borders village in wonderful walking country.

Beer: Belhaven 70 and 80 shilling, Theakston Best Bitter on handpumps.

Accommodation: 2 singles, 4 doubles. B&B £13.50 per person. Half board available. Cards: Amex and Visa.

COLDSTREAM

Newcastle Arms
50 High Street, A697

Licensees: Linda & Walter Douglas
Tel: 0890 2376

Trip and you fall into England in this famous old Borders town with its strong military connections – there is even a Coldstream Guards Museum. The Newcastle Arms is family run and offers a warm welcome in its bars, while the separate dining room serves meals at most times of the day.

Beer: Arrol's 80 shilling and Tetley Bitter on electric pumps.

Accommodation: 1 single, 3 doubles, 1 family room. B&B £13 per person. Children welcome, half price.

INNERLEITHEN

Traquair Arms
Traquair Road, off A72

Licensee: Hugh Anderson
Tel: 0896 830 229

The Traquair Arms is a comfortable stone-built hotel in a quiet Borders town that is popular with hill walkers and anglers. The hotel has open fires, a family welcome, a garden and excellent food lunchtime and evening: Mr Anderson is a trained chef. Meals in the large bar include homemade soup and pâté, tomato and tuna fish salad, Finnan

BORDERS

savoury of flaked smoked haddock with onions, butter, cheese and double cream, omelettes, jacket potatoes with a range of fillings, and such vegetarian dishes as adzuki bean burgers, chilli, mushroom Stroganoff, peanut bake and vegetarian lasagne. Breakfasts are spectacular. The hotel is close to Traquair House, the stately home that keeps its main gates shut until a Stuart returns to the throne. The owners brew the famous strong bottle-fermented beer named after the house and have added a delectable draught beer, too. Brewing is in an 18th-century brew house, and the entire estate is open to visitors. Fishing can be arranged for guests at the hotel and the area is excellent for walkers and golfers. Mr Anderson has a good selection of bottled beers as well as draught, including Greenmantle and Old Jock from Broughton, Traquair House Ale (naturally) and, by the time the guide appears, Caledonian.

Beer: Broughton Greenmantle Ale, Traquair Bear Ale on handpumps.

Accommodation: 2 singles, 7 doubles, 1 family room, 4 en suite. B&B £15-£25 per person. Half and full board available. Off-peak and Weekend Breaks: terms on application. Dogs welcome. Cards: Access, Diners and Visa.

KELSO

Black Swan
Horsemarket. A689

Licensee: Peter Henderson
Tel: 0573 24563

The Black Swan is a cheerful old pub in a typical small Borders town. It has an atmospheric public bar and a comfortable lounge, and serves good lunches and suppers that include soup, roast beef and Yorkshire pudding, chicken and mushroom pie, macaroni cheese, lasagne verde and vegetable lasagne, moussaka, chilli con carne, burgers, curries, fish and chips and, in the evening, duck à l'orange, venison in red wine, steaks and lemon sole. Darts and dominoes are played, but there is no intrusive piped music. There are some facilities for the disabled, and camping can be arranged nearby. The pub is open all day Monday to Saturday and Sunday afternoons.

Beer: Tennent Heriot 80 shilling on handpump.

Accommodation: 3 en suite twins, 1 en suite family room and 1 double, all with colour TVs and tea and coffee making facilities. B&B £17.25 single, £28.75 twin. Half and full board available. Cards: Visa.

MELROSE

Burts Hotel
Market Square, off A7 and A68

Proprietor: Graham Henderson
Tel: 089682 2285 Fax: 089682 2870

Burts Hotel dates from 1772 and is a listed building that has retained its historic charm. There are bars, a residents' lounge, a snooker room, and a pleasant garden in summer. Both Scottish and French dishes are served in the elegant restaurant, while bar meals are available lunchtime and evening. Guests can enjoy walking, fishing, riding, shooting and golf, and can visit several old castles and stately houses in the area.

Beer: Belhaven 80 shilling on air pressure.

Accommodation: 8 singles, 13 doubles/twins, all en suite. B&B £30 single, £52 double. Two-nights dinner B&B £39 per person. Children's room. Pets welcome. Cards: Access, Amex, Diners and Visa.

OXTON

Tower Hotel
Off A68 near Lauder

Licensees: Denis & Hilda Murray
Tel: 05785 235

The Tower is a picturesque old country inn with a striking black and white exterior and stained glass windows. It has public and lounge bars, and a separate dining room, the public bar with a traditional gantry, and a blazing fire on cold days. It is a genuine local, with a strong emphasis on darts and dominoes. All the guest rooms have TVs and tea and coffee making facilities. Food, which ranges from bar snacks to full meals, is available until 9.30 every day.

Beer: Tetley Bitter on handpump.

Accommodation: 3 family rooms. B&B £14 per person. Half and full board available. Children welcome. Family room charged at £31 B&B on a room basis.

PEEBLES

Kingsmuir Hotel
Springhill Road, off A72

Proprietors: Elizabeth, Norman & May Kerr
Tel: 0721 20151

The Kingsmuir is a century-old stately house in leafy grounds on the south side of the Royal Burgh of Peebles. There is a pleasant parkland walk to the high street. The guest rooms in the hotel all have colour TVs, direct-dial phones, private bathrooms and tea makers. The popular bar is one of the busiest in town and has retained its original thick walls that stress the quality of 19th-century workmanship. Traditional Scottish food is served in the bar and the dining room and its quality has won 'Taste of Scotland' awards in 1987, 1988 and 1989. Bar food includes cullen skink soup, steak pie, haggis, neeps and mashed tatties, mince with skirlie pudding, vegetarian casserole, and sandwiches. Dinner may offer such dishes as lentil soup, roasts of lamb, beef and venison, sea fish such as smoked haddock in Mornay sauce, and roast chicken with skirlie stuffing. Peebles is famous for its many tweed and wool shops, and there is also an 18-hole golf course, as well as opportunities for pony-trekking and fishing.

Beer: Broughton Greenmantle Ale and Merlin's Ale on handpumps.

Accommodation: 2 singles, 6 doubles, 2 family rooms. B&B £26 per person sharing. Off-season Weekends £22 per night. Children welcome, no charge under 6. Cards: Access, Amex and Visa.

ST MARY'S LOCH

Tibbie Shiels Inn
A708 Moffat to Selkirk road

Licensees: Jack & Jill Brown
Tel: 0750 42231

Tibbie Shiels is an historic and remote inn on the shores of beautiful St Mary's Loch, one of the most tranquil spots in southern Scotland. Isabella – 'Tibbie' – Shiel was a widow with six children; her husband had worked for the local landlord,

Lord Napier, who established her in the little cottage by the loch to run a hostelry for travellers. Tibbie was a friend of James Hogg, the shepherd poet of Ettrick, and she often played hostess to Hogg, Sir Walter Scott and the literary society of the day. The original old stone cottage is still in use as a bar and restaurant, while a modern extension has waitress service. There is a strong emphasis on home-cooking and local produce; food includes homemade soup, haddock, chips and peas, Yarrow trout, homemade chilli con carne, ploughman's, burgers and sandwiches plus a daily vegetarian special such as bulghur wheat and walnut casserole. Evening meals are available and there is also a splendid afternoon high tea. The loch offers sailing and windsurfing, and the inn is a good base for visiting Grey Mare's Tale waterfall and Abbotsford, the former home of Sir Walter Scott.

Beer: Belhaven 80 shilling and Broughton Greenmantle Ale on handpumps.

Accommodation: 5 doubles, 1 family room. B&B £14 per person. Children welcome, £9 per night under 7 years if sharing with parents. Facilities for the disabled: 5 bedrooms on the ground floor with wheelchair access to bathrooms.

MANORHEAD HOTEL

STOW

Manorhead Hotel
168 Galashiels Road, A7

Licensee: John Pickles
Tel: 05783 201/396

The Manorhead is a 19th-century coaching inn in 1¼ acres of beautifully kept gardens. There is superb food both lunchtime and evening. There are pub games, an open fire and a welcome for families.

Beer: Caledonian 70 shilling and 80 shilling on handpumps.

Accommodation: 1 single, 5 doubles, 1 family room. B&B £18–£22 single, £36–£44 double.

SWINTON

Wheatsheaf Hotel
On B6471, 12 miles north of Berwick

Proprietor: Alan Reid
Tel: 089 086 257

The Wheatsheaf, which faces the village green in Swinton, has a spacious lounge with a long oak settle, a log fire and some agricultural prints on the wall, and a smaller locals' bar with darts, dominoes and a pool table. Mr Reid is an accomplished chef, seafood being his speciality. Bar meals are available lunchtime and evening, with specials chalked on a board. You may find homemade soup, smoked Tweed salmon, baked avocado with seafood, lasagne al forno, steaks, smoked fish pie, fried haddock, chicken or prawn curry, beef and real ale casserole, spinach pancake, Norwegian prawn and cheese salad, and sandwiches. Guest rooms all have colour TVs and tea and coffee making facilities. The Wheatsheaf is a fine base for visiting

Berwick and the region's stunning coastline.

Beer: Greenmantle Ale and 80 shilling on air pressure and handpump.

Accommodation: 3 doubles/twins. B&B £15 per person, £19 single occupancy. Reductions for children sharing with parents. Children's room. Pets welcome but not in public rooms. Cards: Access and Visa.

TWEEDSMUIR

Crook Inn
A701 near Biggar and Moffat

Licensees: Stuart & Mary Reid
Tel: 089 97 272

The Crook is a former drovers' halt and coaching inn. There has been an inn on the site since the 14th century and the present building dates from 1604 and is thought to be Scotland's oldest licensed premises. It was a clandestine meeting place for the outlawed 17th-century Covenanters and takes its name from a landlady named Jeannie o' the Crook who hid a fugitive from the dragoons in a peat stack. Robert Burns wrote his poem 'Willie Wastle's Wife' in the kitchen of the inn, a defamatory piece about the wife of a local worthy. The inn's bar has the original fireplace which was built of stone around a cartwheel that was then set alight to leave the circular hearth. A 20th-century extension has some superb Art Deco touches. Bar food is all homemade from local produce and includes soup, game pie, ploughman's and apple pie. Three-course meals are available, too. Darts, dominoes and crib are played in a separate room. There is a pleasant garden, and a children's play area with climbing frame and slide.

Beer: Broughton Greenmantle Ale on handpump.

Accommodation: 1 single, 7 doubles, 6 rooms with private baths. B&B £26 per person, £44 double. Children welcome, 20% reduction sharing with parents.

YARROW

Gordon Arms Hotel
Junction of A708 and B709

Licensee: Harry Mitchell
Tel: 0750 82222

The Gordon Arms is a delightful old inn by the bridge at Yarrow Water. It was an ale house for drovers and traders and later was the meeting place for such noted local writers as Sir Walter Scott and James Hogg, the Ettrick poet. It was granted a full licence when proposed by Hogg and granted by Scott the magistrate, perhaps not a good example of the even-handed nature of the law. The hotel today has a cheerful bar, lounge and dining room. Food ranges from bar snacks to high tea and full dinner. Bar meals, lunchtime and evening, include homemade soup, ploughman's, sandwiches, haddock, steak pie, salads. grills and a children's menu. Fresh trout is always available and residents can enjoy fishing on the Yarrow and Ettrick rivers and nearby St Mary's Loch and Meggat reservoir. The hotel has an all-day licence seven days a week and there are regular folk evenings.

Beer: Broughton Greenmantle Ale and Tennent Heriot 80 shilling on handpump.

Accommodation: 6 doubles. B&B £16 single, £28.50 double. Children welcome, half price. Dogs allowed.

Good access to the hotel for disabled people. A bunkhouse is being added with low-cost accommodation for walkers.

CENTRAL

BRIDGE OF ALLAN

Queens Hotel
24 Henderson Street, 1 mile from end of M9 at Dunblane roundabout, 2 miles from Stirling

Licensee: Douglas Ross
Tel: 0786 833268

The Queens is an impressive Victorian sandstone building on the main road of this picturesque village. Douglas Ross ensures a warm family welcome for tourists and business people in well-appointed guest rooms, all with colour TVs and tea and coffee making facilities. There are two bars, with the lounge selling a renowned pint of IPA, and the cellar bar a wide range of international beers. Bar snacks are served throughout the day and the bars are licensed until 1am. The Queens also has a beer garden and a basement restaurant serving dinners.

Beer: Arrol's 80 shilling, Tetley Bitter and Younger IPA on handpump and air pressure.

Accommodation: 2 singles, 6 doubles, 2 family rooms. B&B from £20-£25 per person. Half and full board available. Children welcome, half price if sharing. Cards: Access, Amex and Visa.

CALLANDER

Bridgend House Hotel
Bridge End, A81, just off A84

Proprietors: Sandy & Maria Park
Tel: 0877 30130

The Bridgend is a friendly, welcoming country hotel at the foot of Ben Ledi, the gateway to the Trossachs. The hotel has a Tudor façade and luxurious furnishings inside. The emphasis is on quality and tradition; most of the guest rooms have private baths and colour TVs and some of them have four-poster beds. An extensive menu offers Scottish smoked salmon, trout, duck, steaks, and salads (including vegetarian), served until 9.30pm. The hotel is close to the banks of the River Teith and is handy for Stirling Castle, Rob Roy's grave and Loch Katrine. TV nostalgists will recognize Callander as Dr Finlay's 'Tannochbrae'.

Beer: Broughton Greenmantle Ale and Harviestoun 80 shilling on handpumps.

Accommodation: 7 doubles, 1 family room, 5 with private bath. B&B from £10 per person, £20 with bath. Half and full board available. Children welcome, half price 12 and under. Pets welcome.

DRYMEN

Salmon Leap Inn
19 Main Street, just off A811

Licensee: James Bryce-Lind
Tel: 0360 60357

The inn was first known as the Plough and opened in 1759, the year of Robert Burns's birth. It was an alehouse for cattlemen and farmers, and the oldest part of the building, now called the Poachers' Rest, retains the original Hamilton Oak fireplace with wood etchings from Hampden Palace. The name changed in honour of the great salmon leaps at the nearby Pots of Gartness. The inn has a lively bar with a large collection of bric-à-brac, the Poachers' Rest lounge and dining room, and a third bar that serves the beer garden in summer. Food is served in all three bars and includes ploughman's, stuffed pitta bread, lasagne, homemade steak pie, poached salmon steaks, scampi and such puddings as homemade apple pie. There are summer barbecues. The guest rooms all have showers, colour TVs and tea and coffee making equipment.

Beer: Belhaven 80 shilling on air pressure.

Accommodation: 4 doubles, 1 family room (1 double has four-poster bed). B&B from £20 single, £32 double.

KINLOCHARD

Altskeith Hotel
B829 off A81 and A821, near Aberfoyle

Proprietors: Messrs Hamilton & Leeks
Tel: 087 77 266

The hotel's lawns sweep down to beautiful Loch Ard, deep in Rob Roy country, with Ben Lomond glowering over the glen. The Altskeith is a lively, fun-loving hotel with weekend ceilidhs and a wide range of sporting activities. There are lounge and public bars, a residents' lounge and a candle-lit dining room. Bar meals are served, too. The area is ideal for fishing, walking, golf, sailing, windsurfing, pony-trekking, while Stirling Castle, Doune Motor Museum and Glengoyne Distillery are nearby.

Beer: McEwan 80 shilling on handpump.

Accommodation: 5 doubles/twins, 1 family room, 2 rooms with showers. B&B from £17.50 per person, £40 double en suite. Children's room; children welcome to stay, 20% reduction for children under 12 sharing. Cards: Access, Amex, Diners and Visa.

DUMFRIES & GALLOWAY

CANONBIE

Riverside Inn
Signposted from A7

Licensees: Robert & Susan Phillips
Tel: 03873 71512/71295

The Riverside is a lovely old inn in beautiful wooded countryside by the River Esk. There is an old beamed bar reached through an archway from the lounge, cheerful open fires in winter, old pictures of the area on the walls, stuffed wildlife, a long case clock and comfortable seats. Food in the bars and dining room is imaginative and widely praised: you can have home-made beef or lentil broth, quiches, including vegetarian, fresh salmon with spring onion and ginger sauce, a selection of salads, or steak, and the delicious sweets include date pudding and butterscotch meringue. There is a splendid range of local fish in the restaurant. Visitors praise the breakfasts, too.

Beer: Timothy Taylor Landlord and Yates Bitter on handpumps.

Accommodation: 4 twins, 2 doubles, rooms can be let as singles. B&B from £27 per person. Cards: Access and Visa.

DUMFRIES & GALLOWAY

GRETNA

Solway Lodge Hotel
Annan Road, off A74 and A75

Licensee: John G Welsh
Tel: 0461 38266

The Solway Lodge, as its name implies, is close to the Solway Firth. It is slap on the border, and the nearest town is Carlisle. The hotel has a cream-painted exterior with two large porches. Inside there is a comfortable lounge bar that is open all day, including Sunday – so you know you are in Scotland, not England. The welcome is warm and there is excellent bar and restaurant food (restaurant evening only). It is a good base for touring the border area, while Gretna is a pleasant small town that is fortunately shedding its post-war image as the Reno of Great Britain, where teenagers rushed on scooters to get hitched against their parents' wishes.

Beer: Broughton Greenmantle Ale and Tetley Bitter on handpumps.

Accommodation: 10 doubles/twins, all en suite. B&B £27 single, £19 per person sharing. Children half price. Pets welcome (not in public rooms). Cards: Access, Amex, Diners and Visa.

LOCKERBIE

Kings Arms Hotel
29 High Street, town centre, ½ mile off A74

Proprietors: Ian & Wallace Guthrie
Tel: 05762 2410

The Kings Arms is a welcoming 17th-century coaching inn in the heart of Burns country – 'bonny, bonny Galloway', as he described the magnificent scenery. Both Prince Charles Edward Stuart and Sir Walter Scott have stayed in the hotel. It offers substantial, good-value bar snacks and restaurant meals and is the ideal base for coarse fishing on the river or loch; and there are no less than six golf courses within a half-hour's drive.

Beer: McEwan 80 shilling on air pressure.

Accommodation: 3 singles, 5 doubles, 5 twins, 1 family room. B&B £13 single, £25 double. Children welcome, up to 50% reduction.

Somerton House Hotel
35 Carlisle Road; from A74 take slip road into Lockerbie; the hotel is 1 mile from town centre

Proprietors: Mr & Mrs S Ferguson
Tel: 05762 2583/2384

Somerton House is a stately Victorian building made from local red sandstone. It is a listed building and has an ornate plaster cornice and unusual Kauri timber panelling imported from New Zealand at the turn of the century. All the guest rooms have en suite facilities, colour TV and tea and coffee trays. Bar food, lunchtime and evening, includes homemade soup, deep-fried mushrooms in garlic butter, plaice or haddock, curried chicken, minced beef cobbler, ploughman's and sandwiches. The separate restaurant has a 'Taste of Scotland' menu specializing in local fish, meat and game. Guests can enjoy fishing, golf and walks in lovely countryside, and there are many old castles in the area.

Beer: Tetley Bitter on electric pump.

Accommodation: 1 single, 4 doubles/twins, 2 family rooms. B&B £25

DUMFRIES & GALLOWAY

single, £40 double, £45 family room. Children's rooms. Dogs by arrangement. Cards: Access, Air Plus, Amex and Visa.

MOFFAT

Balmoral Hotel
High Street, off A74

Licensees: J Graham & C Bingham
Tel: 0683 20288

The Balmoral is a friendly and family-owned hotel, 200 years old, and set in the picturesque Annan valley. Bar meals, served lunchtime and evening, include homemade steak and kidney pie, Madras curry, chilli con carne, deep-fried haddock, lamb chops, haggis, lasagne, rainbow trout, Solway salmon in season, salads, sandwiches and a daily vegetarian dish. The evening restaurant specializes in fish and game. Moffat, once a spa town and centre of the Scottish woollen trade, is now best known as a small country town in superb countryside, with facilities for fishing, golf, riding, stalking and walking. It is in the heart of Burns Country and some claim that the poet drank in the Balmoral – but then, in common with Dickens and Johnson in London, he seems rarely to have passed a hostelry by!

Beer: Broughton Greenmantle Ale and Tennent Heriot 80 shilling on handpump and air pressure.

Accommodation: 3 singles, 13 doubles/twins, 1 family room, 6 rooms with en suite facilities. B&B £20 single, £25 en suite, £19.50 per person in double, £22 en suite, £45 family room. Children under 6 free. Children's room. Pets welcome. Cards: Access, Amex and Visa.

Black Bull
1 Churchgate, 1 mile off A74

Licensees: Jim & Lynda Hughes
Tel: 0683 20206

The Black Bull is a splendid, 16th-century inn but its roots go back much further. There was a monastery on the site and a papal bull gave the monks permission to build an ale and rest house for pilgrims. The tiled lounge bar of the inn today has old coaching notices and prints while the bar across a courtyard has much memorabilia of the more recent age of steam: the defunct Caledonian Railway ran close to the inn. Between 1682 and 1685 the inn was the headquarters of Graham of Claverhouse ('Bonnie Dundee'): his dragoons ruthlessly put down religious rebels in the area. Robert Burns was a frequent visitor to the Black Bull and scratched his 'Epigram to a Scrimpit Nature' on a window pane (now in a museum in Moscow). Excellent bar food offers homemade soup, shepherd's pie, cheese, potato and bacon hot pot, haggis, fish pie, quiche and salads.

Beer: McEwan 80 shilling and Younger No 3, Theakston Best Bitter on air pressure and handpumps.

Accommodation: 3 singles, 3 doubles all with TVs and tea and coffee makers. B&B £16 single, £30 double. Children welcome. Facilities for the disabled.

BALMORAL HOTEL

LARGOWARD

Staghead Hotel
A915/B940

Licensee: Malcolm Ord
Tel: 033 484 205

The Staghead is an old-world village pub in beautiful countryside close to St Andrews, the home of golf, and to the picturesque fishing village of East Neak. The hotel has a public bar, with darts, dominoes and pool, and the lounge leads to a comfortable sitting room with an open fire and interesting antiques.

Beer: McEwan 80 shilling on handpump.

Accommodation: 1 single, 1 twin, 1 double, 1 family room. B&B £15 per person. Children welcome, half price if sharing.

ST ANDREWS

Russell Hotel
The Scores, off A91

Proprietors: Gordon & Fiona de Vries
Tel: 0334 73447

The Russell is a small, friendly, family-run hotel overlooking St Andrews Bay and close to the Old Course of the Royal and Ancient Golf Club. The hotel's cosy Victorian Bar has a unique atmosphere in which locals, undergraduates, young and old mix freely. The Russell is renowned locally for its splendid bar lunches, while the restaurant serves fresh local produce, including seafood, game and Aberdeen Angus beef. The hotel is a fine base for the golf course, the castle, medieval cathedral and town centre.

Beer: Broughton Greenmantle Ale and McEwan 80 shilling on air pressure.

Accommodation: 5 twins, 2 doubles, 2 family rooms, all with en suite facilities. B&B from £22 per person. Off-season Weekends available: terms on application. Children welcome, free under 12 if sharing, charged for meals.

GRAMPIAN

ABERDEEN

Brentwood Hotel
101 Crown Street, off A92 and A93

Licensee: Jim Byers
Tel: 0224 595440

A stylish modern hotel near the town centre, the Brentwood avoids the plastic 'have a nice day' style of the big hotel chains. The emphasis is on quality and individual attention. Carriages Brasserie is designed as a traditional eating and drinking place with a good choice of food and ale. It is open seven days a week, lunchtime and evening, and children are welcome. Food includes homemade soup, smoked salmon, lasagne, pasta piccanti with chilli sauce, homemade steak and kidney pie, curry, a vegetarian dish of the day, burgers, steaks, salads and grills. Jim Byers is a devoted supporter of real ale and supplies a wide range from the Whitbread stable. The guest rooms are large and beautifully appointed, and excellent breakfasts include local kippers.

Beer: Castle Eden Ale, Flowers IPA, Marston Pedigree Bitter and Wethered Bitter on handpumps plus a regular guest beer.

Accommodation: 33 singles, 27 doubles, 1 family room, 1 suite, all with private baths or showers. B&B £41.50 single, £50 double Monday-Thursday, £20 single, £30 double at weekends. Children welcome, terms by arrangement. Cards: Access, Amex, Diners and Visa.

Ferryhill House
Bon Accord Street

Licensee: Douglas Snowie
Tel: 0224 590867

The Ferryhill is a small, cheerful and attractive Georgian hotel with a large choice of cask beers for the area, some served by traditional tall founts. The other main plus point is that the hotel has no juke box, pool table or television in the bar: 'It is a pub where the art of conversation has not died,' according to one enthusiast. The main bar has large bow windows that overlook the hotel's spacious grounds. There is a hall with more seating, and a plush cocktail bar. Bar food includes soup, stuffed mushrooms, deep-fried brie with redcurrant jelly, steaks, beef Stroganoff, haddock, scampi, jacket potatoes, ploughman's and a set business lunch, currently £4. There is a separate restaurant, too. In warm weather there are tables and chairs on a patio.

Beer: Broughton Greenmantle Ale and Merlin's Ale, McEwan 80 shilling and Younger No 3 and regular guest beers on handpumps and air pressure.

Accommodation: 4 singles, 6 doubles. B&B £20–£25 single, £36–£38 double.

GRAMPIAN

FINDHORN

Crown & Anchor Inn
Off A96, 6 miles from Forres

Proprietors: Roy & Peta Liddle
Tel: 0309 30243

The Crown & Anchor is an 18th-century inn on the edge of Findhorn bay and jetty. The bar, where darts, dominoes, cribbage and backgammon are played, is packed with old photos and prints of the area, and there is a large fireplace with welcoming fires in winter. There are more pictures in the comfortable lounge which also stages folk music on Sunday evenings. Bar food includes soup, ploughman's, sandwiches and toasties, fish and chips and lasagne, and there are children's portions. Residents have the use of the inn's boats on the sandy beach. As well as the excellent draught beers, there is a collection of more than a hundred international beers and a hundred or so different whiskies.

Beer: Brakspear Bitter, Courage Directors Bitter and Wadworth 6X on handpumps plus 3 regular guest beers and draught cider.

Accommodation: 5 doubles/twins. 1 family room, all with private showers. B&B £19 single, £32 double. Children welcome, half price under 12 when sharing.

ROYAL HOTEL, FORRES – *see p 246*

FORRES

Red Lion Hotel
2 Tolbooth Street, A96

Licensees: Robbie & Carol Sutherland
Tel: 0309 72716

The Red Lion, known locally as the 'Red Beastie', is an old hotel rebuilt in 1838, with small cosy bedrooms, including attic rooms. Sadly, after 18 years behind the bar, ill-health forced Jim Storrier to retire in 1989, but he continues to live in Forres and will keep, he says, 'a fatherly eye' on the Sutherlands, who are experienced licensees in the area. The public bar of the hotel has darts, dominoes and cribbage, and there is a quieter, wood-panelled lounge bar and a rare example of a Campbell's Brewery mirror. Forres is a delightful town that takes a vigorous part in the annual 'Britain in Bloom' competition, and is a good base for taking the Whisky Trail or visiting Loch Ness. Known as the Riviera of the North because of its mild climate, Forres has a first-class golf course.

Beer: McEwan 80 shilling and Younger No 3 on air pressure.

Accommodation: 2 singles, 2 doubles. Prices for accommodation had not been fixed as the guide went to press but expect around £12 per person.

Royal Hotel
Tytler Street

Proprietor: B Teasdale
Tel: 0309 72617

The Royal is an imposing three-storey hotel on the west side of the Royal Burgh. The exterior has impressive balconies, dormer windows and sheltering trees, while inside there is a comfortable lounge and a public bar with a cheery log and peat fire. Lunch, high tea and dinner are served, with vegetarian meals a house speciality. All the guest rooms have colour TVs, central heating, radios and tea and coffee making facilities.

Beer: Younger No 3 on air pressure.

Accommodation: 5 singles, 10 doubles, 4 family rooms, 6 with en suite facilities. B&B £20 per person, Weekend £40, Week £140. Special Weekend Breaks 2 people for the price of 1. Children under 15 sharing charged for meals only.

INVERURIE

Thainstone House Hotel
2 miles outside town on A96

Proprietors: Edith & Michael Lovie
Tel: 0467 21643

Thainstone House is a palladian mansion in meadows and woodlands of old Aberdeenshire's Don Valley. The house was designed by the famous local architect Archibald Simpson as a medieval manor house; it was rebuilt in 1820 after a disastrous fire. It was once the ancestral home of James Wilson, a signatory to the American Declaration of Independence. Close by are the ruins of the fortifications where Robert the Bruce's troops rested before the Battle of Barra in 1308. The interior of the hotel is sumptuous, with elegant dining room, lounges, and beautifully appointed guest rooms, including two with four-posters, all with private baths, TVs and tea and coffee making facilities. The bar menu offers soup, marinated Orkney herring, baked avocado and bacon hot-pot, roast sirloin of Aberdeen Angus beef, supreme of chicken in garlic, fresh Don salmon, haddock, escalope of pork Rob Roy filled with haggis, and vegetarian curry. There is a separate restaurant.

Beer: Tennent Heriot 80 shilling on handpump.

Accommodation: 6 doubles, 3 family rooms. B&B £40 single, £55 double. Weekend £70 single, £95 double. Children welcome, if sharing, charged for meals only.

KINCARDINE O'NEIL

Gordon Arms Hotel
North Deeside Road, A93

Licensee: Bryn Wayte
Tel: 03398 84236

The Gordon Arms is an hospitable old inn built around 1810 in one of the oldest villages in Royal Deeside, close to Balmoral Castle. Outside there are impressive chimneys and steeply sloping tiled roofs, inside carefully restored lounges and guest rooms with hand-picked antique furniture that reflects the inn's early 19th-century origins. Food is based on local produce and home cooking and includes inexpensive bar suppers, while vegetarians are catered for with a full menu. The village has a 13th-century church, there are many castles in the area, and there is golf, fishing, shooting, pony-trekking, gliding and water-skiing.

Beer: Theakston Best Bitter and Younger No 3 on handpumps with a regular guest beer.

Accommodation: 5 doubles, 2 family rooms, 3 en suite. B&B from £14 per person. Apply for details of mini-breaks. Children and pets welcome.

STONEHAVEN

Marine Hotel
Shorehead, off A92

Licensee: Philip Duncan
Tel: 0569 62155 Fax: 0569 66691

The Marine is a popular harbour hotel where you can sit outside in summer and watch the boats and the impressive mountainous backdrop while you eat and drink. The hotel is more than a hundred years old and most of the guest rooms overlook the harbour. There is a games room with a pool table and a traditional red phone box. There are also a lounge bar and dining room. The hotel uses fresh local produce and offers morning coffee, lunch, high tea and evening meals. Fresh fish and seafood are the highspots of the menus. There is no specific children's room but they are welcome in the dining room.

Beer: McEwan 80 shilling and Timothy Taylor Landlord on handpumps.

Accommodation: 1 single, 6 doubles, 2 family rooms. B&B £25 single, £30 double. Children welcome, half price (some of the doubles also used as family rooms). Cards: Access, Amex and Visa.

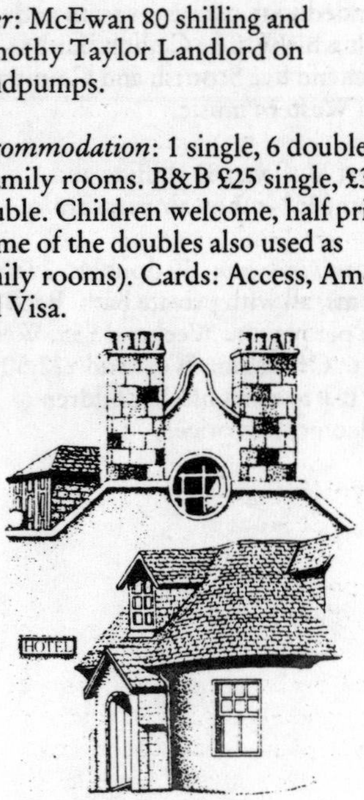

GORDON ARMS HOTEL

FORT WILLIAM

Nevis Bank Hotel
Belford Road, A82

Licensee: Jim Lee
Tel: 0397 5721

Nevis Bank is a cheerful and welcoming hotel on the outskirts of Fort William, a braw, sea-swept and historic old Highlands town. The hotel is conveniently placed at the start of the road up Ben Nevis and on the Road to the Isles. Climbers tackling the famous peak are strongly advised to have a pint in the bar first: better still, have two pints and forget the climb. The hotel has two bars offering a wide range of bar snacks, lunches and suppers. The separate Country Kitchen restaurant offers soup, country pâté, local salmon, Scottish lamb, Aberdeen Angus steaks, salads, and a local delicacy called Cranachan – raspberries blended with oatmeal, cream and malt whisky. The Ceilidh Bar has weekend live Scottish and Country and Western music.

Beer: McEwan 80 shilling and Younger No 3 on air pressure.

Accommodation: 30 doubles, 2 family rooms, all with private bath. B&B £26 per person. Weekend £55, Week £210. Off-season Weekend £22.50 B&B + evening meal. Children welcome, half price.

GLENCOE

Clachaig Inn
Off A82 on old riverside Glencoe road; near Ballachulish

Proprietors: Eileen & Peter Daynes
Tel: 085 52 252

The Clachaig Inn is in one of the most spectacular settings in Britain – the heart of Glencoe, scene of the appalling massacre of the MacDonald clan by the combined forces of the Campbells and English troops in 1692: the inn once bore the sign 'Nae Campbells'. Wooded hillsides give way to the bare, bleak and awesome peak of Aonach Dubh. The inn has stood in its remote setting for some 300 years, but the Daynes have carefully modernized it, and the accommodation is of a high standard and there is now a self-catering lodge as well as the guest rooms in the inn. The dining room seats 50 and serves good Scottish home-cooked food including homemade soup, pâté with oatcakes, sweet herring, vegetarian dish of the day, deep-fried scampi, the Clachaig Sizzler – 8oz rump steak cooked on a cast-iron platter – and a special children's menu. There are two bars, and the lounge has fine views of the west face of the mountain. The Clachaig is open all year and has folk music every Saturday night. It is the ideal base for climbing and walking and there are also seasonal opportunities for fishing and skiing. Some visitors have thought the inn and the accommodation spartan, but others delight in its bleak and remote location.

Beer: McEwan 80 shilling, Younger Scotch Bitter and No 3 on air pressure and regular guest beers.

Accommodation: 2 singles, 17 doubles/twins/family rooms, all with private bath or shower. B&B from £12 per person, £19 with evening meal.Children welcome, half price under 12. There are also 4 self-catering six-berth chalets: £85 to £185 a week.

INVERNESS

Lochardil House Hotel
Stratherrick Road, 1½ miles from town centre

Licensee: Richard Green
Tel: 0463 235995

Lochardil House, on the outskirts of Inverness, is a splendid old mansion house set in five acres of grounds with a sunken garden. It has a partly castellated frontage, sweeping staircases, a quiet cocktail lounge and a genuine locals' bar in the courtyard. The dining room has Gobelin tapestries depicting the biblical story of Esther. Excellent food ranges from homemade soup and sandwiches to lasagne, roast chicken with bacon and oatmeal stuffing, curry, grills, salads, omelettes, and jacket potatoes with a choice of fillings. The delightful guest rooms all have colour TVs and tea and coffee making equipment.

Beer: Younger IPA on air pressure.

Accommodation: 3 singles, 5 doubles, 3 family rooms, all en suite. B&B £42 single, £55 double. Children welcome, £10 per night.

DIRLETON

Castle Inn
½ mile off A198

Licensee: Douglas Stewart
Tel: 062 085 221

Once an important coaching stop on the old Dunbar road to Edinburgh, the Castle Inn now stands in a quiet old Berwickshire village, still offering good ale and victuals to travellers. It has a long, low stucco frontage with tall chimneys and little windowless dormers, like raised eyebrows above the first-floor windows. There is a free-standing inn sign and two porches. The inn looks across the village green to the castle built in 1225, the scene of a major battle during the 'English' Civil War, when it was taken by Cromwell's forces. The village grew around the castle in the 17th century when the sea engulfed the area of the original village and the people moved towards the safety of the battlements. The Castle Inn offers two bars – a public one with fine engraved mirrors and an open fire, and a comfortable lounge also with a blazing welcome on chilly days. There is lunchtime food and service every day, including Sunday afternoons. The main building contains four guest rooms looking out over the green, and a further four are available in the converted stable block. There is also a charming cottage, designated as being of historic interest, which can be let to larger parties.

Beer: Caledonian 70 shilling and McEwan 80 shilling on air pressure.

Accommodation: 3 singles, 5 doubles, 4 rooms en suite. B&B from £15 per person. Children welcome, half price. The cottage has 2 double rooms, kitchen, bathroom and living/dining room with open fire. Cards: Access and Amex.

EDINBURGH

Navaar House Hotel
12 Mayfield Gardens, A7, 1 mile from city centre

Proprietor: A S Thomson
Tel: 031-667 2828

Mayfield is a late 19th-century suburb in the south of Edinburgh. Its houses are big, stately and elegant, and many on the main-road have been converted into hotels. The Navaar has plasterwork in many of the rooms that suggests how ornate the interior must have been originally before it was modernized into a comfortable, urbane roadside hotel conveniently placed for the centre of Old Reekie, with its snooty elegance, magnificent buildings and some of the finest bars in Britain. The bars in the Navaar House are popular with local amateur football, hockey and even cricket teams, and there is live jazz every Tuesday. The bars are open every day and all day until midnight, and food is served both lunchtime and evening. Guest rooms have TVs and tea and coffee makers. As the list indicates, Mr Thomson gives strong support to independent breweries.

Beer: Caledonian 80 shilling, Maclay 80 shilling, McEwan 80 shilling and guest beers on air pressure and handpump including Broughton, Traquair House and beers south of the border.

Accommodation: 2 doubles, 4 family rooms, 5 rooms with showers. B&B £15-£25 per person. Half and full board available. Children welcome, half price. All rooms will be upgraded to full en suite in 1990. Cards: Access, Amex, Diners and Visa.

KIRKLISTON

Newliston Arms Hotel
76 Main Street, B8000, 2 miles off A1 and M8

Licensee: Alexander Nicol
Tel: 031-333 3214

The Newliston is a lively village local two miles from the Forth bridges. It has a thriving and boisterous bar with a panelled ceiling, popular with local folk. Watch for the splendid old tall founts that serve the beer. There is a cheering open fire in winter and bar food lunchtime and evening. Hopetoun House is close by.

Beer: McEwan 70 shilling and 80 shilling on air pressure.

Accommodation: 2 singles, 3 doubles. B&B £12.50 per person. Half and full board available. Week B&B £75. Children welcome, half price.

STRATHCLYDE

AYR

Old Racecourse Hotel
2 Victoria Park, off Racecourse Road, A719

Licensee: John Nicol
Tel: 0292 262873

The hotel is a fine sandstone Georgian town house next to the beach and to golf courses, and a mile from the town centre and new racecourse. It welcomes families. The lounge bar has a vast circular open fire in the centre of the room with a copper canopy fashioned like a whisky still. The hotel serves lunch, high tea and supper and offers local salmon and game when available.

STRATHCLYDE

Other dishes include guacamole with crudités, smoked trout, soups, lobster and crab salads, and homemade apple pie. The hotel is a good base for visiting Burns country, the Burns cottage and the haunted Alloway church.

Beer: McEwan 70 shilling and Younger No 3 on handpumps.

Accommodation: 2 singles, 7 doubles, 3 family rooms, 7 rooms en suite. B&B from £24.75 per person. Children's room; children welcome to stay, half price when sharing.

BIGGAR

Hartree Country House Hotel
1 mile off A702

Proprietors: A Parker & J Phillips
Tel: 0899 21027

Hartree House is a handsome old building dating back to the 14th century and with a striking, partially castellated tower that is half mock-Norman and half mock-French château. The interior includes delightful lounges and dining room and a superb bar that was built in 1885 as a billiard room. There are open fires, and splendid lunches and dinners. Biggar is a charming old market town with the fascinating Gladstone Court Museum that houses old traditional shops and workshops, and Greenhill Covenanters House with relics of the Covenanters.

Beer: Broughton Greenmantle Ale on air pressure.

Accommodation: 10 doubles, 1 family room, all with private bathrooms, colour TVs and tea and coffee making equipment. B&B £33 per person. Weekend £59, Week £189.

BRODICK (ISLE OF ARRAN)

Ormidale Hotel
Knowe Road

Licensee: Tom Gilmore
Tel: 0770 2293

The hotel is a fine Victorian building with superb views over Brodick Bay to the Sleeping Warrior crowned by Goatfell, 2,866 feet above sea level. The Ormidale has a large licensed conservatory with handsome brass beer founts. In summer there are live music events most nights, including folk, discos and jug bands. Good bar meals, with local seafood a speciality, are served lunchtime and evening between Easter and September. There is a children's menu and a play area in the large beer garden. The island is a delight, with deer roaming through the heather and opportunities for fishing, walking, pony-trekking and golf: there are seven courses on the island and the first tee of one is just a few yards from the Ormidale. There are car ferries from Ardrossan to Brodick (booking essential in summer) and a smaller car ferry in summer only between Kintyre and Lochranza in the north of the island.

Beer: McEwan 70 shilling on air pressure.

Accommodation: (Easter-September only; bar open all year) 4 singles, 3 doubles, 1 family room. All rooms equipped with colour TVs. B&B £15.50 per person. Children welcome, half price.

STRATHCLYDE

CASTLECARY

Castlecary House Hotel
Main Street, A80, off M73

Licensee: M Davis
Tel: 0324 840233

Castlecary House is a small village hotel close to Glasgow, with a quiet lounge, busy bar and snugs, and a range of cask beers that constitutes a mini beer festival. It is open all day, including Sundays, and serves both lunch and evening bar meals. Food includes lentil and potato soup, grills, salads, trout, homemade steak and kidney pie, and haddock in beer batter. Accommodation includes rooms in the hotel and 18 cottages, with twin and double rooms.

Beer: Belhaven 80 shilling, Broughton Greenmantle Ale, Harviestoun 80 shilling, Theakston Best Bitter and Old Peculier on handpumps and air pressure.

Accommodation: 8 singles, 9 doubles, 13 rooms with en suite facilities. B&B £15–£25 single, £30–£55 double, terms depend on type of room and facilities: cottage accommodation includes private lounge and own TV and tea and coffee makers.

EAGLESHAM

Eglinton Arms Hotel
Gilmour Street, off A77

Licensee: T Paterson
Tel: 03553 2631

The Eglinton Arms, a popular village local in old Renfrewshire, dates back to the 16th century when it was an important coaching inn. There are reminders of the past in the Stables Bar and the Postillion Restaurant. Darts and dominoes are played in the snug, which has a cheery fire in winter. Good bar food includes homemade soups and pâté, grills, chicken, seafood and poached cod. Cask beer in the lounge bar only.

Beer: McEwan 80 shilling, Younger No 3 on air pressure.

Accommodation: 6 singles, 3 doubles, 5 twins, all with private baths. B&B £43 single, £53 double/twin. Weekend £25 single, £35 double/twin per day.

GLASGOW

Babbity Bowster
16-18 Blackfriars Street, east of the city centre

Proprietor: Fraser Laurie
Tel: 041-552 5055

Fraser Laurie's brilliant creation epitomizes the regeneration of Glasgow as a major cultural centre in Scotland, no longer living in Edinburgh's snooty shadow. Babbity Bowster is bar, café and restaurant rolled into one in an elegant Robert Adam town house on the site of an ancient monastery. The fine re-creation of a medieval inn sign is repeated inside as a wall plaque. There are tall windows, pastel walls, a mass of drawings and photographs of Glasgow and Glaswegians, and a restaurant that also doubles as an art gallery for Glasgow painters. Food ranges from light snacks to full meals, starts with breakfast and goes on until the wee small hours. Try soup, haggis, neeps and tatties, chicken, mushroom or spicy vegetable pies, fresh mussels in wine, filled jacket potatoes, stovies, dish of the day, and such puddings as chocolate and orange fudge cake. There are open fires, outside seating in pleasant weather and live music, including

STRATHCLYDE

traditional fiddlers. The enterprise is named after a Scots kissing dance.

Beer: Maclay 70 shilling, 80 shilling and Porter on air pressure.

Accommodation: 3 singles, 3 doubles, all en suite. B&B £28.50 per person. Full board available. Children welcome to stay. Cards: Access, Amex and Visa.

GOUROCK

Spinnaker Hotel
121 Albert Road. A78, south of town

Licensee: Ann McCartney
Tel: 0475 33107

The Spinnaker is a friendly family-run hotel on the sea front with sweeping views over the Clyde to Dunoon and the distant Highlands. The hotel is a haven of peace with no juke boxes or gambling machines. There is a downstairs bar and dining room, and a cocktail bar on the first floor. A wide range of bar meals are served daily. Sailing, fishing, hill climbing and golf are all available in the area.

Beer: Belhaven 80 shilling on air pressure.

Accommodation: 2 singles, 2 doubles. B&B £12.50 per person, £12 for more than 1 night. Children welcome.

HOUSTON

Houston Inn
North Street, off A761

Licensee: Thomas McKean
Tel: 0505 614315

In the centre of a village near the Clyde, just ten minutes from Glasgow airport and 15 minutes from Loch Lomond, the inn is the oldest pub in Houston and offers a warm welcome. There is a pleasant garden for warm weather, a residents' lounge for families, and lunchtime snacks. It is a good base for walking in the lovely countryside and for visiting Glasgow.

Beer: McEwan 80 shilling on air pressure.

Accommodation: 4 rooms. B&B £16 per person. Cards: Amex.

INVERBEG

Inverbeg Inn
On A82 near Luss, by Loch Lomond

Licensee: Jack Bisset
Tel: 043 686 678

The inn, once known as the Ferry, stands in breathtaking countryside on the west bank of the loch opposite the great craggy slopes of Ben Lomond. The loch ferry calls at the inn's own jetty three times a day in summer. The Inverbeg was once a drovers' alehouse and is still a genuine local with shepherds and fishermen playing dominoes and cribbage in the bar. The lounge bar has sofas and armchairs and a host of prints including one of *The Monarch of the Glen*. There is an evening restaurant, while bar meals are served lunchtime and evening and include homemade soups, meat and fish grills, jacket spuds with a choice of fillings, ploughman's, pizzas, quiche, sandwiches, toasties and salads. A children's menu includes hoops, bangers, beans and fish fingers and chips. As well as the accommodation at the inn, there are sleeping quarters on the cruisers, owned by Mr Bisset, that are for hire on the loch. There are also day trips in season to Dunoon, Oban, Fort William and Glencoe, and the Trossachs.

STRATHCLYDE

Beer: Caledonian 80 shilling on air pressure.

Accommodation: 2 singles, 11 doubles, 1 family room, 7 rooms with private baths. B&B £24 single, with off-season reductions. Children welcome. Facilities for the disabled. Cards: Access, Amex and Visa.

KILMUN

Coylet Inn
Loch Eck, A815

Licensees: R & H Addis
Tel: 036 984 426

The Coylet is a small roadside hotel with imposing dormer windows and superb views of the loch amid the lovely forests of Argyll and the idyllic Cowal peninsula. The Coylet was formerly a coaching inn and parts of the building date back to the 18th century. It offers excellent hospitality with open log fires in winter, a bar, and food lunchtime and evening, and it is a good base for fishing, walking or visiting nearby Dunoon.

Beer: McEwan 80 shilling and Younger No 3 on air pressure.

Accommodation: 1 single, 2 doubles. B&B £14 per person. Children welcome, half price.

WHITING BAY (ISLE OF ARRAN)

Cameronia Hotel
Shore Road, A841

Licensee: William Collingwood
Tel: 0770 7254

The Cameronia is a small and lively family-run hotel overlooking Holy Isle and close to Brodick Castle. There is a comfortable snug, and a steak and wine bar, with a high priority placed on home cooking for both bar and restaurant meals. The hotel is the home of the Cameronia darts team who play badly but with great enthusiasm and raise large amounts of money for charity. There is folk singing every weekend in summer, and ceilidhs and beer and malt whisky tastings in winter.

Beer: Broughton Greenmantle Ale on handpump.

Accommodation: 2 singles, 5 doubles, 1 family room, 1 room with private bath. B&B + evening meal £17 single, £26 double. Half board weekends and weeks available, with golf, fishing and pony trekking holidays by arrangement. Children welcome, terms by arrangement.

HOUSTON INN, HOUSTON – *see p 253*

The Maps

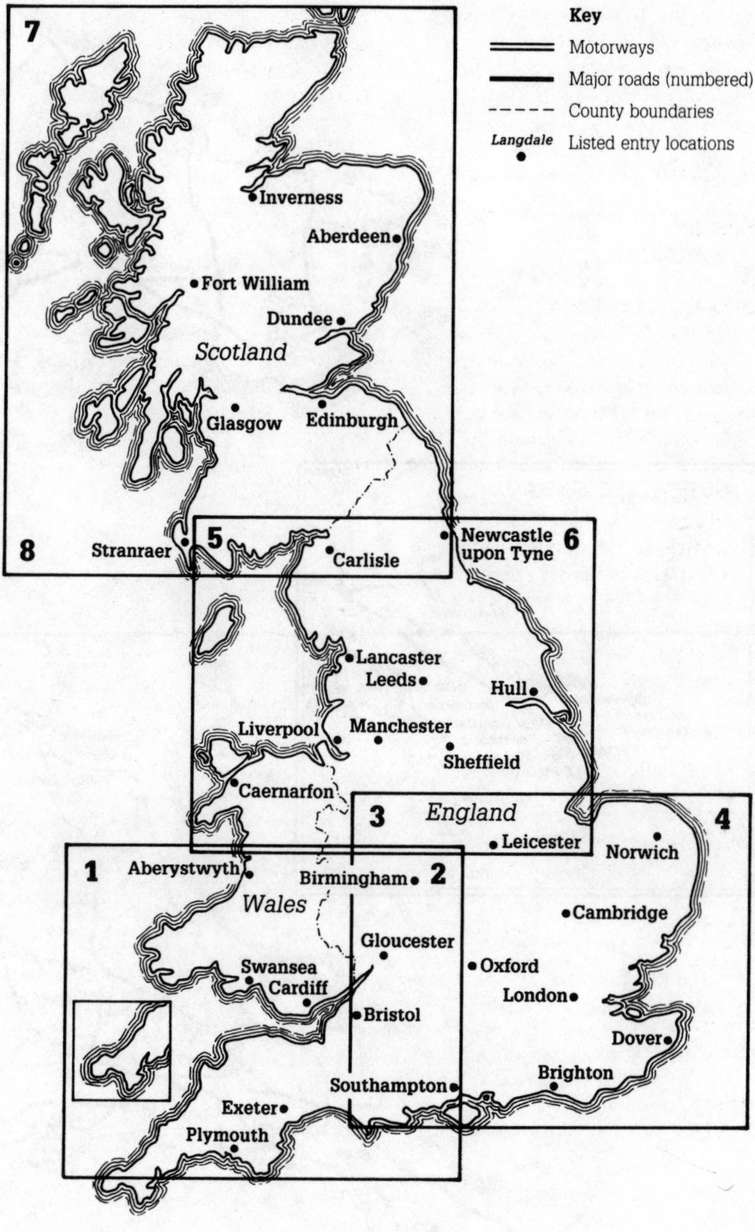
Key
Motorways
Major roads (numbered)
County boundaries
Langdale
Listed entry locations
7
Inverness
Aberdeen
Fort William
Dundee
Scotland
Glasgow
Edinburgh
8
Stranraer
5
Carlisle
Newcastle upon Tyne
6
Lancaster
Leeds
Hull
Liverpool
Manchester
Sheffield
Caernarfon
3
England
4
Leicester
Norwich
1
Aberystwyth
Birmingham
2
Wales
Cambridge
Gloucester
Swansea
Oxford
Cardiff
London
Bristol
Dover
Brighton
Southampton
Exeter
Plymouth

1

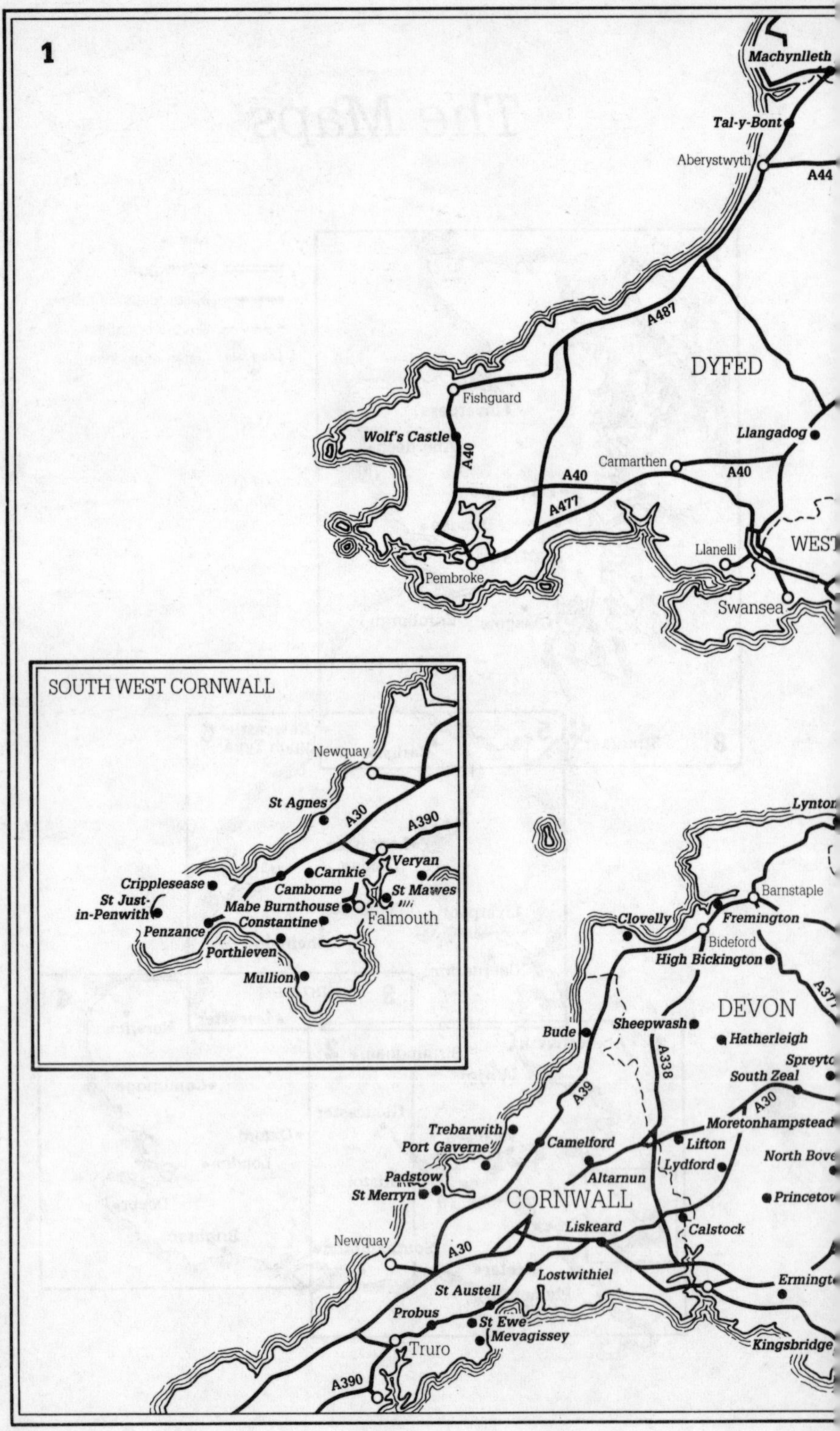
Machynlleth
Tal-y-Bont
Aberystwyth
A44
A487
DYFED
Fishguard
Wolf's Castle
A40
Llangadog
Carmarthen
A40
A40
A477
WEST
Llanelli
Pembroke
Swansea
SOUTH WEST CORNWALL
Newquay
St Agnes
A30
A390
Veryan
Cripplesease
Carnkie
St Just-
in-Penwith
Camborne
St Mawes
Mabe Burnthouse
Falmouth
Penzance
Constantine
Porthleven
Mullion
Lynton
Barnstaple
Clovelly
Fremington
Bideford
High Bickington
DEVON
Bude
Sheepwash
Hatherleigh
A338
South Zeal
A39
A30
Moretonhampstead
Trebarwith
Camelford
Lifton
Port Gaverne
Lydford
Altarnun
Padstow
St Merryn
CORNWALL
Calstock
Liskeard
Newquay
A30
Lostwithiel
St Austell
Probus
St Ewe
Mevagissey
Truro
A390
Kingsbridge

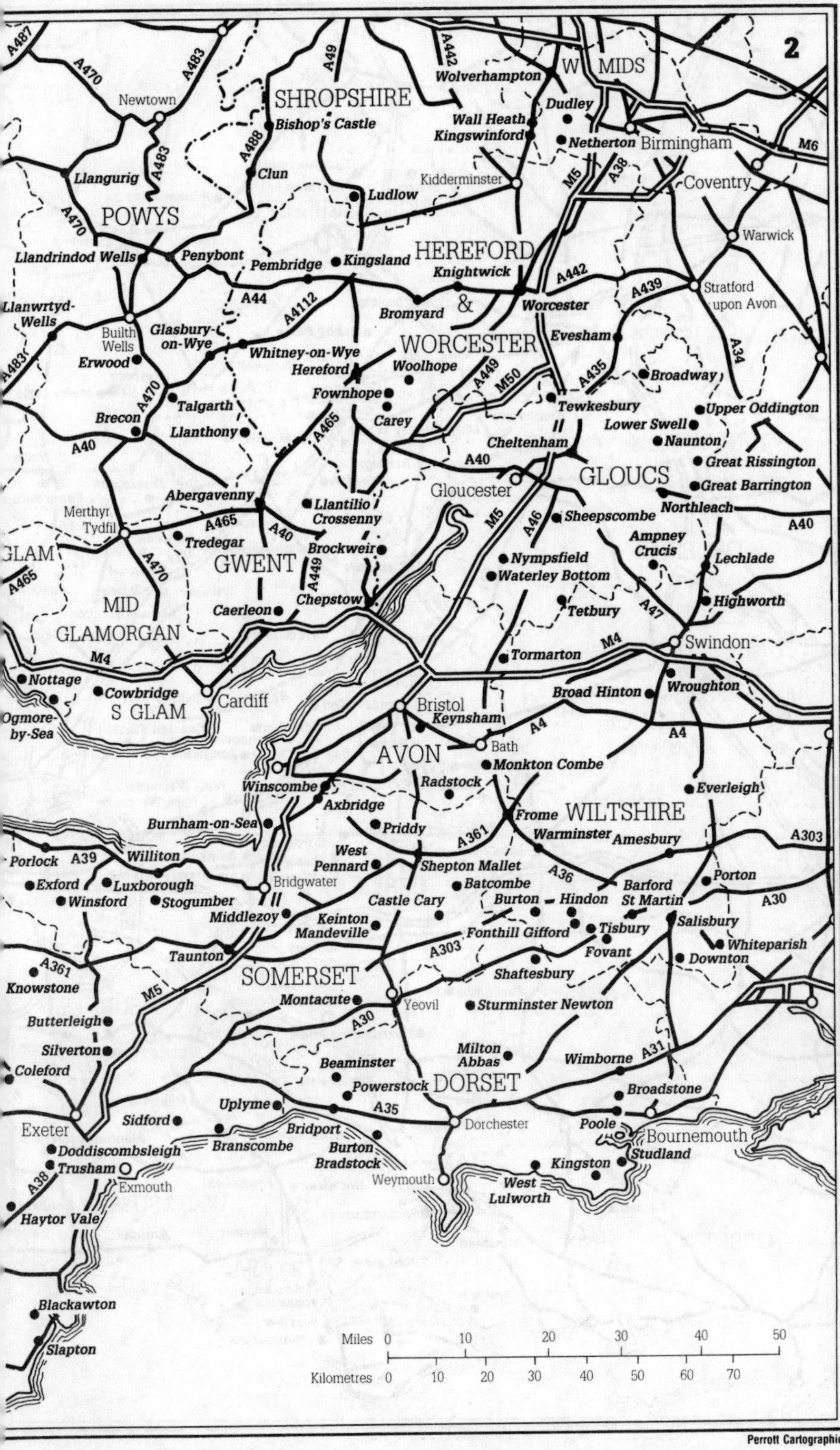

Perrott Cartographics

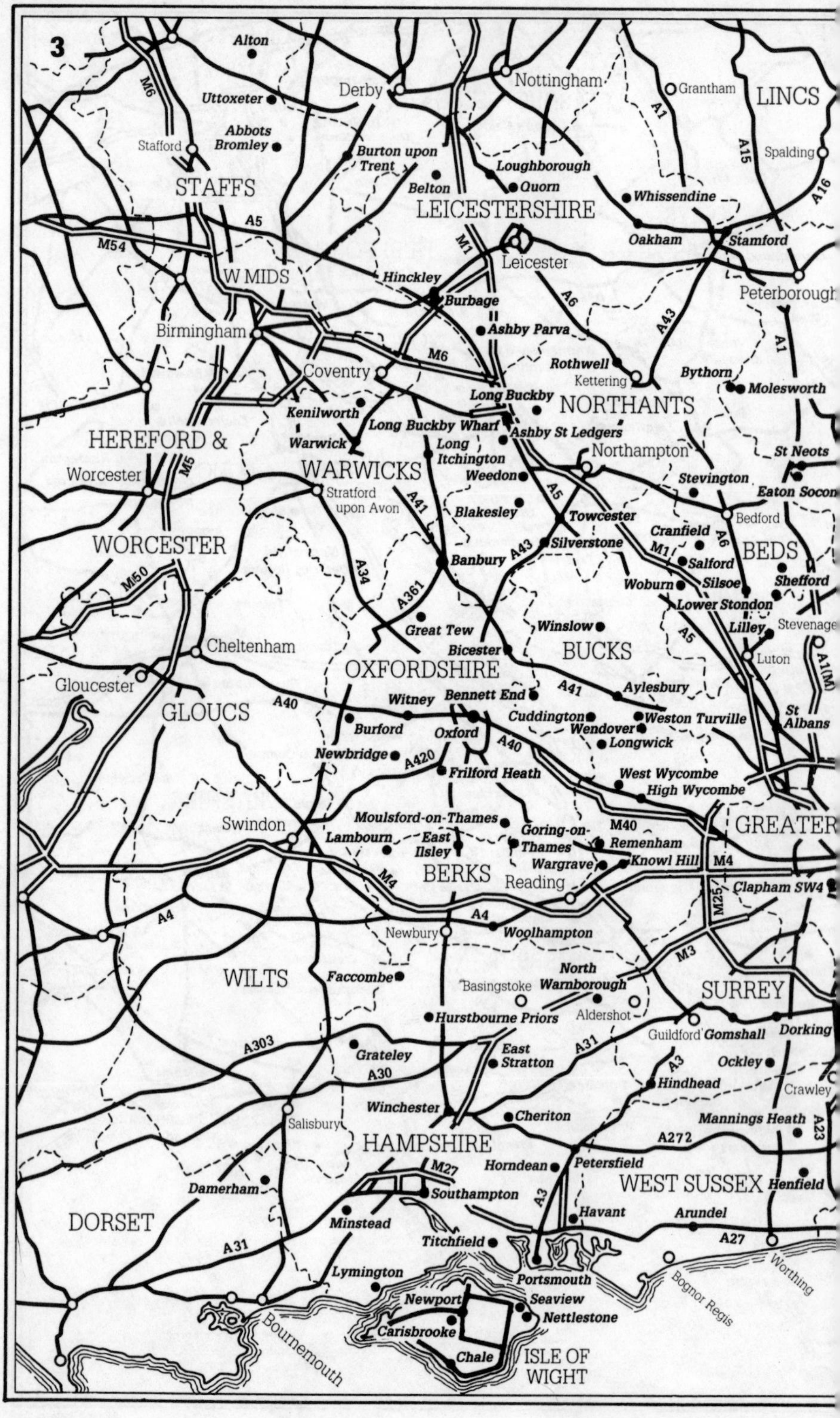
3
Alton
Derby
Nottingham
Grantham
LINCS
M6
Uttoxeter
Abbots Bromley
Stafford
Burton upon Trent
A1
A15
Spalding
Loughborough
Quorn
Belton
STAFFS
Whissendine
A16
LEICESTERSHIRE
A5
M1
Oakham
Stamford
M54
Leicester
W MIDS
Hinckley
Burbage
Peterborough
A6
Birmingham
Ashby Parva
A43
A1
M6
Rothwell
Coventry
Kettering
Bythorn
Molesworth
Long Buckby
NORTHANTS
Kenilworth
Long Buckby Wharf
HEREFORD &
Ashby St Ledgers
Warwick
Long Itchington
Northampton
St Neots
Worcester
M5
WARWICKS
Weedon
Stevington
Eaton Socon
Stratford upon Avon
A41
A5
Blakesley
Bedford
Towcester
Cranfield
WORCESTER
A43
Silverstone
A6
BEDS
Banbury
M1
Salford
M50
A34
Shefford
A361
Woburn
Silsoe
Lower Stondon
Great Tew
Winslow
Lilley
Stevenage
A5
Cheltenham
Bicester
BUCKS
Luton
A1(M)
Gloucester
OXFORDSHIRE
A41
Aylesbury
Bennett End
A40
GLOUCS
Witney
Cuddington
Weston Turville
St Albans
Burford
Oxford
Wendover
A40
Longwick
Newbridge
A420
Frilford Heath
West Wycombe
High Wycombe
Moulsford-on-Thames
M40
GREATER
Swindon
Goring-on-Thames
Lambourn
East Ilsley
Remenham
Wargrave
Knowl Hill
M4
BERKS
M4
Reading
Clapham SW4
M25
A4
A4
Newbury
Woolhampton
M3
WILTS
Faccombe
North Warnborough
Basingstoke
SURREY
Aldershot
Hurstbourne Priors
Guildford
Gomshall
Dorking
A303
East Stratton
A31
Grateley
A3
Ockley
A30
Hindhead
Crawley
Winchester
Cheriton
Salisbury
Mannings Heath
A23
HAMPSHIRE
A272
M27
Horndean
Petersfield
Damerham
WEST SUSSEX
Henfield
Southampton
A3
DORSET
Minstead
Havant
Arundel
A31
Titchfield
A27
Worthing
Lymington
Portsmouth
Bognor Regis
Newport
Seaview
Nettlestone
Bournemouth
Carisbrooke
Chale
ISLE OF WIGHT

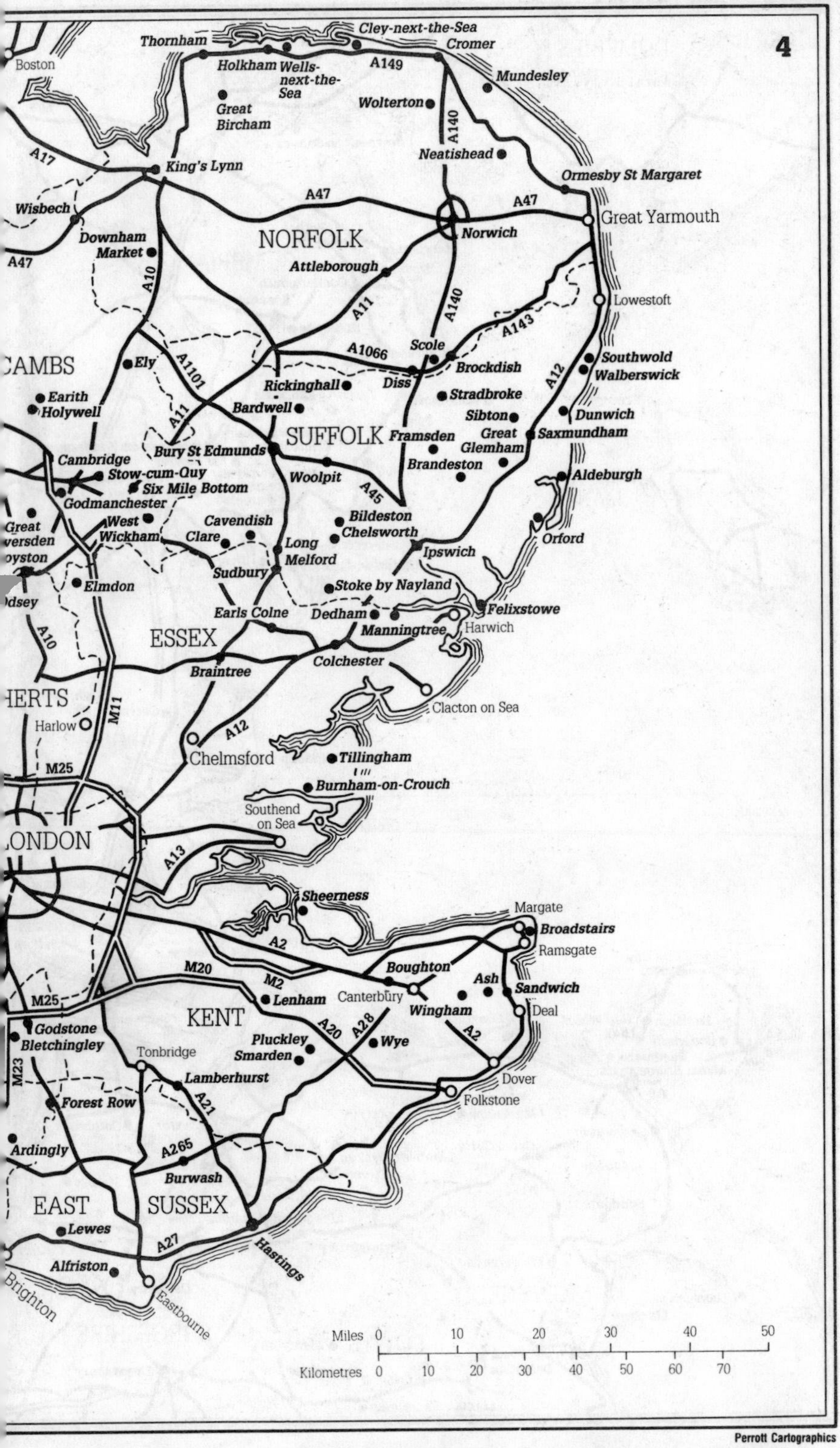

Perrott Cartographics

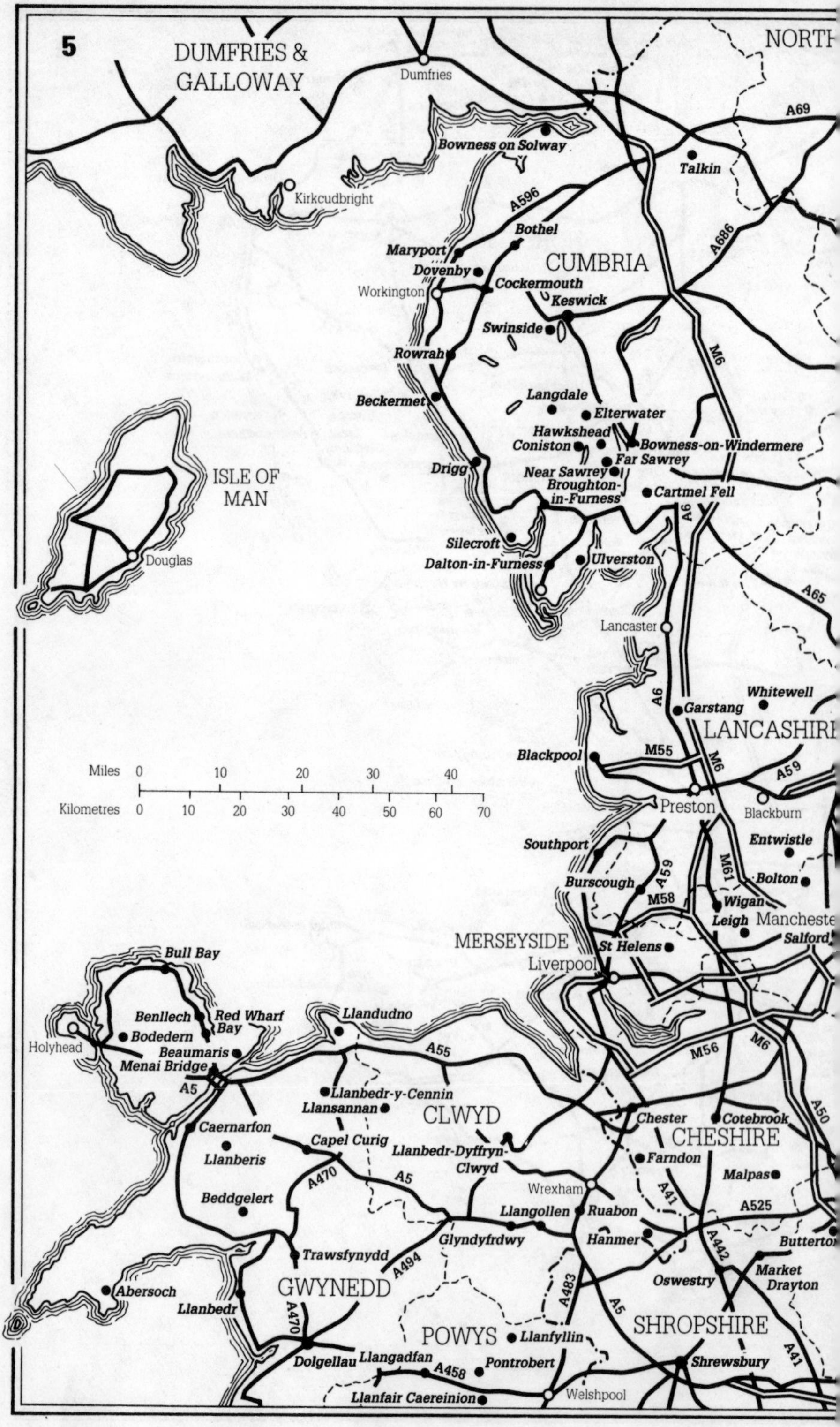
5
DUMFRIES & GALLOWAY
Dumfries
NORTH
A69
Bowness on Solway
Talkin
Kirkcudbright
A596
A686
Bothel
Maryport
CUMBRIA
Dovenby
Workington
Cockermouth
Keswick
Swinside
Rowrah
M6
Langdale
Beckermet
Elterwater
Hawkshead
Coniston
Bowness-on-Windermere
Far Sawrey
Drigg
ISLE OF MAN
Near Sawrey
Broughton-in-Furness
Cartmel Fell
A6
Silecroft
Douglas
Dalton-in-Furness
Ulverston
A65
Lancaster
Whitewell
A6
Garstang
LANCASHIRE
Blackpool
M55
M6
A59
Miles 0 10 20 30 40
Kilometres 0 10 20 30 40 50 60 70
Preston
Blackburn
Southport
Entwistle
A59
M61
Burscough
Bolton
M58
Wigan
Leigh
Manchester
MERSEYSIDE
St Helens
Salford
Liverpool
Bull Bay
Benllech
Red Wharf Bay
Llandudno
Holyhead
Bodedern
Beaumaris
A55
M56
M6
Menai Bridge
A5
Llanbedr-y-Cennin
Llansannan
CLWYD
Chester
Cotebrook
A50
Caernarfon
CHESHIRE
Capel Curig
Llanbedr-Dyffryn-Clwyd
Llanberis
Farndon
A470
A5
Malpas
Wrexham
A41
Beddgelert
Llangollen
Ruabon
A525
Glyndyfrdwy
Hanmer
Butterton
Trawsfynydd
A494
A442
Market Drayton
Oswestry
GWYNEDD
Abersoch
Llanbedr
A483
A5
SHROPSHIRE
A470
POWYS
Llanfyllin
A41
Dolgellau
Llangadfan
A458
Pontrobert
Shrewsbury
Llanfair Caereinion
Welshpool

Perrott Cartographics

7

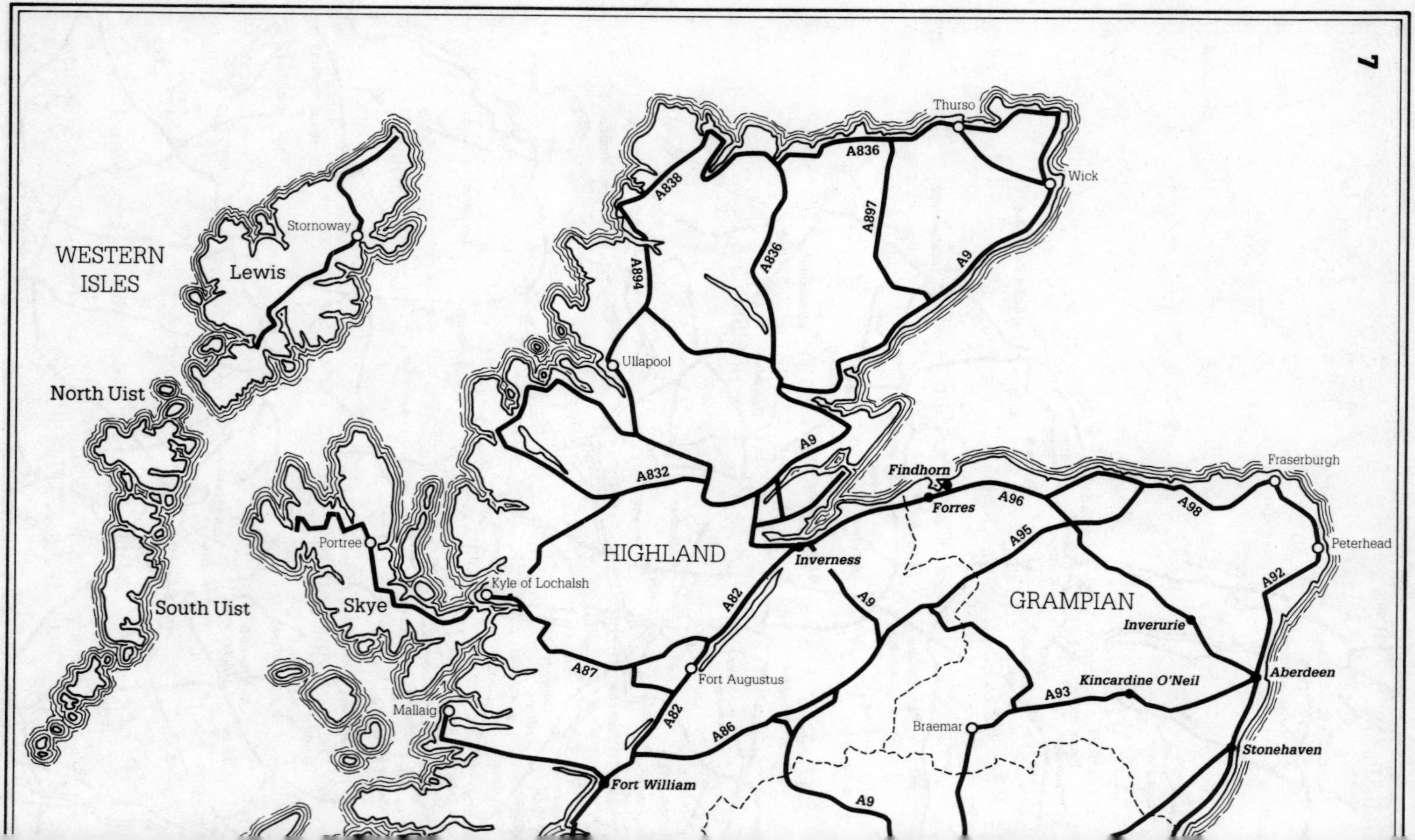
WESTERN ISLES
Lewis
Stornoway
North Uist
South Uist
Skye
Portree
Mallaig
Kyle of Lochalsh
Ullapool
Thurso
Wick
A836
A838
A894
A897
A836
A9
A832
HIGHLAND
Inverness
Findhorn
Forres
A96
A98
Fraserburgh
Peterhead
A95
GRAMPIAN
A9
A82
Inverurie
A92
Aberdeen
Kincardine O'Neil
A93
Fort Augustus
A87
A82
A86
Braemar
Stonehaven
Fort William
A9

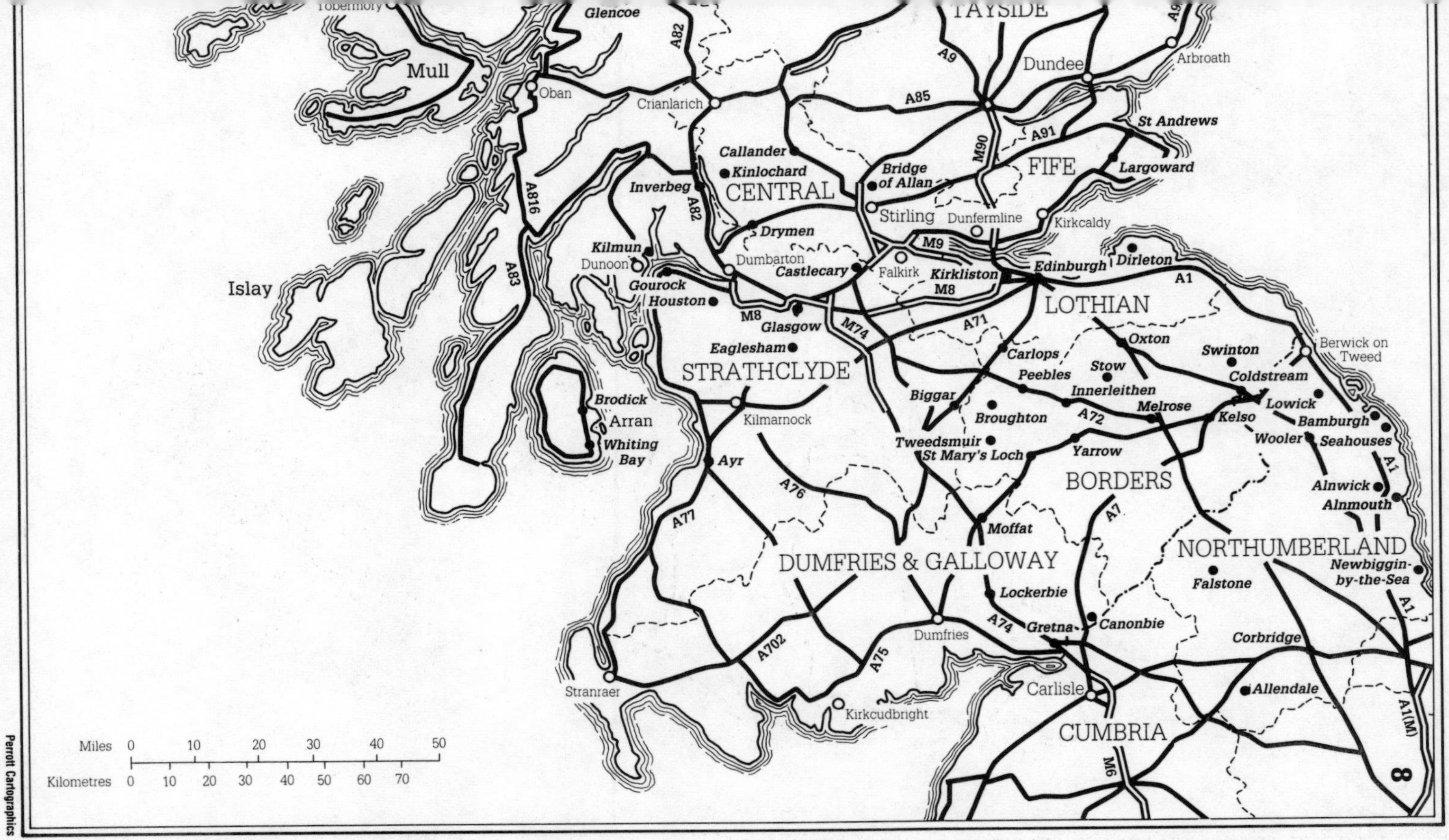

Perrott Cartographics

REPORT FORM

County ______________________________

Town or village ______________________________

Name of pub/hotel ______________________________

Address ______________________________

Location (A or B road) ______________________________

Tel no ______________ Name of licensee ______________

Description of pub (including bars, food, guest rooms and any special facilities) ______________________________

____

____

____

Draught beers (including method of dispense) ______________________________

____

____

Accommodation:

No of single rooms ______ doubles/twins ______ family rooms ______

Cost of B & B per person per day ______ cost for double/twin if price based on room ______________ cost for family room ______________

No of rooms with en suite baths or showers ______________

Can children stay ☐ yes ☐ no Children's reductions ______________

Cost of any special 'breaks', eg off-season, weekend, mid-week ______________________________

Name and address of person recommending ______________________________

____

____

Send to
Roger Protz, CAMRA, 34 Alma Road, St Albans, Herts AL1 3BW

DELETION FORM

County ____________________

Town or village ____________________

Name of pub/hotel ____________________

Address ____________________

____

____

The entry should be deleted for the following reasons:

____

____

____

____

____

____

____

Name and address of person recommending deletion

____

____

____

Send to
Roger Protz, CAMRA, 34 Alma Road, St Albans, Herts AL1 3BW

BOOKS FOR BEER AND PUB LOVERS

CAMRA have a growing list of titles that should be on every pubgoers' bookshelf.

The 1990 *Good Beer Guide*, edited by Andrea Gillies, lists more than 5,000 pubs throughout the British Isles that sell real ale. Complete with a detailed brewery section, £6.95.

CAMRA *Guide to Good Pub Food* by Susan Nowak dispels the myth that pub food is no more than microwaved misery or curly cheese sandwiches. This best selling guide lists pubs throughout Britain serving fresh, imaginative and good-value food, £5.95.

The following well-designed and fully-mapped regional guides are now available:

Best Pubs in London by Roger Protz, £4.95.
Best Pubs in Lakeland by Mike Dunn, £3.95.
Best Pubs in Devon and Cornwall by Tim Webb, £4.95.
Best Pubs in East Anglia by Roger Protz, £4.95.
Best Pubs in North Wales by Mike Dunn, £4.95.
Best Pubs in Yorkshire by Barrie Pepper, £4.95.

If you enjoy going to pubs but don't want to leave the children at home or eat in fast-food burger joints, then you need *Best Pubs for Families* by Jill Adam, some 500 pubs nationwide that offer children's menus, family rooms, gardens and changing facilities for babies, £4.95.

And if you enjoy a good drop as well as real ale then don't miss David Kitton's definitive *Good Cider Guide*, which lists hundreds of pubs, clubs and off-licences that serve the fermented juice of the apple, £5.95.

The Real Ale Drinker's Almanac by Roger Protz (Lochar, £5.95) is a handsome pocket book that gives details of all cask-conditioned beers brewed in Britain, including recipes, ingredients and detailed tasting notes.

Available from all good bookshops or direct from CAMRA, 34 Alma Road, St Albans, Herts AL1 3BW. Add £1 post and packing per volume. Three books or more post free.